from **THE EARTH**
to **THE TABLE**

from THE EARTH
to THE TABLE

JOHN ASH'S *wine country cuisine*

by John Ash with Sid Goldstein

CHRONICLE BOOKS

SAN FRANCISCO

ACKNOWLEDGMENTS

For this revision of the book I've had lots of help. I couldn't have done it without Beth Snow, whose skills with the computer allowed us to reconstruct the original manuscript, bring it up to date, and add some clarity and consistency. Thanks also to Mary Karlin and Mei Ibach for recipe testing. I couldn't forget my literary agent, Sarah Jane Freymann, who keeps me writing.

Finally, my thanks to all those farmers, foragers, fishermen, winemakers, and inspired cooks I've been able to work with for all these years here in the California wine country. I feel blessed to have been a part of this time and place.

— JA

First Chronicle Books LLC edition, published in 2007.

Text copyright © 1995 and 2007 by John Ash and Sid Goldstein.
Library of Congress Cataloging-in-Publication Data available.

ISBN-10: 0-8118-5479-5
ISBN-13: 978-0-8118-5479-5

Manufactured in the United States.

Design and typesetting: McGINTY
Illustrations: Nina Frenkel
Front cover photo: Maren Caruso Photography
Photo assistant: Faiza Ali
Food styling: Kim Konecny
Back cover photo: Susie Cushner

Distributed in Canada by Raincoast Books
9050 Shaughnessy Street
Vancouver, British Columbia V6P 6E5

10 9 8 7 6 5 4 3 2 1

Chronicle Books LLC
680 Second Street
San Francisco, California 94107

www.chroniclebooks.com

CONTENTS

INTRODUCTION

The food production chain is really very simple. We plant it; we grow it; we gather it; we cook it; and then we eat it. When this process occurs with a certain immediacy and a minimum of interference, and if it is nurtured by people who are truly passionate about what they are doing, the results can be glorious.

This book is largely about that process from my perspective in Northern California's verdant wine country. The original version of this book was stimulated in great part by my many-year association with Fetzer Vineyard's Valley Oaks Food and Wine Center. I was able to use the fantastic organic garden there to explore and develop my own skills as a cook and deepen my commitment to sustainable agriculture. Since then I've been able to continue my exploration of fresh, seasonal, ethical foods in the larger context of what is happening not only in the Northern California wine country where I live but in the larger world.

The thrust of this book in its revision continues to be to share the results of this ambitious culinary journey in which I am involved. My hope is to encourage you to reconceive your mental shopping list—to think about what's grown locally and what's in season, and to buy organically and sustainably produced foods whenever possible. Not only is the health of our food supply at stake, but the health and vigor of our planet is being challenged. The flavor of real food, something our ancestors took for granted, is in danger of being denied to us.

CHANGES IN AMERICAN COOKING
I remarked in the original version of this book that Americans were undergoing a profound change in how they thought about and prepared the foods they ate. That revolution continues today at an even faster rate. Ingredients and techniques that were new or exotic in the original book have become commonplace to us now. I included sidebars in the first book extolling exotic ingredients like portobello mushrooms or chipotle chiles that most American cooks are very familiar with now. In my little encampment in Northern California's wine country I have been especially fortunate to be at one of the centers of this revolution. There is a heightened appreciation here of that cornerstone of great food—great ingredients. I am lucky to be in a place that has inspired the nation to a deeper understanding of the importance of knowing intimately the raw materials with which we work.

This book, then, represents my evolution as a cook. It began with my grandmother Maud, with whom I spent a lot of my childhood. In tribute, adaptations of several of her recipes are in this book. Being poor on an isolated mountain ranch in Colorado, she had to use *everything*, and she taught me how to as well. This meant I got an early crash course in such archaic practices as boiling the hooves of calves in order to extract the gelatin. I also learned to appreciate and love the process of cooking. It still seems pretty magical to me that yeast and flour come together to make bread.

Like so many of my contemporaries, I learned to cook formally by studying French cooking both in America and abroad. In the late 1960s and 1970s there was no question that, if you wanted to study the highest order of Western cooking, you went to France to learn your skills and discipline. At that time, if you hadn't "been to France" you were out of the culinary loop. With the exception of a few outposts of indigenous regional cuisine — such as Cajun/Creole in Louisiana, Tex/Mex in the Southwest, or the cooking of the Deep South — that managed to hold their own, fine American cuisine mostly came to us from French or European disciplines and techniques. Wine country cuisine also represents an evolution from those roots, but it has in a relatively short period of a couple of decades taken on an identity of its own.

WHAT IS WINE COUNTRY CUISINE?

I think the very existence of a wine country cuisine is a direct response to the great wines that are being produced here in California. In the early days of wine in California (which really only began in the late 1960s) winemakers tried to duplicate the great wines of Europe, especially those of France. What emerged were big, blockbuster Cabernets and Chardonnays that were so intense they tended to overpower almost any food they accompanied. We cooks tried our best to create dishes that would match these wines. Because of our training at that time, we tended to create variations on French and to some extent Italian dishes, since they were what was most comfortable to us and they also had the tradition of wine as part of their cuisines. It was a gestation period for both winemakers and cooks in California.

Then a curious and wonderful thing happened. For winemakers it was the blind tastings in France in 1976 in which a California Cabernet and Chardonnay beat the best of their French counterparts. For cooks it was beginning to travel to other parts of the world (especially Latin America and Asia) and bring back flavors, ingredients, and techniques that were altogether foreign to the French tradition. We also opened our eyes to the new ingredients beginning to appear in our markets courtesy of the new waves of immigrants, many of whom came from Latin America and Asia. In that sense we began to create our own little culinary global village in California and finally had enough confidence to explore and define territory that was uniquely our own.

Beginning in the 1980s California wines changed dramatically. And this time it was often in response to the food. Big Cabernets and Chardonnays became subtler, more approachable. "Lesser" varieties that better complement the spicy, exotic flavors of ethnic foods (such as Sauvignon Blanc, Gewürztraminer, and Pinot Noir with spicy Asian dishes) became more important. California chefs and winemakers began working together to create harmony and synergy at the table rather than fighting for attention from critics.

During this time, we (both winemakers and cooks) began exploring the unique and rich agricultural microclimates available in the California wine country to grow a broad spectrum of wine grapes and foods. In Sonoma County, my original base of operations, we saw the growth of small family farms devoted to growing all kinds of spectacular new produce and raising animals — such as game birds and organic Sonoma lamb — that fired the cook's imagination. In a real sense we were learning the very thing that had made French and European food and wine so great — the importance of the land and its connection to the cook.

My passion became exploring, with farmers and ranchers, all that could be produced locally. This approach was consistent with my lifelong passion for the farming stage of cooking and for simple preparations. In 1980 when I started my restaurant, John Ash & Company, in Santa Rosa in Sonoma County, I enlisted every grower I could find to supply us with ingredients. (Here, I must recognize and offer my gratitude to Alice Waters and her pioneering efforts at Chez Panisse. She encouraged us all to be proactive in finding wholesome and unusual ingredients.) At first my colleagues and I would sift through seed catalogs each winter and select different varieties just to see if they would grow. Sometimes it worked — sometimes not. But it instilled in me a credo that I believe in even more strongly today: Farming is the first step in cooking. A great cook is only as great as his or her ingredients.

In my view great meals result from spending more time finding great ingredients than in the kitchen preparing them. On its own, a great recipe does not create a unique taste experience. The raw ingredients are the stars of the show.

The role of the cook, then, is like that of a stage director in a play: to coax and encourage the best out of his or her stars — in this case, the vine-ripened tomato, the fresh-from-the-water salmon, the dead-ripe berry, the bundle of fresh, bright basil. Winemakers have a saying that applies equally to food: "The secret of making great wine is to grow great grapes and then not screw them up."

PRESERVATION OF THE LAND

California has a kind of split personality when it comes to taking care of the land. On the one hand it is home to some of the country's most innovative approaches to organic agriculture, natural farming without the use of the "cide" sisters (herbicides, fungicides, insecticides), combined with techniques that recycle and replenish the soil. In recent years mainstream wine-grape growers have embraced disciplines such as biodynamics, which were considered just a few years ago to be a pretty fringe idea. On the other hand California has come to depend on some of the country's most abusive agricultural practices, which involve a vicious circle of ever-increasing amounts of the "cide" sisters and other chemical additives. In this scenario there is never a chance for the land to recover and renew.

In extending my thoughts about the importance of great ingredients to great cooking, then, I would add also that great ingredients come from great land. I strongly believe that the preservation of the planet is directly tied to the food supply. The choices that each of us makes every day about what we eat is like a vote for the planet. It's become a bit of conventional wisdom here in 2007, but when this book was originally published the idea of "voting with your fork" was a pretty new concept. These choices affect the diversity and quality of the food as well as how it is grown or raised, and distributed.

THE IMPORTANCE OF ETHICAL FOOD

In addition to being concerned about the use of chemistry in agriculture, like many of you I worry about the existence of what I call "ethical food." The biological revolution that began in the twentieth century and continues now in the twenty-first has opened the door to such developments as genetic engineering of our foods. I find this troubling because it diverts attention and effort from the preservation of the vast and diverse gene pool that nature has already provided us with and that we are allowing to become extinct. It is this rich pool that has the ability to sustain life. Michael Pollan's wonderful book *The Botany of Desire* talks eloquently about the consequences of not paying attention to natural diversity and selection.

In commercial animal husbandry, as another example, we've all become increasingly aware of practices that we are only beginning to understand — the use of growth hormones, massive doses of antibiotics, and other means to raise animals in ways that are often inhumane, that homogenize and strip flavor, and that have health consequences both for the animal as well as for the consumer. Thankfully, consumer demand in recent years has had a positive effect on how meat is produced. I remember a time in my restaurant when we didn't serve beef because we couldn't find a supplier who raised and processed it naturally and ethically.

This concern about wholesomeness was an important reason that Sid Goldstein and I wrote a book called *American Game Cooking* way back in 1991. One of the basic tenets of the book was that farm-raised game was one of the few remaining meat sources that was not manipulated genetically or chemically and therefore was still a wholesome food.

How food is grown, harvested or slaughtered, fumigated and packaged, stored, shipped, and handled should be of concern to us all, as cooks and eaters as well as residents of the planet. One sensible response is to eat seasonally and locally. We don't really need tasteless tomatoes for salad in December, which can come from halfway around the world. Cabbage, fennel, and citrus can make an equally interesting salad, more in harmony with the season, the ecology, and our appetite.

Another way to cast your vote for ethical forms of agriculture is to patronize local farmers' markets that showcase locally farm-raised seasonal foods. If your city or township doesn't have one, it should. You can help nurture this important movement along by working with your local government, chamber of commerce, state department of agriculture, or USDA extension.

THE IMPORTANCE OF HEALTH AND HEALTHFUL COOKING

In the original edition of this book, I noted that one of the most important new influences facing chefs was a recognition of changing how we cook to embrace healthful eating and longevity. No doubt this was greatly influenced by the fact that I was getting older and that I was finally taking the old adage "you are what you eat" seriously. My early training in French cooking taught me to enrich a sauce or dish by adding more cream or butter or egg yolks or, better yet, all of them! As I cook now, I find that food can be enriched in a myriad of more healthful ways — and that food that starts with great ingredients probably doesn't need to be enriched at all.

The primary health concern then was controlling our fat intake, which I think we'll all remember launched a storm of low-fat products that were supposedly the silver bullet for good health. The controversial USDA "Eating Pyramid" (controversial because pressure from the meat and dairy industries affected the final recommendations) and its recently updated version are at least attempts to bring some understanding to the ever-changing pronouncements of what's good and what isn't. Recent recommendations by the Harvard School of Public Health have given us a clearer picture of what it means to eat in a healthful way, and these have become personal goals and are a touch-stone for many of the recipes in this book. At the same time I've tried to maintain some balance: Food is about pleasure, too, which is my way of saying that I've included a few decadent dishes, and I hope you'll enjoy them, in moderation of course! I remember a time when I was doing a cooking demo with Julia Child for an overflow crowd of admirers and press. She stopped in the middle of her demo and shook her finger at the press assembled there and noted that they were making us a nation of "food hysterics." She exclaimed, "God gave us butter and cream to enjoy." The key, she explained, was to understand your individual metabolism and enjoy everything in moderation and balance. That, with daily exercise, still seems to be very good advice.

THE USE OF RAW EGGS IN COOKING

Traditionally, raw eggs were used to make emulsified sauces such as mayonnaise and aioli. In recent years, however, there has been some concern about eating raw-egg dishes because of possible salmonella contamination. While it is extremely rare for salmonella poisoning to be fatal, the very young, old, or health-compromised should be careful. Interestingly, it is estimated that only 10 percent of the two million cases or so of salmonella poisoning reported each year are caused by raw eggs. Undercooked meat or poultry are much more likely to be the culprits. If you are concerned, however, please be sure to use coddled eggs (eggs that have been heated to at least 145°F) or use flash-pasteurized raw eggs wherever uncooked eggs are called for.

THE NEW MOTHER SAUCES

One of the best examples I can think of that illustrates new American and especially wine country cuisine is what I call the development of the "new mother sauces." Any of you who have spent time cooking traditional French food will no doubt recall the so-called mother sauces (see Julia Child's *Mastering the Art of French Cooking*, Volume One, for a complete description). These included brown sauces derived from brown stocks, white sauces developed from dairy or white stocks, and hot and cold emulsion sauces such as hollandaise or mayonnaise derived from egg yolk and fat combinations. In most of my cooking today the original "mothers," which were often high in butter, cream, and other saturated fats, have been replaced by new, lighter mothers, such as vinaigrettes, salsas, pestos, chutneys, natural stock reductions, and juices. These new mothers come to us from many cuisines, and their appearance indicates a new understanding of how to add flavor and zing to the ever-increasing variety of new foods that are becoming available to us with less fat but — most important — more flavor.

FOOD AS ART

Before I became a chef my training was in art, specifically painting. Looking back on it now, the connection between painting and cooking was pretty direct. I discovered that everything I ever wanted to do on canvas I could also do with food.

Mechanically and intellectually, pushing paint around on a canvas was similar in process to manipulating food on a plate, plus I had the advantage of feeding the body as well as the soul. The enjoyment of food, I believe, is as much visual as it is oral, and like many of my contemporaries I care very much about how food is presented. Many of my recipes have several components, because I love the way certain foods look together as well as how they taste together. That's also why I include suggested garnishes with most of the recipes. It's true I can do things in my restaurant kitchen that I wouldn't expend the energy on in my home kitchen, but even at home I take care with the look of the dish and the look of the plate, because I take pleasure in the activity. Food gives us the opportunity every day to create a masterpiece. And even if each plate doesn't turn out that way, then at least we can enjoy the process of creating it. Cooking can and should remind us of our connection to our bodies, our fellow human beings, and our planet, and the great gifts, delicious ingredients, that God (whoever he or she is) has given us to use.

You will find in these recipes some things familiar and traditional, and some things very new, but all of them are wrapped around a consciousness of this special place where foods and wines are grown together and made in proximity.

What I hope to share with you is my experience, passion, and love for creating wholesome, delicious recipes. In the process, I hope I'll strike a few chords and inspire you to explore your own concept of the natural food chain — from the earth to the table.

As my friend and mentor, the late M. F. K. Fisher, said in her book *The Art of Eating*: "We must eat. If, in the face of that dread fact, we can find other nourishment, and tolerance and compassion for it, we'll be no less full of human dignity. There is a communication of more than our bodies when bread is broken and wine drunk."

— John Ash

SALADS

SALADS *and* WINE

The conventional wisdom is that one doesn't serve wine with salads. Vinegary, acidic dressings and raw greens and vegetables don't usually flatter wine, so why bother?

It may be true that most wines don't do much for iceberg lettuce doused with oil and vinegar (or vice versa), but today's salads are different. Salads are made with a range of greens—romaine and arugula, mâche, frisée, spinach—that are fuller flavored; salads can include grilled vegetables, nuts, meats and fish, and cheeses. They're often the main event, and they can be perfect partners to a full range of wines, from a crisp Sauvignon Blanc to an earthy red.

There are two keys to good salad-wine matches:

1. Make sure there isn't too much acid or vinegar in the dressing; this can kill the fruit in wine. Cut down the amount of vinegar or don't use it at all. For an acid component that's more complementary to wine, you can use citrus juice, a mellow vinegar such as balsamic or rice vinegar, or even wine itself.

2. Look to "bridge" ingredients to connect the salad and wine: That is, include ingredients in the salad whose flavors are a natural complement to the wine. An aged Parmesan cheese is a nice bridge to a buttery, oaky Chardonnay; grilled portobello mushrooms are an earthy bridge to mellow reds like Merlot; fresh pear or melon is a natural with Riesling or Gewürztraminer. In the same way that salads are different creatures from what they used to be, so are wines. A fine old Cabernet from Bordeaux is not a great wine for most salads, but a fresh young California Pinot Noir could be sublime.

GRILLED ASPARAGUS WITH LEMON OLIVE OIL AND PECORINO CHEESE

Serves 4

1 pound fresh asparagus, tough ends discarded

2 tablespoons extra-virgin olive oil

Sea salt, such as Maldon

Freshly ground pepper

3 tablespoons lemon-infused extra-virgin olive oil

½ cup thinly shaved pecorino or Parmigiano-Reggiano cheese

RECOMMENDED WINE
A crisp, clean white wine with no oak and lots of citrus quality would be the ticket here, such as **Sauvignon Blanc**, or **Pinot Gris** or **Pinot Grigio**.

One of the simplest and best ways to cook asparagus is to give it a light coating of olive oil and grill it. Grilling brings out the sweetness, and I prefer it to steaming or boiling, which seems to bring out more of the vegetal notes. I'm convinced too that keeping the asparagus away from water minimizes that interesting condition called "asparagus pee." I won't go any further, but see if it works for you! Add some good olives, thinly sliced meats such as coppa or prosciutto, and maybe a sprinkling of some Fried Capers (page 33) for a delicious antipasti course.

Brush the asparagus with the olive oil and season generously with salt and pepper. Over hot coals or a gas grill preheated to medium-high, grill the asparagus until it takes on a bit of color. Roll and turn so that it's cooked on all sides. Place on a plate and drizzle with the lemon olive oil and scatter the cheese over. Season to taste with salt and pepper. Serve warm or at room temperature.

ASPARAGUS SALAD WITH PICKLED GINGER VINAIGRETTE

Serves 4

RECOMMENDED WINE
An herbal-tinged **Sauvignon Blanc** or **Fumé Blanc** will contrast with the spicy rush of ginger in this dressing.

1 teaspoon chopped shallot

2 tablespoons chopped pickled ginger

3 tablespoons unseasoned rice wine vinegar

2 tablespoons toasted sesame oil

4 tablespoons olive oil

Kosher or sea salt and freshly ground pepper

1½ pounds fresh asparagus

Here's another take on grilled asparagus, this one with some Asian-influenced flavors.

Prepare a charcoal fire. In a small bowl, whisk together the shallot, pickled ginger, rice wine vinegar, sesame oil, and olive oil. Season to taste with salt and pepper. Brush the asparagus with some of the vinaigrette. Grill over hot coals until crisp-tender.

Serve warm or at room temperature, drizzled with the remaining vinaigrette.

GRILLED KALE SALAD

Serves 4

RECOMMENDED WINE
Kale has a very earthy, meaty flavor, so this salad goes well with reds that have an earthy character to them, such as **Pinot Noir**, **Syrah**, **Sangiovese**, or **Chianti**.

1½ pounds Lacinato, Verdura, or other kale, stemmed

⅓ cup extra-virgin olive oil

Kosher or sea salt and freshly ground pepper

3 tablespoons sherry vinegar

This salad was suggested by Jeff Dawson, a renowned gardener I've had the pleasure to work with over the years. It's a simple approach that can be used for any variety of meaty greens. Grilling gives a special smoky flavor, which is heightened by the nutty sherry vinegar. You may not find Lacinato kale in your supermarket, but it is a great variety to track down at the farmers' market or grow in your garden.

Prepare a charcoal fire. Brush the kale leaves very lightly with some of the olive oil. Season with salt and pepper.

Grill the kale leaves over hot coals until they soften and the edges are very lightly charred. In a bowl, toss the kale with the remaining olive oil and the sherry vinegar. Season to taste with salt and pepper.

salt

Salt has many faces and, believe it or not, many flavors. Most salt sold in markets today is rock salt, which is mined from salt deposits left behind by ancient, extinct seas. You can also buy sea salt, which comes from existing seas and is simply sea water that has been evaporated by the sun. One of the most interesting tastings I've ever gone to was a tasting of sea salts from around the world. There was a substantial difference in flavor, depending on location. Some were very mineral while others were almost sweet — so even something as simple as salt can add subtle flavor differences to a recipe. Most tasters (including me) prefer sea salt to ordinary table salt that has been processed in high heat to remove so-called impurities. These impurities are really the trace elements that give sea salt its unique and more complex flavor. Some cooks also believe that sea salt is nutritionally superior to rock salt, but unfortunately there is no truth to this. Any extra minerals that may be in sea salt are in such small amounts that they wouldn't make any dietary difference. In this book I often call for the use of kosher salt. Kosher salt has large, flaky crystals and dissolves much more slowly than ordinary salt — qualities that are helpful in drawing the blood out of meats before cooking, which is a requirement of Jewish dietary law. I like its large crystals as a garnishing salt when you want to see and taste the pure salt flavor.

OTHER SALT MIXTURES:

Dried herbs combined with salt are now widely available in gourmet food shops. They are easy to put together on your own and have the advantage of adding interesting flavors while cutting down on the amount of sodium in your diet, if that's a concern.

Two other salt mixtures that I keep on hand for everyday use are:

Sesame salt (gomasio), from Japanese cooking, is a blend of 4 or more parts toasted, ground sesame seeds to 1 part sea salt. It adds a nutty, earthy note when sprinkled on foods.

Sour salt used in Indian cooking is a blend of 6 or more parts sea salt with 1 part citric or ascorbic acid crystals. It adds a tart-salt flavor that I love with fresh tomatoes and on grilled or sautéed fish.

CUCUMBER-YOGURT SALAD WITH TOYBOX TOMATOES

Serves 6 to 8

RECOMMENDED WINE
An herbal-tinged **Sauvignon Blanc** offers a similar herbal tartness that goes well with the mint, basil, and yogurt flavors in this salad.

when is a pepper a chile?

Recipes can sometimes be confusing in their use of the terms "peppers" and "chiles." In England peppers are known either as "chiles" or "capsicums," and hot ones are called "hot chiles." In Latin America hot peppers are called "chiles" while mild peppers are called "peppers." In the United States the word "peppers" usually refers to the mild bell peppers (pimientos are included in the pepper category as one of the varieties) and "chiles" refers to those peppers that are hot. Furthermore, the original Nahuatl word was "chilli," the Spanish word is "chile," and in English you can find "chili" or "chilli." I've used the Spanish spelling, which is what seems most used in the United States. Whew!

2 medium English cucumbers

Kosher or sea salt

1 cup finely chopped red onion

1 teaspoon minced garlic

½ teaspoon seeded and minced serrano chile

1¼ cups plain yogurt

1 tablespoon chopped fresh basil or 1 teaspoon dried

1 tablespoon chopped fresh mint or 1 teaspoon dried

1 teaspoon cumin seeds, toasted and crushed

¼ teaspoon freshly ground pepper

2 teaspoons sugar

3 tablespoons seasoned rice wine vinegar

¼ cup toasted pine nuts or blanched slivered almonds

2 cups toybox tomatoes or halved cherry tomatoes

Fresh mint sprigs for garnishing

This refreshing salad shines during the summer, when tomatoes are at their peak. Toybox tomatoes are baby red, orange, and yellow tomatoes that have become widely available. (Regular cherry tomatoes will certainly do in their place.) This salad is great for making ahead, since the flavors develop best after about 2 hours in the refrigerator. The combination of cucumbers and yogurt is derived from Indian cuisine, where raita is used as a condiment to calm the palate alongside hot curries.

With a vegetable peeler, remove the skin from the cucumbers in alternating strips, if you want. Cut the cucumbers in half lengthwise and scrape out any seeds with a teaspoon. Cut into ½-inch diagonal slices. Put in a colander in the sink. Lightly sprinkle the cucumber slices with salt, toss, and set aside to drain for at least 1 hour.

In a large bowl, combine the onion, garlic, chile, yogurt, basil, mint, cumin seeds, pepper, and sugar. Rinse the cucumbers and blot dry. In a medium bowl, toss the cucumbers with the rice wine vinegar and add them to the onion-yogurt mixture. Cover and refrigerate for at least 2 hours before serving.

At serving time, stir in the pine nuts and the tomatoes. Serve on chilled plates, garnished with mint sprigs.

BLACK BEAN GAZPACHO SALAD

Serves 8 to 10

2 cups cooked black beans or canned beans, drained and rinsed

2 cups thinly sliced red onion

1 tablespoon finely chopped garlic

2 cups peeled, seeded, and diagonally sliced cucumber

2 cups seeded and diced ripe tomatoes

½ cup diced red bell pepper

½ cup diced yellow bell pepper

2 teaspoons seeded and minced serrano chile

1 cup husked and largely diced tomatillos

1 cup fresh raw corn kernels (1 large ear)

¼ cup chopped fresh cilantro

⅓ cup fresh lime juice

1 tablespoon raspberry or cider vinegar

1 tablespoon bottled hot sauce

¼ cup olive oil

1 cup fresh or canned tomato juice

1 tablespoon chopped fresh oregano or 2 teaspoons dried

Kosher or sea salt and freshly ground pepper

Fresh cilantro sprigs for garnishing

RECOMMENDED WINE
Either a chilled **rosé** or aromatic white like **Riesling** or **Gewürztraminer** provides a nice contrast to this hearty salad.

This is a loose take on a traditional gazpacho soup, with the addition of black beans. It makes a terrific summer lunch salad or hearty first course. While the length of the ingredients list may seem a little daunting and some time is involved in chopping the vegetables, the salad comes together very easily. It's great for a crowd and stores well in the refrigerator for up to 3 days.

In a medium bowl, combine the beans, onion, garlic, cucumber, tomatoes, red bell pepper, yellow bell pepper, chile, tomatillos, corn, cilantro, lime juice, vinegar, hot sauce, olive oil, tomato juice, and oregano. Season to taste with salt and pepper. Chill for at least 2 hours to allow the flavors to blend. Season to taste with additional salt and pepper and add more hot sauce as desired. Serve chilled, garnished with cilantro sprigs.

SUMMER SQUASH SALAD WITH FETA

Serves 6 to 8 as a first course or side dish

RECOMMENDED WINE
A citrusy **Sauvignon Blanc** or crisp **Pinot Gris** or **Pinot Grigio** are nice complements for this garden-fresh salad.

12 ounces zucchini, cut into large dice

8 ounces yellow summer squash, cut into large dice

½ cup drained and coarsely chopped oil-packed sun-dried tomatoes

½ cup sliced Kalamata or Niçoise olives

1 cup largely diced red bell pepper

1½ tablespoons chopped shallot

6 tablespoons olive oil

3 tablespoons raspberry or cider vinegar

1 tablespoon honey

1 tablespoon chopped fresh basil

1 tablespoon chopped fresh mint

3 ounces feta cheese, crumbled

Kosher or sea salt and freshly ground pepper

Anyone who has ever grown zucchini or yellow summer squash knows that you have to be creative to find ways to use all that even a small garden will yield. This Provençal-inspired dish is an excellent accompaniment to grilled seafood or may be served as a first-course salad.

In a large bowl, combine the zucchini, squash, tomatoes, olives, bell pepper, shallot, olive oil, vinegar, honey, basil, mint, and feta. Season to taste with salt and pepper. Refrigerate until ready to serve.

eating seasonally

I can't emphasize enough the value of eating seasonally. By that I mean eating ingredients that are properly available to us during specific seasons. I've never understood why restaurants or markets insist on serving items like tomatoes in winter salads (or why we continue to expect them) when we all know that winter tomatoes are generally pretty awful. Instead, why not serve a winter salad that takes advantage of ingredients that are at their peak in winter? Of course, making that kind of determination has been vastly complicated by jet shipping. Oranges are at their peak in winter, so I think of the recipe following as a winter salad. The downside is that they have to be flown long distances to reach markets anywhere outside Florida or California—no matter what the season. Part of the joy of eating is the anticipation of seasonal foods. For me, the first asparagus of spring or the first raspberries in the summer are a cause for celebration. Eating with the seasons helps ground us and reminds us of our connections to the earth. In *Walden Pond*, Thoreau says: "Live in each season as it passes; breathe the air, drink the drink, taste the fruit, and resign yourself to the influence of each."

FIRE AND ICE MELON SALAD WITH FIGS AND PROSCIUTTO

Serves 8

⅓ cup sugar or honey

¼ cup white wine or water

1 teaspoon seeded and minced serrano chile

1 tablespoon finely diced red bell pepper

1 tablespoon finely diced yellow bell pepper

¼ cup fresh lime juice

1 tablespoon minced fresh mint

2 large honeydew, cantaloupe, crane, or other ripe melon

8 fresh ripe figs, cut in half and fanned

8 paper-thin slices prosciutto

Edible flower petals, such as nasturtium, borage, or daylily, for garnishing (optional)

This is a perfect summertime dish to start a lunch or dinner. The heat of the serrano chiles contrasts with the cool, refreshing melon, and the mint, lime, and salty prosciutto add interesting counterpoints.

In a small saucepan, combine the sugar and wine over medium heat and stir until the sugar is dissolved. Add the chile, red bell pepper, and yellow bell pepper and cool. Stir in the lime juice and mint. Store, covered, in the refrigerator for up to 3 days.

Cut the melons in half and remove the seeds. Cut into decorative shapes and arrange on chilled plates. Spoon the chile syrup over the melon and arrange the figs and prosciutto attractively around. Sprinkle with edible flower petals, if using.

chile heat

The Scoville Scale for measuring the heat level of chiles was developed back at the beginning of the twentieth century by W. L. Scoville. His method involved extracting the heat-producing chemical compounds known as capsaicin, which he then diluted to a point where they were barely detectable to the taste. (Capsaicin is thought to be the most potent of the heat-producing chemicals in chiles.) For example, if a gram of chile extract had to be diluted in 40,000 ml of water and alcohol to be barely perceptible, then that chile was rated at 40,000 Scoville heat units. Although this is not a precise test, since each of us has some differences in sensitivity to chiles, it does give a good estimate of the relative heats of different chiles. Here are some Scoville heat ratings for various popular chiles:

BELL PEPPERS:	0
ANAHEIMS:	800–1,200
POBLANOS:	800–1,200
JALAPEÑOS:	8,000–10,000
SERRANOS:	10,000–18,000
JAPANESE:	25,000–40,000
THAI:	40,000–60,000
PURE CAPSAICIN:	1,000,000

WATERMELON AND RED ONION SALAD

Serves 6

RECOMMENDED WINE
A fruity, slightly sweet **Gewürztraminer** or **Johannesburg Riesling** mirrors the sweet melon and raspberry tastes in this salad.

watermelon

Watermelons are traditionally known for their dark-green exterior and ruby-red flesh, but there is an extraordinary variety of melons available. There are many delicious yellow-fleshed varieties, and the combination of red and yellow melon on a plate is particularly beautiful. I'm especially fond of an heirloom variety called Moon and Stars, which displays a radiant large, yellow oval splash (resembling the moon) and tiny, yellow dots in constellations (the stars) on its green skin. Under the right conditions — a good, warm summer and sandy soil — melons can be grown easily by the home gardener, and many unusual, flavorful melon varieties are available through seed companies (see page 426). Whole watermelons should always be stored at room temperature after being purchased, while cut melons keep better in the refrigerator. Watermelon seeds are edible, by the way. The Chinese roast and salt them to eat as a snack. I've also had them when they've been soaked in soy sauce, lightly dusted with hot pepper, and then roasted at 350°F just until crunchy.

1 tablespoon minced shallots or green onions, white part only

¼ cup raspberry or other fruit vinegar

¼ cup raspberry purée made from fresh or unsweetened frozen berries, puréed and strained

¼ cup fresh orange juice

2 teaspoons honey

¼ cup olive oil

Kosher or sea salt and freshly ground pepper

2 medium sweet red onions, sliced ¼ inch thick and soaked in ice water for at least 30 minutes

2 small bunches watercress, woody stems discarded

8 cups seeded 1-inch cubes watermelon, chilled (use both red and yellow watermelon, if available)

6 large ripe fresh figs, sliced or quartered (optional)

Chopped fresh mint leaves for garnishing

This may sound like an odd combination, but it's one of the most popular summer salads served over the years at my namesake restaurant, John Ash & Company, in Sonoma County, California. Fresh blueberries or blackberries make a wonderful and colorful addition to this salad.

In a medium bowl, whisk together the shallots, vinegar, raspberry purée, orange juice, honey, and olive oil to make a smooth mixture. Season to taste with salt and pepper. Drain the onions, pat dry, and separate into individual rings. Transfer the onion rings to a medium bowl and pour the vinaigrette over. Marinate the onions for at least 30 minutes covered in the refrigerator.

On chilled plates, arrange the watercress and top with the cubed watermelon. Arrange the onions and figs attractively around and drizzle the vinaigrette over. Sprinkle mint leaves over the top and serve immediately.

FENNEL, PEAR, AND PERSIMMON SALAD WITH FIG VINAIGRETTE

Serves 6

3 cups mixed savory greens, such as arugula, watercress, tatsoi, endive, and radicchio

2 firm Fuyu persimmons, peeled and thinly sliced

2 ripe pears, peeled, cored, and cut into wedges

1 fennel bulb, thinly sliced vertically

½ cup pecan halves, lightly toasted

Fig Vinaigrette (recipe follows)

RECOMMENDED WINE
The dressing is fairly sweet, so a fruity white or **rosé** wine with a little bit of residual sugar in it, such as **Riesling**, **Gewürztraminer**, **Chenin Blanc**, or **white Zinfandel** would work well.

This is a wonderful salad for the fall. For a more substantial course, drape some paper-thin slices of prosciutto or coppa around the plate. There are two different varieties of persimmons on the market. I've specified Fuyu persimmons in this recipe because they are fully ripe and really at their peak while they are still firm and thus sliceable. The variety called Hachiya is not ripe until very soft and sweet, and it's usually used mashed or puréed in baking.

Divide the greens among well-chilled plates. Arrange the persimmons, pears, and fennel on and around the greens. Sprinkle with the pecan halves. Drizzle some of the Fig Vinaigrette over all.

FIG VINAIGRETTE
Makes about 1¼ cups

⅔ cup chopped dried figs

½ cup water

½ cup dry white wine

½ cup apple juice or cider

2 teaspoons minced fresh thyme

2 teaspoons black mustard seeds, toasted

1½ tablespoons minced shallot

¼ cup sherry vinegar

⅓ cup olive oil

Kosher or sea salt and freshly ground pepper

In a saucepan, combine ⅓ cup of the figs with the water and bring to a boil. Reduce the heat and simmer, covered, until the figs are soft, about 5 minutes. Cool.

Pour the fig mixture into a blender or food processor and purée. Transfer to a medium bowl. Whisk in the wine, apple juice, thyme, mustard seeds, shallot, vinegar, and olive oil. Season to taste with salt and pepper. Stir in the remaining figs.

ORANGE, OLIVE, AND FENNEL SALAD WITH CRANBERRY VINAIGRETTE

Serves 6

RECOMMENDED WINE
A bright fruity **Gamay**, **Gewürztraminer**, or **white Zinfandel** could all work with this refreshing salad.

3 large navel oranges, peeled and sliced ¼ inch thick

1 large head fennel, sliced paper thin vertically

1 small sweet red onion, peeled and thinly sliced in rings and soaked in ice water if strong

⅔ cup mixed country-style olives, such as Niçoise, cracked green, or Sicilian

Cranberry Vinaigrette (recipe follows)

Fennel sprigs and daikon or sunflower radish sprouts for garnishing

This is a nice salad that takes advantage of ingredients available in the late fall and winter.

Arrange the oranges, fennel, and onion attractively on a plate (the fennel should be right-side up, if possible). Scatter the olives around and drizzle the vinaigrette over. Garnish with the fennel sprigs and sprouts.

~~~~~~

CRANBERRY VINAIGRETTE
Makes about 1¼ cups

1 cup fresh or frozen cranberries

½ cup orange juice

1 tablespoon finely chopped shallot or green onion, white part only

2 tablespoons rice vinegar

1 tablespoon honey

1 tablespoon fresh lime or lemon juice

⅓ to ½ cup canola or neutral olive oil

Kosher or sea salt and freshly ground pepper, preferably white

The idea here is to balance the tart/sweet/salt/ pepper elements to your own taste. If using frozen cranberries, defrost before using. They tend to be difficult to purée in their frozen state.

In a blender or food processor, combine the cranberries, orange juice, shallot, vinegar, honey, and lime juice and purée. With the motor running, slowly add olive oil to the desired consistency. In a medium bowl, strain the purée through a fine-mesh strainer, pushing down on the solids. Season to taste with salt and pepper. Store, covered, in the refrigerator for up to 5 days.

ORANGES, WATERCRESS, AND ENDIVES WITH ASIAN ORANGE VINAIGRETTE

Serves 8

2 large Belgian endives, separated into leaves

4 large seedless oranges, peeled and cut into thick rounds

2 bunches watercress, woody stems discarded

2 cups finely sliced radicchio

Asian Orange Vinaigrette (recipe follows)

Fresh sunflower or daikon sprouts for garnishing (optional)

RECOMMENDED WINE
The sweet-tart-bitter characteristics of this salad would link with one of the aromatic varieties that have the same sweet-tart balance: **Riesling**, **Gewürztraminer**, **Muscat**, or **Viognier**.

This simple, pretty salad focuses on the combination of sweet and slightly bitter tastes along with a flavorful dressing that heightens the flavors dramatically. The vinaigrette will keep up to 5 days covered in the refrigerator and makes an excellent marinade for grilled fish, chicken, or pork.

Arrange the endive leaves, oranges, and watercress attractively on chilled plates. In a medium bowl, toss the radicchio with a couple of tablespoons of the Asian Orange Vinaigrette and mound in the center. Drizzle additional vinaigrette over the rest of the salad and top with the sprouts.

ASIAN ORANGE VINAIGRETTE
Makes a generous ¾ cup

¼ cup frozen orange juice concentrate

2 tablespoons fresh lime juice

2 tablespoons soy sauce, preferably salt reduced

3 tablespoons rice wine vinegar

1 tablespoon peeled and finely chopped fresh ginger

1 teaspoon toasted sesame oil

¼ cup olive oil

1 tablespoon finely chopped green onion, both white and green parts

1½ tablespoons finely chopped fresh cilantro or parsley

Kosher or sea salt and freshly ground pepper

In a blender or food processor, combine the orange juice, lime juice, soy sauce, vinegar, and ginger and process until smooth. Add the sesame oil and olive oil and pulse a few times to form a light emulsion. Transfer to a medium bowl. Whisk in the green onion and cilantro and season to taste with salt and pepper.

TABBOULEH SALAD

Serves 6 or more as a first course

parsleys

There are two kinds of parsley found in the market: curly and flat leaf. They can be used interchangeably, but many cooks prefer the more pronounced herbal flavor of flat leaf. Although we typically think of parsley as a garnish, it makes a wonderful side-dish vegetable when it's cooked briefly in a little stock and then puréed. Lots and lots of parsley is also the key ingredient in tabbouleh salad, which I think is best done with curly-leafed parsley.

4 pounds ripe tomatoes, peeled, halved, and seeded

⅓ cup extra-virgin olive oil

Kosher or sea salt and freshly ground pepper

½ cup fine bulgur wheat

4 cups packed finely chopped fresh parsley, preferably curly leaf

½ cup lightly packed finely chopped fresh mint

3 tablespoons minced green onion, both white and green parts

2 teaspoons minced garlic

2 teaspoons finely grated lemon zest

2 tablespoons fresh lemon juice

Fresh mint sprigs and toasted pine nuts for garnishing (optional)

There is great debate among cooks from the Middle East about the ratio of bulgur wheat to parsley in a tabbouleh. I've been told that it should be at least 8 parts (by volume) parsley to 1 part bulgur. In this version I've made it a bit more bulgur to parsley. The California hook in this salad is the slow-roasted tomatoes. Something magical happens when you cook them for a long time at low temperature—the flavor becomes very concentrated and sweet. They are a perfect foil for the lemony-herbal tabbouleh. Note that bulgur is a cooked product so just needs rehydrating. In Middle Eastern markets it's numbered according to its size: fine is No. 1, medium No. 2, coarse No. 3. Use fine for this recipe. Traditionally, tabbouleh is served with lettuce leaves or pita bread so that you can scoop it up. It's perfectly fine, however, to serve with a fork!

Preheat the oven to 275°F. Arrange the tomatoes cut-side up on a parchment-lined baking sheet, drizzle with 3 tablespoons of the olive oil, and season lightly with salt and pepper. Put in the oven for 3 hours or until tomatoes are somewhat shriveled and slightly browned. Can be made 3 days ahead and stored covered in the refrigerator.

Rinse the bulgur in cold running water until the water runs clear. Drain, put in a medium bowl, and pour enough boiling water over to cover by 1 inch. Allow to sit for 5 minutes, then drain and gently squeeze out the excess water. Either do this in your hands or wrap the bulgur in a clean tea towel and press. Return the bulgur to the bowl and stir in the remaining olive oil, parsley, mint, green onion, garlic, and lemon zest. Season to taste with salt, pepper, and lemon juice. Set aside for at least 20 minutes for the flavors to develop.

Arrange the roasted tomatoes on plates and place a mound of the tabbouleh mixture on top. Garnish with mint sprigs and toasted pine nuts and serve immediately.

Variations: Some Middle Eastern cooks will add pinches of cumin, cinnamon, or allspice to the tabbouleh mixture. Others will add a pinch or two of hot red pepper, such as Aleppo, which is similar in flavor to our ancho chile. Spanish smoked paprika is also an interesting addition.

GOAT CHEESE, FIGS, AND SAVORY GREENS WITH SHERRY-SHALLOT VINAIGRETTE

Serves 4 to 8 as a first course

4 ounces aged goat cheese

4 cups loosely packed mixed savory greens, such as arugula, mizuna, mustard, and watercress

8 small, fresh ripe figs, cut in half and fanned

Sherry-Shallot Vinaigrette (recipe follows)

Mixture of edible flower petals, such as calendula, bachelor's button, or chive, for garnishing

RECOMMENDED WINE

A soft **Riesling** or **Chenin Blanc** with just a touch of residual sugar would go well with the figs and nutty, aged goat cheese. If using a fresh goat cheese, with its tarter flavor, a barrel-aged **Sauvignon Blanc** would work best.

This is one of those very simple recipes that epitomizes summer-sweet figs; rich, aged goat cheese; and an uncomplicated vinaigrette. I particularly like a goat cheese with a little age on it in this salad — it's deep in flavor and has a firm texture. I especially like Laurel Chenel's Crottin or Taupinière (page 421). Try adding slices of ripe pear or apple for an interesting variation.

Slice the cheese into small wedges and set aside. Arrange the greens and figs on chilled plates and dress with the Sherry-Shallot Vinaigrette. Arrange the goat cheese on top and sprinkle with a confetti of edible flower petals.

~~~~~~

SHERRY-SHALLOT VINAIGRETTE

1½ tablespoons fino or Amontillado sherry

1½ tablespoons balsamic vinegar, preferably white

1 teaspoon minced roasted garlic (see page 264)

1 tablespoon minced shallot

¼ cup olive oil

Kosher or sea salt and freshly ground pepper

In a small bowl, whisk together the sherry, vinegar, roasted garlic, shallot, and olive oil until just combined. Season to taste with salt and pepper.

MINTED ROMAINE SALAD WITH BLUE CHEESE AND PECANS

Serves 4

RECOMMENDED WINE
The mint, mustard, and cheese make for a complex flavor combination, which goes best with a crisp, clean, straightforward wine, such as a **Sauvignon Blanc**, **Pinot Grigio**, or a crisp Spanish white like **Albarino**.

4 romaine hearts

1 cup halved cherry tomatoes

¼ cup toasted pecan halves

Blue Cheese and Mint Vinaigrette (recipe follows)

Fresh mint sprigs and additional crumbled blue cheese for garnishing (optional)

This is a simple salad with really punchy flavors to it. It would be a perfect accompaniment to simply grilled chicken or pork.

Cut the romaine hearts crosswise into thick sections. In a large bowl, toss the romaine with the tomatoes, pecans, and Blue Cheese and Mint Vinaigrette. Garnish with mint sprigs and blue cheese, if using.

BLUE CHEESE AND MINT VINAIGRETTE
Makes about 1 cup

¼ cup white wine vinegar

1 tablespoon minced shallot

2 tablespoons Dijon mustard

2 teaspoons minced fresh mint

⅓ cup olive oil

¼ cup apple juice

1 ounce blue cheese, crumbled, such as Point Reyes Farmstead Original Blue or Maytag Blue

Kosher or sea salt and freshly ground pepper

In a medium bowl, combine the vinegar, shallot, mustard, and mint. Whisk in the olive oil and apple juice to form a smooth mixture. Stir in the blue cheese. Season with salt and pepper to taste. Taste carefully first, since blue cheese can be very salty. Store, covered, in the refrigerator for up to 3 days.

Note: For blue cheese sources, see page 421.

WARM RED CABBAGE SALAD WITH PANCETTA AND CALIFORNIA GOAT CHEESE

Serves 6

8 ounces good-quality pancetta, cut into ¼-inch dice

¾ cup water

2 teaspoons roasted garlic (see page 264)

2 tablespoons wild honey

¼ cup champagne vinegar

½ cup olive oil

Kosher or sea salt and freshly ground pepper

1 pound red cabbage, finely shredded

8 ounces California soft ripening or aged goat cheese, cut into attractive wedges

Sunflower or daikon sprouts for garnishing (optional)

RECOMMENDED WINE
The sweet-tart flavors of the warm salad are complemented by an aromatic white like **Riesling**, a chilled **rosé**, or a soft red like **Gamay**.

I love this salad when the weather is cool. When you cook red cabbage with vinegar it turns a beautiful fluorescent red. For the goat cheese I especially like the Bucheret, Camellia, or Crottin from Redwood Hill Farms, or the Humboldt Fog or Bermuda Triangle from Cypress Grove. But use whatever you like.

In a sauté pan, combine the pancetta with the water and cook over medium heat until the water evaporates and the pancetta browns, about 8 minutes. Be sure to stir to brown evenly. Remove and set aside. In the same sauté, pan whisk together the roasted garlic, honey, and vinegar, and then slowly whisk in the olive oil. Season to taste with salt and pepper.

Heat the sauté pan over medium-high heat. Add the cabbage to the honey-vinegar mixture and toss quickly for a minute or two just to warm through. Stir in the pancetta. Place on warm plates. Arrange the goat cheese on top along with sprouts and serve immediately.

Note: For goat cheese sources, see page 421.

GRILLED PORTOBELLO MUSHROOMS ON SAVORY GREENS WITH PARMESAN CHIPS

Serves 6

RECOMMENDED WINE
A rich, barrel-aged **Chardonnay** plays off both the earthiness of the mushrooms and the nutty, toasty cheese chips. If you're a red drinker, choose one with lots of forward fruit and lower tannins, like **Pinot Noir**.

1½ pounds portobello mushrooms

2 tablespoons white balsamic or seasoned rice vinegar

1 tablespoon mashed roasted garlic (see page 264)

2 teaspoons chopped fresh rosemary

2 teaspoons chopped fresh sage

½ cup olive oil

Kosher or sea salt and freshly ground pepper

4 cups mixed young tender savory greens, such as mizuna, arugula, watercress, and red mustard

Mustard Seed Vinaigrette (facing page)

Parmesan Chips (facing page)

I'm specifying portobello mushrooms here because they are widely available. Any other flavorful fresh mushrooms, such as oyster, shiitake, or chanterelle, are delicious in this recipe too. To make this a main course, add some roasted or grilled beets, carrots, and red onions.

Stem the mushrooms and remove the black gills by scraping with a teaspoon. In a small bowl, whisk together the vinegar, roasted garlic, rosemary, sage, and olive oil. Season to taste with salt and pepper. Using a pastry brush, "paint" the mushroom caps liberally with the mixture. Set aside, lightly covered.

Toss the greens with some of the Mustard Seed Vinaigrette and arrange attractively on plates. Drizzle a bit more of the vinaigrette around. Grill the mushrooms quickly over hot coals or in a stove-top grill pan over medium-high heat. Slice the mushrooms thickly on the bias and arrange on top of the greens. Top with Parmesan Chips and serve immediately.

MUSTARD SEED VINAIGRETTE
Makes about ½ cup

2 tablespoons Dijon mustard

1 tablespoon toasted whole mustard seeds

¼ cup seasoned rice vinegar

⅓ cup fresh orange juice

1 tablespoon chopped fresh dill

⅓ cup olive oil

Kosher or sea salt and freshly ground pepper

In a small bowl, whisk together the mustard, mustard seeds, vinegar, orange juice, dill, and olive oil until just combined. Season to taste with salt and pepper. Prepare at least 30 minutes before serving to allow the flavors to marry.

PARMESAN CHIPS
Makes about 12 chips

2 cups freshly grated Parmesan, dry Jack, or Asiago cheese, or a combination

2 teaspoons finely crushed cumin or fennel seeds

To prepare one chip on the stovetop: In a small bowl, combine the cheese and cumin. Heat a large nonstick skillet over medium heat. Sprinkle 2 tablespoons cheese in a lacy round over the bottom of the pan. The cheese will begin to melt and then bubble and lightly brown. Using a fork or spatula, lift by the edges to loosen the chip from the pan. Remove and cool on paper towels for a flat chip. Repeat for the remaining chips.

To prepare multiple chips in the oven: In a small bowl, combine the cheese and cumin. Put the cheese in rounds on parchment or a silicone baking mat on a baking sheet. Bake in a 375°F oven for 6 to 8 minutes or until the chips begin to color. Use a fork to lift the edges and loosen the chips from the pan. Remove and cool on paper towels.

The size of the chip will depend on the amount of cheese you use. Three tablespoons will yield a chip about 4 inches in diameter. Make sure to sprinkle the cheese with a light hand and make them as lacey as possible so that they don't end up too dense and heavy. You can form the chips by draping over a rolling pin or small overturned bowl.

WARM RADICCHIO SALAD WITH LEMON-GARLIC CREAM

Serves 4

RECOMMENDED WINE
A crisp dry white or sparkling wine would go nicely with the crisp-fried, slightly bitter radicchio. Citrusy **Sauvignon Blanc** bridges nicely to the Lemon-Garlic Cream.

panko

Panko is a type of bread crumb that originated in Japan. It is fairly widely available in the United States, especially in Asian markets. I think it is the best dry bread crumb to use, both as an ingredient in recipes and for coating foods for frying or sautéing. When panko is made, the crumb is expanded in a way that makes it very light and crisp, so it doesn't get soggy like ordinary bread crumbs. Furthermore, the crumbs are larger than ordinary commercially available bread crumbs; this helps keep the foods lighter and more delicate. Panko has become one of my pantry staples.

⅓ cup all-purpose flour

2 large eggs

1 tablespoon water

¾ cup coarse dry bread crumbs, preferably panko

½ cup freshly grated dry Jack or Parmesan cheese

1 tablespoon finely chopped mixed fresh herbs, such as chives, parsley, basil, and sage

1 teaspoon kosher or sea salt

½ teaspoon ground white pepper

2 medium heads radicchio, quartered lengthwise

Olive oil for frying

2 cups baby greens, such as arugula, frisée, and mâche

Lemon-Garlic Cream (facing page)

Chopped fresh chives and Fried Capers (facing page) for garnishing

The perfect round shape of radicchio makes it ideal for many uses where other lettuces and greens won't do. In this variation, quartered heads are deep-fried and served with a luscious, garlicky lemon cream. The joy of this dish is biting into the radicchio and tasting the various levels of warmth and crispness inside — a textural treat! If you're really going all-out, deep-fry some capers and scatter them around for garnish.

Spread the flour on a plate. In a shallow bowl, beat the eggs with the water. In another shallow bowl, combine the bread crumbs, cheese, herbs, and salt and pepper. Dredge the radicchio in the flour, shaking off the excess. Coat thoroughly in the egg mixture and then lightly and evenly pat with the bread crumb mixture, shaking off any excess. Refrigerate, uncovered, for at least 30 minutes to help the coating adhere.

In a skillet, pour olive oil to a depth of ¼ inch and heat until the oil shimmers (350°F). Over medium heat, add the radicchio and evenly brown. Transfer to paper towels to drain.

Arrange the baby greens on individual plates and place the fried radicchio on each plate. Drizzle with the Lemon-Garlic Cream and scatter the chives and Fried Capers over the top. Serve immediately while the radicchio is still warm.

LEMON-GARLIC CREAM
Makes about 1 cup

1 large egg

1 tablespoon roasted garlic (see page 264)

2 tablespoons fresh lemon juice

½ to ¾ cup olive oil

Rich Vegetable Stock (page 69) or Chicken Stock (page 66), or water, for thinning

1 tablespoon rinsed and chopped capers, or Fried Capers (at right)

Kosher or sea salt and freshly ground pepper

In a blender or food processor, combine the egg, garlic, and lemon juice. With the motor running, slowly add the olive oil to form an emulsion. The sauce should be thick but not stiff (it should still be pourable). Thin if necessary with stock. Stir in the capers and season to taste with salt and pepper. Store, covered, in the refrigerator for up to 3 days.

FRIED CAPERS

Something magical happens when you quickly deep-fry brine-packed capers. They lose a lot of their vinegar sharpness and become crisp and crunchy — a terrific garnish.

Drain the capers and put them on a paper towel to dry them as much as possible. In a small, deep saucepan, heat ½ inch olive oil until it shimmers (350°F on a frying or candy thermometer). Add the capers to the hot oil and fry for 1 to 2 minutes until they begin to crisp. Fry in batches if doing a lot; otherwise you'll cool the oil down too much. Drain carefully and put on paper towels to absorb excess oil. The capers can be made 3 to 4 hours ahead; keep them uncovered at room temperature.

Note: You also get a bonus here if you haven't scorched the oil. The capers will subtly flavor the oil, and it can be used again to sauté fish, chicken, or vegetables, or wherever you might like the flavor of capers.

WARM VEGETABLE SALAD WITH CHANTERELLE AND PORTOBELLO MUSHROOMS

Serves 4 to 6

RECOMMENDED WINE
A toasty, barrel-aged **Chardonnay**, or a **Pinot Noir**, if you want a red, mirrors the earthy flavors of the mushrooms.

chanterelle mushrooms

Chanterelles, also known as girolles or pfifferlings, are a true wild mushroom that no one has yet figured out how to cultivate. In the United States, most are gathered in the Pacific Northwest everywhere from Northern California to British Columbia. They have a wonderful nutty flavor. Although you can buy them dried or canned, they are best fresh in my opinion. Like most mushrooms, it is best to clean them with a soft brush. Don't immerse them in water unless they are so full of sand and pine needles that you absolutely have to. And don't wrap chanterelles (or any other mushroom) in plastic to store them; they are best stored in the refrigerator in a basket covered with a very lightly moistened cloth or paper towel.

4 tablespoons olive oil

1 cup finely julienned turnip or parsnip

⅔ cup finely julienned carrot

⅔ cup finely julienned red bell pepper

⅔ cup finely julienned fennel

1 tablespoon minced shallots

8 ounces chanterelles, cleaned and sliced ¼ inch thick

2 to 3 large portobello mushrooms, stemmed and black gills removed by scraping with a teaspoon

Kosher or sea salt and freshly ground pepper

2 cups savory young greens, such as arugula, red mustard, watercress, and radicchio

Honey-Lemon Vinaigrette (facing page)

Watercress or fresh chervil sprigs for garnishing (optional)

I love mushrooms and use them as often as I can. Here in the wine country we have access to many varieties of wild mushrooms, which appear after the first rains in the fall. In this recipe I've used wild chanterelles and cultivated portobellos for a double mushroom flavor. For convenience, I've suggested cooking them under the broiler or on the stovetop, but if you can cook them on an outdoor grill, by all means do it.

In a sauté pan, heat 1 tablespoon of the olive oil and sauté the turnip, carrot, bell pepper, and fennel until crisp-tender, about 2 minutes. Set aside and keep warm.

In the same sauté pan, heat 2 tablespoons of the olive oil and sauté the shallots and chanterelles until lightly browned. In a medium bowl, combine with the julienned vegetables.

Preheat the broiler or a stove-top grill pan. Brush the portobellos with the remaining 1 tablespoon olive oil. Season to taste with salt and pepper. Broil or grill the portobellos until softened. Set aside and keep warm.

Toss the vegetables and chanterelles with half the Honey-Lemon Vinaigrette. Divide the greens among the plates. Place the vegetables on top. Thickly slice the portobellos and arrange on the salads. Drizzle with some or all of the remaining vinaigrette and garnish with watercress or chervil, if using.

HONEY-LEMON VINAIGRETTE
Makes about 1 cup

⅓ cup olive oil

2 tablespoons minced shallots

½ cup fresh lemon juice

3 tablespoons honey

Kosher or sea salt and freshly ground pepper

In a sauté pan, heat the olive oil and sauté the shallots until soft but not brown. Set aside in a medium bowl to cool. Whisk in the lemon juice, honey, and salt and pepper to taste. Store, covered, in the refrigerator for up to 1 week.

chervil

One of the subtlest of the herb family, chervil is worth seeking out or even growing in a pot on a sunny window sill. It's a warm herb, in the sense that its parsley-anise flavor and fragrance tend to warm other herbs, or blend and fill in their background.

The flavor and fragrance of chervil resemble myrrh, one of the gifts brought by the Three Wise Men to the baby Jesus. Because of this it became a tradition in Christian Europe to serve chervil soup on Holy Thursday.

PECAN-POLENTA SALAD WITH GRILLED GREEN ONIONS AND CRÈME FRAÎCHE

Serves 6

RECOMMENDED WINE

A barrel-aged **Chardonnay** nicely complements the nutty polenta and the crème fraîche.

ensuring a crisp crust

You'll note that this recipe suggests refrigerating the coated polenta pieces briefly before they are sautéed. This is an important step when using the flour-egg-crumb technique. It is also important to make sure that the oil is the right temperature: The ideal is 350° to 375°F—the point at which the oil shimmers. Placing chilled food in hot oil is key to ensuring a crisp crust around an inside that isn't soggy or greasy.

POLENTA

3 tablespoons unsalted butter

¾ cup minced yellow onion

3 cups rich chicken stock

1 cup polenta

¼ cup freshly grated Asiago cheese

2 tablespoons minced fresh chives

Kosher or sea salt and freshly ground pepper

Olive oil for the pie plate

2 tablespoons all-purpose flour

2 large eggs

1 tablespoon water

¾ cup chopped pecans

⅓ cup coarse dry bread crumbs, such as panko

SALAD

6 large green onions, split lengthwise

½ cup olive oil

Kosher or sea salt and freshly ground pepper

2 tablespoons balsamic vinegar, preferably white

3 cups loosely packed savory greens, such as arugula and frisée

Oven-dried or sun-dried tomatoes for garnishing

½ cup Crème Fraîche (recipe follows)

This robust salad can serve as the centerpiece for the meal. Everything can be made ahead of time and the polenta sautéed just before serving. This is another dish that pairs hot ingredients (the polenta) with cold (the crisp greens) for an intriguing contrast. The oven-dried tomatoes called for as a garnish are made by slicing the tomatoes ½ inch thick. Liberally coat both sides with olive oil and season with salt and pepper. Put in a single layer on a baking sheet lined with parchment paper or a silicon mat and put in a 200°F oven and allowed to dry a bit for 2 to 3 hours. They shouldn't be completely dry but still moist and now full of concentrated tomato flavor. You can certainly use a good, oil-packed sun-dried tomato in place of the oven-dried, but drain before adding.

To make the polenta: In a small saucepan, melt the butter over medium heat and sauté the onion until soft and sweet. Add the stock, increase the heat, and bring to a boil. Slowly sprinkle in the polenta, stirring constantly. Reduce the heat and cook for 10 to 12 minutes, stirring often. The polenta will be thick and soft and will pull away from the sides of the pan when it's done. Stir in the cheese and chives. Season to taste with salt and pepper. Transfer the polenta to an oiled 10-inch pie plate or pan and spread it evenly. Refrigerate for 1 hour. Cut the chilled polenta into even diamond or wedge shapes. Spread the flour on a plate. In a shallow bowl, beat the eggs with the water. In another shallow bowl, combine the pecans and bread crumbs. Lightly dust each polenta piece with flour, dip it into the beaten egg mixture, and then into the pecan mixture, patting to coat evenly. Set on a wire rack and refrigerate until serving time.

To make the salad: Lightly brush the green onions with 1 tablespoon of the olive oil. Season with salt and pepper to taste. Grill or broil until they just begin to color. Set aside.

Whisk together 3 tablespoons of the olive oil and the balsamic vinegar and season to taste with salt and pepper. Toss the greens with the vinaigrette and arrange on chilled plates. In a sauté pan, heat at least 2 tablespoons of the olive oil over medium-high heat and sauté the prepared polenta until golden-brown on both sides. Place on top of the greens along with the green onions and tomatoes. Top with a generous tablespoon of crème fraîche. Finish with a grinding or two of pepper and a sprinkling of salt.

~~~~~~

CRÈME FRAÎCHE

1 cup heavy (whipping) cream, preferably natural and not ultrapasteurized or processed

2 tablespoons buttermilk

1 tablespoon fresh lemon juice

Lots of recipes call for crème fraîche, which is similar to sour cream but smoother and richer. In France, where it originates, its body comes from the natural bacteria in unpasteurized cream. In America, however, this is nearly impossible for us to get unless we milk our own animals, but we can make a good approximation with this simple recipe. Crème fraîche is great for cooking because of its rich flavor and stability— it won't break when heated, unlike sour cream.

In a medium bowl, stir together the cream, buttermilk, and lemon juice. Cover and let sit at room temperature for 6 to 8 hours or until very thick. Store covered in the refrigerator for up to 5 days.

HANGTOWN FRY SALAD

Serves 6

24 small oysters, shucked

1 cup milk

1 cup fine dry bread crumbs, preferably panko

¼ cup yellow cornmeal

1 teaspoon kosher or sea salt

½ teaspoon pure California or New Mexico chile powder

2 tablespoons chopped fresh parsley

12 thin slices pancetta

4 cups loosely packed mixture of baby savory greens, such as arugula, spinach, mustard, and cress

Herbed Egg Crêpes (facing page)

Walnut Oil Vinaigrette (page 43)

"Hangtown" was the other name for Placerville in the California gold country. It got its alternative name during the gold rush, when justice was handed down quickly with a rope. Hangtown fry, the combination of fresh oysters, eggs, and bacon fried together, was a dish that combined rare ingredients for a mountain gold-rush town and reputedly was the dish most often ordered by those who either struck it rich or were about to have their last meal. Much of this can be done ahead and then cooked at the last moment. The bathing of oysters in milk is a step that makes them a little firmer (the action of lactic acid) and also removes any fishiness.

In a medium bowl, combine the oysters and the milk. Let stand, covered, in the refrigerator for up to 3 hours. In a medium bowl, combine the bread crumbs, cornmeal, salt, chile powder, and parsley. Drain the oysters. Roll in the crumb mixture until well coated. Set aside, covered, in the refrigerator on waxed paper.

In a nonstick sauté pan, cook the pancetta until firm and lightly browned but not crisp. Leaving the drippings in the pan, set the pancetta aside and keep warm. In the same pan, quickly sauté the oysters until lightly brown and the edges begin to curl, about 2 minutes.

To serve, attractively arrange the greens on plates. Arrange the strips of Herbed Egg Crêpes on the greens. Place the oysters on top, along with 2 slices of the pancetta. Drizzle each plate with a tablespoon or two of the Walnut Oil Vinaigrette.

HERBED EGG CRÊPES
Makes 3 to 4 crêpes

3 large eggs

2 tablespoons water

1 tablespoon unsalted butter

2 tablespoons minced shallots

2 tablespoons minced fresh basil

2 tablespoons minced red bell pepper

Kosher or sea salt and freshly ground pepper

In a small bowl, beat the eggs with the water until well combined. In a nonstick sauté pan, melt the butter over medium heat and sauté the shallots until soft but not brown. Cool and add to the egg mixture along with the basil and red pepper. Season to taste with salt and pepper.

Heat an 8-inch nonstick skillet over medium heat. Ladle a thin layer of egg mixture into the skillet and cook until just set, about 1 minute. Turn over and cook for 30 seconds more. Turn out onto a cutting board, and cook the remaining eggs in the same manner. Carefully cut into fine, long strips. If you make the crêpes ahead, wrap well after they've cooled and refrigerate them. Allow them to return to room temperature to serve.

DUNGENESS CRAB, CABBAGE, AND APPLE SALAD

Serves 6

RECOMMENDED WINE
The nutty flavors here would go well with the toasty, nutty flavors that one gets with oaky whites such as barrel-fermented **Chardonnay**, **Pinot Blanc**, and aromatic **Viognier**. Look for the next generation of whites that also have some oak influence, like California **Roussane** or **Marsanne**.

24 Belgian endive leaves, about the same size

3 cups very finely shredded green cabbage

1 large tart-sweet apple, such as Gala, peeled, cored, and thinly sliced

¼ cup lightly toasted pistachios or slivered almonds

½ cup Walnut Oil Vinaigrette (page 43)

1 pound fresh cooked Dungeness crabmeat, shredded and picked over to remove any pieces of shell, plus 6 claw-meat portions

2 ounces salmon roe

Fresh daikon or sunflower sprouts for garnishing

Dungeness crab is one of the jewels of the Northern California larder and is used in several recipes in this book. For many here, fresh Dungeness is as much a part of Thanksgiving as turkey is.

Place 4 endive leaves arranged in a square in the center of each plate. In a medium bowl, combine the cabbage, apple, and pistachios and toss with a couple of tablespoons of the Walnut Oil Vinaigrette. Mound in the center of each endive square. Toss the crabmeat with a bit of the vinaigrette and put on top of the cabbage along with a claw-meat portion on top. Drizzle a bit more vinaigrette over all and top with a teaspoon of the caviar and a few sprouts.

LOBSTER AND GRILLED PORTOBELLO MUSHROOM SALAD

Serves 4

Two 1½-pound live Maine lobsters

2 large portobello mushrooms, stemmed and black gills removed by scraping with a teaspoon

2 tablespoons olive oil

Kosher or sea salt and freshly ground pepper

2 cups young savory greens, such as arugula, watercress, mustard, and frisée

Walnut Oil Vinaigrette (page 43)

Salmon roe and fresh chervil sprigs for garnishing (optional)

RECOMMENDED WINE
A rich, barrel-aged **Chardonnay** or **Pinot Blanc** adds a matching richness to this delicious lobster salad.

The rich taste of lobster combined with the earthy, meaty texture of portobello mushrooms is terrific. I've used stock for some of the oil in the Walnut Oil Vinaigrette as a way of reducing the total fat content. (In fact, if you wish to reduce fat in your diet, a concentrated stock can substitute for almost all of the oil in vinaigrettes.) Due to the price of lobsters, this recipe would have to fall into the special-occasion category, but, hey, why not?

In a large stockpot of lightly salted boiling water, plunge the lobsters, head first. Cook for 6 to 8 minutes. Remove them from the pot and cool in cold tap water. Remove the tail and claw meat intact. Set aside.

Prepare a charcoal fire. Generously brush the mushrooms with the olive oil and season with salt and pepper. Quickly grill on both sides until lightly browned and softened. Or, grill in a stove-top grill pan or broil them. Set aside.

Arrange the greens on plates and drizzle with the Walnut Oil Vinaigrette. Cut the portobellos into ¼-inch-thick slices and arrange on the greens. Slice the lobster tails into medallions and fan over the lobster.

Drizzle with a little more of the Walnut Oil Vinaigrette and top with the lobster claw meat (one per plate) and a small spoonful of salmon roe and chervil sprigs, if using.

TEMPURA SOFT-SHELL CRAB SALAD

Serves 6

RECOMMENDED WINE
The crisp-textured vege-
tables and crab should
be mirrored in the wine.
A clean, crisp **Chardonnay**,
a dry **Chenin Blanc**, or a
crisp sparkling wine would
all work well. Although
most people don't know
it, dry sparkling wines
and deep-fried foods are
terrific together.

6 large soft-shell crabs

1 large egg yolk

1 cup ice water

¾ cup flour, preferably a mixture of wheat and
   rice flour

Flour for coating crab

Vegetable oil for deep-frying

2 cups lightly packed mixed savory baby greens,
   such as mizuna, watercress, red mustard, and
   arugula

3 cups finely julienned root vegetables, such as
   carrots, beets, or parsnips, or a combination

½ cup Walnut Oil Vinaigrette (facing page) or
   Honey-Lemon Vinaigrette (page 35)

This is a delightful salad, with lots of crunch from both the raw vegetables and the crisply fried crab. Soft-shell crabs are available fresh from late spring to midsummer. Since they also freeze very well, they are available frozen year-round; ask your fishmonger to order and clean them for you.

Rinse the soft-shell crabs and pat them dry. Set aside.

In a medium bowl, beat together the egg yolk and water until just mixed. Dump the flour in all at once and whisk with a few strokes until the ingredients are loosely combined. The batter will be a little lumpy. Use immediately.

Lightly dust each crab with some flour. In a large saucepan or deep-fryer, pour the vegetable oil to a depth of 2 inches and heat to 350° to 375°F. (It should be shimmering. If it's smoking, it's too hot.) Dip the floured crabs in the tempura batter. Carefully slide the crabs into the hot oil for 3 to 4 minutes or until they are golden brown and crisp. Fry one or several depending on your pan, but do not crowd. Transfer to paper towels to drain. Keep warm.

Arrange the greens on individual plates. Toss the root vegetables with the vinaigrette and place on top. Place a crab on top of this and drizzle with any remaining vinaigrette. Serve immediately.

Note: To julienne vegetables I like to use either a mandoline or a Japanese "turner-slicer"; my favorite is manufactured by Benriner of Japan. It's a great tool that makes long, thin "spaghetti" out of any root vegetable with very little effort.

WALNUT OIL VINAIGRETTE
Makes ¾ cup

¼ cup walnut oil (see Note)

½ teaspoon minced garlic

¼ cup rich chicken stock or shellfish stock

1 teaspoon white wine Worcestershire sauce

1½ tablespoons Dijon mustard

1 teaspoon sherry vinegar

2 teaspoons chopped fresh parsley

2 teaspoons chopped fresh chives

2 teaspoons chopped fresh dill

Kosher or sea salt and freshly ground pepper

This rich-tasting dressing, which has a lower fat content than that of a traditional vinaigrette because stock replaces some of the oil, is a perfect complement to the three warm shellfish-based salads in this book: the Hangtown Fry Salad (page 38), which uses oysters, the Lobster and Grilled Portobello Mushroom Salad (page 41), and the Tempura Soft-Shell Crab Salad (facing page). Once you've tasted how it works with these dishes, you'll think of many other uses for it. Shellfish stock is available frozen in better gourmet shops, and a recipe to make your own (which you can freeze) is included in this book (page 67), but in the absence of either, you can certainly use chicken stock, which everyone who cooks should have on hand. A good-quality canned broth, fat-free, is an acceptable substitute.

In a blender or food processor, combine the walnut oil, garlic, stock, Worcestershire sauce, mustard, and vinegar. Blend until fully combined and creamy. Transfer to a bowl. Whisk in the parsley, chives, and dill. Season to taste with salt and pepper. Store the vinaigrette, covered and refrigerated, for up to 3 days. Bring to room temperature.

Note: Walnut oil, as well as its cousin hazelnut oil, is a robust flavoring agent for vinaigrettes and marinades. The truth about these rich, flavorful oils is that they must be stored in the refrigerator after opening and they can't be kept too long, as they will go rancid, often within 6 months. I particularly like the French Vivier brand, but there are many good ones. Toasted nut oils are expensive but worth it for a special treat, like these salads.

SHRIMP AND ROASTED VEGETABLE SALAD WITH RED PEPPER AND ORANGE VINAIGRETTE

Serves 4 to 6

RECOMMENDED WINE
The sweet shrimp and the roasted vegetables all suggest something that has some barrel influence, like a **Chardonnay**, a fruity **Pinot Noir**, or **Zinfandel**.

VINAIGRETTE

¼ teaspoon coriander seeds, crushed

2 teaspoons chopped fresh thyme

1 medium red bell pepper, charred, skin scraped off with a knife, and finely diced

2 teaspoons finely chopped shallots

4 tablespoons white balsamic or rice vinegar

2 teaspoons finely grated orange zest

¼ cup reduced orange juice or orange juice concentrate

⅓ cup extra-virgin olive oil

Kosher or sea salt and fresh ground pepper

MARINADE

¼ cup chopped fresh parsley

½ cup loosely packed fresh basil leaves, finely chopped

2 tablespoons minced green onion, both white and green parts

1 tablespoon minced garlic

2 teaspoons kosher or sea salt

½ teaspoon freshly ground pepper

¼ teaspoon red pepper flakes

⅓ cup dry white wine

⅔ cup olive oil

SHRIMP

1¼ pounds extra-large shrimp (16 to 20 per pound size), shells on

ROASTED VEGETABLES

2 unpeeled medium beets

1 small celery root, peeled and quartered

2 small carrots

1 medium red onion, root end left on and cut into thick wedges

Olive oil for coating the vegetables

Kosher or sea salt and freshly ground pepper

CABBAGE BASE

2 tablespoons olive oil

3 cups very finely shredded green cabbage

¼ teaspoon crushed celery seeds

Kosher or sea salt and freshly ground pepper

The recipe may seem long, but actually it's very easy and almost all of it can be made ahead of time. The sautéing of the cabbage is the only thing that needs to be done last minute. This is a wonderful main-dish salad for any time of the year, but it reminds me of fall and winter when root vegetables are in abundance. I'm cooking the shrimp in the shell to maximize the flavor and also keep the shrimp moist.

To make the vinaigrette: In a medium bowl, combine the coriander seeds, thyme, bell pepper, shallots, vinegar, orange zest, and orange juice. Whisk in the olive oil to the desired consistency. Season to taste with salt and pepper. Can be made up to a day ahead and stored, covered, in the refrigerator. Bring to room temperature before serving.

To make the marinade: In a small bowl, whisk the parsley, basil, green onion, garlic, salt, pepper, pepper flakes, wine, and olive oil together and allow the flavors to marry for at least 30 minutes before using.

To prepare the shrimp: Slit the shrimp shells down the back, leaving the shells on, to extract more flavor. In a medium bowl, toss the shrimp with the marinade and marinate for up to 2 hours. Remove from the marinade and grill or pan-roast until just done. Remove the shells, leaving the tails on. Set aside.

To roast the vegetables: Preheat the oven to 425°F. In a large bowl, combine the beets, celery root, carrots, and onion and toss the vegetables with olive oil to lightly coat. Season to taste with salt and pepper. In a roasting pan, arrange in a single layer, cover with foil, and roast for 20 minutes, then uncover and allow the vegetables to brown a bit. Remove the vegetables as they are done and set aside. Cut into attractive shapes and set aside.

To make the cabbage base: In a sauté pan, heat the olive oil and sauté the cabbage and celery seeds until the cabbage is just crisp-tender. Season to taste with salt and pepper.

Put a small mound of cabbage in the center of each plate. Arrange the shrimp against the cabbage. Arrange each of the roasted vegetables around the shrimp and spoon the vinaigrette over.

CHOPPED SALAD OF CUCUMBERS, TOMATOES, OLIVES, FETA, AND GARLIC CROUTONS

Serves 4

RECOMMENDED WINE
Salty, tart feta and olives, along with the wine dressing, call for a crisp, lean white, such as **Sauvignon Blanc**, or **Pinot Gris** or **Pinot Grigio**.

4 cups gently packed young arugula

1 medium English cucumber, peeled, seeded, and cut into 1-inch dice (about 3 cups)

3 large, firm ripe tomatoes, stemmed, seeded, and cut into ½-inch dice (about 3 cups)

2 cups meaty black olives, such as Cerignola or Kalamata, pitted and quartered

8 ounces firm feta cheese, cut into large dice

Garlic Croutons (facing page)

Red-Wine Vinegar Dressing (facing page)

Bread salads are famous in both Italy (panzanella) and the Middle East (fattoush) and are a great way to use up day-old bread. I've had versions in which the bread component (which could be bread, lavash, or flat breads like pitas) is mixed in ahead so that it will soak up the vegetable juices and dressing, and others in which it's combined at the last moment so that the bread keeps some of its texture. Here, we're doing the latter to preserve the crunchy texture of the baked bread. The most important thing to remember about bread salads is that they are only as good as the bread that's put into them!

Arrange the arugula on a flat, shallow serving plate and attractively arrange the cucumber, tomatoes, olives, feta, and croutons on top. At serving time, drizzle the dressing over the top and scoop up some of each of the ingredients to serve.

GARLIC CROUTONS

⅓ cup olive oil

2 large garlic cloves, thinly sliced

3 cups 1-inch bread cubes, cut from sturdy day-old bread with crusts removed

2 tablespoons finely chopped fresh parsley

1 teaspoon freshly grated lemon zest

Kosher or sea salt and freshly ground pepper

Preheat the oven to 375°F. In a sauté pan, heat the olive oil over medium heat and sauté the garlic until it just begins to color. Be careful the garlic doesn't burn or it will become bitter. In a medium bowl, toss the bread cubes with the garlic-flavored olive oil and place on a wire rack on a rimmed baking sheet. Toast in the oven until the bread is nicely golden on all sides, about 12 minutes. The croutons should be toasty on the surface but still somewhat soft in the very middle. Remove and toss with the parsley and lemon zest while still warm. Season to taste with salt and pepper. Store airtight for up to 2 days if not using immediately.

RED-WINE VINEGAR DRESSING
Makes about 1 cup

4 tablespoons red- or white-wine vinegar, or fresh lemon juice

1 teaspoon dry or Dijon mustard

2 tablespoons finely chopped shallot or green onion, white part only

½ to ⅔ cup fragrant extra-virgin olive oil

Kosher or sea salt and freshly ground pepper

In a small bowl, whisk together the vinegar, mustard, green onion, and olive oil. Season with salt and pepper, adjusting this very simple dressing to your own taste.

PASTA SALAD WITH SMOKED TROUT AND FRESH DILL

Serves 4 to 6

dill

This herb has a long history of culinary, medicinal, and celebratory uses. The feathery leaves of the plant are used both fresh and dried in salads and often with fish. The seeds, which have a stronger flavor, are more often found in longer-cooking recipes and pickling mixes. Herbalists use both dill leaves and seeds in infusions to dispel flatulence, increase mother's milk, relieve colic in babies, and soothe upset stomachs. Dill was also used as a charm against witches—you could combat an evil spell by carrying a bag of dried dill over your heart.

2 tablespoons freshly grated or prepared horseradish

⅓ cup buttermilk

½ cup Homemade Mayonnaise (facing page)

Kosher or sea salt, freshly ground pepper, and drops of fresh lemon juice

8 ounces rotelle or other corkscrew-shaped pasta

1 cup very thinly sliced sweet red onion

¼ cup chopped fresh dill

1 pound boned and skinned smoked trout, cut into ½-inch pieces

1 cup seeded and thinly slivered ripe Roma tomatoes

1 tablespoon rinsed capers

2 cups lightly packed young arugula or watercress leaves for garnishing

This is one of my favorite summer salads. Any smoked fish you like can be substituted for the trout, such as hot-smoked salmon or tuna.

In a small bowl, combine the horseradish, buttermilk, and Homemade Mayonnaise. Season to taste with salt, pepper, and lemon juice. Set aside for at least 20 minutes for the flavors to develop. You can thin dressing with a little more buttermilk, if you want.

Meanwhile, in a large pot, cook the pasta in salted boiling water until al dente. Drain the pasta and immediately run cold water over it to stop the cooking. Drain again and toss with the buttermilk dressing. Gently stir in the onion, dill, trout, tomatoes, and capers. Season to taste with salt and pepper. Arrange the arugula on chilled plates and top with salad.

HOMEMADE MAYONNAISE
Makes about 1 cup

2 large eggs

½ to 1 teaspoon kosher or sea salt

1 to 2 teaspoons Dijon mustard

2 to 4 teaspoons fresh lemon juice

1 cup olive oil or other vegetable oil

Freshly ground pepper

Homemade mayonnaise is so simple I don't know why anyone buys the commercial stuff. It can be made in a couple of minutes in the food processor or blender and flavored in an infinite variety of ways to enhance the dish you're serving it with. I've listed some of my favorite variations below.

In a blender or food processor, combine the eggs, ½ teaspoon salt, 1 teaspoon mustard, and 2 teaspoons lemon juice. Process the ingredients with 2 or 3 short bursts.

With the motor running, slowly add the olive oil in a steady stream to form a thick emulsion. Taste and season with pepper and additional salt, mustard, and lemon juice as desired. If the mayonnaise is too thick, mix in a little water, stock, or buttermilk. Store, covered, in the refrigerator for up to 1 week.

VARIATIONS
Add the ingredients to the eggs before adding the olive oil.

Caper-Tarragon: 1 to 2 tablespoons rinsed and chopped capers, 2 teaspoons chopped fresh tarragon

Curry-Apple: 2 teaspoons toasted Madras Curry Powder (page 97), ¼ cup finely chopped tart apple, honey to taste

Mustard: 1 to 3 additional tablespoons Dijon mustard, ½ teaspoon grated lemon zest

Red Bell Pepper: ¼ to ⅓ cup finely chopped roasted and peeled red bell pepper (see page 265), drops of bottled hot sauce to taste

Basil: ⅓ cup finely chopped fresh basil

toasting spices

If your spices have spent some time on the shelf, I recommend toasting them lightly before using. You can do this by placing them in a sauté pan over medium heat or in a 375°F oven. It only takes a couple of minutes. Surface oils in spices tend to oxidize and go rancid, and toasting drives off these tired flavors, yielding fresh ones.

ORECCHIETTE SALAD WITH GOAT CHEESE, OLIVES, AND BASIL

Serves 4 to 6

RECOMMENDED WINE
I've always loved the combination of feta and **Fumé Blanc** or **Sauvignon** Blanc. This salad gives me the perfect excuse.

8 ounces orecchiette or other small dried shaped pasta

⅓ cup extra-virgin olive oil

2 tablespoons thinly slivered garlic

¼ teaspoon red pepper flakes

½ cup finely diced red bell pepper

¾ cup slivered Niçoise or Kalamata olives

⅓ cup dry white wine

8 ounces mild California goat feta cheese, crumbled

⅓ cup loosely packed fresh basil leaves, chopped

½ cup lightly toasted pine nuts

Kosher or sea salt and lots of freshly ground pepper

Drops of fresh lemon juice

Lightly toasted pine nuts and fresh basil sprigs for garnishing

One of the things I like most about pasta salads is that you can create a great-tasting dish in about 20 minutes with a few key complementary ingredients. This salad is perfect for a light luncheon but is also wonderful as part of a larger buffet.

In a large pot of lightly salted boiling water, cook the pasta until just al dente. Drain the pasta and immediately run cold water over it to stop the cooking. Transfer to a medium bowl and toss with 2 tablespoons of the olive oil to prevent sticking.

In a medium sauté pan, heat the remaining olive oil over low heat and sauté the garlic until soft but not brown. Add the pepper flakes, bell pepper, olives, and wine. Simmer for 4 to 5 minutes or until most of the wine has evaporated. Remove from the heat, add the pasta, and toss. Stir in the feta, basil, and pine nuts. Season to taste with salt, pepper, and lemon juice.

Serve garnished with pine nuts and fresh basil sprigs.

WHITE BEAN SALAD WITH GRILLED TOMATOES

Serves 6

6 large plum tomatoes, halved and seeded

6 tablespoons extra-virgin olive oil

Kosher or sea salt and freshly ground pepper

1 tablespoon mashed anchovy fillets or anchovy paste

1 tablespoon roasted garlic (see page 264)

2 tablespoons finely grated lemon zest

¾ cup dried white beans, cooked, or 2 cups canned beans, drained and rinsed

1 cup chopped red onion

2 tablespoons rinsed and chopped capers

1 tablespoon chopped fresh mint

3 cups lightly packed young arugula leaves

Fresh mint sprigs for garnishing

RECOMMENDED WINE
A softer-style red like **Pinot Noir** or **Merlot** would be good here. A clean, crisp white like **Sauvignon Blanc** would be a refreshing contrast if you're in the mood for a white wine.

For those looking to add more healthful legumes and beans to their diet, this Mediterranean-influenced salad is a flavorful way to do it. Accompany this with Baked Olives (page 293), a loaf of crusty French bread, and a glass of wine, and you've got a perfect summer supper.

Prepare a charcoal fire or preheat a broiler. In a medium bowl, brush the tomatoes with 2 tablespoons of the olive oil. Season to taste with salt and pepper. Grill the tomatoes over hot coals or broil until lightly colored but still firm. Set aside.

In a large bowl, whisk together the remaining olive oil, anchovy, roasted garlic, and lemon zest. Add the white beans, red onion, capers, mint, and plenty of freshly ground pepper. Toss to combine.

Serve the bean salad on the arugula leaves, surrounded by the grilled tomatoes. Garnish with mint sprigs.

LEMONY POTATO SALAD WITH OLIVES, CORN, AND CASHEWS

Serves 8 to 10

RECOMMENDED WINE
A crisp white like a lighter-style **Chardonnay**, with little or no oak aging, is great with this salad.

zesting citrus

Every kitchen should have a Microplane lemon zester in it. It's an invaluable kitchen tool that I wish I had invented! Before it came to market in the 1990s the usual instruction was to use a vegetable peeler to pull long, thin slices of zest off a lemon, attempting to avoid the bitter white pith beneath the zest. Typically, I was only partially successful at this maneuver.

Kosher or sea salt

4 pounds small red or fingerling potatoes

2 cups corn kernels (2 large ears)

½ cup pitted, slivered Kalamata olives

1 cup chopped unsalted, lightly toasted cashews

½ cup coarsely chopped fresh parsley

Lemon Dressing (recipe follows)

Freshly ground pepper

This is a delicious combination of tart, sweet, and salt, with potatoes as the backdrop. The key here is to dress the cooked potatoes while they are still warm so that they will absorb the lemony dressing. Great for a summer picnic or buffet.

Bring a large pot of salted water to a boil. Add the potatoes, reduce the heat, and simmer the potatoes for 12 to 15 minutes, or until just tender. Don't overcook; the potatoes should be firm but cooked through. Drain the potatoes in cold water and when cool enough to handle, cut into quarters.

In a large bowl, put the quartered potatoes and gently mix in the corn, olives, cashews, and parsley along with the Lemon Dressing. Season to taste with salt and pepper. Don't overmix or the potatoes will break apart. Can be made a day ahead and stored covered in the refrigerator. Best served at room temperature.

LEMON DRESSING

1 tablespoon minced lemon zest

⅓ cup fresh lemon juice

2 tablespoons Dijon mustard

1 tablespoon chopped fresh tarragon or 2 teaspoons dried

½ cup finely chopped green onions, both white and green parts

½ cup extra-virgin olive oil

⅛ teaspoon red pepper flakes

Kosher or sea salt

In a medium, nonreactive bowl, combine the lemon zest, lemon juice, mustard, tarragon, and green onions and whisk thoroughly. Slowly drizzle in the olive oil while whisking. Season with the red pepper flakes and salt to taste.

LEMON RICE SALAD

Makes about 6 cups

3 tablespoons olive oil

¼ cup chopped shallots or green onions, white part only

1 cup basmati or jasmine rice, well rinsed

2 cups Chicken Stock (page 66), Rich Vegetable Stock (page 69), or Corn Stock (page 69)

2 teaspoons grated lemon zest

3 tablespoons fresh lemon juice

¼ cup coarsely chopped fresh herbs, such as cilantro, basil, or mint, or a combination

2 tablespoons minced poached garlic (see page 264)

½ cup finely diced red onion, rinsed in cold water

½ cup diced blanched red bell pepper

⅓ cup lightly toasted pine nuts, pepitas, or chopped cashews

RECOMMENDED WINE
The lemon serves as a great bridge to wines that have a similar lemon flavor, like **Sauvignon Blanc**, **Pinot Gris**, and **Pinot Grigio**, and the whole world of crisp Italian and Spanish whites.

This is a great salad on its own. I also like this as a topping for warm vegetable stews such as Okra, Peppers, and Beans with Lemon Rice Salad (page 291). You'll note that the bell peppers in this recipe are briefly blanched. This means they are dropped into lightly salted simmering water for 30 seconds, then immediately drained. This brief exposure to heat sweetens the pepper and takes away its raw vegetal flavor.

In a deep saucepan, heat 1 tablespoon of the olive oil over medium heat and sauté the shallots until soft but not brown. Add the rice and continue to sauté for 3 to 4 minutes longer, stirring regularly. Add the stock and bring to a boil. Reduce the heat to a simmer, cover, and continue to cook until all the liquid is absorbed (10 to 12 minutes). Remove from the heat, let cool for 5 minutes, then gently fluff with a fork and transfer to a large bowl.

Add the lemon zest, lemon juice, herbs, garlic, red onion, bell pepper, pine nuts, and the remaining 2 tablespoons of the olive oil to the warm rice and gently stir to combine. If not using immediately, cover and refrigerate for up to 2 days. Best served at room temperature.

ROASTED POTATO, BEET, AND ONION SALAD

Serves 6

RECOMMENDED WINE
A crisp **Fumé Blanc** or **Sauvignon Blanc** goes with the green-herb components of the dish and a lighter-style red such as **Pinot Noir** goes with the roasted vegetables. Maybe half a glass of both?

12 fingerling or creamer potatoes

12 garlic cloves

4 tablespoons olive oil

Sprigs of fresh rosemary or thyme

Kosher or sea salt and freshly ground pepper

8 ounces cipollini or pearl onions

12 ounces unpeeled baby red Cioggia or golden beets

1½ tablespoons balsamic vinegar

3 tablespoons olive oil

2 teaspoons chopped fresh chives or parsley

Kosher or sea salt and freshly ground pepper

1 cup loosely packed mixed fresh herbs, such as parsley, chervil, and tarragon

Edible flower petals, if available (see page 418) for garnishing

This is more an approach than a hard and fast recipe. I love the color/flavor/texture mix of potatoes, beets, and onions, but eggplant, asparagus, or carrots could be added or substituted. If you don't have access to baby vegetables, quarter and roast large ones, adjusting the cooking time accordingly. Any mixture of whole herb leaves makes a sprightly addition, but if fresh herbs aren't available, you could always serve the dressed vegetables on a bed of young greens, such as arugula, mustard, and frisée.

Preheat the oven to 375°F. Prepare the vegetables in three separate roasting pans. Halve or quarter the potatoes lengthwise. In a medium bowl, toss the potatoes and garlic cloves with 2 tablespoons of the olive oil and the rosemary and season liberally with salt and pepper. Arrange the potatoes and garlic in a single layer in a roasting pan. Toss the onions with 1 tablespoon of the olive oil and season with salt and pepper in a pan; do the same for the beets in another pan. Cover all three pans tightly with foil and roast the vegetables for 35 to 40 minutes (or until tender), uncovering the potatoes and garlic after 20 minutes to allow them to brown and crisp slightly. Reserve any juices from the beets and onions for the vinaigrette. While the beets are still warm, gently rub their skins off using paper towels.

In a small bowl, whisk the beet and onion juices, balsamic vinegar, olive oil, and chives together. Season with salt and pepper to taste.

Serve the roasted vegetables surrounding a mound of the herbs and drizzle with the vinaigrette. Garnish with the edible flowers. Serve warm or at room temperature.

cooking beets

As you may have surmised from glancing at the recipes in this book, I love beets. I don't think we pay enough attention to most root vegetables, but I really love beets. Too often, old recipes called for boiling beets to death in water (one old cookbook I have specifies 8 hours!). No wonder we grew up disliking beets—the flavor and texture were cooked out of them. Beets have the highest sugar content of any vegetable, and the absolute best (and I think only) way to cook them is to bake or roast them. Alexandre Dumas, in his *Grand Dictionnaire de Cuisine* (published posthumously in 1873), gives this advice: "The best way to cook beets is in the oven. First they should be washed in ordinary brandy. Then they are placed on grills in the brick oven, which is heated as for large loaves of bread. They are left in the oven until it cools, and the following morning cooked again the same way and at the same temperature. The beet is not really cooked until its skin is carbonized." In one small French village that I spent time in years ago, the locals brought their large beets and onions to the boulangerie after the afternoon's bread had come out. The baker would then put these vegetables in the still-hot brick oven and roast them overnight for pickup the next morning. In parts of Italy, roasted beets and onions have for centuries been sold together by street vendors. Roasting caramelizes the sugar in beets and concentrates the flavor. Try it once and you'll never boil a beet again. You'll also find yourself (as I do) looking for ways to utilize this great food.

TOMATOES STUFFED WITH SOUFFLÉED GOAT CHEESE AND SAVORY GREENS

Serves 6

RECOMMENDED WINE
Goat cheese and
Sauvignon Blanc,
of course, are a great
combination. A dry,
crisp sparkling wine
would also work well.

6 firm-ripe medium tomatoes

Kosher or sea salt

4 teaspoons unsalted butter

1½ tablespoons minced shallots

2 teaspoons minced garlic

1½ tablespoons all-purpose flour

⅓ cup half-and-half

1 tablespoon dry sherry

½ cup fresh soft cream cheese or log-style goat cheese

2 large eggs, separated

3 tablespoons minced fresh chives

2 teaspoons minced fresh savory or tarragon

Freshly ground white pepper

3 cups mixed savory baby greens, such as arugula, frisée, watercress, and mizuna

Lemon-Garlic Vinaigrette (facing page)

Basil Oil (page 80) for garnishing (optional)

The combination of warm elements with cool salad greens is seductive and very typical of wine country cooking. The trick of this recipe is that the baking dish for the soufflé is entirely edible.

Cut the tops off the tomatoes and scoop out the seeds and pulp. Sprinkle the insides with salt and invert the tomatoes on paper towels to drain.

In a small saucepan, melt the butter and sauté the shallots and garlic until soft but not brown. Add the flour and continue cooking for 2 to 3 minutes, stirring continuously. Whisk in the half-and-half and sherry and cook for 3 minutes longer, continuously whisking until the mixture is smooth. Transfer the mixture to a medium bowl and let cool slightly. Whisk in the cheese, egg yolks, chives, and savory. Season to taste with salt and pepper.

In a medium bowl, beat the egg whites until they hold stiff peaks. Stir one-fourth of the whites into the cheese mixture to lighten it. Carefully fold in the remaining whites.

Preheat the oven to 400°F. Spoon the soufflé mixture into the tomato shells, mounding it slightly. In a lightly oiled baking dish, place the tomatoes with their sides touching. Bake for 20 to 25 minutes or until the tops are lightly puffed and browned.

Serve the hot tomatoes immediately on a bed of the mixed greens that have been tossed with the Lemon-Garlic Vinaigrette. If you have some basil oil on hand, a drizzle on each plate would add delicious color.

LEMON-GARLIC VINAIGRETTE
Makes about ¾ cup

3 tablespoons white wine vinegar

1 tablespoon fresh lemon juice

2 teaspoons Dijon mustard

½ teaspoon roasted garlic (see page 264)

1 tablespoon light-brown sugar or honey

½ cup extra-virgin olive oil

Kosher or sea salt and freshly ground pepper

In a medium bowl, whisk together the vinegar, lemon juice, mustard, roasted garlic, sugar, and olive oil. Season to taste with salt and pepper. Store any unused vinaigrette (you won't need it all for this recipe) tightly covered in the refrigerator for up to 5 days.

PORK TENDERLOIN SALAD WITH ROASTED BEET VINAIGRETTE

Serves 6 to 8 as a main course

RECOMMENDED WINE
The sweet berrylike flavor of the beets and the molasses-based marinade suggest a softer, fruity red such as **Pinot Noir**, but I think a peppery **Zinfandel** would provide a nice contrast with this dish.

Two 12-ounce pork tenderloins, trimmed

Orange-Molasses Marinade (facing page)

2 tablespoons olive oil

6 cups mixed baby greens, such as arugula, mizuna, and red mustard

Grilled red onion rings for garnishing

Roasted Beet Vinaigrette (facing page)

This main-course salad has been a personal favorite for a long time. I particularly like the quality of roasted beets, as the natural sugars of the beets intensify during the roasting process. This salad is vividly red and green, a stunning visual statement as well. The marinade is delicious on a wide range of meat and poultry, but for the flavor to develop here, the pork needs to be marinated for at least 4 hours, so plan ahead.

In a baking dish, combine the pork tenderloins and the Orange-Molasses Marinade, turning to coat. Marinate, covered, in the refrigerator for 4 to 6 hours, turning occasionally.

Preheat the oven to 400°F. Remove the tenderloins from the marinade and pat dry. In a large sauté pan, heat the olive oil over high heat and quickly sear the pork on all sides. Lower heat and continue to cook on the stove or in the oven until just done, about 6 to 8 minutes. Do not overcook. The pork should remain slightly pink and juicy.

Arrange the greens attractively on the plates. Garnish with the grilled onions and drizzle with the Roasted Beet Vinaigrette. Slice the tenderloin on the bias and arrange on top. Serve immediately.

ORANGE-MOLASSES MARINADE

1 tablespoon olive oil

1½ cups chopped red onions

1½ tablespoons chopped garlic

1 teaspoon cracked pepper

½ cup balsamic vinegar

1¼ cups fresh orange juice

⅓ cup molasses

1 tablespoon toasted and crushed coriander
  seeds

1 tablespoon grated orange zest

Kosher or sea salt and freshly ground pepper

In a small saucepan, heat the olive oil. Sauté the onions and garlic until lightly browned. Add the pepper, vinegar, orange juice, molasses, coriander seeds, and the orange zest. Bring to a boil. Reduce the heat and simmer for 5 minutes. Remove from the heat and cool before using. Season to taste with salt and pepper.

ROASTED BEET VINAIGRETTE
Makes about 1½ cups

1 pound large red beets, unpeeled

2 tablespoons olive oil

Kosher or sea salt and freshly ground pepper

¾ cup rich chicken stock, fat removed

2 tablespoons balsamic vinegar

1 teaspoon sherry vinegar (optional)

2 teaspoons honey

½ teaspoon crushed aniseeds

Preheat the oven to 375°F. Lightly oil the beets with 1 tablespoon of the olive oil. Put in a roasting pan and season with salt and pepper. Roast in the oven until cooked through and the skins begin to shrivel, about 40 minutes, depending on the size of the beets.

While still warm, remove the beet skins by rubbing with a towel. Cut into ¼-inch dice and set aside.

In a blender or food processor, combine the chicken stock and half the beets, and purée. Transfer the purée to a medium bowl. Whisk in the balsamic vinegar, sherry vinegar, honey, aniseeds, and remaining olive oil. Season to taste with salt and pepper. Stir in the remaining diced beets.

Store, covered, in the refrigerator up to 3 days. Best served warm or at room temperature.

GRILLED ASPARAGUS AND STEAK SALAD WITH HOISIN VINAIGRETTE

Serves 6 as a main course

1 tablespoon peppercorns

2 teaspoons coriander seeds

2 teaspoons fennel seeds

1 teaspoon kosher or sea salt

Olive oil for coating the steak and the asparagus

1 pound thick-cut top sirloin or New York strip steak

1 pound young, pencil-sized asparagus

Kosher or sea salt and freshly ground pepper

3 cups baby peppery greens, such as cress, arugula, and mustard

1 large mango, peeled, pitted and cut into wedges, or 2 large navel oranges cut into thick rounds

Hoisin Vinaigrette (recipe follows)

Finely sliced sweet red onions soaked briefly in ice water, and daikon sprouts for garnishing

You can no doubt tell by now that I love asparagus. This is a fast, healthful main course with lots of flavor. This recipe can also be done using a stove-top grill pan instead of a charcoal grill.

With a spice grinder, grind together the peppercorns, coriander seeds, fennel seeds, and salt to make a fine powder. Oil the steak lightly and coat lightly but evenly with the peppercorn mixture. Set aside for at least 30 minutes.

Lightly oil the asparagus and season to taste with salt and pepper. Set aside.

Grill the steak over hot coals until rare. Keep warm and the grill asparagus until crisp-tender. Arrange the asparagus, greens, and mango attractively on plates. Slice the steak thinly across the grain and arrange on top. Drizzle the Hoisin Vinaigrette over and garnish with onions and daikon sprouts.

HOISIN VINAIGRETTE
Makes about ½ cup

2½ tablespoons hoisin sauce

1½ teaspoons sodium-reduced soy sauce

1 teaspoon Dijon or Chinese mustard

2 tablespoons white wine vinegar

1 teaspoon minced garlic

2 teaspoons peeled and minced fresh ginger or galangal

2 tablespoons light olive oil

3 to 4 tablespoons fat-free chicken stock

Kosher or sea salt and freshly ground pepper

In a blender or food processor, combine the hoisin sauce, soy sauce, mustard, vinegar, garlic, ginger, olive oil, and chicken stock. Pulse 2 or 3 times to combine, adding enough stock for the desired consistency. Season to taste with salt and pepper. Store, covered, in the refrigerator for up to 3 days.

FRESH CORN, ORZO, AND SMOKED CHICKEN SALAD WITH PINE NUTS

Serves 6 to 8 as a main course

2 teaspoons red pepper flakes

½ cup seasoned rice wine vinegar

2 tablespoons light corn syrup

2 bay leaves

3 tablespoons fresh lime juice

4 ounces dry orzo or other grain-shaped pasta

2 tablespoons olive oil

12 ounces smoked chicken or Corned Chicken (page 198), julienned

2½ cups fresh raw corn kernels, white or yellow (2 to 3 large ears)

¼ cup chopped fresh basil

½ cup chopped green onions, both white and pale green parts

½ cup julienned red bell pepper, blanched for a couple of seconds in boiling water

Kosher or sea salt and freshly ground pepper

½ cup toasted pine nuts

Fresh basil sprigs and lime wedges for garnishing

RECOMMENDED WINE
I love matching corn with a **Chardonnay** that has not been over-oaked. The fresh, sweet fruit flavors of the wine mirror those of the sweet corn.

pine nuts

It goes by many names: pignoli, pignolia, piñon, pinocchio, and Indian nut, as well as pine nut. The seeds of all pine trees are probably edible, but the best culinary pine nuts come from the European stone pine and the piñon tree of the American Southwest. Pine nuts have a very long culinary history. They were found among the foods in the ruins of Pompeii, and they are mentioned in the works of Virgil, Theocritus, and Ovid, who referred to them as one of the great aphrodisiacs of his time. Their rich flavor is at its best after they've been lightly toasted. Shelled pine nuts, because of their high oil content, can become rancid fairly quickly. Buy them at a store that has a rapid turnover and be sure to store them tightly sealed in a cool, dark place. I keep pine nuts in the refrigerator or freezer.

This makes an excellent lunch salad or light supper for summer, and it can be made ahead of time and chilled. Smoked chicken is widely available, and this might just be an excuse to make Corned Chicken. Any smoked meat or fish would be tasty in this salad. If the corn isn't perfectly young, sweet, and tender, I suggest blanching it for a few seconds and cooling it before using.

In a small saucepan, combine the pepper flakes, vinegar, corn syrup, bay leaves, and lime juice. Bring to a simmer and cook for 5 minutes. Remove from the heat and cool. Remove and discard the bay leaves. In a pot of lightly salted boiling water, cook the orzo until al dente. Drain the pasta and immediately run cold water over it to stop the cooking. Drain again, scoop into a large bowl, and toss with the olive oil.

Add the dressing and lightly toss to combine. Add the smoked chicken, corn, basil, green onions, and red pepper. Toss to combine and season with salt and pepper to taste. Refrigerate for an hour or so for the flavors to marry. Serve the salad sprinkled with pine nuts and garnished with basil sprigs and lime wedges.

SOUPS

SOUPS *and* WINE

As with salads, the conventional wisdom is that wine isn't traditionally served with soup, but I've included wine recommendations for each of the soups in this chapter because for me soup often is the meal, and I think wine can be a perfect beverage to serve with it. The choice of wine should reflect complementing flavors in the soup. As you'll note, many of the soups contain wine as an ingredient, which is a good tip-off that wine can work very well as an accompaniment.

Besides looking for linking flavors, I think it's important to select a wine that has a similar body or mouth-feel to the soup: For example, a creamy pumpkin or butternut squash soup really works best with a rich-bodied, creamy-tasting, barrel-aged Chardonnay and probably doesn't work well with a light-bodied, tart Sauvignon Blanc. Keep in mind that soups—even broth-based soups—are full-bodied taste experiences because of the way soup coats the mouth; choose a wine with a similar mouth-feel.

Two notes on soup making: Soups come in two basic styles — chunky, where the solid ingredients retain their distinctiveness, and smooth, where the ingredients are cooked together and then puréed. For soups that are to be puréed, it's a good idea to let the soup base cool slightly or even completely before transferring it to the blender or food processor, because an accident involving a high-powered motor and boiling hot liquid is not pleasant. In fact, most soups benefit from being cooled completely, even refrigerated overnight, before heating and serving: The flavors have a chance to develop and it is much easier to remove the fat — this is especially necessary for soups made with meat.

STOCKS

Good homemade stocks are really very easy to make and are the basis for good soups and sauces. I look on stock making as a rainy-day project—something to do when I'm going to be around the house for a few hours. Stocks don't take much attention—just an occasional check to make sure they aren't boiling hard (which causes them to get cloudy) and are developing the flavors you want.

Although I've included recipes for several stocks, I believe that you really need to know how to make only two stocks: chicken, to cover all your meat and fish needs, and a good vegetable stock. In addition to the stocks included here, note that there are several other stocks attached to specific recipes (e.g., the Vegetarian Red Chile Stock on page 287), which can be used in a number of ways.

About the stock recipes:

1. All of the recipes yield about 1 gallon of stock. If storage space is a problem in your refrigerator or freezer, then reduce the strained stocks uncovered over high heat by up to half. Not only will they require less space, but their flavors will be more concentrated and intense.

2. If you anticipate that you are going to reduce the stocks either for storage or to make a sauce, then don't add any salt, pepper, or strong spice or herb. In the reduction those flavors will become too dominant. Wait until the dish is nearing completion to do the final seasoning and flavoring.

3. Fresh fruit and vegetable juices can substitute wholly or in part for stocks in many recipes. Once you start using a juicer you'll come up with your own favorite combinations.

4. For simple stocks, remember to save the cooking liquid from potatoes and beans. They can provide the base for a stock that can then include fresh herbs, chiles, or what have you.

CHICKEN STOCK (WESTERN VERSION)

5 to 6 pounds meaty chicken parts, such as wings, backs, and necks, or a large stewing hen, quartered

2 tablespoons vegetable oil

2 cups chopped onions

1 cup chopped carrots

1 cup chopped celery

4 large garlic cloves, unpeeled

1 cup chopped mushrooms, any kind

2 cups dry white wine

2 large bay leaves

2 cloves (optional)

½ teaspoon peppercorns

6 quarts water

Rinse the chicken and set aside. In a stockpot, heat the vegetable oil over medium-high heat. Sauté the onions, carrots, celery, garlic, and mushrooms until the vegetables are lightly browned. Add the chicken, wine, bay leaves, cloves (if using), peppercorns, and enough water to cover the chicken by at least 3 inches. Bring to a boil. Reduce the heat and simmer slowly, partially covered, for 1½ to 2 hours, carefully skimming off any scum or froth that rises to the surface. Remove from the heat, cool slightly, and strain carefully. Refrigerate the stock and remove the fat layer. Store, covered, in the refrigerator for up to 5 days or freeze for up to 3 months.

CHICKEN STOCK (ASIAN VERSION)

5 to 6 pounds meaty chicken parts, including feet, if available

6 whole green onions, smashed

8 quarter-sized slices fresh ginger

6 quarts water

Rinse the chicken and add to a stockpot along with the green onions and ginger. Add enough water to cover the chicken by at least 3 inches and bring to a boil. Reduce the heat and simmer slowly, partially covered, for 1½ to 2 hours. Carefully skim off any scum or froth that rises to the surface. Remove from the heat, cool slightly, and strain carefully. Refrigerate the stock and remove the fat layer. Store, covered, in the refrigerator for up to 5 days or freeze for up to 3 months.

EASY SHELLFISH STOCK

One tip that I always give in my cooking classes is to never throw away shrimp shells. There is as much or more flavor in the shell as there is in the meat of the shrimp. If you are peeling raw shrimp for a recipe, always save the shells and store them in a plastic bag in your freezer. Then, when you need to make a good fish or shellfish stock, all you have to do is to take one of your basic chicken stocks (or even canned low-salt, fat-free chicken stock) and add as many shrimp shells as you have. You might also include a good splash or two of dry white wine, then bring to a boil, reduce the heat, and simmer for 5 minutes. Strain and discard the shells and now you have a delicious stock for your favorite fish soup or sauce.

A final admonition — never, never use bottled clam juice (even though a recipe may suggest it). It has a very salty, metallic taste and I think it's thoroughly disagreeable. If you don't have shrimp shells to make this simple stock, then you are better off just using your homemade (preferably) or canned chicken stock.

TRADITIONAL FISH STOCK

6 pounds absolutely fresh fish bones, trimmings, and heads

2 tablespoons olive oil

2 cups chopped onions

1 cup chopped carrots

2 garlic cloves, smashed

2 cups dry white wine

1 cup coarsely chopped fresh parsley leaves and stems

2 large bay leaves

1 teaspoon whole coriander seeds

1 tablespoon chopped fresh lemon zest

6 quarts water

Choose mild white fish for this stock. Oily, heavier-flavored fish such as salmon or tuna are often too strong for a basic all-purpose stock.

Rinse the fish well and remove the gills if using the heads. Set aside. In a stockpot, heat the olive oil over medium heat. Sauté the onions, carrots, and garlic until the vegetables are just beginning to color. Add the fish, wine, parsley, bay leaves, coriander seeds, lemon zest, and water and bring to a boil. Reduce the heat and simmer, partially covered, for 30 to 45 minutes. Carefully skim any scum or froth that rises to the surface. Remove from the heat, cool slightly, and strain. Refrigerate the stock and remove any fat. Store, covered, in the refrigerator for 3 days or freeze for up to 2 months.

LAMB OR OTHER MEAT STOCK

6 to 8 pounds cracked lamb shanks and meat trimmings, most of the fat removed

2 medium onions, quartered

2 large carrots, chopped

2 celery stalks, chopped

1 head garlic cloves, separated but unpeeled

2 cups hearty red wine

2 bay leaves

1 bunch fresh parsley leaves and stems, coarsely chopped

2 teaspoons dried thyme

1 teaspoon peppercorns

¼ cup tomato paste or 1 cup canned tomatoes

6 quarts water

The procedure is the same for most brown meat stocks, such as beef, venison, and pork. To make sure the stock has enough flavor, add some meat trimmings along with the bones.

Preheat the oven to 450°F. In a roasting pan, put the shanks, trimmings, onions, carrots, celery, and garlic and roast for 45 to 50 minutes or until the shanks are nicely browned. Turn the shanks and vegetables occasionally.

Transfer the shanks and vegetables to a large stockpot, leaving fat behind. Pour off the fat from the roasting pan and put the pan over medium heat. Pour in the wine, scraping up any of the browned bits on the bottom. Add to the stockpot, along with the bay leaves, parsley, thyme, peppercorns, and tomato paste. Add enough cold water to cover the shanks by at least 2 inches and slowly bring to a boil. Reduce the heat and simmer, partially covered, for 4 to 6 hours. Check occasionally to make sure the shanks are covered with liquid. Be sure to skim any froth or scum that rises to the surface. Strain the stock carefully, refrigerate, and remove the fat from the surface. Store, covered, in the refrigerator for up to 5 days or freeze for up to 3 months.

RICH VEGETABLE STOCK

⅓ cup olive or canola oil

8 cups chopped onions or leeks, or both

4 cups chopped carrots

2 cups chopped celery, including tops

¼ cup chopped garlic

4 cups chopped mushrooms, such as cremini

6 quarts water

2 cups dry white wine

4 cups seeded and diced fresh tomatoes or canned diced tomatoes

2 teaspoons peppercorns

3 bay leaves

2 cups coarsely chopped fresh parsley leaves and stems

In a large stockpot, heat the olive oil over medium-high heat. Sauté the onions, carrots, celery, garlic, and mushrooms until the vegetables are very lightly browned. Or, you can toss the vegetables with the oil, spread out in a single layer, and roast in a preheated 400°F oven to lightly brown. Be sure to stir and turn occasionally.

Add the water, wine, tomatoes, peppercorns, bay leaves, and parsley. Bring to a boil, immediately reduce the heat, and simmer, partially covered, for 2 hours. Carefully strain and cool. Store, covered, in the refrigerator for up to 5 days or freeze for up to 3 months.

CORN STOCK

8 large ears fresh corn

2 tablespoons olive oil

6 cups chopped onions

4 cups chopped carrots

2 cups chopped celery

2 tablespoons chopped garlic

2 cups dry white wine

2 bay leaves

½ teaspoon peppercorns

6 quarts water

You can also add fresh or dried chiles, or toasted cumin or coriander seeds, or a combination, for variation.

Remove the kernels from the ears of corn and reserve both the corn and the cobs. In a stockpot, heat the olive oil over medium heat. Sauté the onions, carrots, celery, and garlic until the vegetables are just beginning to brown. Break the corn cobs into 2 or 3 pieces each and add to the pot along with the wine, bay leaves, peppercorns, and enough water to cover all by at least 3 inches. Bring to a boil, then reduce the heat and simmer for 1½ hours. Strain the stock, pressing on the vegetables and cobs to extract all the liquid, return the liquid to the stockpot, and add the reserved corn kernels. Simmer for an additional 25 to 30 minutes. Strain and cool. Store, covered, in the refrigerator for up to 5 days or freeze for up to 3 months.

MUSHROOM STOCK

1 ounce dried porcini mushrooms or field blend dried mushrooms, soaked in 2 cups warm water for 20 minutes

½ cup (1 stick) unsalted butter, or more

4 to 5 pounds fresh mushrooms

4 cups chopped onions

3 tablespoons chopped garlic

3 cups chopped carrots

3 large bay leaves

2 teaspoons chopped fresh rosemary

2 teaspoons peppercorns

3 cups canned diced tomatoes, including juice

2 cups dry white wine

6 quarts water

This is a great stock to make when your market is offering half-price, over-the-hill mushrooms — those that have opened up completely and are getting soft (but not moldy). Buy a lot of them and store them in the freezer if you don't have time to make the stock right away. Add to this any mushroom stems and pieces or leftover wild mushrooms you might have. The secret here is to sauté the mushrooms in small batches so they have a chance to brown, which intensifies their flavor dramatically.

Drain the mushrooms, reserving the soaking water, and chop. In a stockpot, melt half the butter and sauté the fresh and reconstituted mushrooms, in batches if necessary, until they are well browned and most of the liquid has evaporated. Remove the mushrooms and set aside. Add the remaining butter to the stockpot and sauté the onions, garlic, and carrots until lightly browned. Add the bay leaves, rosemary, peppercorns, tomatoes, wine, and water and bring to a boil. Reduce the heat and simmer, partially covered, for 1 hour. Strain, pushing down on the solids, and refrigerate. Remove the fat layer. Store, covered, in the refrigerator for up to 5 days or freeze for up to 3 months.

TOMATO STOCK

7 to 8 pounds ripe tomatoes

Olive oil for sautéing

4 cups chopped red onions

2 cups chopped mushrooms, such as cremini

2 tablespoons slivered garlic

1 cup chopped carrots

2 cups dry white wine

3 large bay leaves

¼ cup tomato paste or chopped dried tomatoes

2 teaspoons peppercorns

½ teaspoon fennel seeds

¼ teaspoon saffron threads (optional)

6 quarts water

Preheat the oven to 400°F. Put the tomatoes in a single layer in a lightly oiled baking pan. Roast in the oven for about 30 minutes until the tomatoes are very lightly browned. Set aside.

In a stockpot, heat a tablespoon or two of olive oil over medium heat. Sauté the onions, mushrooms, garlic, and carrots until just beginning to color. Add the wine, bay leaves, tomato paste, peppercorns, fennel seeds, saffron (if using), roasted tomatoes, and water and bring to a boil. Reduce the heat and simmer, partially covered, for 2 hours. Remove from the heat, cool slightly, and strain, pressing on the solids. Chill the stock and remove any fat. Store, covered, in the refrigerator for up to 5 days or freeze for up to 3 months.

juices

An alternative or interesting addition to stocks is fresh vegetable and fruit juices. Juicers vary, but I like the kind that capture all the pulp and provide a clear, sparkling juice. If your juice is cloudy, slowly heat it in a saucepan just to simmer. Skim away the froth that rises and then strain the liquid through cheesecloth or a coffee filter. There are no hard and fast rules to substituting juices for some or all stocks. Here are some ideas to encourage you:

• Use a combination of chicken stock and fresh fennel juice to poach chicken breasts for salad.

• Use fresh carrot or red bell pepper juice as a beautiful garnish to ladle around a risotto.

• Intensify the flavors of corn and mushroom stocks by adding the juices of each at the end, and roast the corn or mushrooms first to add even more flavor.

• Use fresh juices as a basis for vinaigrettes or marinades.

• Reduce the juices until they become syrupy and use to drizzle over grilled or roasted meats, cooked vegetables, or fresh fruits.

Yields, of course, vary depending on the fruit, herb, or vegetable used and the type of juicer, but I usually figure on about 1 cup of juice for each pound of product.

ROASTED BUTTERNUT SQUASH SOUP WITH LIME CRÈME FRAÎCHE

Serves 8

RECOMMENDED WINE
The creamy, sweet flavors in this recipe mirror the flavors found in aromatic whites like **Viognier**, **Riesling**, and **Gewürztraminer**. One of the sweeter-style **Chardonnays** with moderate oak aging could also work nicely.

3 tablespoons unsalted butter

3 cups chopped yellow onions

3 cups roasted butternut squash

6 cups rich chicken or vegetable stock

1½ tablespoons lightly toasted, Madras Curry Powder (page 97)

¼ teaspoon freshly grated nutmeg

1 tablespoon honey

1 cup half-and-half or heavy (whipping) cream

3 tablespoons dry sherry

Kosher or sea salt and freshly ground pepper

Toasted pepitas (pumpkin seeds) or almonds, and chopped fresh chives, for garnishing

Lime Crème Fraîche (recipe follows)

Butternut squash is generally available and the most flavorful of the winter hard squashes. Its dense flesh takes very well to roasting or baking. To roast: Preheat the oven to 400°F. Cut the squash in half, remove the seeds, and lightly paint with olive oil or melted butter. Roast cut-side up in the oven for 40 to 45 minutes or until the flesh is soft and very lightly caramelized.

In a large sauté pan, melt the butter and sauté the onions until very soft but not brown. Transfer to a food processor and process, in batches if necessary, the onions and roasted squash. In a large saucepan, whisk together the onion-squash purée, stock, curry powder, nutmeg, and honey. Bring to a simmer and cook for 10 to 15 minutes, stirring occasionally. Stir in the half-and-half and sherry. Season to taste with salt and pepper.

Ladle the soup into warm soup bowls. Garnish with the pepitas, chives, and a drizzle of Lime Crème Fraîche.

LIME CRÈME FRAÎCHE

1 cup Crème Fraîche (page 37)

2 teaspoons finely grated lime zest

1 tablespoon fresh lime juice

Kosher or sea salt and freshly ground pepper

In a medium bowl, mix the crème fraîche, lime zest, and lime juice. Season to taste with salt and pepper. Refrigerate for at least 1 hour for flavors to develop. Can be stored, covered, in the refrigerator for up to 3 days.

BEET SOUP WITH MINT

Serves 6 to 8

2 pounds beets, unpeeled

2 tablespoons olive oil

Kosher or sea salt and freshly ground pepper

4 to 5 cups rich chicken or vegetable stock

1 tablespoon fresh lemon juice

1 tablespoon honey

½ teaspoon toasted, crushed caraway seeds

¼ teaspoon ground cloves

¼ cup chopped fresh mint

Stirred plain yogurt and fresh mint sprigs for garnishing (optional)

RECOMMENDED WINE

Beets are so naturally sweet that any fruity wine with a bit of matching residual sugar would work, such as whites like **Riesling** or pinks like **White Zinfandel** or similar wines made in that style.

This is a very simple, earthy soup with beautiful color. It's one that I like to serve in little demitasse cups to begin the meal, and it's equally good hot or cold. Be careful in adding honey so that the soup doesn't get too sweet. Roasted beets are very sweet on their own.

Preheat the oven to 375°F. In a roasting pan, lightly coat the beets with the olive oil and season to taste with salt and pepper. Cover with foil and roast for 30 to 40 minutes or until the flesh is soft. Remove, cool, and peel away the skins with a paring knife or by rubbing with a rough towel.

In a food processor or blender, purée the beets with 4 cups stock, lemon juice, honey, caraway seeds, cloves, and mint. Season to taste with salt and pepper. Add more stock if a thinner consistency is desired. Serve hot or cold. Garnish with a dollop of yogurt and a sprig of fresh mint, if using.

FIVE LILIES CHOWDER

Serves 8

RECOMMENDED WINE
Sauvignon Blanc with its herbal, citrusy flavors would be great with this dish.

3 tablespoons olive oil

4 cups diced yellow onions

¼ cup sliced shallots

1 tablespoon chopped garlic

1 cup dry white wine

1 bay leaf

6 cups rich Chicken Stock (page 66) or Mushroom Stock (page 70)

Kosher or sea salt and freshly ground pepper

2 teaspoons finely chopped fresh thyme or 1 teaspoon dried

2 teaspoons finely chopped fresh oregano or 1 teaspoon dried

½ cup finely diced celery

1 cup finely sliced leeks, both white and tender green parts

2 tablespoons dry sherry

2 tablespoons minced fresh chives

Gremolata (page 86) for garnishing (optional)

The "Five Lilies" here refers to the onions, shallots, leeks, garlic, and chives—all members of the lily, or allium, family. In addition to being very tasty, this soup is low in fat. The trick to this dish is not to overcook the vegetables added at serving time; they should have some crunch left. To turn this into a main-course soup, add some cooked wild rice, sautéed mushrooms, or any other favorite vegetable, or a combination.

In a medium saucepan, heat the olive oil and sauté the onions, shallots, and garlic until they soften and just begin to color, about 5 minutes. Transfer half the onion mixture to a blender or food processor. Purée and return to the pan. Add the wine, bay leaf, and stock and simmer for 10 minutes. Season to taste with salt and pepper. (The soup base may be prepared in advance to this point and stored, covered, in the refrigerator for up to 3 days or frozen for up to 3 months and reheated before finishing.)

Just before serving, add the thyme, oregano, celery, leeks, and sherry to the hot soup base. Bring to a simmer and cook for 2 minutes. Do not overcook; the vegetables should retain their crunchy texture. Remove the bay leaf, stir in the chives, and garnish with a sprinkling of the gremolata, if using.

LENTIL "CAPPUCCINO"

Serves 8 to 10

½ ounce dried porcini mushrooms, soaked in 1 cup warm water for 20 minutes

2 tablespoons olive oil

½ cup chopped celery

1 cup chopped carrots

1 cup chopped onion

1 cup stemmed and chopped cremini or shiitake mushrooms

½ cup chopped leeks, white part only

1 tablespoon chopped garlic

6 cups rich Lamb Stock (page 68) or Mushroom Stock (page 70)

1 cup dry white wine

1 large bay leaf

1 tablespoon chopped fresh oregano or 1 teaspoon dried

1 teaspoon cumin seeds, toasted and crushed

1¼ cups black or brown lentils, picked over

Kosher or sea salt and freshly ground pepper

Steamed milk (if you have an espresso machine) or unsweetened, lightly whipped cream, flavored with a few drops of truffle oil (optional)

Chopped fresh chives for garnishing (optional)

RECOMMENDED WINE
This is a rich, earthy dish and could go with an earth-red wine such as **Pinot Noir** or **Syrah**.

This is a whimsical approach to soup in a coffee cup that I served at a James Beard House dinner many years ago. Because the color of the soup is similar to coffee, I played with the idea of adding a dollop of steamed milk or whipped cream to make it look like cappuccino. If you wanted to be really decadent, a shaving or two of fresh truffle to mimic chocolate could complete the presentation.

Drain, rinse, and coarsely chop the mushrooms. Set aside.

In a large saucepan, heat the olive oil over medium heat. Sauté the celery, carrots, onion, cremini mushrooms, leeks, garlic, and porcini until the vegetables are soft and lightly colored. Add the stock, wine, bay leaf, oregano, cumin seeds, and lentils. Simmer for 40 to 45 minutes or until the lentils are very soft. Remove the bay leaf and season to taste with salt and pepper. Transfer to a blender or food processor. Purée, in batches if necessary, and strain through a medium-mesh strainer. Adjust the consistency, if you want, by adding more stock.

Serve in warm 6-ounce coffee cups with a saucer. Garnish with steamed milk and chopped chives, if using.

SPICY BLACK BEAN CHOWDER WITH PINEAPPLE-BANANA SALSA

Serves 8 to 10

RECOMMENDED WINE
You can either mirror the hearty flavors with a peppery **Zinfandel** or **Syrah** or contrast them with an aromatic white like **Riesling** or **Viognier**. White Zinfandel or an herbal **Fumé Blanc** or **Sauvignon Blanc** would also be fun.

2 tablespoons olive oil

4 cups chopped onions

¼ cup chopped garlic

½ cup chopped celery

2 pounds smoked ham hocks

1¾ cups black beans, soaked overnight and drained

6 cups rich Chicken Stock (page 66) or Vegetable Stock (page 69)

2 cups fresh orange juice

2 tablespoons pure chile powder, such as ancho

1 tablespoon seeded and minced serrano chile

2 bay leaves

1 tablespoon chopped fresh thyme or 1½ teaspoons dried

1 teaspoon fennel seeds

1½ tablespoons chopped fresh oregano or 2 teaspoons dried

½ teaspoon ground cloves

1 teaspoon ground cinnamon

Kosher or sea salt and freshly ground pepper

3 cups seeded and diced fresh tomatoes or canned diced tomatoes, including juice

⅓ cup chopped fresh cilantro

Pineapple-Banana Salsa (facing page)

Fresh cilantro sprigs for garnishing (optional)

This hearty chowder draws heavily from Latin American flavors, such as Brazilian and Cuban. The hot-sweet spice flavors are typical of those cuisines. The Pineapple-Banana Salsa is also delicious on grilled fish and chicken. (And if you're grilling fish or chicken, also grill the pineapple and red onions that are used for the salsa.)

In a stockpot, heat the olive oil and sauté the onions, garlic, and celery until they just begin to color. Add the ham hocks, beans, stock, orange juice, chile powder, chile, bay leaves, thyme, fennel seeds, oregano, cloves, and cinnamon. Bring to a simmer and cook, partially covered, until the beans are tender, about 1 hour. (At this point, the soup can be stored covered in the refrigerator overnight, if you want, to develop the flavors and to congeal the fat so that it is easily removed.)

Skim any fat from the soup. Remove the bay leaves and ham hocks and discard any skin or fat from the hocks. Pull off and shred the meat from the hocks and return it to the soup. Heat the soup through and season to taste with salt and pepper. Just before serving, stir in the tomatoes and cilantro. Top each serving with a spoonful of the Pineapple-Banana Salsa and garnish with a cilantro sprig, if using.

PINEAPPLE-BANANA SALSA
Makes about 1½ cups

½ cup diced fresh pineapple

⅓ cup diced ripe but firm banana

¼ cup minced red onion

¼ cup diced orange segments

2 teaspoons seeded and minced serrano chile

2 tablespoons chopped fresh cilantro

1 tablespoon fresh lime juice

Drops of olive oil

In a medium bowl, gently combine the pineapple, banana, red onion, orange, chile, cilantro, lime juice, and olive oil. Refrigerate for at least 30 minutes to allow the flavors to blend.

WINE COUNTRY BORSCHT

Serves 8

RECOMMENDED WINE
The natural sweetness of the beets suggests an earthy and fruity red wine, such as **Pinot Noir**, **Zinfandel**, or **Gamay**.

3 tablespoons olive oil

3 pounds lean stewing beef, such as brisket or tri-tip (also called triangle tip or sirloin tip), cut into 1½-inch cubes

1½ cups chopped carrots

1½ cups chopped onions

2 tablespoons chopped garlic

½ cup chopped celery

5 cups peeled and diced raw red beets

2 cups seeded and diced tomatoes

8 cups rich Beef Stock (page 68) or Mushroom Stock (page 70)

3 cups dry red wine

1½ teaspoons fennel seeds

2 teaspoons chopped fresh thyme or 1 teaspoon dried

¼ cup balsamic vinegar

Kosher or sea salt and freshly ground pepper

3 tablespoons finely chopped fresh parsley

1½ cups diced red potatoes, with skin on

2½ cups finely shredded green cabbage

1 teaspoon crushed caraway seeds

2 cups roasted, peeled, and finely diced beets (optional)

Sour cream for garnishing (optional)

This is a rich stew that is a meal in a bowl, particularly when accompanied by crusty French bread. In this recipe we've made the presentation a little more elegant by straining out the cooking vegetables and adding separately cooked potatoes and cabbage at the end to give more color and texture. I recommend making the soup a day ahead and refrigerating it overnight: This makes it easier to remove the fat layer and you can then prepare the beets, potatoes, and cabbage just before you reheat the soup.

In a stockpot, heat 2 tablespoons of the olive oil. Add the beef in batches and quickly brown on all sides. Remove the meat and set aside. Add the carrots, onions, garlic, and celery and sauté until the vegetables are lightly colored. Return the beef to the pot and add the raw beets, tomatoes, stock, wine, fennel seeds, and thyme. Bring to a boil. Reduce the heat and simmer, partially covered, for 1½ to 2 hours or until the beef is very tender. Occasionally skim off the fat.

Strain the soup carefully, pressing down gently on the meat and vegetables to extract as much liquid as possible. Set aside the beef and discard the remaining vegetables, if you want. Return the beef and strained liquid to the stockpot. (The soup can be made ahead to this point and stored, covered, in the refrigerator overnight.) Add the balsamic vinegar and season with salt and pepper to taste. Stir in the parsley and keep warm.

In a separate saucepan, in lightly salted boiling water, cook the potatoes until just tender, about 5 minutes. Drain and keep warm. In a medium sauté pan, heat the remaining 1 tablespoon of the olive oil. Sauté the cabbage and caraway seeds until crisp-tender, about 2 minutes.

Ladle the borscht into warm soup bowls. Add the roasted beets (if using), potatoes, and sautéed cabbage. Garnish with a dollop of sour cream, if using.

FRESH PEA SOUP WITH TARRAGON AND LEMON CRÈME FRAÎCHE

Serves 6 to 8

3 tablespoons olive oil or unsalted butter

1 cup chopped onion

2 cups chopped leeks, both white and tender green parts

½ cup chopped celery

¼ cup chopped carrot

1 tablespoon chopped garlic

6 cups rich Vegetable Stock (page 69) or Chicken Stock (page 66)

½ cup dry white wine

4 cups shelled fresh spring peas or frozen peas

Kosher or sea salt

2 tablespoons chopped fresh tarragon

3 cups lightly packed shredded romaine or other deep green lettuce

Freshly ground pepper

A dollop of Lime Crème Fraîche (page 72), tarragon leaves, and a drizzle of Fennel Oil (page 81) for garnishing (optional)

RECOMMENDED WINE
The fresh licorice flavor of tarragon is a great link to **Sauvignon Blancs** with their herbal, green flavors.

We tend to think of pea soup as a hearty winter dish. This version is made from fresh peas and is perfect in spring and early summer when peas are at their peak. You can serve the soup warm or cold depending on the weather. If serving warm, plan to serve it shortly after it's reheated in order to preserve the bright green color and flavor.

In a stockpot, heat the olive oil and sauté the onion, leeks, celery, carrot, and garlic until soft but not browned. Add the stock and wine and bring just to a boil. Reduce the heat and simmer for 10 minutes.

In a separate saucepan, add the peas to lightly salted boiling water and cook for 3 minutes or until crisp-tender. Drain immediately and plunge into cold water to stop the cooking and retain the color. Drain again. Add the peas and the tarragon to the soup and simmer for 3 minutes more or until peas are soft. Off the heat, allow the mixture to cool slightly and then add the lettuce so that it just begins to wilt.

Purée in a food processor or blender and strain through a medium-mesh strainer, pressing down on the solids. Thin if you want with additional stock. Season to taste with salt and pepper.

Serve the soup warm or cold, with a dollop of the Lime Crème Fraîche, tarragon leaves, and Fennel Oil, if using.

infused oils

Once you start playing with these, I think you'll become as hooked on them as I am. For me, they are part of the basic pantry and add not only color but often intense and unusual flavor to a wide variety of foods. They are easy to make, and I always have a few stored in the refrigerator in handy squirt bottles so that I can squirt a rainbow of color and flavor on almost anything.

I've divided the infused oils into ingredient categories. As you'll note, however, the approach is basically the same. I encourage you to come up with your own combinations—even mix categories if you want. A couple of other comments:

There is nothing sacred about the quantities you use, so adjust according to your taste. For the oil I usually use a good olive or canola oil. Both of these are neutral in flavor and a good carrier for the infusion. I don't generally use extra-virgin olive oil unless that is a flavor component I want in the final infusion. I suggest storing your infused oils in the refrigerator because I think it keeps them fresher tasting. Most oils tend to solidify when cold. If this happens, simply put in a pan of warm water or in the microwave for a few seconds before using.

LEAFY HERB OILS
(such as basil, mint, chive, cilantro, parsley, and shiso)

2 cups lightly packed herbs, large stems removed first

1 to 2 cups olive oil

Kosher or sea salt and freshly ground white pepper

Blanch the herbs in lightly salted, boiling water for 2 to 3 seconds. Drain and immediately plunge into ice water to stop the cooking and set the color. This blanching step inactivates the enzymes that cause the herbs to turn brown and develop an oxidized flavor.

Squeeze the herbs dry, chop, and add to a blender or food processor along with enough oil to cover. Blend to make a thick paste. Pour into a clean tall jar and cover with up to 2 inches of oil. Stir well and store, covered, in the refrigerator for at least 8 hours and preferably for a day or two depending on the intensity of color and flavor desired. Season with a little salt and pepper if you want and store, covered, in the refrigerator for up to 3 weeks.

SPICE OILS

(such as chile, curry, saffron, mustard, ginger, fennel, cumin, coriander, cinnamon, and juniper berry)

Lightly toast whole (preferably) or ground spices in a dry pan over medium heat for a minute or two. This refreshes them, helping to drive off any rancid oils or flavors. If using whole spices, grind after toasting. Add enough oil to make a thick paste and then put in a clean jar and cover with a couple of inches of oil. Stir and allow to infuse for at least 2 days at room temperature. When the desired taste and color are achieved, carefully strain through cheesecloth or a very fine-mesh strainer and store, covered, for up to 2 months.

DRIED FRUIT AND VEGETABLE OILS

(such as apricots, sun-dried tomatoes, and dried mushrooms)

Purée the dried fruits or vegetables in a blender with enough oil to cover and make a thick paste. Put in a clean jar and cover with a couple of inches of oil and stir to combine. Allow to sit for a couple of days or until the desired flavor and color are achieved. Strain to remove all of the sediment and store, covered, for up to 2 months, preferably in the refrigerator.

MUSSEL, LEEK, AND WHITE BEAN CHOWDER

Serves 6

RECOMMENDED WINE
A rich white like a barrel-aged **Chardonnay** or **Pinot Blanc** would go well here.

mussels

Mussels found in the market today all come from farm-raised sources and are much more uniform, meatier, and cleaner than those gathered in the wild. Also, because the farms are regularly inspected, you don't have to worry about red tides and other contamination. Mussels are raised on both the east and west coasts of America and are readily available. One of the simplest and best fish stocks you can make involves simply poaching mussels in white wine and then straining the liquid through cheesecloth to remove any debris.

3 tablespoons olive oil

2 cups thinly sliced leeks, white part only

2 tablespoons finely slivered garlic

3 pounds mussels, scrubbed and beards removed

1 cup dry white wine

4 cups Fish Stock (page 67), Chicken Stock (page 66), or Vegetable Stock (page 69)

1 cup cooked cannellini, borlotti, or baby lima beans

1 cup seeded and diced fresh ripe or canned tomatoes

1 tablespoon chopped fresh parsley

1 tablespoon chopped fresh basil

Kosher or sea salt and freshly ground pepper

Drops of fresh lemon juice

2 cups lightly packed baby spinach

Red Pepper Aioli (page 168) for garnishing (optional)

This is reminiscent of the fish stews found around the Mediterranean. Any cooked white beans can be used. The flavor of the soup will be greatly influenced by the stock you use. Try the Corn Stock (page 69), Easy Shellfish Stock (page 67), or Tomato Stock (page 71).

In a large saucepan, heat the olive oil and sauté the leeks and garlic until soft but not brown. Add the mussels, wine, and stock. Simmer, covered, until the mussels open, about 3 minutes. Discard any unopened mussels. Remove from the heat. Strain, reserving both the stock and the vegetables. Return the stock to the pan.

Remove the mussels from their shells and discard the shells. Return the mussels, leeks, and garlic to the pan with the stock. Add the beans, tomatoes, parsley, and basil. Heat to warm through. Season to taste with salt and pepper and drops of lemon juice.

To serve, place a few spinach leaves in deep soup bowls. Ladle the hot soup over the spinach. Garnish with a dollop of Red Pepper Aioli, if using.

MY GRANDMOTHER'S WHITE BEAN SOUP

Serves 10 to 12

2 cups dried Great Northern beans or navy beans

2 tablespoons olive oil

2 cups thinly sliced onions

2 tablespoons chopped garlic

1 cup diced carrots

1 cup diced celery

8 cups rich Chicken Stock (page 66) or Vegetable Stock (page 69)

2 cups dry white wine

1 pound meaty smoked ham hocks

2 teaspoons dried thyme

1 teaspoon fennel seeds

2 large bay leaves

½ teaspoon red pepper flakes

3 cups seeded and diced fresh ripe tomatoes or canned diced tomatoes, including juice

3 tablespoons chopped fresh parsley

2 cups finely shredded green cabbage

Freshly grated Parmesan or dry Jack cheese for garnishing

My friends tease me about how often I say "my grandmother's" this or that, but the truth is that my grandmother was the one who instilled in me a real passion for cooking. Living in the mountains of Colorado, she knew how to whip up a hearty bean soup to combat the bone-chilling weather. Here's to you, Grandma.

Sort through the beans to remove any debris. Rinse thoroughly and soak overnight in enough water to cover the beans by at least 3 inches. Alternatively, use the quick-soak method explained in the margin.

In a stockpot, heat the olive oil and sauté the onions, garlic, carrots, and celery until they just begin to color. Add the stock, wine, ham hocks, thyme, fennel seeds, bay leaves, and pepper flakes. Bring to a simmer and cook, partially covered, for 30 to 40 minutes or until the beans are tender. Add the tomatoes and parsley. Remove from the heat. (At this point, the soup can be stored, covered, in the refrigerator overnight, if you want, to develop the flavors and to congeal the fat so that it is easily removed.)

Skim any fat from the soup. Remove the bay leaves and the ham hocks, discard any skin or fat, shred the meat, and return it to the soup. Heat to a simmer. Just before serving, stir in the cabbage. Serve the soup and pass the Parmesan cheese.

RECOMMENDED WINE
I like the rustic quality of **Zinfandel** with this extremely hearty soup.

the quick-soak method for cooking beans

In my cooking classes, I find that the main reasons students give most often for not cooking and eating more dried beans is the long overnight soaking time usually recommended. Several years ago the USDA came up with a technique that helps deal with this. It enables you to be ready to cook dried beans in an hour.

It's very simple: First, wash the dried beans thoroughly and pick through to remove any debris. (Remember dried beans are a natural agricultural product that comes to us right from the field.) Put the washed beans in a deep pot and cover with at least 3 inches of cold water, and bring it to a boil over high heat. As soon as the water boils, remove from the heat and let it sit for at least 1 hour. What we're looking for here is that the beans are plump, with no wrinkled skins. Drain the beans, add fresh water, and finish the cooking.

OYSTER-SPINACH CHOWDER

Serves 8

RECOMMENDED WINE
The rich, creamy soup would go well with a barrel-fermented and aged **Chardonnay** that has some malolactic fermentation, which gives a creamy, buttery quality to the wine to match up to the soup.

1 tablespoon unsalted butter

1 tablespoon olive oil

4 ounces pancetta or lean bacon, diced

3 cups thinly sliced onions

2 cups thinly sliced leeks, white part only

3 garlic cloves, very thinly sliced

6 cups rich Shellfish Stock (page 67) or Chicken Stock (page 66)

2 teaspoons chopped fresh thyme or 1 teaspoon dried

2 cups thickly sliced small new potatoes

2 cups cream or No-Cream Cream (facing page)

¼ cup dry sherry

Kosher or sea salt and freshly ground pepper

4 cups lightly packed baby spinach

1 tablespoon grated lemon zest

1 pound small shucked, drained oysters (about 2½ cups)

Tiny garlic croutons and chopped fresh chives for garnishing (optional)

Over the past few years I've gravitated away from rich, cream-based soups, but every once in a while I can't resist. I'm using cream in this recipe, but a very delicious and healthful alternative is the No-Cream Cream recipe that follows. Be sure your oysters are small. If you get large ones, marinate them in milk in the refrigerator for a couple of hours and then rinse to remove strong flavors. Cut into bite-sized portions before adding to the chowder.

In a stockpot, heat the butter and olive oil and sauté the pancetta until browned. Remove and drain on paper towels. Discard all but 2 tablespoons of fat.

Add the onions, leeks, and garlic to the pot and sauté until soft but not brown. Add the stock and thyme, bring to a boil, then reduce heat and simmer for 5 minutes. Add the potatoes and simmer for 5 minutes or until the potatoes are almost done. Add the cream and sherry and season to taste with salt and pepper. Heat through but do not boil so that cream won't take on a cooked flavor. Divide the spinach, zest, oysters, and reserved pancetta among warm bowls. Ladle the hot soup over and garnish with croutons and chives, if using. Serve immediately.

NO-CREAM CREAM
Makes about 2½ cups

2 teaspoons olive oil

½ cup chopped yellow onion

⅓ cup rice, preferably medium- or short-grain, which is starchier

2 cups rich fat-free chicken stock or vegetable stock

1 cup dry white wine

Kosher or sea salt and freshly ground white pepper

OK, I confess . . . I do love cream, and in my early training in France the mantra always was "if you want to enrich a dish, add some cream, and to make it even better, whisk in some butter and egg yolks"! I do use some cream if it adds a desirable richness to the final dish, but it can be too much of a good thing. A great alternative that allows you to cut down on cream in part or fully and still have most of the richness and mouth-feel that cream provides is this very low-fat No-Cream Cream.

In a saucepan, heat the olive oil over medium heat and sauté the onion until soft but not colored. Add the rice and sauté 2 minutes longer, stirring regularly. Add 1 cup of the stock and the wine and simmer, covered, until the liquid is mostly absorbed and the mixture is very soft, about 20 minutes. Cool slightly, transfer the mixture to a blender, and purée. With the motor running, add more stock until you reach the desired consistency. Season to taste with salt and pepper. Make a double batch and freeze it in 1-cup portions; it keeps for up to 4 months, frozen.

ITALIAN GARLIC AND BREAD SOUP WITH POACHED EGGS

Serves 6 to 8

RECOMMENDED WINE
The Italian heritage here calls out for a crisp white like **Pinot Gris** or **Pinot Grigio**, or **Pinot Bianco**. For something different a sparkling dry **Prosecco** would also be fun.

½ cup extra-virgin olive oil

3 large garlic cloves; 2 peeled and halved lengthwise, 1 peeled and bruised

6 thick slices crusty Italian bread, such as ciabatta

6 large eggs

6 cups rich Chicken Stock (page 66) or Vegetable Stock (page 69)

⅓ cup dry Marsala or sherry

Kosher or sea salt and freshly ground pepper

3 cups lightly packed baby spinach or arugula

2 cups peeled, seeded, and diced ripe tomatoes

Gremolata (recipe follows)

½ cup freshly grated Parmesan or pecorino cheese

This is typical of simple peasant-style soups served all around the Mediterranean. It's also the kind of soup your grandmother might have made when you had a bad cold. You could add almost anything else you'd like to the soup depending on what's in season or what needs to be used up in your refrigerator! A good rich stock is required.

In a sauté pan, heat the olive oil over medium heat and sauté the halved garlic until lightly browned. Remove the garlic and discard. Sauté the bread slices on both sides until golden brown, in batches if necessary. Rub with the bruised garlic. Set aside.

Poach the eggs in barely simmering water until the whites are just set and then immediately put in a large bowl of ice water to stop the cooking. You can prepare both the toasted bread and the eggs 3 to 4 hours ahead, if you want.

In a stockpot, heat the stock and Marsala to boiling and season to taste with salt and pepper. Divide the spinach and tomatoes among the bowls and place a bread slice on top of each bowl. Using a slotted spoon, place a poached egg on top of each bread slice and ladle the hot stock over. Sprinkle the gremolata and Parmesan cheese over and serve immediately.

GREMOLATA

3 tablespoons minced poached garlic (see page 264) or 1 tablespoon minced raw garlic

¼ cup chopped fresh parsley

1 tablespoon chopped fresh mint or basil

1 tablespoon finely grated lemon zest

In a small bowl, combine the garlic, parsley, mint, and lemon zest. This can be done an hour or two ahead.

TOMATO-CURRY SOUP WITH RISO AND BASIL-MINT PESTO

Serves 8

1 tablespoon olive oil

2 cups ¼-inch diced onion

1 tablespoon chopped garlic

1 tablespoon or more good curry powder, such as Madras Curry Powder (page 97)

One 32-ounce can diced tomatoes, (including juice), preferably Muir Glen

4 cups flavorful Chicken Stock (page 66) or Vegetable Stock (page 69)

1 cup dry white wine

1 tablespoon minced fresh ginger

1 teaspoon whole fennel seeds

¼ teaspoon red pepper flakes

Kosher or sea salt and freshly ground pepper

⅓ cup riso pasta, cooked al dente

Basil-Mint Pesto (recipe follows) for garnishing (optional)

RECOMMENDED WINE
The soup is richly flavored and fairly acidic and so demands a wine with similar acidity. A crisp, clean, un-oaked **Chardonnay** would work here, as would a crisp sparkling wine. Alternatively, a slightly sweet, lower-alcohol **Gewürztraminer** would be an interesting contrast to the spicy heat from the chile and curry. If you would like red wine, a soft, lower-tannin **Pinot Noir** could work as long as the pepper spice isn't overwhelming.

This is a simple recipe, easily put together at the last moment. Remember that curry powders vary greatly in strength. Taste carefully to decide if you want more. Riso is pasta shaped like rice. Orzo or any other small shaped pasta can be used. To turn this into a main-course soup, you could add shellfish such as shrimp or scallops, smoked chicken, or even grilled portobello mushrooms. The Basil–Mint Pesto makes a nice addition and can be made ahead. The soup will still be delicious without it.

In a stockpot, heat the olive oil over medium heat and sauté the onion, garlic, and 1 tablespoon curry powder until just beginning to color. Add the tomatoes, stock, wine, ginger, fennel seeds, and pepper flakes and simmer for 10 minutes. Season to taste with salt and pepper and additional curry powder. Just before serving, add the riso and simmer for a couple of minutes more. Serve in warm soup bowls, swirled with a dollop of Basil-Mint Pesto, if using.

BASIL-MINT PESTO
Makes about 1 cup

2 cups firmly packed fresh basil leaves

⅓ cup loosely packed fresh mint leaves

1 tablespoon finely chopped garlic

3 tablespoons lightly toasted pine nuts or chopped almonds

⅓ cup olive oil

⅓ cup freshly grated Parmesan or Asiago cheese

2 tablespoons heavy (whipping) cream or rich chicken or shellfish stock

Kosher or sea salt and freshly ground pepper

Plunge the basil and mint leaves into a pan of boiling water for 5 to 10 seconds. Immediately drain and plunge into a large bowl of ice water to stop the cooking and set the bright green color. Drain and squeeze out excess water. In a food processor or blender, combine the basil mixture, garlic, pine nuts, and olive oil and purée. Transfer to a medium bowl and stir in the cheese and cream. Season to taste with salt and pepper. The mixture should be thick and not runny. Store, covered, in the refrigerator for up to 5 days.

canned tomatoes

Except for the summertime window, I prefer canned tomatoes to fresh. They are picked when they are truly ripe (they are not gassed green ones). Diced canned tomatoes in juice are widely available and now even come in two sizes: regular and petite dice. Among the many brands of canned tomatoes, the one that always seems to win blind taste tests is Muir Glen. In compliance with our current full-disclosure policy, I must tell you that I have no association with them. I do, however, think they are the best-tasting canned tomato product on the market, and if that isn't enough they also come from certified organic farms.

HOMINY SOUP WITH SALAD

Serves 6

RECOMMENDED WINE
A nice aromatic white with just a tiny touch of residual sugar would be nice here, such as **Riesling**, **Gewürztraminer**, or **Chenin Blanc**.

3 tablespoons olive oil

2 cups sliced onions

2 tablespoon slivered garlic

2 teaspoons ground cumin

1 teaspoon seeded and finely diced serrano or jalapeño chile

¼ cup masa harina (see Note)

5 cups Chicken Stock (page 66) or Vegetable Stock (page 69)

3 cups canned diced tomatoes, including juice, preferably Muir Glen

1 tablespoon dried oregano, preferably Mexican

4 cups cooked white or yellow hominy

Kosher or sea salt and freshly ground pepper

Bottled hot sauce of your choice (optional)

SALAD

3 cups finely sliced green cabbage

1 cup sliced radishes

1 large avocado, diced

½ cup fresh cilantro leaves or tender stems

2 limes, cut into wedges for squeezing over

This simple soup uses hominy, or posole, as the Mexicans call it. It's a hearty soup that, for me, is a meal, since it includes both the soup and the salad in one bowl! You could embellish it with cooked shrimp, chicken, or spicy sausage. Canned hominy is perfectly acceptable, but if you have the time, your own home-cooked hominy will have more corn flavor. You can also use whatever salad ingredients you like.

In a stockpot, heat the olive oil and sauté the onions, garlic, cumin, and chile until soft but not browned. Blend the masa harina with the stock until smooth and then add to the stockpot along with the tomatoes, oregano, and hominy. Bring to a boil, then reduce the heat and simmer for a few minutes. Season to your taste with salt and pepper and drops of hot sauce.

Ladle the soup into bowls and pass the cabbage, radishes, avocado, cilantro, and lime wedges for everyone to add to their liking.

Note: Masa harina is lime-treated dried field corn that has been ground into a flour. It is the basic flour used to make masa, the dough for tortillas and tamales, and is widely available in Mexican markets as well as many supermarkets. Hominy is the whole corn that has also been treated with lime to remove its tough hull.

CHILLED CORN, JICAMA, AND BUTTERMILK SOUP WITH SHRIMP

Serves 6 to 8

3 tablespoons olive oil

1½ cups chopped onions

2 teaspoons minced garlic

2 teaspoons peeled and minced fresh ginger

1 teaspoon high-quality curry powder, such as Madras Curry Powder (page 97)

½ teaspoon seeded and minced serrano chile

¾ cup diced new potatoes

½ cup dry white wine

2 cups Chicken Stock (page 66) or Easy Shellfish Stock (page 67)

⅔ cup half-and-half or heavy (whipping) cream or No-Cream Cream (page 85)

4 cups buttermilk

2 tablespoons fresh lime juice

3 cups fresh sweet corn kernels (3 large ears, preferably roasted or grilled first)

3 tablespoons chopped fresh cilantro

1 cup diced jicama

12 ounces cooked bay or rock shrimp

Kosher or sea salt and freshly ground pepper

Tabasco or other hot pepper sauce

Chopped fresh chives for garnishing

RECOMMENDED WINE
The tart buttermilk and lime are natural partners with a wine of similar qualities, like **Sauvignon Blanc**, unoaked **Chardonnay**, or crisp Italian and Spanish whites like **Pinot Gris** and **Albarino**.

jicama

A native of Central and South America, jicama is now grown widely throughout the Pacific Rim. It is a fleshy, crisp, sweet root that ranges in size from less than a pound to 5 pounds or more. I think it is best eaten raw, although some Mexican dishes call for it to be stir-fried or steamed. It does need to be peeled. It makes a great raw addition to a salad and has an excellent affinity for tart-sweet vinaigrettes. Jicama is a good alternative for fresh water chestnuts in Chinese cuisine, as it has a similar sweet, crunchy flavor and texture. It is generally available year-round, especially in Latin American and Asian markets.

The potato and curry base of this soup can be made ahead in a larger quantity and frozen for use at any time. Any combination of raw vegetables can be used, such as cucumbers, red onions, and sweet peas. The quality of the buttermilk is key to the flavor of the dish. A good "Bulgarian" cultured buttermilk is what I like, or look for a good goat buttermilk.

In a large saucepan, heat 2 tablespoons of the olive oil over medium heat and sauté the onions, garlic, ginger, curry, and chile until soft but not brown. Add the potatoes, wine, and stock and bring to a boil. Reduce the heat and simmer until the potatoes are very tender. Remove from the heat and cool. In a blender or food processor, purée the cooled soup base. Refrigerate for up to 2 days, if making ahead.

Add the half-and-half, buttermilk, lime juice, corn, cilantro, jicama, and shrimp to the chilled soup base. Season to taste with salt, pepper, and drops of Tabasco sauce.

Serve cold, garnished with chopped chives.

CHILLED FRESH TOMATO SOUP WITH SUMMER RELISH

Serves 6

RECOMMENDED WINE
Fumé Blanc and **Sauvignon Blanc** really express the flavors and aromas of a summer vegetable garden. The mint and basil are a perfect match for the fresh green herbal flavors of these wines.

4 pounds ripe tomatoes, coarsely chopped

¼ cup balsamic vinegar

Kosher or sea salt and freshly ground white pepper

Summer Relish (recipe follows)

1 large avocado, cut into 6 to 8 fans

Crème Fraîche (page 37) or yogurt

Fruity extra-virgin olive oil and fresh mint or basil sprigs for garnishing (optional)

Unfortunately, regular hothouse tomatoes don't work in this recipe. Wait until summer heirloom tomatoes are in season and select the most flavorful, vine-ripened ones you can find. This is a great excuse to visit your local farmers' market. For variety I will sometimes add up to a cup of freshly juiced cucumber, sweet red bell pepper, or carrot to the soup mixture. Also, a drizzle of fresh herb oil in place of the olive oil would be a nice touch.

Purée the tomatoes in a food processor and force through a medium-mesh strainer with a rubber spatula to catch all the seeds and skins. Season to your taste with vinegar, salt, and pepper. Cover and refrigerate until very cold.

Ladle the soup into chilled soup bowls. Place 1 or 2 tablespoons of the Summer Relish in the center and garnish with avocado, a dollop of Crème Fraîche, and a drizzle of olive oil around an herb sprig, if using.

~~~~~~

SUMMER RELISH

1 tablespoon chopped fresh basil

2 teaspoons chopped fresh mint

¼ cup diced red onion

3 tablespoons diced red bell pepper

¼ cup seeded and diced cucumber, preferably lemon cucumber

2 teaspoons extra-virgin olive oil

Kosher or sea salt and freshly ground pepper

In a medium bowl, gently stir the basil, mint, onion, bell pepper, cucumber, and olive oil together. Season to taste with salt and pepper.

CORN SOUP WITH CRAB

Serves 4 to 6

2 tablespoons unsalted butter

1½ cups chopped onions

1 cup chopped carrots

¼ cup chopped celery

2 teaspoons chopped garlic

3½ cups corn kernels (3 to 4 large ears)

1 star anise pod

Big pinch saffron threads

5 cups fat-free Chicken Stock (page 66)

Kosher or sea salt and freshly ground pepper

8 ounces fresh Dungeness lump crabmeat, shredded and picked over to remove any pieces of shell

2 tablespoons finely chopped fresh chives

RECOMMENDED WINE
Sweet corn and crab are ideal with a sweeter-style **Chardonnay** that is not overpowered by oak.

This healthful recipe calls for crab, but you could use whatever sweet shellfish is available to you, such as lobster or shrimp. If you wanted to go whole hog, you could of course garnish with a squiggle of Crème Fraîche (page 37), caviar, or something similar!

In a deep saucepan or stockpot, melt the butter over medium heat and sauté the onions, carrots, celery, and garlic until soft but not brown, stirring occasionally, for about 5 minutes. Add the corn, star anise, and saffron and continue to cook and stir for another 5 minutes.

Add the stock and bring to a boil. Reduce the heat to a simmer and cook for 10 minutes. Discard the star anise and purée the soup in a blender or food processor, being careful to do so at low speed and with the blender jar only half filled (hot liquids expand dramatically, so be careful!). You'll need to do this in batches.

Strain the soup through a medium-mesh strainer, pushing down on the solids, and return to the pan. Season to taste with salt and pepper and reheat. Ladle into warm soup bowls, top with the crab and chives, and serve.

MEXICAN ONION SOUP

Serves 6 to 8

RECOMMENDED WINE
When onions cook slowly they become very sweet. The sweetness, coupled with the chile heat, suggests one of the aromatic white wines like **Riesling**, **Gewürztraminer**, **Viognier**, or **Muscat**.

3 tablespoons olive oil

3 pounds onions, thinly sliced

2 tablespoons slivered garlic

1 teaspoon crushed cumin seeds

1 teaspoon crushed coriander seeds

1 teaspoon chopped fresh oregano

3 tablespoons pure ancho, Chimayo, or California chile powder

1 cup dry red wine

7 cups rich Chicken Stock (page 66) or Vegetable Stock (page 69)

¼ cup masa harina (see Note, page 88)

Kosher or sea salt and freshly ground pepper

Very thinly sliced fried tortilla strips, Cilantro Pesto (recipe follows), and grated queso añejo cheese, for garnishing (optional)

This is an interesting twist on the traditional French onion soup using flavors from Mexico. For an interesting variation, I sometimes place a toasted croûte on top of the soup, add grated Pepper Jack, and brown under the broiler or with a propane torch. If you want to go all the way you might want to drizzle on a little Cilantro Pesto. I've included that recipe below.

In a stockpot, heat the olive oil and slowly sauté the onions and garlic until they are richly browned. This will take 30 to 45 minutes. Add the cumin, coriander, oregano, and chile powder and sauté for 2 to 3 minutes longer until fragrant. Add the wine and stock and bring to a simmer. In a small bowl, whisk the masa harina with a little stock or water to prevent lumping and then whisk into the soup. Continue to simmer for another 10 minutes or so, stirring often. Season to taste with salt and pepper. Serve in warm soup bowls garnished with fried tortilla strips, Cilantro Pesto, and cheese, if using.

CILANTRO PESTO
Makes about 1¼ cups

3 cups packed tender stems and leaves of fresh cilantro

1 tablespoon chopped poached garlic or roasted garlic (see page 264)

2 tablespoons toasted pepitas or blanched almonds

3 tablespoons grated Mexican cheese, such as queso fresco or queso añejo

½ teaspoon minced jalapeño chile

⅓ cup olive oil

Kosher or sea salt and freshly ground pepper

Blanch the cilantro in lightly salted boiling water for 5 seconds and then immediately plunge into ice water to stop the cooking and set the color. Drain well, squeeze dry, and chop coarsely. In a food processor or blender, combine the cilantro, garlic, pepitas, cheese, chile, and olive oil and process until nearly smooth. Season to taste with salt and pepper. Store, covered, in the refrigerator for up to 2 days.

THAI-INSPIRED TOMATO NOODLE SOUP WITH SHRIMP

Serves 6 to 8

One 2-ounce packet cellophane (mung bean) or thin rice noodles (vermicelli)

7 cups Easy Shellfish Stock (page 67) or Chicken Stock (page 66)

2 tablespoons Asian fish sauce

1 tablespoon Asian chile-garlic sauce

3 cups canned diced tomatoes, including juice

2 tablespoons brown sugar

1 pound medium shrimp (31 to 35 per pound), shelled and deveined

¼ cup fresh lime juice

¼ cup diagonally sliced green onion, both white and green parts

2 teaspoons toasted sesame oil

½ cup loosely packed fresh cilantro leaves

3 tablespoons Fried Garlic (recipe follows)

RECOMMENDED WINE
The hot, sweet, spicy, tart flavors here would go best with a fruity, unoaked chilled white wine like typical **Rieslings**, **Gewürztraminers**, and California **Viogniers**.

This is a simple soup that uses mung bean or rice noodles, Asian fish sauce, and chile-garlic sauce, all of which are readily available in any Asian market and increasingly in large supermarkets with ethnic food sections. For the chile sauce, Lee Kum Kee brand from Hong Kong is widely distributed. You can also certainly substitute other noodles like Japanese soba or even angel hair (capellini). Since these take longer to cook, prepare them ahead (follow package directions) and add to the soup just as you serve it.

Place the noodles in a medium bowl, cover with hot water, and soak until softened, 20 to 25 minutes. Drain the noodles and dump in a tangle on a cutting board. Cut through crosswise and lengthwise to form roughly 6-inch lengths. Set aside.

In a stockpot, combine the stock, fish sauce, chile-garlic sauce, tomatoes, and sugar. Bring to a boil, reduce heat, and simmer for a minute or two. Add the shrimp and simmer for a minute or until they turn pink. Divide the noodles among warm bowls. Ladle the hot soup and shrimp over the noodles and sprinkle lime juice, green onion, and drops of sesame oil on top. Finally, top with cilantro and Fried Garlic just as you begin to eat.

FRIED GARLIC

Garlic can be fried up to a day ahead and stored airtight.

Heat ½ inch peanut or olive oil over medium heat to 350°F. Add garlic and cook until golden brown. It will take 5 minutes or so. If oil is too hot, garlic will burn and become bitter so you might try a tester slice first. Garlic chips are a great addition to salads and to all kinds of dishes, like Tuna Sicilian Style with Roasted Cauliflower and Green Beans (page 160).

MENDOCINO GAZPACHO

Serves 8 to 10

RECOMMENDED WINE
A chilled dry **rosé** wine would be perfect with this. Dry rosés from all over the world have really taken off lately, and you'll find a selection in good wine shops. In California you'll see rosés made from several red wine grapes, like **Syrah**, **Sangiovese**, **Grenache**, and **Zinfandel**.

6 cups tomato juice, preferably homemade

2 cups rich Chicken Stock (page 66), Fish Stock (page 67), or Vegetable Stock (page 69)

3 tablespoons soy sauce

3 tablespoons rice vinegar

2 cups peeled, seeded, and diced English or lemon cucumber (about 12 ounces)

½ cup finely chopped red onion

2½ cups seeded and diced ripe red or yellow tomatoes, or a combination

1 head poached, toasted, or roasted garlic, finely chopped (see page 264)

2 teaspoons seeded and minced serrano chile

1 medium yellow bell pepper, charred, peeled, and diced

1 medium red bell pepper, charred, peeled, and diced

1 medium poblano chile, charred, peeled, and diced

2 to 3 tablespoons fruity olive oil

Fresh lime juice

Kosher or sea salt and freshly ground pepper

Garlic Croutons (facing page)

Chopped fresh cilantro or mint, or a combination, and avocado slices for garnishing (optional)

The traditional recipe for Spanish gazpacho calls for puréeing all the vegetables along with some bread to add body and texture. I prefer mine more like a chowder, and instead of incorporating the bread into the soup, I like to make it into garlicky croutons to use as a garnish. You could make this a meal by adding some cooked shrimp or, my favorite, lobster. Other vegetables are fair game, too, like a little crisp jicama or young zucchini.

In a nonreactive container, combine the tomato juice, stock, soy sauce, rice vinegar, cucumber, red onion, tomatoes, garlic, serrano chile, yellow bell pepper, red bell pepper, poblano chile, and olive oil. Season to taste with the lime juice, salt, and pepper. Refrigerate for at least 2 hours for the flavors to marry. Check the taste and add more salt and pepper if needed. Serve topped with Garlic Croutons, cilantro, and avocado, if using. Can be made up to 2 days ahead and stored, covered, in the refrigerator.

GARLIC CROUTONS

⅓ cup olive oil

2 large garlic cloves, bruised with the side of a knife

2 cups ½-inch bread cubes, cut from good day-old bread with crusts removed

2 tablespoons minced fresh parsley

1 teaspoon freshly grated lemon zest

Kosher or sea salt and freshly ground pepper

Preheat the oven to 375°F. Heat the olive oil in a sauté pan over medium heat and sauté the garlic until it just begins to color. Be careful the garlic doesn't burn or it will become bitter. Toss the bread cubes with oil and put on a wire rack on top of a rimmed baking sheet. Toast in the oven until bread is nicely golden on all sides. The croutons should be toasty on the surface but still somewhat soft in the very middle. Remove and toss with the parsley and lemon zest. Season to taste with salt and pepper while still warm. Store airtight if not using immediately.

CURRIED APPLE AND MUSSEL CHOWDER

Serves 6

RECOMMENDED WINE
This is a terrific match with fruity **Gewürztraminer**, since the sweet spice and fruit in the chowder mirror the same flavors in the wine.

3 tablespoons olive oil

3 cups peeled and ½-inch-diced tart green apples

1 tablespoon slivered garlic

1 large red onion, coarsely chopped (2½ cups)

2 cups ½-inch diagonally sliced leeks, both white and tender green parts

2 to 3 tablespoons Madras Curry Powder (facing page)

1 cup dry white wine

5 cups rich Shellfish Stock (page 67) or Chicken Stock (page 66)

2 cups apple juice

1 teaspoon toasted and crushed coriander seeds

1 teaspoon toasted and crushed fennel seeds

1½ cups thinly sliced fresh fennel

3 pounds mussels, scrubbed and beards removed

Big pinch cayenne pepper (optional)

Fennel fronds for garnishing (optional)

This soup is fast to make. We used to gather fresh mussels along our California coast in the fall and winter. Unfortunately, concerns about pollution, especially from land-based run-off, has curtailed that. Farm-raised mussels are an excellent alternative. They are constantly monitored and much more uniform than their wild cousins. Fresh, farm-raised mussels are generally available year-round, but you probably will have to order ahead.

In a sauté pan or large saucepan, heat 1 tablespoon of the olive oil over medium-high heat and sauté the apples until just beginning to brown but still firm. Set aside.

Heat the remaining oil and sauté the garlic, onion, leeks, and curry until just beginning to soften but not brown. Add the wine, stock, apple juice, coriander seeds, and fennel seeds and simmer for 5 minutes. Add the fennel and mussels and cover and simmer until the mussels open, about 3 minutes. Add the apples and cayenne pepper (if using), and heat through. Save 18 mussels in their shells for garnish. Remove the meat from the remaining mussels and divide among 6 warm bowls. Arrange the mussels in their shells in the bowls and ladle the hot chowder over. Serve immediately, garnished with fennel fronds, if you like.

MADRAS CURRY POWDER

1 ounce coriander seeds

1 ounce cumin seeds

1 ounce fenugreek seeds

1 ounce poppy seeds

1 ounce cardamom seeds

¼ ounce mustard seeds

½ ounce crushed dried chile (see Note)

1 cinnamon stick, broken into small pieces

½ ounce ground ginger

1 ounce ground turmeric

The world of curry is as diverse as the cultures that use it and as personal as the people making it. Curries range from mild, as in the curries of Indonesia, to fiery hot Thai and Indian curries. The basic curry called for in this book and in most recipes is a mild to medium-hot Indian-style curry powder. You should definitely make your own! Curry powders should begin with toasted whole spices, which are then ground finely and stored in airtight containers. Toasting brings out the rich flavor of the spice. Once ground, the spices begin to lose their subtle flavors and aroma quickly, so you should plan to use up whatever you've made within 3 months. Most commercial curries are simply mixtures of spices that have not been toasted, and who knows how long ago they were ground.

Here is a basic curry mixture that you can make at home. Health food stores are usually a good source for whole spices at a reasonable price, but be sure to investigate any Asian or Caribbean markets in your area.

Preheat the oven to 375°F. Put the coriander seeds, cumin seeds, fenugreek seeds, poppy seeds, cardamom seeds, mustard seeds, chile, and cinnamon stick in a baking pan and toast for 3 to 4 minutes or until the spices are fragrant, then cool. In a spice grinder or with a mortar and pestle, grind to a powder. Transfer to a small bowl. Stir in the ginger and turmeric. Store in an airtight container in the refrigerator or freezer for up to 3 months.

Note: The heat of the chile will determine the heat of the curry. Use ancho, pasilla, or chile negro for a milder curry or red pepper flakes from any of the hot chiles, such as chipotle, for a fiery version.

APPLE-HERB VICHYSSOISE

Serves 6 to 8

RECOMMENDED WINE
A fruity, sweet-style **Chardonnay** with a minimum of oak aging or a **Riesling** or **Chenin Blanc** with just a bit of residual sugar.

1 tablespoon olive oil

1½ cups chopped leeks, white part only

½ cup chopped onion

¼ cup chopped celery

1 pound tart-sweet apples, such as Fuji or Gala, peeled and chopped

8 ounces boiling potatoes, peeled and chopped

3 cups rich Vegetable Stock (page 69) or Chicken Stock (page 66), fat removed

½ cup dry white wine

¼ cup apple brandy, such as Calvados, or medium-dry sherry, such as Amontillado

2 cups half-and-half, heavy (whipping) cream, or No-Cream Cream (page 85)

2 tablespoons minced fresh chervil

2 tablespoons minced fresh chives

1 tablespoon minced fresh tarragon

1 tablespoon minced fresh mint

Kosher or sea salt and freshly ground white pepper

Finely diced apples, chervil sprigs, chive flowers, and a drizzle of Chive Oil (page 80) for garnishing (optional)

One of the first serious cookbooks I remember buying many years ago was Albert Stockli's Splendid Fare, *written after he had retired from the Four Seasons in New York City. He was a real fan of vichyssoise with fruit in it — so this recipe is a tribute to him.*

In a large stockpot, heat the olive oil and sauté the leeks, onion, celery, and half the apples until soft but not brown. Add the potatoes, stock, and wine. Simmer, partially covered, until the vegetables are very soft. Remove from the heat. Add the brandy and the remaining apples. Transfer to a blender or food processor and purée, in batches if necessary, until very smooth. Strain through a medium-mesh strainer. Add the half-and-half, chervil, chives, tarragon, and mint and refrigerate until well chilled. Season to taste with salt and pepper just before serving. Can be made up to 1 day ahead and stored, covered, in the refrigerator.

Serve in chilled soup bowls, garnished with apples, chervil sprigs, chive flowers, and chive oil, if using.

BLUE CHEESE AND APPLE SOUP

Serves 6 to 8

2 tablespoons unsalted butter

⅓ cup minced shallots or green onions, white part only

3 cups peeled and diced tart-sweet apples, such as McIntosh, Gala, or Fuji

½ cup dry white wine

3 cups rich Vegetable Stock (page 69) or Chicken Stock (page 66)

8 ounces creamy blue cheese, such as sweet Gorgonzola, Cambozola, Maytag Blue, diced

1¼ cups half-and-half

Kosher or sea salt and freshly ground pepper

Drops of fresh lemon juice

Minced fresh chives and a drizzle of hazelnut or walnut oil for garnishing (optional)

RECOMMENDED WINE
A big, luscious barrel-fermented and aged **Chardonnay** is a great choice here to go with the apple and rich cheese flavors. These flavors should embrace the toasty, creamy nuances in the wine.

Apples and a tangy blue cheese are a great combination, so why not in soup? This rich combination is best served in small quantities. The key is to choose a flavorful blue cheese that is creamy, such as Point Reyes Original Blue (see page 421). If you like more apple flavor, then substitute a good organic apple juice for some of the stock or wine.

In a medium saucepan, melt the butter and sauté the shallots until soft but not brown. Add the apples and continue to cook until they just begin to soften. Add the wine and stock and bring to a boil. Reduce the heat and simmer for 5 minutes. Add the cheese and half-and-half and stir over gentle heat until the cheese melts and the mixture is smooth. Season to taste with salt, pepper, and lemon juice. Do not boil, as the soup will develop a curdled appearance. Should you desire a smoother consistency, you may purée the soup, adding more stock.

Serve either hot or cold. Garnish with the minced chives and hazelnut oil, if using.

POBLANO AND SMOKED CHICKEN CHOWDER WITH HOMINY

Serves 6 to 8

RECOMMENDED WINE

The chile heat and tartness of the tomatillos plays wonderfully off the fruity, lower-alcohol wines with good acidity and a bit of residual sugar, like **California Riesling, Gewürztraminer**, or **Chenin Blanc**. The new **Viogniers** from California, which are typically made in a very ripe style, also work here.

2 tablespoons olive oil

4 cups sliced yellow onions

2 large poblano chiles, seeded and cut into thin strips

1 tablespoon finely slivered garlic

3 cups husked and halved tomatillos

½ teaspoon fennel seeds

½ teaspoon cumin seeds

½ teaspoon coriander seeds

2 teaspoons dried oregano, preferably Mexican

2 cups diced and seeded fresh tomatoes or canned diced tomatoes, including juice

7 cups rich Chicken Stock (page 66), Corn Stock (page 69), or Vegetable Stock (page 69)

12 ounces julienned smoked chicken

¾ cup fresh cooked or canned and drained hominy

Kosher or sea salt and freshly ground pepper

¼ teaspoon ground cinnamon

¼ cup coarsely chopped fresh cilantro

Thinly sliced and fanned avocado and fresh cilantro sprigs for garnishing (optional)

This is a hearty soup that could be the centerpiece of a meal. The flavor of the poblano chile is even better if you char and peel it first. If you do, add it in when you add the tomatillos. Poblanos are widely available all year-round, especially in areas that have a Mexican population of any size. They are often mislabeled "pasilla," which is not a fresh chile but a dried one. Cinnamon and other sweet spices are used often in Mexican cooking to add aroma and subtle complexity. Add just as you are serving the soup so that the aromatics can kick into gear.

In a saucepan, heat the olive oil and sauté the onions, chiles, and garlic until soft but not brown, about 5 minutes. Add the tomatillos, fennel seeds, cumin seeds, coriander seeds, oregano, tomatoes, and stock. Simmer gently for 15 minutes. Add the smoked chicken and hominy. Simmer to heat through. Season to taste with salt and pepper and stir in the cinnamon and chopped cilantro.

Ladle into warm soup bowls and garnish with the avocado slices and cilantro sprigs (if using), and serve immediately.

ROASTED EGGPLANT SOUP WITH BELL PEPPERS

Serves 8

1 large eggplant, peeled or not as you please, cut into ½-inch-thick rounds

2 tablespoons chopped garlic

½ cup loosely packed fresh basil leaves

¼ cup chopped green onions, white part only

⅛ teaspoon red pepper flakes

½ cup olive oil

2 cups chopped red bell peppers

1½ cups chopped red onions

Kosher or sea salt and freshly ground pepper

1 cup seeded and diced ripe fresh tomatoes or canned diced tomatoes

6 cups Tomato Stock (page 71) or Chicken Stock (page 66)

Fresh young basil sprigs and freshly shaved Asiago or Parmesan cheese for garnishing

Basil Oil (page 80) for garnishing (optional)

RECOMMENDED WINE
A good **Fumé Blanc** or **Sauvignon Blanc**, or **Pinot Gris** or **Pinot Grigio**, with bright acidity bridges nicely to this earthy soup.

This is one of my oldest and most favorite soups. It originated as a clear tomato broth with slices of roasted eggplant and vegetables in it; the soup was transformed accidentally when I appeared as a guest chef in a restaurant in Chicago, and the kitchen staff decided it was easier to purée it. I found I liked it better their way too. The soup is particularly wonderful in the summer, when the bounty of peppers, eggplant, onions, and tomatoes bursts forth in our gardens and farm markets.

Preheat the oven to 375°F. Oil a baking sheet and arrange the eggplant on it in a single layer. In a food processor, combine the garlic, basil, green onions, pepper flakes, and 6 tablespoons of the olive oil. Process briefly to make a smooth mixture. Spread evenly over the eggplant slices and bake for 15 to 18 minutes or until the eggplant is soft and lightly browned. Remove, coarsely chop, and set aside.

In a small sauté pan, heat the remaining olive oil and sauté the peppers and onions until softened. Season to taste with salt and pepper. Transfer to the food processor. Add the tomatoes and reserved eggplant and pulse 5 or 6 times to chop. Add the stock and continue to pulse until puréed. The soup should be smooth but still have just a bit of texture. (Don't use a blender. I think it makes the soup too smooth.) The soup can be prepared up to this point and stored covered in the refrigerator for up to 2 days. Heat, season to taste with salt and pepper, and serve garnished with basil sprigs, cheese, and a drizzle of Basil Oil, if using.

RADICCHIO SOUP WITH SMOKED GOAT CHEESE

Serves 4

RECOMMENDED WINE
Several wines could work here, offering both contrast and similarity. A rich barrel-aged **Chardonnay** would match up with the cheese. A softer-style red with lower tannins, like **Pinot Noir**, would bridge to the earthy, slightly bitter radicchio. Maybe a half glass of each?

⅓ cup extra-virgin olive oil

1 small head radicchio, quartered and sliced thinly

Kosher or sea salt and freshly ground pepper

2 tablespoons finely sliced garlic

2 tablespoons finely sliced shallots

One 15-ounce can diced tomatoes, including juice, preferably Muir Glen

½ cup hearty red wine

3 cups rich Chicken Stock (page 66) or Vegetable Stock (page 69)

2 cups ½-inch bread cubes, cut from good-quality peasant-style bread, crusts removed

4 ounces smoked goat Cheddar, cut into ¼-inch dice

¼ cup loosely packed fresh basil leaves, coarsely chopped.

This is a very simple soup but brings together interesting contrasting flavors — bitter from the radicchio and smoky from the cheese — that I think are delicious and intriguing. The cheese I like to use for this is the smoked goat Cheddar from Redwood Hill Farms (see page 421). You could use any good smoked cheese, such as smoked mozzarella.

In a deep saucepan, heat 2 tablespoons of the olive oil over medium-high heat and sauté the radicchio for a minute or two, just until it just starts to wilt. Season lightly with salt and pepper. Remove and set aside.

Add 2 more tablespoons olive oil to the pan and sauté the garlic and shallots until softened but not brown. Add the tomatoes, wine, and stock and bring to a boil, then reduce the heat and simmer for 5 minutes or so. Season to taste with salt and pepper.

Meanwhile, toss the bread cubes with the remaining olive oil. In a large sauté pan, quickly sauté the bread cubes over medium-high heat until they are golden brown. Add more oil if necessary. Can be made a day ahead.

Stir the radicchio into the hot soup. Divide the cheese and bread cubes among large soup bowls and ladle the soup over. Sprinkle the basil over the top and serve immediately.

Note: If making the soup ahead, do not add the radicchio until serving time. The soup will become too bitter if the radicchio is left in for more than a few minutes.

LAVENDER-BLUEBERRY SOUP

Serves 8 or more

2 quarts fresh or IQF blueberries

1 cup dry red wine

1½ cups water

6 tablespoons fragrant honey

¼ cup frozen orange juice concentrate

1½ tablespoons dried lavender flowers
(see sidebar)

Zest and juice of 1 large lemon

One 4-inch cinnamon stick

½ teaspoon freshly ground pepper

¼ teaspoon ground cloves

Crème Fraîche (page 37), whole blueberries, and
fresh mint sprigs for garnishing (optional)

Fruit soups are traditional fare in Scandinavian cuisines. Here, the floral quality of the lavender adds an interesting flavor note to the blueberries. If fresh blueberries are not available, you can use IQF (individually quick-frozen without sugar), preferably wild ones, which you can find in supermarkets. Add the honey a bit at a time to make sure the soup doesn't end up being too sweet. It's not supposed to be a dessert! The soup can be served hot or cold. I haven't puréed the soup, but you could do so, then push it through a medium-mesh strainer for a more elegant texture.

In a stockpot, combine the blueberries, wine, water, honey, orange juice, lavender, lemon zest, lemon juice, cinnamon stick, pepper, and cloves. Bring just to a boil, then reduce the heat and simmer for 8 minutes. Remove the cinnamon stick. Can be served hot or cold. Garnish with a dollop of Crème Fraîche and a sprinkling of fresh blueberries and a mint sprig, if using.

RECOMMENDED WINE
A fruity, slightly sweet **Gewürztraminer** echoes the fruity-floral notes in the soup.

lavender

Lavender flowers are wonderfully fragrant and add a lot of character to savory dishes. They are inexpensive and can be purchased in most health food stores. (Be sure that the lavender you're using is intended for cooking. Do not use lavender that has been sprayed or designed for use in sachets.) Store lavender in a sealed container in your pantry. Lavender flowers make a particularly good dry marinade, or rub, for poultry or fish (like Seared Ahi Tuna with a Lavender-Pepper Crust on page 155). Culinary lavender (both flowers and leaves) is used to flavor vinegars, oils, and jellies, and when infused into a sugar syrup it makes an interesting ice or sorbet. It is also a key ingredient in that famous French mixture, herbes de Provence.

Historically, lavender was known as the herb of love. It worked both ways, however: On the one hand, it was considered an aphrodisiac; on the other, a sprinkle of lavender water on the head purportedly kept the wearer chaste.

PASTAS, GNOCCHIS, PIZZAS, *and* RISOTTOS

PASTA *and* WINE

Matching wine with pasta is all about what accompanies the pasta and not about the pasta itself. We all have had the experience of enjoying a red wine with a hearty red sauce and a delicate white wine with a fish pasta that had no cream in it. Let the primary ingredient and flavor be your guide here.

PENNE WITH GRILLED ASPARAGUS AND TOMATOES

Serves 6

½ cup extra-virgin olive oil

1 pound young, tender asparagus

12 plum tomatoes, halved, seeded, and coarsely
    chopped

Kosher or sea salt and freshly ground pepper

4 tablespoons roasted garlic (see page 264)

8 anchovy fillets, rinsed and finely chopped

½ cup chopped fresh basil

3 tablespoons chopped fresh parsley

1 tablespoon chopped fresh mint

½ teaspoon red pepper flakes

1 pound penne or other tube-shaped dried pasta

Freshly grated Parmesan cheese and Fried
    Capers (page 33) for garnishing (optional)

RECOMMENDED WINE
Try a crisp, clean
Sauvignon Blanc with
herbal notes; it's a great
match to this dish. A crisp
Italian or Spanish white
would also be delicious.

This is a simple and very flavorful pasta with some zing. It's the grilling of the vegetables that makes it special. If asparagus is not available, try using thin-sliced fennel bulb or even black kale (see page 285).

Prepare a charcoal fire. Using 2 tablespoons of the olive oil, lightly oil the asparagus and tomatoes and season to taste with salt and pepper. Grill over hot coals until just tender but well marked. Cut the asparagus diagonally into 2-inch lengths and set aside. In a medium bowl, toss the tomatoes, roasted garlic, anchovies, basil, parsley, mint, pepper flakes, and the remaining olive oil together.

In a large pot of lightly salted boiling water, cook the pasta until just al dente. While the pasta is cooking, heat the tomato mixture in a large sauté pan. When the pasta is done, drain and add to the pan along with asparagus. Toss to combine. Season to taste with salt and pepper. Serve immediately, garnished with Parmesan cheese and Fried Capers, if using.

PURSLANE AND PENNE

Serves 4

RECOMMENDED WINE
A crisp **Sauvignon Blanc** or dry **Chenin Blanc** are good choices.

4 ounces lean smoky bacon, cut crosswise into ¼-inch-wide strips

8 ounces penne or other tube-shaped dried pasta

⅓ cup extra-virgin olive oil

12 ounces young purslane, woody stems removed

2 tablespoons red wine vinegar, plus additional for seasoning

½ teaspoon sugar

2 cups seeded and diced ripe plum tomatoes

½ cup finely diced feta cheese

Kosher or sea salt and freshly ground pepper

Foraging for wild foods has always had a personal attraction for me. It started years ago when I read Euell Gibbons' classic Stalking the Wild Asparagus *and Billy Joe Tatum's* Wild Foods Cookbook and Field Guide. *Purslane is basically a weed (*Portulaca oleracea*) that grows in many parts of the country. It has the texture of a succulent and a tart, citric flavor. My grandmother and I used to gather it often and cook it with lamb's-quarter (*Chenopodium album*), another wild green. It is best when young, before it gets woody, from late spring to early summer. It is one of those humble peasant ingredients that is beginning to appear in upscale markets and restaurants. Purslane is worth buying or foraging when you see it. In Italy, young purslane leaves are often sprinkled on tomato salads.*

In a sauté pan, cook the bacon until crisp. Using a slotted spoon, remove the bacon to paper towels and set aside. Discard all but 2 tablespoons of the bacon fat.

In a large pot of lightly salted boiling water, cook the penne until just al dente. Drain and toss with 1 tablespoon of the olive oil. Keep warm.

In a large skillet or wok over medium-high heat, heat the reserved bacon fat. Quickly sauté the purslane until just tender but not limp, about 2 to 3 minutes. Add the 2 tablespoons of vinegar and the sugar and cook for 30 seconds more. Add the cooked pasta, remaining olive oil, tomatoes, feta, and bacon, and toss just to combine. Season to taste with salt and pepper and additional drops of vinegar. Serve immediately.

RIGATONI WITH ROASTED CAULIFLOWER AND PARSLEY PESTO

Serves 6

1 medium cauliflower (2 pounds or so), sliced ½-inch thick vertically

Extra-virgin olive oil for brushing the cauliflower

Kosher or sea salt and freshly ground pepper

8 ounces rigatoni or other tube-shaped dried pasta

Parsley Pesto (recipe follows)

¾ cup pitted, slivered oil-cured black olives, such as Niçoise, Kalamata, or Cerignola

1 cup cooked cannellini, borlotti, or other heirloom beans

Thinly shaved Asiago or Parmesan cheese and fresh mint sprigs for garnishing

RECOMMENDED WINE
The rich green pesto is great with **Sauvignon Blanc**.

I think of this as a fall or winter dish, but it could just as easily be served as part of a summer buffet. Roasting cauliflower, like roasting the root vegetables discussed in other recipes, brings out sweet flavors that you'd never get by steaming or boiling. You'll encounter roasted cauliflower again with tuna on page 160. Obviously, I love it. Slivered sun–dried tomatoes are also a nice addition to this recipe.

Preheat the oven to 425°F. Brush both sides of the cauliflower with olive oil and season liberally with salt and pepper. Arrange in a single layer on a baking sheet. Put in the oven and roast for 15 to 20 minutes or until the cauliflower is lightly browned and tender. Break into large irregular pieces and set aside.

In a large pot of lightly salted boiling salted water, cook the pasta until just al dente. Drain, reserving ½ cup of the cooking water. Toss the hot pasta with the Parsley Pesto, cauliflower, olives, and beans, adding a bit of the reserved water if the mixture seems dry. Top with cheese and mint. Serve warm or at room temperature.

~~~~~~

PARSLEY PESTO
Makes a generous cup

4 cups packed fresh parsley leaves and tender stems

1 tablespoon chopped poached or roasted garlic (see page 264)

2 tablespoons toasted pine nuts or slivered almonds

2 tablespoons freshly grated Parmesan or Asiago cheese

Grated zest of 1 lemon

⅓ cup olive oil

Kosher or sea salt and freshly ground pepper

Blanch the parsley in lightly salted, boiling water for 5 seconds and then immediately plunge into ice water to stop the cooking and set the color. Drain, squeeze dry, and chop coarsely. In a food processor or blender, combine the parsley, garlic, pine nuts, cheese, lemon zest, and olive oil and process until smooth. Season to taste with salt and pepper. Store, covered, in the refrigerator for up to 5 days or freeze for up to 3 months.

BOW TIES WITH FETA, OLIVES, AND GOLDEN RAISINS

Serves 4 to 6

RECOMMENDED WINE
The infinitely versatile fruit-iness and acidity of **Fumé Blanc** or **Sauvignon Blanc** provides the necessary counterpoint for this pasta.

3 tablespoons olive oil

1 cup thinly sliced small red onion

1 cup slivered red or yellow bell pepper

2 teaspoons thinly sliced garlic

One 28-ounce can diced tomatoes, including juice

⅔ cup pitted, slivered Kalamata olives

½ cup golden raisins

½ cup dry white wine

2 tablespoons rinsed capers

2 tablespoons chopped fresh basil or 2 teaspoons dried

1 teaspoon seeded and minced serrano chile or ¼ teaspoon red pepper flakes

Kosher or sea salt and freshly ground pepper

8 ounces bow tie–shaped dried pasta, such as farfalle

¼ cup minced fresh parsley

½ cup crumbled feta cheese

The interplay of salty olives and feta with sweet golden raisins makes for an intriguing palate teaser. This combination evokes memories of a long-ago summer spent in Greece.

In a large sauté pan, heat 2 tablespoons of the olive oil. Sauté the onion, bell pepper, and garlic until the vegetables are soft but not brown, about 10 minutes. Add the tomatoes, olives, raisins, wine, capers, basil, and chile. Simmer, uncovered, for 10 to 12 minutes, or until slightly thickened. Season to taste with salt and pepper. Keep warm.

In a large pot of lightly salted boiling water, cook the pasta until just al dente. Drain and toss with the remaining 1 tablespoon olive oil and parsley. Top with the sauce and feta and serve immediately.

CORKSCREW PASTA WITH EGGPLANT, TOMATOES, AND FRESH MOZZARELLA

Serves 4

2 medium unpeeled eggplants (1½ pounds), cut into ½-inch-thick rounds

2 tablespoons extra-virgin olive oil, plus additional for brushing eggplant

Kosher or sea salt and freshly ground pepper

3 large ripe tomatoes (1¼ pounds), cut into ½-inch dice

2 tablespoons red wine vinegar, plus additional for seasoning

1 tablespoon chopped poached garlic (see page 264) or 1 teaspoon chopped raw garlic

2 tablespoons rinsed capers

¼ cup coarsely chopped fresh basil

1 pound dried corkscrew pasta, such as fusilli

8 ounces fresh mozzarella packed in water, drained and cut into ¼-inch dice

(see page 264)

RECOMMENDED WINE
Crisp whites, like **Sauvignon Blanc**, or **Pinot Gris** or **Pinot Grigio**, or softer-style (lower-tannin) reds, like **Pinot Noir** or **Grenache**, complement this dish.

This is my favorite fast summertime pasta. It's essential that you have good, juicy ripe tomatoes for this recipe. Eggplant can also be grilled if you don't want to use the oven. Grilled zucchini could be added or take the place of the eggplant.

Preheat the oven to 400°F. Brush the eggplant rounds with olive oil and put in a single layer on a baking sheet. Season liberally with salt and pepper. Roast in the oven until soft and lightly browned on top but still holding their shape, about 18 minutes. Remove, cool, and cut the eggplant into 1-inch dice and set aside.

In a large bowl, toss together the tomatoes, the 2 tablespoons olive oil, the vinegar, garlic, capers, and basil. Season to taste with salt and pepper and more vinegar.

In a large pot of lightly salted boiling water, cook the pasta until just al dente. Drain the pasta, reserving ½ cup of the cooking water. Toss the hot pasta with the tomato mixture and add some of the reserved hot water if it seems a little dry. Add the cheese and toss gently until the cheese begins to soften. Add the eggplant and toss and serve immediately.

FUSILLI WITH COLLARDS, BACON, AND GARLIC

Serves 4 to 6

RECOMMENDED WINE
For a counterpoint to
the slight bitterness of
the greens and saltiness
of the bacon, try a crisp
Fumé Blanc or **Sauvignon
Blanc**. If you wanted something red, a lower-tannin
wine with subtle herbal
notes, such as a **Merlot**,
Pinot Noir, or **Sangiovese**,
would be great.

1½ pounds collard greens, Swiss chard, or kale, woody stems discarded, coarsely chopped

5 ounces good smoked bacon, coarsely chopped

2 tablespoons extra-virgin olive oil

1½ cups thinly sliced red onions

½ teaspoon seeded and minced serrano chile

2 tablespoons slivered garlic

½ cup sliced Niçoise, Kalamata, or other oil-cured black olives

½ cup rich Chicken Stock (page 66) or Vegetable Stock (page 69)

1 pound fusilli or other corkscrew-shaped dried pasta

2 tablespoons balsamic vinegar

Kosher or sea salt and freshly ground pepper

Freshly grated or shaved Parmesan cheese for garnishing

Except for the olives, this pasta is reminiscent of a Southern "mess of greens." It's a delicious, simple wintertime dish.

Blanch the greens in lightly salted boiling water for 2 minutes to soften. Drain and rinse in cold water to stop the cooking and set aside.

In a skillet, cook the bacon over medium heat until browned. Using a slotted spoon, remove the bacon to paper towels and pour off all but 2 tablespoons of the fat. Add the olive oil, onions, chile, and garlic to the pan and sauté until just beginning to brown. Add the olives, blanched greens, and stock and cook, covered, over medium heat until the greens are tender. The collards will take the longest to cook. Keep warm.

In a large pot of lightly salted boiling water, cook the fusilli just until al dente. Drain and toss with the greens mixture and bacon. Season to taste with the vinegar, salt, and pepper. Garnish with Parmesan cheese. Serve immediately.

CONCHIGLIE WITH SWEET AND SOUR LAMB

Serves 6

4 tablespoons olive oil

3 pounds boneless lamb shoulder, well trimmed and cut into 1-inch cubes

Kosher or sea salt and freshly ground pepper

2½ cups sliced onions

1 tablespoon slivered garlic

½ cup finely diced carrot

½ cup finely diced fennel bulb or celery

2 cups seeded and diced tomatoes

½ cup red wine vinegar

⅓ cup golden raisins

1 tablespoon light-brown sugar

2 cups rich Lamb Stock (page 68) or Chicken Stock (page 66)

½ cup dry white wine

1 tablespoon chopped fresh rosemary or ½ teaspoon dried

1 teaspoon ground cinnamon

1 pound conchiglie or other shell-shaped dried pasta

⅓ cup minced fresh parsley

Toasted pine nuts for garnishing

RECOMMENDED WINE

Try a low-tannin red wine such as a **Pinot Noir** or **Merlot** with this dish. A light, fruity white wine, such as a **Riesling** or **Chenin Blanc** with just a touch of residual sugar (1 percent or so), also works, because it mirrors the slight sweetness and sweet-spice aromas in the dish.

Conchiglie is one of the seemingly endless number of pasta shapes; they look like little conch shells. You can, of course, use any shape of dried pasta you please, or try this sauce with the fresh Gremolata Pasta (page 117). The sauce in this dish is magnificent, and I would suggest making a double batch so you can freeze one for later use. Like most stewed meat sauces, this one tastes even better a day or two after being made.

In a heavy-bottomed pot, heat 3 tablespoons of the olive oil over medium-high heat and brown the lamb quickly and evenly, seasoning lightly with salt and pepper. Do this in batches, if necessary. Remove the meat and set aside. Add the onions, garlic, carrot, and fennel to the pot and sauté over medium heat until just beginning to color. Return the meat to the pot and add the tomatoes, vinegar, raisins, sugar, stock, wine, rosemary, and cinnamon. Simmer for 1½ to 2 hours or until the meat is very tender. Skim off the fat. Season to taste with salt and pepper and adjust the sweet-and-sour elements with sugar and vinegar. Keep warm.

At serving time, in a large pot of lightly salted boiling water cook the pasta until just al dente. Drain and transfer to a serving bowl. Toss with the remaining 1 tablespoon olive oil and the parsley. Ladle the lamb sauce over the pasta and garnish with toasted pine nuts.

ORECCHIETTE WITH RED WINE–BRAISED RABBIT

Serves 6

RECOMMENDED WINE
This simple, hearty dish would be great with the pepper and spice flavors of Zinfandel.

½ ounce dried porcini mushrooms, soaked in 1 cup warm water for 20 minutes

1 large rabbit (4 pounds), cut into quarters

Kosher or sea salt and freshly ground pepper

⅓ cup olive oil

8 ounces chanterelle, oyster, or shiitake mushrooms, stemmed and quartered

1 cup sliced yellow onion

3 tablespoons slivered garlic

½ cup diced carrot

½ cup thinly sliced celery

1/3 cup sliced drained sun-dried tomatoes

2 cups hearty red wine

2 cups seeded and diced ripe fresh tomatoes

1 teaspoon minced fresh thyme

1 teaspoon minced fresh sage

4 cups rich rabbit or chicken stock

⅓ cup finely chopped fresh parsley, preferably flat leaf

¼ cup chopped fresh basil

8 ounces orecchiette or other small, shaped dried pasta

Fresh basil or mint sprigs and shaved Asiago, Parmesan, or dry Jack cheese for garnishing

I love rabbit and don't know why more Americans don't buy it. Its lean, delicate flavors are delicious. This is a hearty peasant-style dish that certainly suggests fall and winter. For a more elegant presentation, bone out the loins and sauté them briefly along with the liver. Slice and arrange attractively with the rest of the garnishes on top of the pasta. If you can't find rabbit, chicken works well too. Orecchiette, or "little ears," pasta is widely available. You can use whatever shape of pasta you like, however.

Drain the mushrooms and chop. Season the rabbit pieces liberally with salt and pepper. In a large, heavy-bottomed saucepan, heat the olive oil and quickly brown the rabbit. Remove and set aside. Add the mushrooms, onion, garlic, carrot, and celery, in batches if necessary, and sauté until very lightly browned.

Return the rabbit to the pan and add the sun-dried tomatoes, wine, fresh tomatoes, thyme, sage, and the stock and bring to a simmer. Cover and simmer until the rabbit is tender and begins to pull away from the bones easily, 45 to 50 minutes. Remove the rabbit, separate the meat from the bones, discard the bones, cut the meat into bite-sized pieces, and set aside. Strain the stock, reserving the vegetables, and return the stock to the pan. Bring to a boil and cook over high heat for 8 to 10 minutes to reduce and thicken slightly. This also concentrates the flavors. Season to taste with salt and pepper. Add the reserved meat and vegetables and heat through. Stir in parsley and basil just before serving.

Meanwhile, in a large pot of lightly salted water, cook the pasta until just al dente. Drain and toss with the rabbit sauce. Garnish with basil sprigs and shaved cheese.

FIOCHETTI WITH LEEKS AND SMOKED SALMON

Serves 4

2 tablespoons unsalted butter

2 tablespoons olive oil

2 cups sliced leeks, white part only

1 cup rich Chicken Stock (page 66), Shellfish Stock (page 67), or Vegetable Stock (page 69)

⅓ cup dry white wine

1 tablespoon Dijon mustard

1 cup cream or No-Cream Cream (page 85)

1 tablespoon grated lemon zest

Kosher or sea salt and freshly ground black pepper

3 tablespoons chopped fresh dill

8 ounces fiochetti or other small, shaped dried pasta

8 ounces smoked salmon, cut into wide strips

5 ounces smoked mozzarella or Gouda cheese, cut into ¼-inch dice

Dill sprigs and Fried Capers (page 33) for garnishing (optional)

RECOMMENDED WINE
A complex, barrel-aged **Chardonnay** or **Pinot Blanc** will mirror the smoky flavors of the cheese and have enough body to balance this dish.

This dish is reminiscent of one prepared for me during a trip to Norway several years ago. In addition to the ingredients below, the chef added some sautéed chanterelles and a garnish of a few tart huckleberries. Fiochetti is a tiny butterfly-shaped pasta with serrated edges. Use whatever fun shape you like.

In a large skillet, melt the butter with the olive oil over medium heat and sauté the leeks until translucent but not brown, about 10 minutes. Set aside. In a saucepan, combine the stock, wine, mustard, cream, and lemon zest and reduce over medium-high heat to a light sauce consistency, about 8 minutes. Season to taste with salt and pepper and stir in the fresh dill.

Meanwhile, in a large pot of lightly salted boiling water, cook the pasta until just al dente. Drain the pasta and toss with the sauce, leeks, salmon, and mozzarella. Serve immediately, garnished with dill sprigs and Fried Capers, if using.

BASIC PASTA

Yields about 1 pound pasta

making fresh pasta

Traditional Italian pasta is a combination of flour and eggs and nothing else. Marcella Hazan, in her excellent book *Marcella's Italian Kitchen*, makes the point succinctly: "Olive oil, salt, colorings, seasonings have no gastronomic reason for being in pasta. Some, such as olive oil, which makes the pasta slicker, are wholly undesirable and a detriment to good pasta."

Fresh flour is, of course, the most important ingredient in making good pasta. Italians make pasta out of hard-wheat (durum) flour, also known as semolina, but depending on the region, they will sometimes use some portion of all-purpose flour. The durum has a higher gluten content, which is desirable when making pasta with a machine. Different flours produce different flavors and textures in the pasta, so you might try both types and decide which you like better.

Being a little less of a purist than Marcella, I love experimenting with fresh herbs and other seasonings in pasta to add some highlights.

2 cups unbleached all-purpose flour or durum
semolina flour

3 large eggs

Drops of water as needed

FOOD PROCESSOR METHOD

Put the flour in the bowl of the food processor. With the motor running, add the eggs, one at a time. Continue processing for 10 seconds after the last egg has been added. Add drops of water if the dough seems too dry. Turn out onto a lightly floured work surface and knead for 6 to 8 minutes or until the dough is smooth and satiny and springs back when pressed with a finger.

HAND-MIX METHOD

Put the flour in a mound on a work surface. Form a well in the center and break the eggs into the well. Mix the eggs with a fork. Pulling from the sides of the well, gradually incorporate the flour into the eggs. Continue to mix until the dough forms a ball, adding drops of water as necessary. Begin kneading the dough, pushing the dough with the heel of your hand. Knead until soft and satiny. Most important, the dough should spring back when poked with your finger. This will take 10 to 15 minutes of continuous kneading.

Divide the dough into 4 pieces, wrap in plastic wrap, and refrigerate for at least 45 minutes. The dough may also be frozen at this point; thaw in the refrigerator before proceeding.

Roll by hand or with a hand-cranked pasta machine, according to the manufacturer's directions.

SPINACH-BASIL PASTA

3 cups lightly packed spinach leaves

1 cup lightly packed fresh basil leaves

2 cups unbleached all-purpose flour

2 large eggs

In a saucepan of lightly salted boiling water, blanch the spinach and basil for 5 seconds. Remove and immediately plunge into ice water to set the color. Drain, pat dry, and then squeeze in a towel to remove any excess liquid. Chop very fine and add to the pasta as the eggs are incorporated into the flour. Proceed as directed on facing page.

CARROT-SAGE PASTA

¼ cup fresh carrot purée or juice

2 teaspoons minced fresh sage

2 cups unbleached all-purpose flour

2 large eggs

Add the carrot purée and sage to the eggs as they are incorporated into the flour. Proceed as directed on facing page.

GREMOLATA PASTA

2 teaspoons finely grated lemon zest

1 tablespoon minced garlic

1 tablespoon minced fresh parsley

2 cups unbleached all-purpose flour

2 large eggs

Add the lemon zest, garlic, and parsley to the eggs as they are incorporated into the flour. Proceed as directed on facing page.

SAFFRON–WHITE WINE PASTA

¼ cup dry white wine

¼ cup water

1 teaspoon crumbled saffron threads

2¼ cups unbleached all-purpose flour

2 large eggs

In a small saucepan, combine the wine, water, and saffron. Bring to a boil. Remove from the heat and let cool. Strain, if you wish, and add the liquid to the eggs as they are incorporated into the flour. Proceed as directed on facing page.

PASTA RAGS WITH ARUGULA AND PANCETTA

Serves 4

RECOMMENDED WINE
The earthy, salty notes from the pancetta and pecorino coupled with the bitterness from the arugula are fun bridges to clean, crisp lemony white wines like **Sauvignon Blanc** and **Pinot Grigio** and earthy reds like **Sangiovese** and **Syrah**.

⅓ cup extra-virgin olive oil

4 ounces pancetta, cut into ¼-inch dice

1 heaping cup sliced onion (1 small onion)

1 pound fresh pasta, cut into irregular shapes

1 quart lightly packed young arugula

Kosher or sea salt and freshly ground pepper

¼ cup finely shaved pecorino cheese (optional)

Originally this recipe came about because I wanted to make use of the leftover scraps of fresh pasta from making pasta shapes. Use one of the fresh pastas on page 117 and simply cut them into fairly large irregular shapes.

In a large sauté pan, heat the olive oil over medium-high heat and sauté the pancetta and onion until golden brown, about 5 minutes. Set aside and keep warm.

In a large pot of salted boiling water, cook the fresh pasta until al dente, about 3 minutes. Drain and add to the pancetta mixture. Put the pan back on medium heat and add the arugula, tossing to combine and just wilting the arugula slightly. Season to taste with salt and pepper. Serve immediately, with a topping of shaved cheese, if using.

PASTA WITH FRESH TOMATOES, SHRIMP, AND ZUCCHINI

Serves 4

½ cup fruity olive oil

2 teaspoons finely chopped garlic

1 tablespoon finely grated lemon zest

½ teaspoon red pepper flakes

3 cups diced ½-inch-diced zucchini

12 ounces medium (31 to 35) shrimp, shelled and deveined, shells reserved

1 tablespoon unsalted butter

½ cup chopped onion

⅓ cup dry white wine

4 cups ripe cherry tomatoes, preferably different colors, halved

¼ cup chopped fresh flat-leaf parsley

Kosher or sea salt and freshly ground pepper

Fresh lemon juice for seasoning

1 pound fresh Gremolata Pasta (page 117), cut into fettuccine

RECOMMENDED WINE
An uncomplicated white wine with nice acidity to link to the lemon juice in this dish would work nicely. Unoaked **Chardonnay**, **Sauvignon Blanc**, dry **Riesling**, or a nice dry sparkling wine would all work here.

Here's a simple dish that takes advantage of ripe tomatoes from your garden or the farmers' market. This is also a chance to experiment with other fresh herbs like chervil or tarragon in place of, or in combination with, the parsley. You could shave a little salty cheese like pecorino as a garnish if you wanted, but I think I like it best without cheese.

In a medium bowl, combine the olive oil, garlic, lemon zest, and red pepper flakes. Add the zucchini and shrimp and toss to coat. Set aside to marinate for at least 30 minutes. In a sauté pan, heat the butter over medium heat and cook the onion until just lightly browned, about 4 minutes. Add the wine and reduce until lightly thickened.

Add the zucchini and shrimp mixture and cook until the zucchini has softened just a bit and the shrimp are pink. Stir in the tomatoes and parsley and season to taste with salt, pepper, and drops of lemon juice.

Meanwhile, in a large pot of salted boiling water, cook the pasta until just al dente. Drain and toss with the sauce. Serve immediately.

CURRIED SWEET POTATO RAVIOLI

Serves 4 to 6

RECOMMENDED WINE
The heat from the curry is softened and rounded with a fruity white wine such as **Riesling**, **Viognier**, or **Chenin Blanc**.

1½ pounds sweet potatoes

3 tablespoons unsalted butter

⅓ cup minced shallots or green onions, white part only

1 tablespoon good-quality curry powder, such as Madras Curry Powder (page 97)

½ cup dry white wine

½ cup heavy (whipping) cream

1 tablespoon chopped fresh parsley

1 tablespoon chopped fresh chives

1 teaspoon minced fresh mint

Kosher or sea salt and freshly ground pepper

1 pound fresh pasta sheets

2 cups hot rich Chicken Stock (page 66)

The sweet potato filling used here has a myriad of other uses: by itself as a garnish for roasted meats, as a filling in deep-fried wontons, or as a soup base, thinned with stock and cream to make a lovely soup. I particularly like it in these ravioli, which are served here in a simple stock; they could also be tossed with fresh herb butter and a little grated Parmesan or pecorino cheese.

Roast the sweet potatoes in a 375°F oven until soft, about 1 hour. Cool and remove the skins. With a potato masher or food mill (don't use a food processor), mash the potatoes and set aside. You should have about 2 cups.

In a saucepan, melt the butter and sauté the shallots and curry powder until the shallots are soft but not brown and the curry is fragrant. Add the wine, bring to a boil, and reduce to 2 tablespoons or so. Add the mashed sweet potatoes and cream. Stir to combine thoroughly and heat the mixture through. Remove from the heat and stir in the parsley, chives, and mint. Season to taste with salt and pepper. Cool.

Cut the pasta sheets into strips about 4 inches wide. Place a row of rounded tablespoonfuls of potato mixture along the bottom half of the long pasta strip at 1-inch intervals. Fold the top half of the strip over to enclose the filling. Cut the ravioli with a knife, or a fluted cutter if you have one. Seal the dough around the filling by pressing gently with your finger to expel any air. If the dough is very fresh, it should stick to itself. If the dough has dried out at all, paint a little water around the filling and then seal. (Ravioli can be made ahead and stored, frozen, for up to 2 months. Defrost in the refrigerator before proceeding.)

Put the ravioli in lightly salted boiling water and simmer until they begin to float, about 3 to 4 minutes. Remove the ravioli carefully with a slotted spoon and divide among warm soup bowls. Ladle in enough hot stock just to moisten the ravioli and serve immediately.

EGGPLANT–GOAT CHEESE RAVIOLI

Serves 6

Two 1½-pound unpeeled globe eggplants, cut into ¾-inch-thick rounds

2 tablespoons olive oil, plus additional for brushing

Kosher or sea salt and freshly ground pepper

½ cup minced shallots or green onions, white part only

1 tablespoon chopped garlic

1 cup crumbled fresh goat cheese

⅓ cup freshly grated Parmesan or dry Jack cheese

⅓ cup finely chopped toasted pine nuts or almonds

3 tablespoons finely chopped fresh basil

1 pound fresh pasta, rolled into thin sheets

Melted butter, or Creamy Tomato Sauce (page 123), or Warm Basil Cream (page 151)

Shaved Parmesan cheese and fresh basil leaves cut into fine chiffonade for garnishing (optional)

RECOMMENDED WINE

A lighter-style red wine such as a **Gamay** or **Sangiovese** works well with this dish; for contrast, try a fresh, clean **Fumé Blanc** or **Sauvignon Blanc** with little or no oak. In fact, try a glass of both!

Grilled eggplant and goat cheese are one of my favorite flavor combinations. Use any fresh goat cheese you can find, but be on the lookout for those wonderful cheeses from Laurel Chenel, Bodega Goat Cheese, or Redwood Hill Farms (see page 421). I've suggested two different sauces. Go all out and serve the ravioli with both.

Brush the eggplant rounds liberally on both sides with olive oil. Season with salt and pepper and grill or broil (or roast in a preheated 400°F oven) for 12 minutes or so until lightly browned and softened. Chop and set aside. Heat the remaining 2 tablespoons olive oil and sauté the shallots and garlic until soft but not brown. Remove from the heat, cool, and add to a food processor with the eggplant, goat cheese, Parmesan cheese, pine nuts, and basil and pulse 3 or 4 times to combine. The mixture should still have some texture. Season to taste with salt and pepper.

Cut the pasta sheets into strips about 3 inches wide. Put a row of rounded tablespoonfuls of the eggplant-cheese mixture along the bottom half of each pasta strip at 1-inch intervals. Fold the top half of the strip over to enclose the filling. Cut the ravioli apart using a knife, or a fluted cutter if you have one. Seal the ravioli around the filling by pressing gently with your finger to expel any air. Make sure the dough is well sealed. If the dough is very fresh, it should stick to itself easily. If the dough has dried out at all, paint a little water around the filling and then seal. (Ravioli can be made ahead and stored, frozen, for up to 2 months. Defrost in the refrigerator before proceeding.)

Put the ravioli in lightly salted boiling water and simmer until the ravioli begin to float, about 4 minutes. Drain and serve with melted butter, or with Creamy Tomato Sauce or Warm Basil Cream, or both. To do this, drizzle the sauce decoratively around the ravioli. Garnish with shaved Parmesan cheese and basil chiffonade (if using), and serve immediately.

TONNARELLI WITH DUNGENESS CRAB SAUCE

Serves 4

RECOMMENDED WINE
A rich white like a barrel-aged **Chardonnay** or **Pinot Blanc** is a great complement to this luscious dish. Be sure the wine isn't too fat, however, and has some nice acidity and citrus notes to help cut through the richness of the sauce.

1 pound fresh pasta, rolled into sheets

4 tablespoons olive oil

¼ cup minced shallots or green onions, white part only

2 teaspoons minced garlic

¾ cup dry white wine

2 cups rich fish or shellfish stock

¾ cup heavy (whipping) cream

3 tablespoons dry sherry

1 tablespoon tomato paste

Kosher or sea salt and freshly ground pepper

3 cups thickly sliced oyster or shiitake mushrooms

1 pound fresh Dungeness crabmeat, shredded and picked over to remove any pieces of shell

3 tablespoons chopped fresh chives

1 tablespoon finely grated lemon zest

½ cup peeled, seeded, and diced ripe tomato or halved cherry tomatoes

This very rich dish comes from the wrong end of the nutrition pyramid, but it's a worthwhile treat when fresh Dungeness or your local crab is available. You could also substitute any other fish or shellfish such as cooked shrimp, lobster, or scallops. To add a little green texture, I often throw in some crisply cooked sugar snap or snow peas. Tonnarelli refers to a flat, irregularly cut (but essentially square) pasta. You can use any pasta shape you like.

Cut the pasta sheets into 1-inch squares. Loosely cover with waxed paper and set aside.

In a large saucepan, heat 2 tablespoons of the olive oil over medium heat and sauté the shallots and garlic until soft but not brown. Add the wine and stock, and bring to a boil, and reduce the liquid by half. Add the cream, sherry, and tomato paste and return to a boil. Cook, uncovered, to reduce to a light sauce consistency, about 8 minutes. Season the sauce to taste with salt and pepper. In a sauté pan, heat the remaining 2 tablespoons olive oil over high heat and sauté the mushrooms until lightly browned. Add the crabmeat, chives, lemon zest, and sautéed mushrooms to the sauce and keep warm.

In a large pot of lightly salted boiling water, cook the pasta until just al dente, 3 to 4 minutes. Drain and gently toss with the crab sauce and tomato. Spoon into warm bowls and serve immediately.

SHRIMP AND FRESH HERB SPAETZLE WITH CREAMY TOMATO SAUCE

Serves 4 to 6

8 ounces shrimp, shelled and deveined

¾ cup heavy (whipping) cream

1 cup all-purpose flour

1 large egg

2 tablespoons chopped mixed fresh herbs, such as parsley, basil, and chives

Kosher or sea salt and freshly ground pepper

2 tablespoons olive oil plus additional for coating

Creamy Tomato Sauce (recipe follows)

Chopped fresh parsley and Basil Oil (page 80) for garnishing (optional)

Spaetzle is a staple in German and Austrian cooking. Because of its national origins we don't think of it as a pasta, but it certainly is a member of the pasta family. Spaetzle is traditionally made with only flour or with a flour and potato mixture; it is poached and then sautéed. Other rich shellfish could be used in place of the shrimp. I also like smoked salmon as an alternative.

Purée the raw shrimp in a food processor. Add the cream and purée until smooth. Add the flour, egg, herbs, salt, and pepper and pulse to make a smooth batter. The dough will be pretty stiff. I find that the easiest way to deal with it is to put it into a pastry bag with ¼-inch opening at the tip. Simply squeeze out, cutting off ½-inch-long noodles into a pot of salted boiling water. Cook the spaetzle for 2 to 3 minutes or until they float to the surface. Drain and cool immediately under cold running water. The spaetzle can be made ahead to this point. Toss with a few drops of olive oil and store, covered, in the refrigerator for up to 24 hours.

When ready to serve, in a sauté pan heat the 2 tablespoons olive oil over medium-high heat and sauté the spaetzle until lightly browned and crispy. Drain on paper towels and keep warm. Spoon the Creamy Tomato Sauce onto warm plates and pile the spaetzle on top. Sprinkle with chopped parsley and a drizzle of Basil Oil, if using.

CREAMY TOMATO SAUCE

Makes about 3 cups

2 tablespoons olive oil

½ cup minced red onion

⅓ cup dry white wine

¾ cup rich Shellfish Stock (page 67) or Chicken Stock (page 66)

One 14-ounce can diced tomatoes, drained

1 teaspoon chopped fresh rosemary

½ cup heavy (whipping) cream or No-Cream Cream (page 85)

Kosher or sea salt and freshly ground pepper

In a saucepan, heat the olive oil and sauté the onion until just beginning to color. Add the wine, stock, tomatoes, and rosemary and cook over medium-high heat for 5 to 6 minutes to moderately reduce. Strain the sauce through a medium-mesh strainer, pushing down on the solids. Return the liquid to the pan, add the cream, and reduce if needed to the desired sauce consistency. The sauce should have some body but not be too thick. Season to taste with salt and pepper. Can be made a day or two ahead and stored, covered, in the refrigerator.

RICOTTA-HERB GNOCCHI WITH TWO SAUCES

Serves 4 to 6

RECOMMENDED WINE
The earthy notes of **Pinot Noir** are magical with the flavors of the Wild Mushroom Cream. A toasty barrel-aged **Chardonnay** works well as a white wine alternative.

1 pound fresh whole-milk ricotta, drained (see Note)

⅓ cup unbleached all-purpose flour

½ teaspoon freshly ground white pepper

4 tablespoons minced mixed fresh herbs, such as tarragon, chives, and chervil

½ teaspoon ground fennel seeds

½ teaspoon kosher or sea salt, plus additional for salting the cooking water

Large pinch freshly grated nutmeg

Chive flowers and fresh herb sprigs for garnishing (optional)

Wild Mushroom Cream (facing page)

Spinach-Arugula Pesto (facing page)

I love gnocchi because they are easy to prepare and can be made well ahead of time and then frozen. This dish uses two sauces: a rich Wild Mushroom Cream and a refreshing Spinach-Arugula Pesto for balance. You don't have to use both, but it's fun, and they can be made ahead.

In a food processor, combine the ricotta, flour, white pepper, herbs, fennel seeds, ½ teaspoon salt, and the nutmeg. Process until combined. Or you can knead by hand for 4 to 5 minutes, or until very smooth. The dough should be somewhat sticky. (If it is too sticky, add a little bit of flour, but be careful about adding too much or the gnocchi may become heavy.)

Divide the dough into egg-sized portions and roll into logs about ½ inch thick. With a sharp knife, cut the logs into ¾-inch pieces. (If you'd like, you can roll the pieces up the back of a fork to create the traditional ridged surface.) Put the gnocchi on floured waxed paper on a baking sheet. Refrigerate, uncovered, for at least 30 minutes. (The gnocchi may also be frozen at this point; freeze in a single layer on the baking sheet and then store in tightly closed sealable plastic bags.)

Bring 4 quarts of lightly salted water to a gentle boil. Carefully put the gnocchi in the water, in batches if necessary, and simmer until they rise to the surface, about 2 to 3 minutes. Cook for 1 minute longer and then remove with a slotted spoon and drain. The gnocchi may be made to this point up to 2 hours in advance; rinse them in cold water and toss gently with a little olive oil to prevent sticking. Reheat with a little olive oil in a sauté pan or a hot oven.

Gently combine the gnocchi with the Wild Mushroom Cream and put on warm plates. Drizzle Spinach-Arugula Pesto over the top. Garnish with chive flowers and herb sprigs, if using.

Note: Draining ricotta rids the cheese of excess water, undesirable in a recipe like this.
To drain ricotta, simply scoop it into a fine-mesh strainer, or into a colander or strainer lined with a double thickness of well-rinsed cheesecloth. Suspend the strainer over a bowl and store, covered, in the refrigerator at least 6 hours or overnight, stirring at least 2 or 3 times.

WILD MUSHROOM CREAM
Makes about 2 cups

½ ounce dried morels or porcini mushrooms, soaked in 1 cup warm water for 20 minutes

1 cup finely chopped fresh shiitake or other wild mushrooms

2 tablespoons olive oil

3 tablespoons minced shallots or green onions, white part only

½ cup dry white wine

1½ cups heavy (whipping) cream

1 tablespoon minced fresh parsley

1 tablespoon Dijon mustard

Kosher or sea salt and freshly ground pepper

Remove the mushrooms from the soaking liquid and reserve the liquid. Chop the soaked mushrooms and set aside with the fresh wild mushrooms.

In a saucepan, heat the olive oil and sauté the shallots until very lightly colored. Add all the mushrooms and sauté over medium-high heat until the mushrooms have lightly browned. Add the wine and reserved soaking liquid and reduce the liquid uncovered over high heat for 5 minutes. Add the cream and reduce to a light sauce consistency. Stir in the parsley and mustard. Season to taste with salt and pepper and keep warm.

SPINACH-ARUGULA PESTO
Makes about 1 cup

3 cups packed spinach or arugula leaves, or a combination

1 tablespoons toasted chopped almonds or pine nuts

2 tablespoons freshly grated Parmesan cheese

2 teaspoons finely grated lemon zest

½ cup olive oil

Kosher or sea salt and freshly ground pepper

Blanch the spinach in boiling salted water for 5 to 10 seconds. Drain, plunge into cold water to stop the cooking, and drain again. Squeeze as much water as you can from the spinach and chop. Add to a food processor or blender along with almonds, cheese, and lemon zest and pulse a couple of times. With the motor running, add the olive oil to the desired consistency. Add just enough oil to make a smooth paste. Season to taste with salt and pepper. Store, covered, in the refrigerator for up to 3 days or freeze for up to 3 months.

GRATIN OF PROSCIUTTO AND CHARD GNOCCHI WITH TOMATO-EGGPLANT SAUCE

Serves 6

RECOMMENDED WINE
This dish calls out for a red wine with Italian heritage. Seek out an Italian or California **Sangiovese**, **Nebbiolo**, **Barbera**, or **Dolcetto**.

2 tablespoons olive oil

2 pounds Swiss chard, center stems removed and finely chopped

2 tablespoons chopped fresh basil or 1 teaspoon dried

2 cups whole-milk ricotta, drained (see page 124)

1¼ cups freshly grated Parmesan, Asiago, or pecorino cheese

⅔ cup chopped prosciutto

2 large egg yolks, lightly beaten

4 tablespoons all-purpose flour, plus additional for dusting

½ teaspoon freshly grated nutmeg

Kosher or sea salt and freshly ground pepper

3 tablespoons unsalted butter, melted

¼ cup fresh bread crumbs

2 teaspoons grated lemon zest

Tomato Eggplant Sauce (facing page)

Fresh basil sprigs and Basil-Mint Oil (page 80) for garnishing (optional)

This is a great make-ahead dish: You can prepare the gnocchi and sauce a couple of hours ahead, then finish at the last moment under the broiler.

Heat the olive oil over medium heat and sauté the chard for 3 to 4 minutes, or until completely wilted. You should have about 2 cups.

In a food processor, combine the chard, basil, ricotta, ¾ cup of the Parmesan cheese, and the prosciutto. Add the egg yolks, the 4 tablespoons flour, and the nutmeg. Pulse just to combine, being careful not to purée. Season to taste with salt and pepper. The mixture will be very soft and sticky.

Flour your hands generously and form the mixture into small logs, about 6 inches long and ½ inch wide. Cut into 1-inch lengths. Put on a floured baking sheet and refrigerate, uncovered, for at least 30 minutes. (The gnocchi may also be frozen at this point; freeze in a single layer on the baking sheet until hard and then store in tightly closed sealable plastic bags.)

Working in batches, if necessary, gently place the gnocchi in lightly salted simmering water. Gently cook the gnocchi for 2 to 3 minutes or until they rise to the surface. With a slotted spoon, transfer them to a lightly buttered ovenproof gratin dish large enough to hold the gnocchi in one layer. Paint with the remaining melted butter. Mix the remaining ½ cup Parmesan cheese with the bread crumbs and lemon zest and sprinkle evenly over the buttered gnocchi.

Put the gnocchi under a preheated broiler, about 3 inches from the heat, and lightly brown. Spoon the Tomato-Eggplant Sauce onto warm plates and place the hot gnocchi on top. Garnish with fresh basil sprigs and drizzle the Basil-Mint Oil decoratively around, if using. Serve immediately.

TOMATO-EGGPLANT SAUCE

1¼ pounds eggplant

2 tablespoons olive oil, plus additional for brushing the eggplant

Kosher or sea salt and freshly ground pepper

1½ cups minced onions

1 tablespoon roasted garlic (see page 264)

½ cup finely diced cremini or shiitake mushrooms

½ cup dry white wine

One 35-ounce can plum tomatoes

1 cup rich chicken stock or mushroom stock

2 teaspoons dried oregano

1 teaspoon fennel seeds

¼ teaspoon red pepper flakes

Balsamic vinegar

Preheat the oven to 400°F. Slice the eggplant lengthwise into ½-inch-thick slices, brush lightly with olive oil, and season both sides with salt and pepper. Put in a single layer on a baking sheet and roast for 10 to 12 minutes or until soft and lightly browned. Chop and set aside.

In a saucepan, heat the 2 tablespoons olive oil and sauté the onions, roasted garlic, and mushrooms until they just begin to color. Add the wine, tomatoes, stock, oregano, fennel seeds, and pepper flakes and simmer for 15 minutes, stirring occasionally to break up the tomatoes. Add the tomato mixture and eggplant to a food processor and pulse to the desired sauce consistency. Season to taste with salt and pepper and drops of balsamic vinegar. You can also process the mixture more and strain through a medium-mesh strainer to make a smoother sauce, if you prefer. The sauce can be stored, covered, in the refrigerator for up to 3 days.

BASIC PIZZA DOUGH

Makes one 14-inch or two 8-to-10-inch pizzas

pizza

Good pizza, like good pasta, depends on a good dough. I have included two variations on pizza dough, and I like both for the different qualities of the crusts they make. Basic Pizza Dough results in a plain, thin, crisp crust, making it a good foil for more elaborate toppings. The Pizza Dough with Sun-Dried Tomatoes and Herbs creates a crust that is a bit thicker and, because it includes lots of flavorful ingredients, is best suited to simple toppings such as a scattering of freshly grilled vegetables or garden-ripe tomatoes with a drizzle of fresh pesto. Both pizza doughs can be made ahead of time and stored in sealable plastic bags for a day or two in the refrigerator or up to a month in the freezer. If frozen, defrost overnight in the refrigerator before using. Following the dough recipes, I've included a few of my favorite pizza toppings.

I also love a fresh pizza dough spread with a generous layer of one of the several pestos in this book and topped with a scattering of good olives. This can be done quickly, especially if you've made the pizza dough ahead of time and have it available from the freezer.

1 package active dry yeast

¾ cup warm water (100°F)

2 tablespoons olive oil

¼ cup coarse rye or whole-wheat flour

1¾ cups all-purpose flour, plus additional as needed

1 teaspoon kosher or sea salt

Coarse cornmeal for sprinkling on the pan

In a small bowl, sprinkle the yeast over the warm water and let sit for 8 to 10 minutes or until foamy. In a food processor with the plastic or metal blade, an electric mixer fitted with the dough hook, or by hand, combine the yeast mixture, 1 tablespoon olive oil, rye flour, the 1¾ cups all-purpose flour, and salt. Mix until the dough forms a ball. If the dough is very sticky, add a little extra flour. Continue to knead for about 1 minute in the food processor, about 3 minutes in the electric mixer, or about 4 to 5 minutes by hand, until the dough is smooth and satiny.

Smear a large bowl with the remaining tablespoon of olive oil. Put the dough in the bowl and turn it to coat with the oil. Cover with plastic wrap and let the dough rise in a warm place until it has doubled, 1 to 2 hours. Lightly flour a work surface and roll the dough into a 14-inch circle. Sprinkle cornmeal on a pizza pan or baking sheet and put the dough on it. Cover with a towel and allow to rest for 30 minutes.

Preheat the oven to 475°F. Spread the pizza with the topping you're using and bake in the oven on the top rack for 10 to 12 minutes, or until the dough is nicely browned and the topping is hot.

PIZZA DOUGH WITH SUN-DRIED TOMATOES AND HERBS

Makes one 14-inch or two 8-to-10-inch pizzas

1 package active dry yeast

1 cup lukewarm water (100°F)

1 teaspoon sugar

2 tablespoons chopped mixed fresh herbs, such as basil, thyme, oregano, parsley, and chives, or your favorites

2 tablespoons minced sun-dried tomatoes

¼ cup plus 1 tablespoon extra-virgin olive oil

2 teaspoons kosher or sea salt

3 cups all-purpose flour, plus additional for kneading

Coarse cornmeal for sprinkling on the pan

In a small bowl, sprinkle the yeast over the warm water, then sprinkle the sugar onto the yeast, and let sit for 8 to 10 minutes or until foamy.

In a food processor with the plastic or metal blade, an electric mixer fitted with the dough hook, or by hand, combine the yeast mixture, herbs, tomatoes, the ¼ cup olive oil, salt, and the 3 cups flour. Process in short bursts until the mixture forms a ball. Or mix the ingredients by hand.

Remove the dough from the food processor and knead on a lightly floured work surface until smooth and elastic. The time will vary depending on the method used to make the dough. (Hand-mixed dough may need more kneading.) If the dough is very sticky, use a little extra flour.

Smear a large bowl with the remaining 1 tablespoon olive oil. Put the dough in the bowl and roll it around to coat with oil. Cover with plastic wrap and let the dough rise in a warm place until it has doubled, 1 to 2 hours. Lightly flour a work surface and roll the dough into a 14-inch circle. Sprinkle cornmeal on a pizza pan or baking sheet and put the dough on it. Cover with a towel and allow to rest for 30 minutes. Preheat the oven to 475°F. Scatter the desired topping over the pizza. Bake in the oven on the top rack for about 20 minutes or until the crust is golden brown and well puffed.

SIMPLE PIZZA SAUCE

Makes about 4 cups

4 cups canned plum tomatoes, including heavy
    purée

2 tablespoons extra-virgin olive oil

2 tablespoons thinly slivered garlic

¼ teaspoon red pepper flakes

¼ cup coarsely chopped loosely packed fresh
    basil leaves

Kosher or sea salt and freshly ground pepper

In a food processor, pulse the tomatoes briefly 2 or 3 times to coarsely chop. Or do it by hand. Set aside.

Heat the olive oil in a skillet over medium heat and sauté the garlic and pepper flakes until the garlic is softened but not brown. Add the tomatoes, including the purée, and basil, bring to a simmer, and cook for 5 minutes or until lightly thickened. Season to taste with salt and pepper. Store, covered, in the refrigerator for up to 7 days, or freeze indefinitely.

BLUE CHEESE AND CARAMELIZED ONION PIZZA WITH SAGE

Makes enough topping for one 14-inch or two 8-to-10-inch pizzas

1 recipe Pizza Dough with Sun-Dried Tomatoes and Herbs (page 129)

4 tablespoons extra-virgin olive oil

1½ pounds yellow onions, thinly sliced

Kosher or sea salt and freshly ground pepper

12 ounces creamy blue cheese, such as Point Reyes Farmstead Original Blue or an Italian Gorgonzola dolce, crumbled

¼ cup fresh sage leaves

Prepare the Pizza Dough with Sun-Dried Tomatoes and Herbs. Preheat the oven to 500°F, preferably with a pizza stone or brick-oven insert in the oven.

In a deep, heavy-bottomed pan, heat 3 tablespoons olive oil and sauté the onions until golden brown, stirring regularly to prevent burning. This may take 15 minutes. Season to taste with salt and pepper.

Scatter the onions evenly over the top of the prepared dough. Scatter the blue cheese and sage leaves on top and drizzle with remaining tablespoon of olive oil. Bake the pizza on the stone for about 15 minutes or until the dough is puffed, golden, and cooked through.

POTATO, RED ONION, ARUGULA, AND BRIE PIZZA

Makes enough topping for one 14-inch or two 8-to-10-inch pizzas

RECOMMENDED WINE
Brie is great with lush red wines such as **Pinot Noir** or **Syrah**.

1 recipe Basic Pizza Dough (page 128)

3 tablespoons olive oil

2 cups sliced red onions

Kosher or sea salt and freshly ground pepper

12 ounces red potatoes, thinly sliced

½ cup freshly grated Parmesan cheese

6 ounces Brie, thinly sliced

1 cup loosely packed arugula leaves

1 medium red bell pepper, charred, peeled, and finely chopped

Prepare the Basic Pizza Dough. Preheat the oven to 500°F preferably with a pizza stone or brick-oven insert in the oven. In a deep, heavy-bottomed pan, heat the olive oil and sauté the onions until crisp-tender. Season to taste with salt and pepper. Set aside.

In a medium saucepan, blanch the potatoes in lightly salted boiling water until crisp-tender, about 3 minutes. Cool in ice water to stop the cooking, drain, and pat dry.

Sprinkle the Parmesan cheese over the dough. Layer the potatoes evenly on top, followed by the onions and the slices of Brie. Season to taste with salt and pepper.

Bake the pizza for 12 to 15 minutes on the top rack. Scatter the arugula and red pepper on top and slice and serve immediately.

SPICY PORK PIZZA WITH BASIL-MINT PESTO

Makes enough topping for one 14-inch or two 8-to-10-inch pizzas

1 recipe Basic Pizza Dough (page 128)

2 tablespoons olive oil

12 ounces coarsely ground pork shoulder

¼ cup chopped red onion

1 teaspoon minced garlic

¼ teaspoon cayenne pepper

½ teaspoon ground cumin

1 teaspoon dried oregano

2 cups coarsely grated mozzarella cheese

⅓ cup Basil-Mint Pesto (page 87)

⅓ cup slivered Kalamata, Niçoise, or other oil-cured black olives

⅓ cup crumbled feta cheese

⅓ cup coarsely chopped fresh basil or mint for garnishing (optional)

RECOMMENDED WINE

A crisp, cool white like **Sauvignon Blanc**, or **Pinot Gris** or **Pinot Grigio**, would be perfect with the lively flavors of mint and salty, tart feta in this pizza.

This spicy pizza can be made with a variety of meats: I've done it with pork, lamb, and turkey. It is also delicious with chopped prawns or rock shrimp, which I suggest adding halfway through baking so they won't overcook.

Prepare the Basic Pizza Dough. Preheat the oven to 500°F, preferably with a pizza stone or brick-oven insert in the oven.

In a large sauté pan, heat the olive oil over medium-high heat and sauté the pork, onion, garlic, cayenne pepper, cumin, and oregano until the pork is almost completely cooked through. Drain off the fat and set aside. Spread the mozzarella evenly over the prepared dough. Crumbling the meat mixture, spread it evenly over the cheese. Top with the pesto and the olives. Bake the pizza on the top rack until the crust is brown and the cheese is melted, 12 to 15 minutes. Just before removing the pizza from the oven, sprinkle with the feta and basil, if using. Serve immediately.

DOUBLE OLIVE AND PEPPER PIZZA WITH PROSCIUTTO

Makes enough topping for one 14-inch or two 8-to-10-inch pizzas

RECOMMENDED WINE
This dish calls out for a red wine with Italian heritage. Seek out an Italian or California **Sangiovese** or **Barbera**.

1 recipe Basic Pizza Dough (page 128)

⅔ cup Simple Pizza Sauce (page 130)

8 ounces mushrooms, thinly sliced

1 small red bell pepper, chopped

½ cup sliced green olives, such as Cerignola or Lucques

½ cup sliced black oil-cured olives, such as Kalamata

4 ounces prosciutto, coarsely chopped

½ cup freshly grated Parmesan cheese

¼ cup chopped fresh basil

½ teaspoon red pepper flakes

This is a perfect Sunday night pizza: full of flavor, great for the family, easy to prepare. Sliced into smaller pieces, it also makes for delicious appetizers.

Prepare the Basic Pizza Dough. Preheat the oven to 500°F, preferably with a pizza stone or brick-oven insert in the oven.

Spread the Simple Pizza Sauce evenly over the dough. Scatter the mushrooms, bell pepper, green olives, black olives, and prosciutto all over the dough. Sprinkle the Parmesan cheese, basil, and pepper flakes evenly over the top. Bake for 10 to 20 minutes, depending on thickness of the crust.

ASPARAGUS, ROASTED GARLIC, AND LEMON RISOTTO

Serves 6

3 tablespoons unsalted butter

¼ cup sliced shallots

1½ cups Arborio rice

1 cup sliced shiitake mushrooms

3 tablespoons chopped roasted garlic (see page 264)

½ cup dry white wine

5 to 6 cups Vegetable Stock (page 69) or Chicken Stock (page 66), heated

2 cups ¼-inch diagonally sliced young asparagus, tips reserved

1 tablespoon finely grated lemon zest

⅓ cup chopped fresh chives

⅓ cup freshly grated Parmesan or Asiago cheese

Kosher or sea salt and freshly ground pepper

Drops of fresh lemon juice

Additional shaved Parmesan cheese and deep-fried basil sprigs (see Note) for garnishing (optional)

RECOMMENDED WINE

Using the similarity strategy, I'd look for a wine that has lemony, herbal flavors since those are the up-front impressions that this dish presents. They are softened a bit by the cheese and the mushrooms, which add a richness, but still the overall impression is bright, clean, clear flavors. Yummm! Wines that exhibit this flavor style are **Sauvignon Blancs**, **Pinot Grigios**, and unoaked **Chardonnays**.

Risottos have become a signature dish of the wine country. They are infinitely versatile, and I particularly like the addition of seasonal vegetables. The spring asparagus used here must be young and tender, since it's added at the last minute and barely cooked.

In a medium saucepan, melt the butter over medium heat and sauté the shallots until soft but not brown. Add the rice and mushrooms and cook, stirring often, until rice is translucent, about 3 minutes.

Add the roasted garlic, wine, and enough stock to cover rice mixture and cook, stirring constantly, until liquid is nearly absorbed. Continue adding hot stock in this manner, stirring all the time and letting the rice absorb the stock before adding more. Begin testing the rice after about 12 minutes. You're looking for the rice to be creamy and not gummy. The center of each rice grain should still have some texture and bite (al dente). This will take 16 to 18 minutes total. Stir in the asparagus and cook for a minute of two longer. Then stir in the lemon zest, chives, and cheese. Season to taste with salt, pepper, and drops of lemon juice. Serve in warm bowls, garnished with shaved Parmesan cheese and deep-fried basil sprigs, if using.

Note: To deep-fry basil or any leafy herb, wash and carefully dry the leaves or sprigs. In a sauce pan, heat ½ inch olive or canola oil over medium heat until it just shimmers (350°F). Drop the sprigs into hot oil and be careful—even when dry they will spatter. You'll see them change color just a bit. Turn and continue to cook until crisp but not browned. The whole process should take less than a minute. Drain and place on a folded paper towel to absorb the oil. The herbs can be fried an hour or two ahead.

If I had to choose only one food to live on, it would be rice. Although rice is an important agricultural crop in California, Americans are way behind the rest of the world in consumption. Happily, the popularity of rice has increased dramatically in recent years, due in great part to dishes like risotto.

Anyone who can cook can make risotto. Marie Simmons, in her insightful book *Rice, the Amazing Grain*, succinctly describes the process: "To make risotto the rice is first sautéed in fat and then simmering broth is added slowly while the mixture is stirred. The rice expands as it absorbs the broth, and the friction of the stirring softens the outside of the grain, forming a creamy almost sauce-like consistency. The center of the rice remains firm to the bite or al dente." That's all it takes. You can experiment with different broths and additions (vegetables, cheeses, bits of meat), but don't improvise with the process.

The key to good risotto is the right variety of rice. Classically, Italian Arborio is used, but you can make a wonderful risotto with California medium-grain rice. The primary differences between Italian and California rice are in the sturdiness of the grain and the price, since the Italian is much more expensive. California medium-grain rice is softer and not as sturdy as Italian Arborio. If you decide to use it, stir only occasionally and add the liquid in no more than three doses, rather than a half cup at a time. If you stir California rice too much it becomes soft and mushy and loses the classic risotto bite.

Since making risotto typically takes 25 to 30 minutes of steady stirring, home cooks sometimes consider it impractical both for entertaining and for family dinners. Not so! It's a great excuse to get everybody in the kitchen with you. Also, a trick used in restaurants is to prepare the risotto in two stages: Cook it to the point where half the liquid has been added; then spread the rice out as thinly as possible on a baking sheet to cool. It can keep this way covered in the refrigerator for up to a day. To complete the risotto, return the rice to the pan and continue adding the remaining liquid in appropriate increments. The goal for great risotto is to have every grain soft and creamy on the outside from the steady stirring but still with a little bit of texture on the inside so that it will keep its shape. When risotto gets to that point you must sit down and eat it. Wait 10 minutes and it continues to slowly cook, turning into what Julia Child might have called a "mucilaginous mush"!

CARROT RISOTTO

Serves 6

3 tablespoons unsalted butter

½ cup minced shallots

1½ cups Arborio rice

½ cup dry white wine

1½ cups grated carrots

5 to 6 cups Vegetable Stock (page 69), heated

2 tablespoons minced fresh parsley

2 tablespoons minced fresh tarragon

1 tablespoon minced fresh marjoram

½ cup freshly grated Parmesan cheese

2 tablespoons fresh lemon juice

Sautéed wild mushrooms, such as oyster or chanterelle for garnishing (optional)

RECOMMENDED WINE
The sweetness of the carrots goes well with a white or red with just a touch of residual sugar, such as **Gewürztraminer** or **Gamay**.

Carrots add a sweetness and beautiful orange color to this risotto. The addition of the lemon juice helps balance that sweetness. I have included an alternative version, for the fun of it, that uses fresh fennel and carrot juices in place of the vegetable stock.

In a medium saucepan, melt the butter over medium heat and sauté the shallots until soft but not brown. Add the rice and sauté evenly until rice is translucent, about 3 minutes. Add the wine and stir over medium heat until it is absorbed. Stir in the carrots and begin adding the hot stock by ½-cup increments, stirring constantly. When each addition is absorbed, add the next ½ cup, until the stock is mostly (or all) incorporated and the risotto is creamy but not overcooked. Stir in the parsley, tarragon, marjoram, and the Parmesan cheese. Add the lemon juice to taste. Serve garnished with wild mushrooms, if using.

Variation: For a richer wintertime version (and another use for your juicer), substitute the following for 3½ cups of the vegetable broth (follow instructions for whatever juices you may have).

1¾ cups fresh carrot juice

1¾ cups fresh fennel juice

1½ cups grated carrots, reserved until the end of the recipe

Combine the vegetable juices with 1½ to 2½ cups stock and heat to a simmer. Proceed as above. Add the grated carrots at the end along with the herbs and Parmesan cheese.

NEW WORLD RISOTTO

Serves 6 to 8

RECOMMENDED WINE
A complex barrel-aged wine like **Chardonnay**, **Pinot Blanc**, or **Viognier** would be a great match for this dish, especially if you decide to go whole-hog and use the corn broth.

4 tablespoons olive oil

1 cup minced onion

¼ cup slivered garlic

1½ cups Arborio rice

1 teaspoon toasted cumin seeds

¼ teaspoon red pepper flakes

½ cup dry white wine

5 to 6 cups Corn Stock (page 69) or Vegetable Stock (page 69), heated

2 cups corn kernels (2 large ears)

½ cup diced tomatillos

¼ cup diced red bell pepper

¼ cup diced yellow bell pepper

½ cup sliced tiny rounds green beans

½ cup diced yellow squash

½ cup freshly grated dry Jack, Parmesan, or Asiago cheese, or a combination

¼ cup chopped fresh cilantro

Kosher or sea salt and freshly ground pepper

Carrot-Corn Broth (facing page)

Deep-fried basil sprigs (see page 135) for garnishing (optional)

"New World" in this recipe refers to the ingredients that were unique to the Americas. Margaret Visser in her book Much Depends on Dinner *notes how, over and over again, early explorers were amazed at the ingenuity and efficiency of the native farmers. Iroquois and other tribes would prepare the earth in mounds and plant corn. A few days later they would plant beans and squash. When the plants emerged from the mound, the corn grew straight and strong, the beans climbed the corn, and the squash trailed down the side of the mound and covered the flat land between, keeping it shaded and moist. This recipe honors that kinship of these three ingredients and includes others from the New World larder. I've added the Carrot-Corn Broth to this recipe, but the risotto is equally good without it. I'm just gilding the lily and also encouraging you to use that juicer!*

In a deep saucepan, heat the olive oil over medium heat and sauté the onions and garlic until soft but not brown. Add the rice, stir to coat with oil, and sauté until the rice is opaque, about 3 minutes. Add the cumin seeds and pepper flakes.

Add the wine and cook until all the liquid is absorbed. Add the hot stock in ½-cup portions, stirring after each addition until the liquid is almost absorbed. When the risotto is almost done, and you judge that only a couple more additions are needed, add the corn, tomatillos, red bell pepper, yellow bell pepper, green beans, and squash. Continue stirring and adding stock until the vegetables are tender and the rice is creamy but not overcooked. Stir in the cheese and cilantro. Season to taste with salt and pepper. Scoop into the center of warm soup bowls, surrounded by a small ladle of the Carrot-Corn Broth. Top with basil sprigs (if using), and serve immediately.

CARROT-CORN BROTH
Makes 2 cups

¾ cup corn juice (4 cups sweet corn kernels, cut
  from 4 large ears)

1 cup carrot juice (12 ounces carrots)

1½ tablespoons unsalted butter at room
  temperature

Drops of hot sauce

Kosher or sea salt and freshly ground pepper

In a small saucepan, warm the corn juice and carrot juice over medium heat to just below the simmer. Whisk in the butter and drops of hot sauce. Season to taste with salt and pepper. Keep warm.

Note: For variation, you can add poached garlic (see page 264) to the carrots to be juiced, substitute red bell pepper juice for some of the carrot juice, or add an infusion of saffron simmered for a few minutes in a little white wine. If I feel really decadent, I substitute 2 teaspoons of truffle oil for the butter.

SUN-DRIED TOMATO AND OLIVE RISOTTO

Serves 4 to 6

RECOMMENDED WINE
This is a rich dish that can, because of the olives and sun-dried tomatoes, match up well with a hearty red wine. My favorite match would be with a peppery California **Zinfandel**. The fresh mint is also a flavor echo in **Cabernet**.

4 tablespoons extra-virgin olive oil

1 cup minced white onion

1 tablespoon minced garlic

2 cups Arborio rice

1 cup dry white wine

5 to 6 cups rich Chicken Stock (page 66) or Vegetable Stock (page 69), heated

¾ cup peeled, seeded, and diced plum tomatoes

⅓ cup drained and slivered, oil-packed sun-dried tomatoes

¼ cup chopped Kalamata, Niçoise, or other oil-cured olives

1 tablespoon small capers, rinsed

⅓ cup loosely packed mint leaves, chopped

2 tablespoons chopped fresh parsley

1 cup freshly grated Parmesan or pecorino cheese

Freshly ground pepper

Fresh mint sprigs for garnishing

Sun-dried tomatoes can vary widely in both sweetness and saltiness. Those from Italy often are a lot saltier than those produced in California. If the olives seem excessively salty, rinse them before adding. If you decide to use pecorino, remember that it is often pretty salty, too. The point I'm obviously trying to make here is to be aware of the salt in this dish.

In a large saucepan, heat the olive oil over medium heat and sauté the onion and garlic until soft but not brown. Add the rice and stir, coating the rice grains with the oil, for 5 minutes or so. The grains will turn opaque and "click" against the side of the pan.

Add the wine and stir and cook until the liquid is absorbed. Add the hot stock in ½-cup increments, stirring until the liquid is almost all absorbed. Continue until the stock is mostly (or all) incorporated and the risotto is creamy but not overcooked. Add the plum tomatoes, sun-dried tomatoes, olives, capers, mint, and parsley and cook for a minute or two to warm through. Stir in the cheese along with a grinding or two of pepper and serve immediately in warm bowls, garnished with mint sprigs.

RISOTTO WITH GRILLED RADICCHIO

Serves 6 to 8

2 tablespoons extra-virgin olive oil

1 medium head (8 to 10 ounces) fresh radicchio, quartered

Kosher or sea salt and freshly ground pepper

3 tablespoons unsalted butter

1 large red onion, finely chopped (about 2 cups)

1 tablespoon finely sliced garlic

2 cups Arborio or other superfino rice, such as Carnaroli or Vialone Nano

½ cup dry white wine

5 to 6 cups good-quality Chicken Stock (page 66) or Vegetable Stock (page 69), heated

1 cup freshly grated Parmigiano-Reggiano cheese, plus additional for garnish

1 tablespoon finely grated lemon zest

3 tablespoons lightly toasted pine nuts (optional)

RECOMMENDED WINE
The smoky radicchio and buttery cheese would be great with a peppery **Zinfandel** or a red Italian varietal like **Sangiovese**, **Barbera**, or **Dolcetto** from Italy or California.

Radicchio adds a pleasant little bitter bite to the rich risotto. Grilling it adds a little smokiness and tempers the bitterness a bit. A little finely diced and crisp-cooked pancetta is a nice addition stirred in just before serving.

Brush or drizzle the olive oil on the radicchio and season lightly with salt and pepper. On a medium-hot grill or in a stove-top grill pan, grill the radicchio until lightly colored and just beginning to soften, 3 to 4 minutes total. You want the radicchio to still have a bit of texture. Cool and slice the radicchio very finely and set aside.

In a large skillet, melt the butter over medium heat and sauté the onion and garlic until soft but not brown, about 4 minutes. Add the rice and stir to coat with the butter, cooking for about 3 minutes until rice begins to turn opaque. Stir in the wine and enough stock to cover rice. Continue to stir until most of the liquid has been absorbed and then add another cup of hot broth, stirring until nearly absorbed. Continue in this manner until the rice is al dente, tender but still firm in the center. This will take about 18 to 20 minutes.

Stir in half the radicchio, 1 cup cheese, and lemon zest. Season to taste with salt and pepper. Scatter the remaining radicchio and the pine nuts, if using, over the top and serve immediately, passing additional cheese.

FISH *and* SHELLFISH

FISH *and* WINE

There is a wonderful affinity between wine and fish and shellfish. The delicate flavors of fish usually call for subtle white wines, but earthy ingredients — wild mushrooms, tomatoes, bay leaves, olives — and cooking techniques such as grilling can make fish and shellfish perfect with a red wine, too.

Rich shellfish stews are another example of red wine–friendly fish dishes. In fact, most fish preparations that are in the Mediterranean style or influenced by Mediterranean cooking have an affinity for lighter-style red wines. I've been asked a few times what my last meal would be if I had a choice. There's no question—a piece of grilled wild king salmon and a glass of good California Pinot Noir.

A note on the recipes in this section (and throughout the book): You'll notice that many of the recipes contain marinades plus a sauce or two. Please don't be deterred by the length of some of the recipes. I've given you the elements that I like to assemble for the final dish, but the results will be (nearly!) as good if you choose to prepare only one or two of the elements. For example, Grilled Salmon with Roasted White Corn Salsa and Warm Basil Cream (page 150) is terrific unmarinated and accompanied with either the salsa or the basil cream.

EATING RESPONSIBLY AND SUSTAINABLY FROM THE SEA

For a number of years I've been honored to be part of a yearly weekend program put on in May by the Monterey Bay Aquarium in Monterey, California, called "Cooking for Solutions." This program highlights the aquarium's educational initiative, "Seafood Watch Consumer Guide." The aim of this program is to raise consumer awareness about the importance of choosing sustainably harvested or farmed seafood in markets and restaurants. On a wallet-sized card called "Choices for Healthy Oceans," they recommend which seafoods to buy or avoid, helping consumers to become active proponents of environmentally friendly seafood.

Why should we care? Well, what's happened is that the increased consumer demand for seafood is depleting fish stocks around the world and harming the health of the oceans. Today, according to the U.N. Food and Agriculture Organization, nearly 70 percent of the world's fisheries are fully fished or overfished. Consumer purchasing power can support sustainable fisheries and fish farms while relieving pressure on overfished populations. In other words, the choice you make when you purchase seafood is an important vote for the future health of the oceans.

What does it mean to be sustainable? Sustainable seafood is fish or shellfish caught or farmed in ways that can be practiced now and in the future, without jeopardizing the survival of any species or the integrity of the ecosystem. See page 425 for more information and resources for seafood sustainability.

SMOKED SALMON CHEESECAKE WITH A WALNUT CRUST

Serves 12

CRUST

2 cups panko or other coarse, dry bread crumbs

¾ cup finely chopped toasted walnuts

¼ cup finely grated Parmesan or Asiago cheese

1 tablespoon chopped fresh dill or
   1 teaspoon dried

⅓ cup unsalted butter, melted, plus more for
   the pan

FILLING

3 tablespoons unsalted butter

1 yellow onion, minced

1¾ pounds cream cheese at room temperature

⅓ cup half-and-half

⅔ cup grated Gruyère or Asiago cheese

½ teaspoon kosher or sea salt

¼ teaspoon freshly ground white pepper

4 large eggs, separated

8 ounces good-quality smoked salmon,
   finely chopped

RECOMMENDED WINE

This rich cheesecake probably needs a wine of some richness too, like a barrel-fermented and aged **Chardonnay** or **Pinot Blanc**.

This makes an elegant first course or lunch main course. For lunch, a small slice of this rich, savory cheesecake with a salad of baby greens would be plenty. When this cake is ready to take from the oven, a toothpick inserted in the center will come out clean.

To make the crust: In a medium bowl, combine the bread crumbs, walnuts, Parmesan cheese, and dill and stir gently. Drizzle the butter in slowly while stirring to lightly coat the bread crumbs. They should still be loose and not compacted. Press the crumb mixture into the bottom and up the sides of a buttered 9-inch springform pan. (The crust will not come all the way up the sides of the pan.) Refrigerate.

To make the filling: Preheat the oven to 350°F. In a small sauté pan, melt the butter and sauté the onion until soft but not brown. Set aside. Using an electric mixer fitted with the paddle attachment, or by hand with a wooden spoon, in a large bowl blend the cream cheese, half-and-half, sautéed onion, cheese, and salt and pepper until smooth. Beat in the egg yolks one at a time. In a separate medium bowl, beat the egg whites to stiff but not dry peaks. Fold in the salmon. Carefully fold the beaten whites into the cream cheese mixture. (It should have the consistency of a thick batter. If it's too stiff, add a little milk or cream.) Pour into the prepared pan. Bake for 1 hour and 10 minutes or until set. Remove from the oven and allow to cool in the pan.

Remove the ring from the springform pan and cut the cheesecake into slices with a warm knife. Serve at room temperature.

FISH TACOS WITH CITRUS SALSA AND CABBAGE SLAW

Serves 4

RECOMMENDED WINE
A light, fruity well-chilled white wine, such as a **Chenin Blanc**, **Riesling**, or **Sémillon**, would hit the mark with this dish.

⅓ cup olive oil

1 tablespoon pure chile powder, such as ancho or chipotle

1 tablespoon fresh lime juice

Kosher or sea salt and freshly ground pepper

1½ pounds skinless fillets of halibut, sea bass, or tuna

8 flour or corn tortillas, freshly grilled or steamed

Cabbage Slaw (recipe follows)

Citrus Salsa (facing page)

Cilantro Aioli (facing page)

Fresh cilantro sprigs

Fish tacos have become all the rage in recent years, especially in southern California and Baja California, where they originated. This is a delicious recipe in which all of the components can be made ahead of time and the fish grilled at the last moment. The Cabbage Slaw, Citrus Salsa, and Cilantro Aioli are sort of a "gilding of the lily" as Grandmother would have said. Traditionally, finely shaved cabbage and radishes, a squeeze of lime, and a squirt of crema or sour cream would be what you'd get, and you could certainly go that simpler route here, too.

Prepare a charcoal fire or preheat a stove-top grill. In a small bowl, whisk together the olive oil, chile powder, and lime juice and season to taste with salt and pepper. Brush liberally on the fillets. Grill the fish until it is just done. Put a warm grilled tortilla on each plate. Top with the Cabbage Slaw, a portion of the grilled fish, a heaping tablespoon or two of the Citrus Salsa, a spoonful of the Cilantro Aioli, and a sprig or two of cilantro. Fold over and eat immediately.

~~~~~~

CABBAGE SLAW

4 cups finely shredded green cabbage

2 tablespoons kosher or sea salt

⅓ cup thinly sliced red bell pepper

⅓ cup thinly sliced red onion

¼ cup finely sliced fresh mint or basil

2 tablespoons seasoned rice wine vinegar

1 to 2 tablespoons fresh lime or lemon juice

1 teaspoon sugar

1 tablespoon olive oil

Freshly ground pepper

In a colander, toss together the cabbage and salt, put a plate on top, and weight it with heavy cans or a bag of sugar. Let drain at room temperature for at least 2 hours. Rinse and drain cabbage and pat it dry. In a medium bowl, combine the the cabbage with the bell pepper, red onion, and mint. In a small bowl, whisk together the vinegar, lime juice, sugar, and olive oil until the sugar has dissolved. Season to taste with pepper. Toss with the cabbage mixture and refrigerate. Can be made up to 24 hours in advance.

CITRUS SALSA

3 large navel oranges, peeled and segmented

1 lemon, peeled and segmented

1 lime, peeled and segmented

2 teaspoons chopped fresh cilantro

1 teaspoon seeded and minced serrano chile

2 teaspoons seasoned rice wine vinegar

1 tablespoon olive oil

Kosher or sea salt and freshly ground pepper

In a medium bowl, combine the orange, lemon, and lime segments. Add the cilantro, chile, vinegar, and olive oil and gently toss to combine. Season to taste with salt and pepper.

CILANTRO AIOLI

1 teaspoon rinsed capers

½ cup packed chopped fresh cilantro

1 tablespoon minced blanched garlic or roasted garlic (see page 264)

4 tablespoons minced green onions, green part only

1 teaspoon seeded and minced serrano chile

1 large egg

½ cup olive oil

Kosher or sea salt and freshly ground pepper

In a blender, combine the capers, cilantro, garlic, green onions, chile, and egg and purée. With the motor running, slowly drizzle in the olive oil until the aioli is emulsified. Scoop the aioli into a small bowl and season with salt and pepper to taste. This may be prepared a day in advance and kept tightly covered in the refrigerator.

JAPANESE-STYLE GRILLED SALMON WITH SOBA NOODLE SALAD

Serves 4

RECOMMENDED WINE
Soft reds like **Pinot Noir** or **Merlot** are nice with this salmon as long as you don't allow it to become too sweet. A drier-style **Gewürztraminer** or **Riesling** is also delicious with this dish.

MARINADE

¼ cup soy sauce

¼ cup sake or dry white wine

¼ cup mirin

2 tablespoons sugar

3 tablespoons chopped green onion, both white and green parts

3 tablespoons peeled and chopped fresh ginger

Grated zest and juice of 1 small lemon

Four 5-ounce fillets of salmon, with skin on

Soba Noodle Salad (facing page)

This approach with salmon works equally well on fresh halibut or sea bass. I serve the resulting fish hot or at room temperature, either as the center of the plate or as part of a salad. If you are doing this fish on the barbeque, a technique that I find helpful is to place the fish skin side down on a sheet of heavy aluminum foil and cook it indirectly and covered over medium heat. The foil prevents the fish from sticking or burning caused by the sugar in the marinade. If you are broiling, do the same thing and be careful not to get the fish too close to the broiler element so that it can cook without burning. I'd allow at least 4 inches between the fish and the heat source.

To make the marinade: In a medium bowl, combine the soy sauce, sake, mirin, sugar, green onion, ginger, lemon zest, and lemon juice, stirring to dissolve the sugar. In a medium bowl, pour the marinade over the fish and marinate in the refrigerator for 2 to 4 hours. Turn the fish occasionally.

Prepare a charcoal grill or preheat a broiler. Remove the fish from the marinade and pat dry. Grill or broil on both sides until just done, about 4 to 5 minutes per side. Be careful not to overcook. Salmon should still be translucent in the center. Serve warm or at room temperature, with the Soba Noodle Salad.

SOBA NOODLE SALAD

DRESSING

¼ cup dashi or fat-free chicken stock

¼ cup soy sauce

⅓ cup rice vinegar

1 tablespoon sugar

2 teaspoons toasted sesame oil

SALAD

4 ounces dried soba noodles

½ cup finely julienned daikon or breakfast radishes

1 cup loosely packed daikon radish sprouts

¾ cup diagonally sliced green onions, both white and green parts

1 tablespoon toasted sesame seeds

Japanese seven-spice powder (optional)

To make the dressing: In a small bowl, combine the dashi, soy sauce, vinegar, sugar, and sesame oil.

To make the salad: In a large pot, bring 2 quarts lightly salted water to a boil over high heat. Separate the noodles and drop them into the boiling water, stirring once or twice. When the water begins to boil, add 1 cup cold water. Repeat this procedure twice, cooking until the noodles are just tender, 3 to 4 minutes. Drain in a colander. Rinse with cold water until completely cooled, rubbing gently with your hands to remove all surface starch, and drain well.

Toss the noodles with the dressing and arrange the daikon, sprouts, green onions, sesame seeds, and a dash of seven-spice powder, if using, over the top.

GRILLED SALMON WITH ROASTED WHITE CORN SALSA AND WARM BASIL CREAM

Serves 6

RECOMMENDED WINE
Chardonnay seems to have a special affinity for sweet corn, so in concert with the salmon's richness and the creamy texture of the sauce, a well-balanced Chardonnay would be delicious here.

4 tablespoons olive oil

1 tablespoon finely grated lemon zest

2 tablespoons chopped fresh mint

Six 6-ounce ½-inch-thick wild salmon fillets or steaks

Kosher or sea salt and freshly ground pepper

Roasted White Corn Salsa (facing page)

Warm Basil Cream (facing page)

Fresh cilantro or mint sprigs for garnishing

This dish epitomizes cooking in the wine country. Of course, our California wild-caught king salmon is the salmon of choice here (no farm raised!). The Roasted White Corn Salsa can be made a day ahead, but the Warm Basil Cream needs to be made just before serving.

In a small bowl, whisk together the olive oil, lemon zest, and mint. Rub the mixture over the salmon and liberally season with salt and pepper. Marinate the salmon for 1 hour in the refrigerator.

Prepare the grill. Remove the fish from the marinade, pat dry, and grill until just done, about 4 to 5 minutes per side. Place on warm plates with a heaping tablespoon or two of Roasted White Corn Salsa on top, warm Basil Cream all around, and a garnish of herb sprigs.

ROASTED WHITE CORN SALSA
Makes about 2½ cups

2 cups sweet white corn kernels (2 large ears)

¼ cup olive oil

Kosher or sea salt and freshly ground pepper

⅓ cup finely diced red bell pepper

⅓ cup finely diced red onion

⅓ cup chopped fresh cilantro or basil, or
   a combination

1 teaspoon seeded and minced serrano chile

1 tablespoon sherry or cider vinegar

1 teaspoon fresh lemon juice

1 teaspoon honey

Preheat the oven to 425°F. Toss the corn with the olive oil and lightly season with salt and pepper. Spread out in a single layer on a baking sheet and roast in the oven until very lightly browned. Alternatively, you can grill the ears of corn over coals or on a stove-top grill pan until colored and then cut kernels from the cob. In a medium bowl, combine the corn, bell pepper, red onion, cilantro, chile, vinegar, lemon juice, and honey. Cover and store in the refrigerator for up to 3 days.

WARM BASIL CREAM
Makes about 1¼ cups

1 tablespoon olive oil

¼ cup chopped shallots or green onions, white
   part only

2 tablespoons chopped garlic

½ cup dry white wine

2 cups rich shellfish or chicken stock

¼ teaspoon fennel seeds

1 cup heavy (whipping) cream

1½ cups lightly packed fresh basil leaves

Kosher or sea salt and freshly ground pepper

Fresh lemon juice for seasoning

½ cup peeled, seeded, and finely diced Roma
   tomatoes (optional)

In a saucepan, heat the olive oil and sauté the shallots and garlic until soft but not brown. Add the wine, stock, and fennel seeds, bring to a boil, and reduce by half. Add the cream and reduce to a light sauce consistency. Strain and add to a blender.

Blanch the basil leaves momentarily in boiling salted water then plunge immediately into ice water to stop the cooking and set the color. Squeeze dry. Add the blanched basil to the blender and process until smooth. Return the contents to the saucepan and keep warm. Season to taste with salt, pepper, and drops of lemon juice. Stir in the tomatoes just before serving, if using.

*farmed versus
wild fish*

As more of the world's waters are overfished or become polluted, we see the growth of farm-raised fish. Most of the salmon offered in our markets today is farm-raised. Is one better than the other?

Almost all cooks I know who have had experience with both would without question pick a wild salmon over a farm-raised one. The texture and flavor are better, and the wild salmon is also less fatty than its farm-raised cousin.

The downside to farm-raised salmon from both an ecological and a health standpoint unfortunately has been widely documented. See page 425 for all the latest information. A final thought here: Not all farm-raised fish and shellfish are bad. There are many success stories of ethical aquaculture.

SALMON CURED WITH TEQUILA AND HERBS

Servings will depend on its use

RECOMMENDED WINE
I'd choose either a crisp sparkling wine or a lean, crisp **Sauvignon Blanc**, a **Pinot Gris** with good acidity and herbal highlights, or one of the increasingly available unoaked **Chardonnays**.

One 3-to-4-pound salmon fillet, all bones removed, skin on

¼ cup kosher or sea salt

3 tablespoons sugar

1 tablespoon grated lemon zest

2 teaspoons freshly ground pepper

⅔ cup mixed fresh herbs, such as basil, tarragon, parsley, chives, mint, chervil, and cilantro

⅓ cup good tequila

This preparation, essentially a New World gravlax, is delicious. I like to use the thinly sliced salmon for canapés and to layer on warm grilled flat bread with a scattering of thinly sliced sweet red onions, fresh salmon caviar, and a dollop of good sour cream or Crème Fraîche (page 37). This salmon is also delicious used to make those wonderful old-fashioned tea sandwiches with fresh herb butter and thinly sliced cucumbers.

Line a pan just large enough to hold the salmon with a layer of cheesecloth. Lay the salmon on top of the cheesecloth, skin-side down.

Mix the salt, sugar, lemon zest, and pepper and sprinkle evenly over the salmon. Chop the herbs coarsely and scatter over the fish. Wrap tightly in cheesecloth and sprinkle with the tequila. Turn the fish skin-side up and cover with plastic wrap. Put in the refrigerator and allow to cure for 2 to 3 days.

Gently wipe off the marinade ingredients and slice very thinly on an angle, leaving the skin behind.

Note: To give the salmon a firmer texture, put a smaller pan or tray, weighted with bricks or canned goods, on top of the wrapped salmon while it's curing.

SALMON IN A FENNEL CRUST WITH A ROASTED RED PEPPER–BLOOD ORANGE VINAIGRETTE

Serves 4

1½ tablespoons crushed fennel seeds

½ teaspoon crushed white peppercorns

1 teaspoon kosher or sea salt

Four 6-ounce ½-inch-thick salmon fillets or steaks

3 tablespoons olive oil

4 cups lightly packed mixed baby salad greens

Roasted Red Pepper–Blood Orange Vinaigrette (recipe follows)

RECOMMENDED WINE
This full-flavored recipe requires a complex, rich white wine, such as a **Chardonnay**, or a red wine with lots of flavor but not a lot of tannins, like **Pinot Noir** or **Merlot**.

The flavors of fennel seeds, roasted peppers, and blood oranges somehow express the cooking of the wine country. If blood oranges are not available, regular oranges or pink grapefruit can be substituted. The recipe makes more vinaigrette than you'll probably use—save it for another salad. It also make a delicious marinade for fish or chicken.

In a small bowl, combine the crushed fennel seeds, peppercorns, and salt. Rub the salmon with 1 tablespoon of the olive oil and lightly coat both sides of the salmon with the spice mixture. In a large sauté pan, heat the remaining olive oil over medium heat. Sauté the salmon and cook until lightly browned, about 4 minutes. Turn and brown on the other side for 2 to 3 minutes or until just cooked through. The salmon should still be pink in the center. Toss the greens with some of the vinaigrette and place on plates. Top with the salmon and serve.

blood oranges

Until recent years, blood oranges were grown almost exclusively around the Mediterranean; now they are grown fairly extensively in California. Their name is derived from the color of their flesh, which can range from rosy to very deep burgundy. Blood oranges have a unique tart-sweet flavor and are definitely worth seeking out.

ROASTED RED PEPPER–BLOOD ORANGE VINAIGRETTE

1 large red bell pepper, roasted, peeled, and chopped

1 tablespoon finely chopped shallot or green onion, white part only

⅔ cup blood orange juice

½ teaspoon crushed fennel seeds

2 teaspoons minced fresh thyme or 1 teaspoon dried

1 tablespoon sherry vinegar

2 tablespoons toasted hazelnut oil (optional)

⅔ cup extra-virgin olive oil

Kosher or sea salt and freshly ground white pepper

In a blender, combine the bell pepper, shallot, orange juice, fennel seeds, thyme, sherry vinegar, and hazelnut oil (if using), and purée. With the motor running, slowly add the olive oil to emulsify and thicken—you may not need to use all of it. Season to taste with salt and white pepper. If too thick, thin with additional orange juice.

SALMON CAKES

Serves 8 as an appetizer

RECOMMENDED WINE
These meaty, succulent salmon cakes would be wonderful with a soft red or **rosé** wine or a buttery Chardonnay.

8 ounces fresh salmon filet, skinned and boned

2 ounces fresh uncooked shrimp

1 large egg white, beaten

2 tablespoons finely diced red or yellow bell pepper, or a combination

1 tablespoon finely chopped green onion, both white and green parts

2 teaspoons finely grated lemon zest

½ teaspoon seeded and minced jalapeño chile

2 teaspoons mayonnaise

2 teaspoons rinsed and chopped capers

⅓ cup panko or other coarse dry bread crumbs, plus additional for dredging

Kosher or sea salt and freshly ground pepper to taste

Olive oil for sautéing

Since we use a lot of salmon in the wine country, there always seem to be a few small pieces left over. I developed this recipe to take advantage of those tidbits. I often serve these cakes on a bed of savory salad greens and garnish them with a dollop of aioli or one of the other homemade mayonnaises. You'll note that I call for the salmon to be both diced and finely chopped. This gives some texture to the finished cake.

Divide the salmon in half. Cut half the salmon into ¼-inch dice and very finely chop the other half. Cut the shrimp into ¼-inch dice. In a medium bowl, combine the diced salmon, chopped salmon, shrimp, egg white, bell pepper, green onion, lemon zest, chile, mayonnaise, capers, and the ⅓ cup bread crumbs. It should just hold together and at the same time not be too dense and heavy. Add more bread crumbs or mayonnaise if needed. Season to taste with salt and pepper. Divide the mixture and pat to form into 8 cakes no thicker than 1 inch. (The salmon cakes may be prepared in advance to this point. Store, uncovered, in the refrigerator for up to 4 hours.) Season more bread crumbs with salt and pepper and dredge the salmon cakes. In a large sauté pan, pour in olive oil to a depth of ⅛ inch. Heat the oil and sauté the cakes until golden brown, about 3 minutes per side.

SEARED AHI TUNA WITH A LAVENDER-PEPPER CRUST

Serves 8

1½ pounds center-cut ahi tuna

1 teaspoon kosher or sea salt

2 teaspoons black peppercorns

1 teaspoon white peppercorns

2 teaspoons fennel seeds

1½ teaspoons dried lavender flowers

3 tablespoons olive oil

4 cups savory greens and fresh herbs, such as mâche, arugula, cress, and chervil

Mustard Seed Dressing (recipe follows)

Deep-fried basil leaves (see page 135) for garnishing (optional)

(see page 135)

RECOMMENDED WINE
A crisp **Sauvignon Blanc** would match up with the acidity and herbal flavors in this dish. A fruity **Pinot Noir** or **Grenache** would also work nicely if you want to serve a red wine.

This makes an elegant first course using our old tuna friend, "ahi," as the Hawaiians call it, or yellowfin. The crust is especially interesting because of the lavender, a highly aromatic flower usually used in cosmetics. In moderation, it's also an interesting culinary herb, being one of the key ingredients in the French herbes de Provence mixture. I also use this mixture on beef steaks, such as filets, cooked rare.

Trim and cut the tuna into strips approximately 2 inches thick and 2 inches wide. Using a mortar and pestle, rolling pin, or a spice grinder, finely crush the salt, black peppercorns, white peppercorns, fennel seeds, and lavender. Lightly oil the tuna pieces with 2 teaspoons of the olive oil and coat lightly but evenly with the lavender-pepper mixture. In a skillet, heat the remaining olive oil over high heat and quickly sear the tuna on all sides, about 3 minutes, total. Don't overcook; the tuna should be very rare inside. Let the tuna rest for 5 to 10 minutes before slicing.

Attractively arrange the greens on chilled plates. Drizzle with Mustard Seed Dressing. Slice the tuna thinly and arrange on top of the dressed greens. Garnish with deep-fried basil leaves, if using.

MUSTARD SEED DRESSING
Makes about ⅔ cup

4 tablespoons whole-grain mustard

2 tablespoons olive oil

2 teaspoons toasted mustard seeds

2 tablespoons seasoned rice vinegar

3 tablespoons vegetable stock or water

1 teaspoon honey

Kosher or sea salt and freshly ground pepper

In a small bowl, whisk together the mustard, olive oil, mustard seeds, vinegar, stock, and honey. Season to taste with salt and pepper.

TUNA "SANDWICHES" WITH RAISINS, HERBS, AND CAPERS IN A FRESH TOMATO BROTH

Serves 4

RECOMMENDED WINE
Crisp whites like **Sauvignon Blanc** and **Pinot Gris** or **Pinot Grigio** would be great here. We're seeing initial experimentation in California with other whites from the Mediterranean, like **Vermentino**. Or try a soft red like **Pinot Noir** or **Carignane**, a variety that used to be planted widely in California and is still available. Look for Mediterranean counterparts that are widely produced.

½ cup extra-virgin olive oil

1 cup minced red onion

3 tablespoons minced garlic

3 tablespoons dry bread crumbs, preferably panko

2 tablespoons rinsed and finely chopped capers

3 tablespoons golden raisins, plumped in ½ cup water for 15 minutes, drained, and chopped

2 tablespoons chopped fresh parsley

2 teaspoons chopped fresh mint

1 tablespoon chopped fresh basil

⅓ cup freshly grated Parmesan cheese

Kosher or sea salt and freshly ground pepper

1½ pounds tuna, cut into eight 3-by-5-by-¼-inch pieces

2 tablespoons balsamic vinegar

Fresh Tomato Broth (facing page)

Fried herb sprigs, such as basil or parsley, and Basil Oil (page 80) for garnishing (optional)

Variations of this dish can be found all around southern Italy and Sicily. The flavor of the broth depends on using sweet ripe tomatoes. If your tomatoes are not up to snuff, try oven roasting them first to develop their flavor, or use good-quality canned tomatoes to make the juice. Ideally, the broth should be relatively clear. Tuna acceptable for this recipe are troll-caught bigeye or yellowfin. Ask your fishmonger to cut the slices specified in this recipe.

In a sauté pan, heat 3 tablespoons of the olive oil and sauté the onion and garlic until soft but not brown. Transfer the mixture to a medium bowl and stir in the bread crumbs, capers, raisins, parsley, mint, basil, and Parmesan cheese. Season to taste with salt and pepper. Toss the mixture with 2 tablespoons of the olive oil to lightly coat the bread crumbs. The mixture should just hold together when squeezed. If not, add a few more drops of oil. Lay 4 tuna slices out flat and spread them evenly with the mixture. Top with the remaining tuna slices and secure with toothpicks, if necessary. In a small bowl, whisk the remaining olive oil with the balsamic vinegar and brush the bundles generously with the mixture. Season to taste with salt and pepper. Can be prepared 3 hours ahead and stored, covered, in the refrigerator.

Grill the bundles over medium-hot coals, about 3 minutes per side. Alternatively, they can be broiled or pan roasted. Be careful not to overcook. Place the bundles in large, warm soup bowls and ladle the Fresh Tomato Broth around. Top with a fried herb sprig and drizzle Basil Oil over the broth, if using. Serve immediately.

FRESH TOMATO BROTH
Makes about 1¼ cups

1½ cups fresh tomato juice, all pulp and solids removed

⅔ cup rich shellfish or chicken stock

½ cup coarsely chopped fresh basil

Drops of fresh lemon juice

Kosher or sea salt and freshly ground white pepper

2 to 3 tablespoons unsalted butter at room temperature

In a small saucepan, bring the juice, stock, and basil to a gentle boil and cook for 5 minutes to reduce slightly and concentrate the flavors. Strain through a fine-mesh strainer. Season to taste with lemon juice, salt, and pepper. Whisk in the butter and keep warm.

GRILLED AHI TUNA WITH JAPANESE NOODLES, GINGER-SOY SAUCE, AND WASABI MOUSSE

Serves 4

RECOMMENDED WINE
A fruit-forward white wine like **Chenin Blanc** or **Gewürztraminer**, or a soft red with low tannins, such as **Gamay**, or a **rosé**, would be an ideal accompaniment to this Asian-influenced dish.

Four 1-inch-thick center-cut ahi tuna steaks

2 tablespoons olive oil

Kosher or sea salt and freshly ground pepper

1½ tablespoons minced garlic

2 tablespoons minced fresh ginger

½ teaspoon seeded and minced serrano chile or ¼ teaspoon red pepper flakes

½ teaspoon minced lemon zest

½ cup rice wine vinegar

⅓ cup low-sodium soy sauce

½ cup chicken stock, all fat removed

2 teaspoons sugar

1 pound soba or somen noodles

½ cup diagonally sliced green onions, both white and pale green parts

Wasabi Mousse (facing page)

Chive Mixture (facing page)

Ahi is yellowfin tuna, which is the tuna most often used in Japanese restaurants for sushi and sashimi. Its beautiful deep, dark red, firm-fleshed meat truly is the beef of the sea. "Ahi" is the term used in Hawaii to describe this variety of tuna, and I think it sounds more appealing than "yellowfin." I originally prepared this dish for an article on low-fat cooking in Bon Appètit *magazine. The recipe was coupled with the Five Lilies Chowder (page 74) and fresh fruits to provide a menu in which only 14 percent of the calories come from fat. (That version, however, didn't include the Wasabi Mousse.) Low fat isn't the only reason to try this: I think it's very tasty and it's simple! The Wasabi Mousse and the Chive Mixture may be made up to 2 hours in advance.*

Prepare a medium charcoal fire or preheat a stove-top grill.

Rub the tuna steaks with 1 teaspoon of the olive oil and lightly season with salt and pepper. Set aside. In a small saucepan, heat the remaining olive oil over medium heat and sauté the garlic and ginger until they just begin to color. Add the chile, lemon zest, vinegar, soy sauce, stock, and sugar and bring to a boil. Reduce slightly. Remove from the heat and set aside. Keep warm.

Cook the noodles in lightly salted boiling water until just al dente, according to package directions. Drain and transfer to a medium bowl. Toss with half the ginger–soy sauce mixture and with the green onions.

Grill the tuna on both sides until just done, about 2 to 3 minutes per side (the center should remain very pink). Remove and keep warm.

Serve the tuna steaks on a bed of the noodles and drizzle with the remaining ginger-soy sauce. Spoon a dollop of the Wasabi Mousse on the ahi and sprinkle with the Chive Mixture. Serve immediately.

WASABI MOUSSE

1½ teaspoons wasabi powder

½ cup heavy (whipping) cream

Kosher or sea salt

Fresh lemon juice

In a medium bowl, whisk the wasabi powder into the heavy cream. Lightly season with salt and drops of lemon juice. Whisk until the mixture is stiff.

CHIVE MIXTURE

2 tablespoons minced fresh chives

2 teaspoons minced lemon zest

2 teaspoons minced fresh mint

½ teaspoon seeded and minced serrano chile

In a small bowl, mix the chives, lemon zest, mint, and chile together.

TUNA SICILIAN STYLE WITH ROASTED CAULIFLOWER AND GREEN BEANS

Serves 4

RECOMMENDED WINE
A crisp white wine such as **Sauvignon Blanc**, or **Pinot Gris** or **Pinot Grigio**, would be terrific. Also seek out white regional varietals like **Vermentino**, **Fiano**, or **Greco**.

1 pound sushi-grade tuna, cut into ¾-inch cubes

⅓ cup fragrant extra-virgin olive oil

1 tablespoon thinly sliced garlic

¼ cup white wine vinegar

1 cup seeded and diced firm ripe tomato or halved cherry tomatoes

2 teaspoons finely grated lemon zest

1½ teaspoons dried oregano flowers or regular dried oregano

½ teaspoon red pepper flakes

Kosher or sea salt

Roasted Cauliflower (recipe follows)

8 ounces young, tender green beans, cooked crisp-tender in boiling salted water

2 tablespoons halved fresh young mint leaves

⅓ cup green olives, such as picholine

The flavors here are fresh and simple, and this dish can be made ahead. If you've never had roasted cauliflower — it will change your life! I've poached the tuna in water here, but you could also poach it for about 5 minutes in olive oil heated to 180°F.

In a large saucepan, bring 8 cups of lightly salted water to a boil. Drop the tuna into the water, lower the heat to a simmer, and cook for 1 minute. Drain and put in a single layer on a platter to cool.

In a small saucepan, heat the olive oil over medium heat and sauté the garlic until very lightly browned and crisp. Be careful not to overcook or the garlic will become bitter. Pour the garlic and olive oil into a medium bowl and cool. Stir in the vinegar, tomato, lemon zest, oregano, and pepper flakes. Season to taste with salt. Pour the marinade over the cooled tuna and set aside. Let stand for a couple of hours for the flavors to blend.

Arrange the Roasted Cauliflower, green beans, mint leaves, and olives attractively on a serving plate. Place the tuna mixture on top and pour the vinaigrette over.

~~~~~~

ROASTED CAULIFLOWER

1 small head cauliflower

⅓ cup fragrant walnut or extra-virgin olive oil

Kosher or sea salt and freshly ground pepper

Preheat the oven to 375°F. Remove the green leaves from the cauliflower and vertically cut into ½-inch-thick slices. Brush both sides of the slices liberally with the walnut oil and season lightly with salt and pepper. Lay the slices in a single layer on a clean, well-oiled baking sheet and roast in the oven for 25 to 30 minutes or until the top of the cauliflower is lightly browned and tender. The bottoms will be a deeper golden brown. Remove from the oven. Serve warm or at room temperature.

STURGEON WITH PANCETTA, CAPERS, PARSLEY, AND LEMON

Serves 6

2 tablespoons olive oil

4 ounces pancetta, cut into ¼-inch dice

Six 5-ounce sturgeon fillets

Kosher or sea salt and freshly ground pepper

¼ cup all-purpose flour

3 tablespoons minced shallots

1 tablespoon minced garlic

½ cup dry white wine

1 cup rich fish stock or shellfish stock

2 tablespoons fresh lemon juice

2 tablespoons unsalted butter

⅔ cup seeded and diced tomatoes

2 tablespoons minced fresh parsley

3 tablespoons rinsed capers

RECOMMENDED WINE

The smoky, salty flavors of the pancetta and capers require a crisp, citrus-tinged **Fumé Blanc** or **Sauvignon Blanc** for contrast.

capers

A staple of Mediterranean cooking since their introduction by the Greeks in 600 B.C., capers have a prominent place in wine country cuisine. They are pickled or salt-cured flower buds of the sun-loving caper shrub (a relative of the rose). They are hand-harvested during the early spring, which accounts for their relatively high cost. Their slightly bitter flavor, the reason we like them, comes from the formation of capric acid, which is developed when they are pickled or salted.

Sturgeon is a fish with excellent flavor. It is a great sport fish in California, although it is becoming scarce and is now farm raised in several locations, including the upper Sacramento River where it is raised to produce caviar. Caviars from the traditional sources in the Caspian and Black Seas are now banned in the United States, so as farms expand to produce more caviar we'll also see more sturgeon in the market. If you can't find sturgeon, any firm-fleshed fish, such as halibut, sea bass, mahi mahi, or domestic swordfish will do. Imported swordfish should not be used.

In a large sauté pan, heat the olive oil over medium heat and cook the pancetta until lightly browned. Remove and reserve.

Liberally season the sturgeon with salt and pepper and then dust with the flour. Sauté until golden brown on both sides and cooked through, about 8 minutes depending on thickness. Unlike salmon, sturgeon must be thoroughly cooked. Check with the point of a knife. Remove and keep warm.

Add the shallots and garlic and cook until softened, about 2 minutes. Add the wine, stock, and lemon juice and over high heat reduce to a light sauce consistency. Remove from the heat, whisk in the butter to form a light emulsion, and then stir in the tomatoes, parsley, capers, and pancetta. Season to taste with salt and pepper. Serve the fish on warm plates, topped with the sauce.

PACIFIC ROCK COD STEWED WITH ORANGES, TOMATOES, AND OLIVES

Serves 4

RECOMMENDED WINE
A crisp white wine with good acidity and some herbal notes would work well with this dish. Wines made in this style include most **Sauvignon Blancs**, unoaked **Chardonnays**, drier-style **Rieslings**, and **Pinot Grigio** or **Pinot Gris**. If you like red wine, choose one with low tannins and lots of fruit, like **Pinot Noir**.

2 tablespoons olive oil

2 cups thinly sliced red onions

1 tablespoon slivered garlic

1 cup canned diced tomatoes, including juice

¾ cup dry white wine

½ teaspoon kosher or sea salt

¼ teaspoon freshly ground pepper

3 tablespoons slivered Kalamata or Gaeta olives

2 large navel oranges, peeled and cut into segments

1 pound halibut or sea bass fillets

2 tablespoons chopped fresh chives and 2 ounces feta cheese, drained and thinly sliced, for garnishing (optional)

This is a recipe that I've always enjoyed because it's easily prepared. In California, rock cod (a rockfish, not a cod) is also known as "red snapper," another misnomer, since it bears no relationship to the true red snapper from the Gulf of Mexico. I think this name was originally a marketing ploy — "Pacific red snapper" sounds a lot more enticing and expensive than "red rock cod." Unfortunately, we've learned that rock cod caught off our California coast have been overfished, so choose a good firm white fish, such as halibut, sea bass, or even scallops, that is sustainably harvested. Hook and line–caught rock fish from Alaska and British Columbia are okay if you can find them.

In a large sauté pan, heat the olive oil over medium heat and sauté the onions and garlic, stirring occasionally, until the onions are just beginning to color, about 3 minutes.

Add the tomatoes, wine, salt, and pepper and bring to a boil. Reduce the heat and simmer for 2 minutes. Stir in the olives and oranges and lay the fillets over the mixture in a single layer, spooning some of the vegetable mixture over the top.

Cover and simmer until the fish is just cooked through, about 5 minutes. The time will depend on how thick the fish is. Garnish with chives and feta, if using.

HALIBUT IN A SPICY COCONUT BROTH

Serves 4

Four 6-ounce ¾-inch-thick fillets halibut

Kosher or sea salt and freshly ground pepper

3 tablespoons olive oil

1 cup chicken stock

1½ cups well-stirred coconut milk

½ cup Laksa Paste (recipe follows)

6 cups lightly packed young spinach

Daikon or other savory sprouts, such as sunflower, for garnishing

RECOMMENDED WINE
The coconut milk and curry spice are delicious with lower-alcohol (meaning those that have a little residual sugar after fermentation) aromatic white wines like California **Viognier** or **Riesling**.

This delicious dish can be made with any fresh, meaty, and sustainable fish. The spicy coconut milk–based curry mixture called laksa is originally from Indonesia and Malaysia; this is my California version.

Preheat the oven to 475°F. Pat the halibut dry and season lightly with salt and pepper. In an ovenproof sauté pan (preferably nonstick), heat 2 tablespoons of the olive oil over medium-high heat and quickly sauté the halibut on one side until nicely browned. Turn the fish over and put the pan in the oven for 4 to 5 minutes or until just cooked through.

While the fish is cooking, in a small saucepan, heat the stock and coconut milk and bring to a simmer. Stir in the Laksa Paste and keep warm.

In a large skillet, heat the remaining tablespoon of olive oil over medium-high heat and stir-fry the spinach until just beginning to wilt, about 1 minute. Place the spinach in the centers of warm shallow bowls and top with halibut. Ladle the broth around, top with sprouts, and serve immediately.

LAKSA PASTE
Makes about 1 cup

2 tablespoons Asian chile-garlic sauce

⅓ cup chopped shallots

⅓ cup chopped and toasted macadamia nuts or blanched almonds

¼ cup peeled and finely chopped fresh ginger

2 tablespoons coriander seeds, crushed

1 teaspoon shrimp paste or 2 tablespoon Asian fish sauce

Grated zest and juice of 2 limes

2 teaspoons sugar

2 tablespoons vegetable oil

1 teaspoon toasted sesame oil

½ cup coconut milk

In a blender, combine the chile-garlic sauce, shallots, macadamia nuts, ginger, coriander seeds, shrimp paste, lime zest, lime juice, sugar, vegetable oil, and sesame oil and process for a minute or two or until very smooth. In a small saucepan, cook the purée over medium heat for 4 to 5 minutes, stirring constantly. It should be very fragrant. Stir in the coconut milk and cook for 2 to 3 minutes more. Store, covered, in the refrigerator for up to 5 days, or freeze for up to 3 months.

Note: Chile-garlic sauce is available in Asian markets and the Asian section of some supermarkets. Lee Kum Kee from Hong Kong is a widely distributed brand.

SHELLFISH IN A SAFFRON-SCENTED STOCK

Serves 6

RECOMMENDED WINE
This is a rich dish that requires a rich wine. An elegant, barrel-aged **Chardonnay, Viognier,** or **Pinot Blanc** would be great!

saffron

Saffron, the world's most expensive and exotic spice, is the stigma of a small purple crocus called *Crocus sativus*; it can be harvested only by hand. It is estimated that it takes over a quarter million crocus flowers to yield one pound of saffron. Luckily, very little saffron is needed to flavor a dish. It yields an intense color and flavor like nothing else in the world. Most saffron comes from Spain, where it is used to flavor many dishes, the most famous of which is paella. It is also an essential ingredient in bouillabaisse in southern France and risotto milanese in Italy.

MARINADE

¼ cup finely chopped fresh parsley

¼ cup chopped fresh basil

1 tablespoon minced shallot or green onion, white part only

2 teaspoons minced garlic

1 teaspoon minced fresh oregano or ½ teaspoon dried

1½ teaspoons kosher or sea salt

½ teaspoon red pepper flakes

1 tablespoon finely grated orange zest

⅓ cup dry white wine

⅓ cup extra-virgin olive oil

12 extra-large shrimp (16 to 20 per pound), shelled and deveined

12 large sea scallops, rinsed and side muscle removed

STOCK

4 cups Easy Shellfish Stock (page 67)

1 cup dry white wine

½ teaspoon saffron threads

2 bay leaves

¼ cup julienned leek, white part only

¼ cup julienned carrot

24 mussels, scrubbed and debearded

Chopped fresh chives and finely sliced strips of nori (dried seaweed) for garnishing (optional)

This elegant presentation for shellfish looks even better in deep, wide-rimmed white bowls. For the full visual effect, make the stock as clear as possible. Use whatever selection of fish and shellfish you want as long as they are absolutely fresh!

To make the marinade: In a medium bowl, prepare the marinade by combining the parsley, basil, shallot, garlic, oregano, salt, pepper flakes, orange zest, wine, and olive oil. Add the shrimp and scallops and marinate, covered, in the refrigerator for up to 1 hour. Prepare a charcoal fire or preheat a stove-top grill pan. Remove from the marinade, wipe off most of it, and grill quickly over hot coals until just done, 1 to 2 minutes. Be careful not to overcook. The shellfish should be slightly translucent in the middle. Set aside.

To make the stock: Meanwhile, in a large saucepan, bring the stock, wine, saffron, and bay leaves to a boil. Reduce the heat and simmer for 5 minutes to develop the saffron aroma and color. Strain carefully. In another large pot, quickly blanch the julienned leek and carrot in lightly salted boiling water (just 5 seconds) and remove. Pour off most of the water, return to a boil, and steam the mussels until just open. (Discard any that don't open.)

Divide the shrimp, scallops, mussels, leek, and carrot among warm soup bowls. Ladle the steaming stock over the seafood. Garnish with chives and nori, if using.

CALAMARI BRUSCHETTA WITH TOMATOES, GOAT CHEESE, AND MINT

Serves 4

⅓ cup plus 2 tablespoons extra-virgin olive oil, plus additional for the toasts

3 tablespoons fresh lemon juice

2 tablespoons chopped fresh basil

Kosher or sea salt and freshly ground pepper

1 pound cleaned small calamari bodies, separated from tentacles

3 or 4 medium-firm ripe plum tomatoes, halved and seeded

1 small red onion, cut into ¼-inch-thick rounds

1 tablespoon roasted garlic (see page 264)

2 tablespoons coarsely chopped fresh mint

2 tablespoons chopped fresh chives

Red wine vinegar

4 ounces aged goat cheese or feta, crumbled

1 crusty Italian or French baguette, cut into ½-inch-thick slices

Small fresh mint leaves and Fried Capers (page 33) for garnishing (optional)

RECOMMENDED WINE
The classic combination of goat cheese and **Sauvignon Blanc** is further enhanced by the fresh mint and seafood in this dish.

Calamari, or squid, were historically a major fish resource for California, especially around Monterey Bay. Overfishing, climate changes, and other factors have significantly reduced the squid population off the California coast.

In cooking calamari there is no in-between—either you cook them very briefly or simmer them for a long time. Anything in between results in a tough, chewy, and thoroughly uninteresting (not to say inedible) product. This recipe uses the fast-cook method and can also be done under a hot broiler if you don't want to fire up the grill, but the smoky flavor the grill adds is a real plus. This is also a wonderful mixture to use, without the toasts, on hot or cold pasta dishes.

In a large bowl, combine the ⅓ cup olive oil, lemon juice, basil, 1 teaspoon salt, and a grinding or two of pepper and whisk together. Add the squid bodies and tentacles and marinate for 1 hour at room temperature.

Prepare a charcoal fire or preheat the broiler. Remove the squid from the marinade and reserve the marinade. Over hot coals or under the broiler, grill the bodies and tentacles until they just begin to firm and turn opaque, only a few minutes. Be careful not to overcook or the calamari will be tough. Slice the bodies into bite-sized rings and the tentacles into bite-sized portions. Set aside. (Do not refrigerate.)

Add the tomatoes and onion to the reserved marinade, stir to coat, then drain and grill briefly. Coarsely chop them and then put them in a large bowl with the calamari, garlic, mint, chives, vinegar, and the 2 tablespoons olive oil. Season to taste with salt and pepper. Gently stir in the goat cheese. Lightly paint the bread with the remaining olive oil and grill over hot coals until lightly toasted with grill marks. Put a heaping tablespoon or two of the calamari mixture on each toast and garnish with a mint leaf and Fried Capers, if using.

CIOPPINO

Serves 8

RECOMMENDED WINE
This is a dish friendly to just about every imaginable wine. I'd use either a crisp white or the same red used to make the stew.

¼ cup olive oil

3 cups chopped onions

3 tablespoons chopped garlic

1 cup chopped carrots

⅔ cup chopped celery or fennel

3 cups canned peeled whole or diced tomatoes, including juice

2½ cups hearty red wine, such as Zinfandel, Cabernet, or Sangiovese

6 cups Easy Shellfish Stock (page 67) or low-salt chicken stock

3 large bay leaves

¼ cup chopped fresh basil

1 tablespoon chopped fresh oregano

2 teaspoons fennel seeds

½ teaspoon red pepper flakes

Kosher or sea salt and freshly ground pepper

1 whole Dungeness crab (about 2 pounds), cleaned and chopped into sections

1½ pounds mussels, scrubbed and debearded

2 pounds rock fish fillets, cut into 1-inch cubes

16 medium shrimp, shelled and deveined (freeze the shells for stock!)

8 thick slices sourdough bread, brushed with garlic-infused olive oil (page 47) and toasted

¼ cup chopped fresh parsley

Cioppino, a rich, flavorful fish stew, is a dish closely identified with San Francisco. Though some think that it was invented there, most food historians believe that it came to the City by the Bay via early Italian fishermen who emigrated there from northern Italy, specifically Genoa. The name itself is thought to have come from the Genovese word ciuppin *or* giuppin, *and in fact may be simply a corruption of the Genovese word* suppin, *which translates to "little soup" or "little cup of soup." The romantic picture often conjured up about cioppino was that it was typically made on board the small fishing boats as they returned back home with their catches through the Golden Gate into San Francisco Bay on their way to Fisherman's Wharf. If you've ever been on San Francisco Bay, you know it is often pretty rough, and somehow the image of a big pot of hot, simmering stew twisting and turning on a small boat battered by the waves sounds a little dangerous to me! In this recipe I find that the most flavorful result comes from using a combination of fresh fish and shellfish. A shopping list that you could use would be 2 to 3 pounds fresh fish fillets such as halibut or sea bass; 3 pounds shellfish or crustaceans such as clams, mussels, and crab; and 1 pound shrimp. This is just a guide but will at least give you a general idea of quantity. You'll note too that I've suggested straining the aromatic herbs and vegetables out of the soup base before adding the fish. If you like the texture of the veggies and don't want to do this—then don't! Also remember to add the various fish and shellfish separately so that you can control their cooking time. The idea is to cook them so that all retain their best texture.*

In a deep soup pot, heat the olive oil over medium heat and sauté the onions, garlic, carrots, and celery until lightly browned. Add the tomatoes, wine, stock, bay leaves, basil, oregano, fennel seeds, and pepper flakes. Bring to a boil, then reduce the heat to a simmer, and cook partially covered for 15 to 20 minutes. Strain, discarding the solids, and return the broth to the pot. Season to taste with salt and pepper. Can be made ahead at this point and refrigerated or frozen for later use.

Add the crab and mussels to the broth and cook over medium heat until the mussels open, about 5 minutes. Add the fish and shrimp and cook for another 3 to 4 minutes or until the fish is just cooked through. Place a piece of toasted sourdough in the bottom of each warm soup bowl and ladle the soup on top. Sprinkle the parsley over all and serve immediately.

GRILLED SHRIMP WRAPPED IN ZUCCHINI WITH A RED PEPPER AIOLI

Serves 8 as an appetizer or 4 as a main course

RECOMMENDED WINE
A crisp clean white such as **Sauvignon Blanc**, an un-oaked **Chardonnay**, a dry **Riesling**, or a **Pinot Gris** with good acidity would be great here. A chilled soft red such as **Gamay** or a dry **rosé** could also work nicely.

16 extra-large shrimp (16 to 20 per pound)

3 tablespoons olive oil

¼ cup dry white wine

2 teaspoons grated lemon zest

1 teaspoon minced fresh oregano or ½ teaspoon dried

1 teaspoon minced fresh garlic

¼ teaspoon red pepper flakes

½ teaspoon kosher or sea salt

4 zucchini, sliced very thinly lengthwise to yield 16 slices

16 large fresh basil leaves

16 rosemary branches, leaves removed halfway on the stem, or bamboo skewers soaked in water for 30 minutes

Red Pepper Aioli (recipe follows)

Lemon wedges for garnishing (optional)

This is a great way to use up the abundance of zucchini that always seems to hit us in midsummer.

Shell and devein the shrimp, leaving the tails on. In a large bowl, whisk together the olive oil, wine, lemon zest, oregano, garlic, pepper flakes, and salt. Add the shrimp and marinate in the refrigerator for up to 2 hours. Meanwhile, blanch the zucchini slices in boiling salted water for 5 seconds and cool immediately in ice water. Pat dry and set aside.

Drain the shrimp and discard the marinade. Wrap each shrimp first with a basil leaf, then with a zucchini slice. Skewer with the rosemary, or a bamboo skewer, catching the end of the zucchini to help hold it in place. Grill for 4 to 5 minutes, turning once or twice until the shrimp are just done.

Serve with a dollop of Red Pepper Aioli on the shrimp or in a ramekin on the side, and garnish with lemon wedges to squeeze over, if using.

~~~~~~

RED PEPPER AIOLI
Make about 1½ cups

2 large egg yolks

1 tablespoon or more chopped, roasted, or poached garlic (see page 264)

2 roasted, peeled, and chopped red bell peppers

2 tablespoons Dijon mustard

⅔ cup olive oil

Fresh lemon juice

Kosher or sea salt and freshly ground pepper

Drops of hot sauce

Add the egg yolks, garlic, bell pepper, and mustard to a blender or food processor. With the motor running, slowly add the olive oil to form an emulsion. The mixture should be thick but not stiff. Season to taste with lemon juice, salt, pepper, and hot sauce. Store, covered, in the refrigerator for up to 3 days.

GRILLED SHRIMP WITH MELON-PINEAPPLE SALSA

Serves 4 to 6

1 pound extra-large shrimp (16 to 20 per pound)

¼ cup light olive oil

2 teaspoons minced or pressed garlic

1 tablespoon minced green onion, both white and green parts

½ teaspoon finely chopped fresh oregano or ¼ teaspoon dried

½ teaspoon kosher or sea salt

¼ teaspoon red pepper flakes

3 tablespoons dry white wine

Melon-Pineapple Salsa (recipe follows)

1 small ripe avocado, peeled, pitted, and cut into fans, and fresh cilantro sprigs for garnishing

RECOMMENDED WINE
The sweet shrimp and fruity Melon-Pineapple Salsa mirror beautifully wines like California and German **Rieslings** and **Gewürztraminers**, French **Chenin Blancs**, and California **white Zinfandel**, all of which have similar fresh fruit flavors and sweetness.

In this dish, the shrimp can be served warm right off the grill or at room temperature and included as part of a summer buffet. You can either shell the shrimp as suggested or grill them with the shell on, which I think adds a lot of flavor. To grill with shell on, simply take a pair of scissors and snip the shell along the back so that you can remove the intestinal vein.

Shell and devein the shrimp, leaving the tails on. Whisk together the olive oil, garlic, green onion, oregano, salt, pepper flakes, and wine and marinate the shrimp for a maximum of 2 hours, covered, in the refrigerator. Skewer the shrimp together, if desired, to facilitate turning them during grilling.

Grill or broil the shrimp quickly, about 1 to 2 minutes per side, until they just turn pink. Be careful not to overcook. Shrimp should remain slightly transparent in the middle. Divide the Melon-Pineapple Salsa among plates and place the shrimp attractively on top, along with the avocado and cilantro.

MELON-PINEAPPLE SALSA
Makes about 2 cups

1 cup diced melon

1 cup diced fresh pineapple (see Note)

½ teaspoon seeded and minced serrano chile

1 tablespoon finely diced sweet red onion

1 tablespoon olive oil

2 tablespoons fresh lime or lemon juice

2 teaspoons honey

2 teaspoons chopped fresh cilantro

Kosher or sea salt and freshly ground pepper

In a medium bowl, carefully stir together the melon, pineapple, chile, and red onion. In a small bowl, whisk together the olive oil, lime juice, and honey and pour over the fruit mixture. Gently stir in the chopped cilantro. Season to taste with salt and pepper.

Note: For additional flavor, lightly oil and grill thick slices of pineapple before cutting it up.

NEW WORLD SHRIMP COCKTAIL WITH ROASTED OR GRILLED VEGETABLES

Serves 4

RECOMMENDED WINE
This dish, as well as most containing some heat from chiles, goes well with aromatic white wines. These include **Riesling**, **Gewürztraminer**, **Viognier**, **Muscat**, and **Sauvignon Blanc**. Choose one with ripe, rich fruit flavors.

3 Roma tomatoes, halved and seeded

4 large tomatillos, husk removed

1 small red onion, peeled and quartered

2 jalapeño chiles, halved and seeded

1 large red or orange bell pepper, halved and seeded

1 large poblano chile, halved and seeded

1 large ear corn, husk and silk removed

Olive oil for coating

Kosher or sea salt and freshly ground pepper

1 pound extra-large shrimp (16 to 20 per pound), shelled and deveined

½ cup fresh lime juice

⅓ cup fresh orange juice

¼ cup tomato juice

2 teaspoons brown sugar

1½ teaspoons kosher or sea salt

Drops of hot sauce

GARNISH

2 tablespoons ¼-inch diagonally sliced chives or green onions, green part only

¼ cup fresh cilantro leaves

½ cup unsalted popcorn

1 small avocado, peeled, pitted, and cut into 4 fans

Jicama, peeled and cut into long, thin spears (optional)

Peppers, tomatoes, chiles, and of course "mother corn" were all part of the New World pantry. I've called for shrimp here, but you could use any fresh shellfish of your choice, such as scallops, oysters, or mussels. Make sure the container you serve the cocktail in is clear glass so you can see all the colors of the food. I love to do this in a large martini or margarita glass. To carry the corn theme to its ultimate, I also sometimes add corn nuts to the garnish. Don't be put off by the relatively long list of ingredients. Basically all I'm doing here is roasting (or grilling) several vegetables, chopping them up, and puréeing half of them to make a sauce and using the other half in the cocktail along with the shrimp.

Preheat the oven to 500°F and line a rimmed baking sheet with aluminum foil. Brush the tomatoes, tomatillos, red onion, jalapeño chiles, bell peppers, poblano chile, and corn with the olive oil and season to taste with salt and pepper. Put the vegetables, cut-side down, in the pan and put the pan in the oven. Roast the vegetables until they just take on a little color, removing them by type as they do. The tomatoes and tomatillos will take 5 minutes, the peppers about 8 minutes. Set aside to cool as they are done.

Meanwhile, in a large saucepan, bring to a boil 6 cups of lightly salted water. Add the shrimp and immediately turn off the heat. Allow the shrimp to sit in the water for 2 minutes, or until they are pink and the very center of the shrimp meat is still slightly translucent. Immediately drain the shrimp and submerge in a large bowl of very cold water. When cool, drain and transfer the shrimp to a large bowl and set aside.

Slip the skins off the tomatoes and peppers and, along with onions and tomatillos, coarsely chop, keeping each separate. Cut the corn off the cob and set aside with the other vegetables. Put half these vegetables in a blender with the lime juice, orange juice, tomato juice, brown sugar, and salt. Blend until smooth. You should have about 2½ cups. Strain through a medium-mesh strainer, pushing down on the solids and discard any remaining solids. Season to your taste with drops of hot sauce.

Serve in martini glasses or glass bowls, attractively arranging half the remaining vegetables, including the corn. Arrange all but 4 of the shrimp on top and spoon some of the sauce over. Sprinkle on half the chives and cilantro. Add a final layer of roasted vegetables and sauce and top each with a shrimp. Sprinkle on the remaining chives and cilantro and finally the popcorn. Finish by adding avocado fans and spears of jicama (if using), to suggest swizzle sticks! Serve immediately.

ROCK SHRIMP CAKES WITH SALSA CRUDA

Serves 4

RECOMMENDED WINE
A fruity aromatic wine like **Riesling** or **Viognier** would be my choice here with the sweet shrimp and hot chile flavors. Alternatively, a **Sauvignon Blanc** also works, marrying with the greens and herbs.

1 pound rock shrimp

¼ cup dry white wine

1 large egg, beaten

½ cup coarse bread crumbs, preferably panko, plus additional to coat the cakes lightly

5 tablespoons mayonnaise

1 teaspoon dry mustard

2 tablespoons minced fresh parsley

2 tablespoons minced green onion, both white and green parts

2 teaspoons white wine Worcestershire sauce

Drops of Tabasco or other hot sauce

2 teaspoons ground dried shrimp (optional)

Kosher or sea salt and freshly ground pepper

Clarified butter or vegetable oil for sautéing

2 cups savory salad greens

Salsa Cruda (facing page)

Roasted Tomatillo and Avocado Sauce (optional) (facing page)

Fresh cilantro sprigs and slices of ripe avocado for garnishing

Rock shrimp are native to the southeastern United States and are so-named because they have a rock-hard shell that is generally removed mechanically, causing the shrimp to have a broken appearance. The flavor of rock shrimp is phenomenal, however. When cooked, they have all the richness, flavor, and texture of lobster meat, at a much lower price. While rock shrimp are generally available, you can substitute regular shrimp if necessary. Be sure not to overcook either shrimp. Rock shrimp tend to cook in about half the time of regular shrimp. I've called for the use of some dried shrimp in the recipe. This is available in both Mexican and Asian markets and in those sections of some supermarkets. It's a great way of adding even more shrimp flavor if you can find it.

When I make this dish, I often use a green sauce, which I put in a squeeze bottle and squirt decoratively around the edge of the plate. You certainly don't have to add it, but I wanted to share the recipe with you because it's one of my favorite sauces with fish, poultry, and roasted vegetables.

In a large sauté pan over medium-high heat, combine the rock shrimp and wine and cook for 1 minute. The shrimp will still be translucent and half done. Drain the shrimp, saving the cooking liquid, cool shrimp, and chop coarsely.

Combine the egg, the ½ cup bread crumbs, mayonnaise, mustard, parsley, green onion, Worcestershire sauce, Tabasco sauce, and dried shrimp, if using. Fold in the rock shrimp and their cooking liquid and season with salt and pepper to taste. Form into 8 cakes. Coat both sides lightly with additional crumbs and refrigerate, uncovered, for at least a few minutes or up to 2 hours ahead.

In a large sauté pan, melt the butter and sauté the cakes until lightly brown on both sides. Remove the cakes and keep warm. Divide the greens among 4 plates. Place the shrimp cakes on the greens and top with Salsa Cruda. Garnish with the Roasted Tomatillo and Avocado Sauce (if using), cilantro sprigs, and avocado slices.

SALSA CRUDA
Makes about 1 cup

12 ounces ripe tomatoes, seeded and diced

⅓ cup diced red onion

1 tablespoon olive oil

1 teaspoon seeded and minced serrano chile

2 tablespoons chopped fresh cilantro

1 teaspoon finely chopped fresh mint (optional)

Fresh lime or lemon juice

Pinch of sugar

Kosher or sea salt and freshly ground pepper

In a medium bowl, combine the tomatoes, red onion, olive oil, chile, cilantro, mint (if using), lime juice, and sugar. Season to taste with salt and pepper. Allow the flavors to blend for at least 1 hour before using. Store, covered, in the refrigerator up to 2 days.

ROASTED TOMATILLO AND AVOCADO SAUCE
Makes about 1½ cups

12 ounces tomatillos, husked

1 small onion, quartered

1 serrano or jalapeño chile, seeded

4 garlic cloves, peeled

3 tablespoons olive oil

½ teaspoon whole coriander seeds

½ teaspoon cumin seeds

Kosher or sea salt and freshly ground pepper

1 large avocado (10 to 12 ounces), peeled, pitted, and chopped

¼ cup chopped fresh cilantro

½ cup Chicken Stock (page 66) or Vegetable Stock (page 69)

Preheat the oven to 375°F. In a medium bowl, toss the tomatillos, onion, chile, and garlic cloves with the olive oil and put in an ovenproof baking dish. Sprinkle the coriander seeds and cumin seeds on top along with a light seasoning of salt and pepper. Toss again.

Roast, uncovered, for about 30 minutes or until the tomatillos and onion are lightly browned and soft. Cool slightly and transfer to a food processor or blender, being sure to include all the juices and browned bits from the dish.

Add the avocado and cilantro and process briefly. With the motor running, add enough stock to make a nice, smooth sauce. Season to taste with salt and pepper. Serve warm or at room temperature. The sauce can be made up to 1 day in advance but is best served soon after it is made. Store, covered, in the refrigerator.

ROCK SHRIMP TAMALES WITH FOUR-PEPPER CREAM

Serves 4

RECOMMENDED WINE
With dishes that have a lot of flavor and spice, I like softer, fruity, aromatic wines, like **Gewürztraminer**, **Riesling**, or **Viognier**.

8 large dried corn husks (see Note)

MASA

¼ cup (½ stick) unsalted butter at room temperature

2 cups masa harina

1 teaspoon baking powder

1 teaspoon kosher or sea salt

1 tablespoon finely chopped chipotle in adobo sauce

¼ cup canola or olive oil

1 cup hot chicken stock or shellfish stock

FILLING

2 slices bacon, finely diced

½ cup finely chopped poblano chile

2 tablespoons minced red onion

1 teaspoon minced garlic

½ cup chicken stock or shellfish stock

8 to 10 ounces rock or bay shrimp, coarsely chopped

½ teaspoon adobo sauce

1 tablespoon chopped fresh cilantro

Four-Pepper Cream (recipe follows)

Cilantro sprigs and diced bell pepper for garnishing

I am fascinated by wrapped foods in general and tamales in particular. At one point I even wanted to write a global tamale book, describing different types of doughs and fillings. My better judgment prevailed, but this zesty contribution was one of the results. For other tamale inspirations, see Sticky Rice "Tamales" with Star Anise Beef or Pork (page 234) and Mediterranean Polenta Tamales with Ratatouille Filling and Pepper-Corn Cream Sauce (page 276).

Soak the corn husks in warm water for 30 to 40 minutes to soften.

To make the masa: Using an electric mixer fitted with the paddle attachment, or by hand with a wooden spoon, in a large bowl beat the butter until light and fluffy. Add the masa harina, baking powder, salt, and chipotle. Mix until well blended. With the motor running, slowly add the canola oil and the hot stock. Continue mixing until you hear a slapping sound, about 2 minutes. The dough will be soft. Set aside. You can do this all by hand with a wooden spatula, but it will take some energy!

To make the filling: In a large sauté pan over medium heat, sauté the bacon until translucent. Add the chile, onion, and garlic and sauté slowly until tender, about 3 minutes. Add the stock, shrimp, and adobo sauce. Cook, stirring, until the shrimp are barely cooked through, about 1 minute. Remove from the heat, strain, set the solids aside, and return the liquid to pan. Over high heat, reduce the liquid until syrupy and add to the shrimp mixture. Add the chopped cilantro and stir to combine.

Remove the husks from the water, drain, and pat dry. Spread out the corn husks on a dry work surface. Pinch off an egg-sized piece of the masa mixture. Pat it into the corn husk, flattening the dough to about 4 inches square and ¼ inch thick, leaving a border of husk at least ½ inch wide around the perimeter of the dough. Spread a tablespoon of the filling lengthwise in the center of the dough. Fold the husk together until the edges overlap and the masa and its filling are completely enclosed by the husk. Gently flatten the top and bottom of the husk and fold the ends up to enclose. Repeat with the other 7 husks. Place, folded-side down, in a steamer over boiling water and steam, covered, for 45 minutes.

Open the husks to reveal the tamales and place on warm plates. Spoon the Four-Pepper Cream over the tamales and garnish with cilantro sprigs and diced pepper. Serve immediately.

Note: Dried corn husks are available in Mexican markets and also by mail order. For sources, see page 424.

FOUR-PEPPER CREAM
Makes 2 to 3 cups

2 tablespoons olive oil

¼ cup chopped shallots

2 teaspoons seeded and chopped serrano chile

¾ cup dry white wine

2 cups rich Shellfish Stock (page 67) or Chicken Stock (page 66)

¾ cup heavy (whipping) cream

2 tablespoons finely diced red bell pepper

2 tablespoons finely diced yellow bell pepper

2 tablespoons finely diced poblano chile

Kosher or sea salt and freshly ground white pepper

Drops of fresh lemon or lime juice

In a medium sauté pan, heat the olive oil and sauté the shallots and serrano chile until soft but not brown. Add the wine and stock and bring to a boil. Continue to boil until the mixture is reduced by half. Add the cream and continue to boil until the mixture is reduced to a light sauce consistency. Stir in the red bell pepper, yellow bell pepper, and poblano chile. Season to taste with salt, pepper, and drops of lemon juice. Serve warm. Four-Pepper Cream can be made up to a day ahead and stored covered in the refrigerator.

masa harina, cornmeal, and polenta

It's easy to see why these terms are confusing, but they shouldn't be used interchangeably. They are really different things!

Masa harina is corn that has been dried, treated with limewater, and then ground to make a flour. Widely available in supermarkets, it is an ingredient in the prepared dough used to make corn tortillas and tamales.

Ordinary ground cornmeal of the kind used in this country, primarily for making cornbread, dusting bread and pizza pans, and coating foods for frying, does not go through the limewater processing and lacks the flavor and texture necessary to make good tortillas or tamales.

Polenta, the Italian dish of cooked cornmeal served either as mush or cooled and sliced, is made from either very finely ground or coarsely ground cornmeal. Ground cornmeal labeled "polenta" is available at gourmet food stores and markets that carry Italian products. If you can't find this product, you can certainly substitute regular (coarse yellow) cornmeal.

SCALLOP SEVICHE WITH CILANTRO, LIME, AND SERRANO CHILES

Serves 4 as an appetizer

RECOMMENDED WINE
The lime notes of the seviche would be nicely balanced by the zingy acidity of a crisp **Sauvignon Blanc** or a dry sparkling wine from California or **cava** from Spain.

8 ounces absolutely fresh sea or bay scallops, cut into uniform cubes or slices

2 tablespoons minced green onion, both white and green parts

½ teaspoon seeded and minced serrano or jalapeño chile

1 tablespoon chopped fresh cilantro

1 teaspoon kosher or sea salt

4 tablespoons fresh lime juice

½ teaspoon sugar

1 tablespoon olive oil

Seviche is the best-known dish that "cooks" fish through the use of acidity, without heat. A number of different acidic elements will work, but lime juice and vinegar are the two most popular. In this dish, the scallops are marinated for a couple of hours, which causes a change in the actual protein structure of the shellfish, simulating the effect of cooking with heat. After more than 4 hours, the fish "overcooks" and becomes mushy and dry, so you can't really do this ahead.

This is a very simple dish to put together and can be used in a number of different ways. I like the seviche rolled up in crisp romaine or iceberg lettuce leaves and eaten out of hand, like a kind of Latin American spring roll. The seviche is also delicious served on crisp corn or flour tortilla wedges with a spoonful of Salsa Cruda (page 173) on top.

In a medium bowl, combine the scallops, green onion, chile, cilantro, salt, lime juice, sugar, and olive oil. Cover and refrigerate. Let the seviche "cook" for 2 hours or to taste.

GRILLED SCALLOPS WITH FENNEL, RED PEPPER, AND LEMON-TARRAGON VINAIGRETTE

Serves 4

1 large fennel bulb, tops removed

Olive oil for coating

Kosher or sea salt and freshly ground pepper

12 jumbo dayboat sea scallops (about 1¼ pounds), side muscle removed

2 red bell peppers, charred, peeled, and cut into triangles

1 cup crisp-cooked tender seasonal vegetables, such as snow peas, asparagus tips, fava beans, or English peas, or a combination

Lemon-Tarragon Vinaigrette (recipe follows)

Sprigs of fresh tarragon or chervil and rinsed fresh salmon roe for garnishing (optional)

RECOMMENDED WINE
A **Sauvignon Blanc** or **Fumé Blanc** captures the fresh, lemony flavors in the vinaigrette. Tarragon is also a great link to Sauvignon Blanc.

This is a relatively simple dish that lends itself to all kinds of seasonal ingredients. Note that dayboat, or dry-pack, scallops are specified in the recipe. These are scallops that are not put in a brine of any sort—simply harvested and placed in wet muslin bags and shipped daily.

Slice the fennel lengthwise into thin fans. Brush with the olive oil and season to taste with salt and pepper. Grill over hot coals until marked and crisp-tender. Arrange on plates. Lightly oil and season the scallops and grill until just done, about 2 minutes per side. Be careful not to overcook—the centers should still be slightly translucent. Arrange on top of the fennel along with the bell peppers and seasonal vegetables. Drizzle a tablespoon or two of Lemon-Tarragon Vinaigrette over each serving and garnish with tarragon sprigs and salmon roe, if using. Serve immediately.

LEMON-TARRAGON VINAIGRETTE
Makes about 1 cup

1 teaspoon finely grated lemon zest

⅓ cup fresh lemon juice

1 tablespoon minced shallot

1 tablespoon chopped fresh tarragon

2 teaspoons honey

⅓ cup olive oil

Kosher or sea salt and freshly ground white pepper

In a small bowl, whisk together the lemon zest, lemon juice, shallot, tarragon, and honey, and then slowly whisk in the olive oil to form a lightly thickened vinaigrette. Season to taste with salt and pepper. Store, covered, in the refrigerator for up to 5 days.

SEARED DAYBOAT SCALLOPS WITH SAUTÉED APPLES AND VANILLA-SCENTED SAUCE

Serves 4

RECOMMENDED WINE
This is a classic dish to highlight the apple-vanilla flavors and creamy texture of a barrel-fermented and aged **Chardonnay**.

½ ounce dried porcini mushrooms, soaked in 1 cup warm water for 20 minutes

1 pound jumbo dayboat scallops

Kosher or sea salt and freshly ground white pepper

5 tablespoons unsalted butter

1 cup chopped cultivated white mushrooms

½ cup chopped shallots or green onions, white part only

2 cups peeled and julienned tart green apples (Pippin or Granny Smith)

1 cup dry white wine

3 cups Easy Shellfish Stock (page 67)

1½-inch piece vanilla bean, split lengthwise

1 cup heavy (whipping) cream

1 teaspoon Dijon mustard

1 tablespoon olive oil

Fresh chervil sprigs, rinsed fresh whitefish or salmon caviar, and Oven-Dried Apple Slices (facing page) for garnishing (optional)

The quality of the scallops is crucial to this dish, and again dayboat scallops are called for. The recipe also calls for a split vanilla bean. You'll need only half here. The other half you can put in your sugar jar to make vanilla sugar. It can stay there indefinitely. You can also substitute the No-Cream Cream (page 85) for the heavy cream in this recipe.

Drain the porcini mushrooms and chop. Remove any side muscles from the scallops, rinse, pat dry, and lightly season with salt and pepper. Set aside.

In a medium saucepan, melt 2 tablespoons of the butter over medium heat and sauté the white mushrooms and shallots until just beginning to color. Add 1 cup of the apples, the wine, stock, and vanilla bean and reduce by half over medium-high heat, about 10 minutes. Add the cream and mustard and reduce to a light sauce consistency. Strain the sauce through a fine-mesh strainer, pushing down on the solids, and discard the solids. Season to taste with salt and pepper. Keep the sauce warm.

In a sauté pan, melt 2 tablespoons of the butter with the olive oil over high heat and sear the scallops quickly on both sides, about 3 minutes total. The scallops should still be slightly translucent in the center. Set the scallops aside and keep warm. In a clean pan, heat the remaining butter and sauté the remaining apples for a minute or two until crisp-tender. Be careful not to overcook; the apples should still be firm.

Arrange the apples and scallops attractively on warm plates. Spoon the warm sauce over and garnish with chervil, caviar, and Oven-Dried Apple Slices, if using.

OVEN-DRIED APPLE SLICES

Preheat the oven to 250°F. Peel and slice apples in very thin rounds with a mandoline or similar device. Dip into orange or pineapple juice and then pat dry. Place in a single layer between sheets of parchment on a baking sheet. Put in the oven for 15 to 20 minutes or until apples are softened. Remove the top layer of parchment, return to the oven, and allow the apples to dry completely, about 1 hour longer. Remove and store in an airtight container.

DUNGENESS CRAB IN WINE AND VERMOUTH

Serves 2 as a main course or 4 as an appetizer

One 3-to-4-pound cooked Dungeness crab

4 ounces unsalted butter

⅔ cup dry vermouth

½ cup dry white wine

1½ cups clear fish or chicken stock

3 tablespoons thinly sliced garlic

2 teaspoons minced fresh ginger

1½ tablespoons soy sauce

1 tablespoon fresh lemon juice

2 teaspoons sugar

2 teaspoons cornstarch dissolved in 1 tablespoon water

¼ cup chopped fresh parsley or a combination of parsley and chives

Freshly ground pepper

RECOMMENDED WINE
I've had this dish with both a good, full-bodied **Chardonnay** and with a good amber ale; I like them both.

This simple dish celebrates one of the real treasures of the Northern California, Oregon, and Washington coasts—Dungeness crab! I think it's the best but, unfortunately it's not generally available outside these areas. You can substitute other crab such as king crab. Fresh mussels, clams, and shrimp can also be substituted or added to the mix. Serve with a big stack of napkins and lots of crusty French bread.

Clean, crack, and separate the crab into sections and set aside.

In a saucepan, combine the butter, vermouth, wine, stock, garlic, ginger, soy sauce, lemon juice, sugar, and cornstarch mixture. Simmer, covered, for 5 minutes or so. Add the crab and parsley and warm the crab through. Season to taste with pepper.

Ladle the crab and broth into large bowls and serve immediately.

SCALLOPS WITH CELERY ROOT SALAD

Serves 8

RECOMMENDED WINE
The sweet scallops and the creamy celery root salad are a natural accompaniment to a creamy, barrel-aged **Chardonnay**, **Pinot Blanc**, or **Sauvignon Blanc**.

8 jumbo dayboat scallops (1½ pounds)

2 tablespoons olive oil, plus additional for the baking sheet

Big pinch hot paprika or cayenne pepper

Kosher or sea salt and freshly ground pepper

Celery Root Salad (recipe follows)

3 to 4 ounces fresh salmon caviar (or sturgeon caviar if you're feeling flush!)

Fresh chervil or dill sprigs for garnish

This makes a beautiful starter course. The key is to use absolutely fresh dayboat, or dry-pack, scallops. The salad here is one of my favorites and is delicious on its own. Celery root can also vary widely. Pick one that is heavy for its size, which means there won't be a hole in the center. Taste the celery root after cutting, and if it seems tough or too strongly flavored then blanch it for a few seconds in salted boiling water followed by a dunk in ice water to retain its crunch.

Preheat the broiler. Slice each scallop horizontally into 3 rounds. Arrange the slices in individual overlapping cloverleaves on an oiled baking sheet. Mix the olive oil and paprika together and brush on the scallops. Season very lightly with salt and pepper and broil until heated through, about a minute or so.

Mound the Celery Root Salad on plates and set the scallop cloverleafs on top. Top with caviar and chervil sprigs and serve immediately.

Note: Alternatively, you can simply sear the scallops on both sides and place them whole on top of the salad.

CELERY ROOT SALAD

1 large (1 to 1½ pounds) celery root

1 cup mayonnaise

¼ cup buttermilk

2 tablespoons Dijon mustard

2 tablespoons whole-grain Dijon mustard

1 tablespoon fresh lemon juice

2 teaspoons sherry or brown rice vinegar

Kosher or sea salt and freshly ground pepper

Peel, thinly slice, and cut the celery root into thin julienne. In a medium bowl, mix together the mayonnaise, buttermilk, Dijon mustard, whole-grain Dijon mustard, lemon juice, and vinegar until smooth. Stir in the celery root to evenly coat. Season to taste with salt and pepper. This is best done at least an hour ahead and refrigerated for the flavor to develop.

CRAB GRATIN

Serves 4 as a first course or 8 as part of a tapas menu

¼ cup fragrant olive oil

1 cup finely chopped onion

¾ cup finely diced carrots

1 tablespoon finely chopped garlic

3 cups canned diced tomatoes, including juice

¾ cup shrimp stock (made from chicken stock and shrimp shells)

3 tablespoons brandy, preferably Spanish

½ cup dry sherry, such as Spanish fino or Amontillado

½ teaspoon hot Spanish paprika (pimentón)

1 large bay leaf

3 tablespoons chopped fresh parsley

12 ounces fresh or frozen crabmeat, shredded and picked over to remove any pieces of shell

Kosher or sea salt and freshly ground pepper

Unsalted butter for the ramekins and the topping

1 cup dry bread crumbs, preferably panko

½ cup finely grated hard cheese, such as Manchego or Idiazabal from Spain or dry Jack from California

RECOMMENDED WINE
If we were being true to the Spanish influence here we'd have this with a glass of medium-dry sherry, like **Amontillado**. A very crisp, dry white like **Sauvignon Blanc**, or **Pinot Gris** or **Pinot Grigio**, or a dry sparkler like a **cava** from Spain would also be nice.

This is a simple dish with the flavors of Spain that is easily prepared ahead. In Spain, they would use the meat from the spider crab. Living in Northern California, I of course use our local Dungeness. Use whatever is available to you.

In a deep sauté pan, heat the olive oil over medium heat and sauté the onion, carrots, and garlic. Cook for 5 minutes, stirring, until the vegetables soften and begin to color lightly. Add the tomatoes, stock, 2 tablespoons of the brandy, the sherry, paprika, and bay leaf and bring the sauce to a boil. Reduce the heat and simmer for 15 minutes, uncovered, or until the vegetables are soft and the sauce has thickened.

Discard the bay leaf and purée the sauce in a blender or with an immersion blender. Strain through a medium-mesh strainer, pushing down on the solids, and return to the pan. Add the remaining tablespoon of the brandy and bring to a simmer. Stir in the parsley and crab. Season to taste with salt and pepper.

Preheat the oven to 425°F. Spoon the mixture into buttered ramekins. In a small bowl, mix together the bread crumbs and cheese and sprinkle on top. Dot with butter and bake in the oven until the top is lightly golden, about 10 minutes for small tapas-sized ramekins and 20 minutes for larger ones. If the crab mixture is hot, simply top with the bread crumb mixture and run under a hot broiler for a couple of minutes to brown the topping. Serve hot.

CRAB WONTONS WITH ORANGE-CHIPOTLE SAUCE

Makes 40 wontons

RECOMMENDED WINE
A **Riesling** or **Gewürztraminer** with a little residual sugar would be great with this eclectic dish. The orange-blossom and spice flavors in the wines are accentuated by the Orange-Chipotle Sauce, and the wines' fruitiness would help to mellow and balance the heat in the sauce.

½ cup golden raisins

1 cup dry white wine

3 cups fresh or frozen Dungeness crabmeat, shredded and picked over to remove any pieces of shell

1 cup fresh corn kernels (1 large ear), or frozen corn kernels

¾ cup finely diced red bell pepper

¼ cup chopped fresh chives or green onion, both white and green parts

1 tablespoon olive oil

¼ cup chopped fresh cilantro

1 teaspoon ground toasted cumin

1 tablespoon minced fresh ginger

2 tablespoons minced fresh oregano

1 tablespoon finely grated lime zest

Kosher or sea salt and freshly ground pepper

80 wonton wrappers

Cornstarch or rice flour for dusting

Peanut, corn, or canola oil for deep-frying

Cilantro sprigs for garnishing

Orange-Chipotle Sauce (facing page)

China and Mexico meet in California in this delicious, unusual dish. The wontons and sauce can be made ahead of time and frozen, if desired. To freeze the wontons, put them uncovered in a single layer on a baking sheet lined with waxed paper and freeze until hard. The wontons can then be carefully placed in freezer bags. Thaw in the refrigerator before frying.

In a small bowl, combine the raisins and the wine. Let stand at room temperature for 2 hours or more to soften and plump.

Preheat the oven to 250°F. Drain the raisins and discard the wine. In a large bowl, combine the plumped raisins with the crab, corn, bell pepper, chives, olive oil, cilantro, cumin, ginger, oregano, and lime zest. Season to taste with salt and pepper. Put 1 tablespoon crab filling in the middle of each of 40 wonton wrappers. Lightly brush the edge of each wrapper with water and put a second wrapper on top, pressing the edges together to seal completely. Dust a sheet of waxed paper with cornstarch and put the wontons on top.

In a large saucepan, heat about 3 inches of oil to 350°F on a candy or deep-fry thermometer. Put the wontons in the hot oil in batches and deep-fry for 2 minutes or until golden brown and puffed. Remove carefully and drain on paper towels, then put in a warm oven while finishing the rest of the wontons. Garnish with fresh cilantro sprigs and serve immediately with Orange-Chipotle Sauce.

ORANGE-CHIPOTLE SAUCE
Makes about ½ cup

1 small red bell pepper, roasted and peeled

3 tablespoons thawed frozen orange juice concentrate

3 tablespoons fresh lime juice

1 teaspoon sherry or cider vinegar

2 teaspoons honey

½ teaspoon toasted ground cumin

1 teaspoon minced chipotle in adobo sauce (see sidebar)

¼ cup olive oil

Kosher or sea salt

In a blender or food processor, combine the bell pepper, orange juice concentrate, lime juice, vinegar, honey, cumin, and chipotle and purée. With the motor running, slowly add the oil to form a smooth sauce. You may not need to use the full ¼ cup. Season to taste with salt. The sauce can be made up to 2 days ahead and stored, covered, in the refrigerator. It if separates, buzz it up briefly in the blender to recombine.

chipotle chiles

Chipotle chiles are jalapeños that have been dried and smoked. Using them, you get the double hit of hot spice and smoke. They can be purchased in their dry form, or canned as "chipotles in adobo sauce," in which they are stewed with a little tomato, garlic, vinegar, and other spices. Chipotles in adobo sauce are readily available in Mexican markets and now widely available in the Mexican food aisle of the supermarket. Chipotles are pretty powerful, so if you have a low threshold for heat, add a little less than the recipe calls for. You can always add more. If you're like me, however, you'll soon be using them in everything. An easy way to store canned chipotles after you've opened them is to chop or purée them quickly and put in a sealable freezer bag. Seal and flatten, and then freeze. Now you can pinch off a piece to add to recipes whenever you want.

OYSTERS ON THE HALF SHELL WITH PICKLED GINGER SALSA

Serves 4 to 6

RECOMMENDED WINE
A crisp, lean California **brut** sparkling wine or a citrusy **Sauvignon Blanc** would be a great match here.

24 fresh oysters, such as Hog Island, Preston Point, Fanny Bay, or any good half-shell oyster

Pickled Ginger Salsa (recipe follows)

Absolutely fresh oysters on the half shell are one of God's best gifts to us. In California, we get them from several oyster farms ranging from Tomales Bay, north of San Francisco, all the way up to British Columbia. A single variety, Miyagi from Japan, makes up most of what is cultivated in this region. It is an amazingly adaptable creature and will take on varying characteristics depending on where and how it is grown. (It also takes on the name of the area it's farmed in.)

Shuck each oyster by carefully inserting the point of an oyster knife at the hinge end of the shells, cup-side down, and twisting. Don't lose the juices. Free the oyster from the bottom shell by gently sliding a knife underneath it. Top with a teaspoon of the Pickled Ginger Salsa and slurp down.

~~~~~~

PICKLED GINGER SALSA
Makes about 1 cup

¼ cup peeled and diced jicama

¼ cup peeled, seeded, and diced cucumber

¼ cup finely diced red onion

3 tablespoons chopped pickled ginger

1 tablespoon seasoned rice wine vinegar

2 teaspoons fresh lime or lemon juice

1 tablespoon chopped fresh cilantro

1 teaspoon toasted sesame seeds

¼ teaspoon sugar

Kosher or sea salt and freshly ground pepper

In a medium bowl, combine the jicama, cucumber, red onion, ginger, vinegar, lime juice, cilantro, sesame seeds, and sugar. Season to taste with salt and pepper. Cover and refrigerate. This salsa is best used within a couple of hours of making.

food and love

The two have always been connected—an intimate dance of the senses. I know in my own experience that the most memorable (and sensuous) times of my life have all been around food.

For all of recorded history, claims have been made that certain foods increase sexual potency and desire. The Chinese tout shark fin and bird's nest soups (made from real ones). The French made Champagne and wine essential to the process (which I definitely approve of). The Scots swear by haggis— minced sheep innards mixed with oatmeal and spices and then stuffed into a sheep's stomach and boiled for 4 hours. (They obviously have a different sense of sensuality!) Other cultures include cocoa and chocolate (forbidden by the Aztecs to their women), pine nuts (according to Ovid), hippopotamus snout and hyena eyes (from Pliny), and, of course, oysters. Caviar, snails, and the eggs, glands, and sexual organs of all kinds of birds, animals, and fish have been credited with special powers. Even prunes were so highly regarded as an aphrodisiac in Elizabethan times that they were served free in brothels.

Foods from the garden that have been endowed with special sexual potential at one time or another include apples, figs, bananas, cucumbers, leeks, peppers, tomatoes, and potatoes. (The obvious connection is that many of them resemble human genitalia!) The noted anthropologist Peter Farb observed that the association between food and sex has probably existed since humans started walking upright. Eating brings people into close proximity in a situation that does not call for defensive tactics; the table, after all, is less fraught than the bed. Eating can bind a couple more effectively than sex simply because people have dinner more often and more predictably than they have sex. M. F. K. Fisher notes in her wonderful little book *An Alphabet for Gourmets* that "gastronomy has always been connected with its sister art of love. [Passion and sex is the] come-and-go, the preening and the prancing, the final triumph or defeat, of two people who know enough, subconsciously or not, to woo with food as well as flattery."

There are physiological reasons for us to connect the two desires: For one, the same very sensitive structures, called Krause's end bulbs, are found in both the taste buds of the mouth and in the sensitive parts of our sexual organs. (This could explain why sexual desire and delicious food aromas both cause our mouths to water.) But, for me, the connection is both subtler and more all-encompassing than physiology can explain. It is the total sensuality of cooking and eating—the way I experience food as something to be touched and smelled, my love of its look and sound and savor—that makes it a sensual experience as well.

BARBECUED OYSTERS WITH A ZESTY BARBECUE SAUCE

Serves 12

RECOMMENDED WINE
A soft red like **Pinot Noir** or **Gamay**, a crisp sparkling wine, or a locally brewed beer, especially a pale ale, would go beautifully here.

BARBECUE SAUCE

3 tablespoons olive oil

2 cups minced onions

1 tablespoon minced garlic

1 tablespoon ground cumin

1 tablespoon ground ginger

1 tablespoon kosher or sea salt

1 teaspoon freshly ground pepper

1 cup apple cider vinegar

1 cup fresh orange juice

3 bay leaves

4 cups catsup

1 cup dark molasses

1 teaspoon Tabasco or other hot sauce

¼ cup dark-brown sugar

¼ cup hoisin sauce

½ cup (1 stick) unsalted butter, cut up

Kosher or sea salt and freshly ground pepper

6 dozen large oysters, in their shells

During the spring and fall, I love to go to Tomales Bay, where oysters of all sizes are grown. We take the larger oysters (which are up to 6 or more inches long and just too fleshy to eat raw), put them on the grill until they just pop open, and then slather them with a warm, zesty barbecue sauce. As they say, "It doesn't get any better than this!" The recipe makes more than enough sauce for 6 dozen large oysters. The sauce is also great brushed on grilled chicken or ribs.

In a large saucepan, heat the olive oil over medium heat and sauté the onions and garlic until soft but not brown. Stir in the cumin, ginger, salt, pepper, vinegar, orange juice, bay leaves, catsup, molasses, Tabasco sauce, brown sugar, hoisin sauce, and butter. Bring to a simmer and cook for 20 to 30 minutes, stirring occasionally, until thick. Remove the bay leaves, season to taste with salt and pepper, and keep the sauce warm.

Place the oysters in their shells on a hot grill. As soon as they pop open, spoon the warm barbecue sauce over them and serve immediately. Some will open rather quickly, in a couple of minutes. Others, you may have to help along with a flat knife. Discard those that do not open.

MUSSELS BAKED WITH SERRANO CHILES AND FRESH MOZZARELLA

Serves 6 as an appetizer

2 cups dry white wine

2 tablespoon unsalted butter

3 dozen large mussels, scrubbed and debearded

2 tablespoons olive oil plus additional for bread crumbs

6 ounces pancetta or thick-sliced bacon, finely diced

2 tablespoons minced garlic

¼ cup minced shallots or green onions, white part only

2 teaspoons seeded and minced serrano chile

6 tablespoons minced fresh parsley

6 tablespoons dry white bread crumbs

6 ounces fresh mozzarella cheese, thinly sliced

1 large bunch spinach, washed, large stems discarded

I really love mussels. In addition to their great taste, they are also relatively inexpensive. As with clams and oysters, the shells should be tightly closed when you purchase mussels, since this indicates they are still alive and fresh. Use the mussels as close to the time of purchase as possible. You'll have leftover liquid from poaching the mussels in this recipe. It's a delicious stock for soups and sauce, so definitely save it.

In a medium pot, bring the wine and butter to a boil over high heat. Add the mussels and cover. Shaking the pan occasionally, cook the mussels until the shells just begin to open, about 3 minutes. Discard any unopened mussels. Using a slotted spoon, remove the mussels and set aside. Strain the poaching liquid through a fine-mesh strainer and reserve. Remove and discard the top shell from the mussels. Replace any mussels that have been dislodged from their shells during cooking.

In a sauté pan, heat the 2 tablespoons olive oil and cook the pancetta until crisp. Drain on paper towels. Add the garlic, shallots, and chile to the pan and sauté until soft but not brown, about 2 to 3 minutes. Transfer to a small bowl and cool a bit. Add the pancetta and parsley and stir to combine. In a medium bowl, combine the bread crumbs and a few drops of olive oil to very lightly coat them.

Place the prepared mussels in a single layer in a shallow casserole or other ovenproof pan. Moisten each with a few drops of the reserved poaching liquid. Divide the pancetta mixture evenly on top of the mussels. Cover each mussel with a thin slice of mozzarella. Sprinkle the oiled bread crumbs on top. Preheat the broiler. Put the mussels under the broiler until the cheese just melts and lightly browns, about 3 minutes.

While the mussels are browning, pour ⅓ cup of the reserved poaching liquid into a sauté pan. Heat over medium-high heat and add the spinach, stirring for a minute to just wilt. Divide the wilted spinach into small beds on each plate; arrange 6 mussels on top of each. Serve immediately.

RECOMMENDED WINE

A crisp **Sauvignon Blanc** or unoaked **Chardonnay** would be a good counterpoint to the spicy, cheesy mussels.

serrano chiles

The serrano is a small, medium-hot green chile with a little more fire than a jalapeño. They are widely available in grocery stores. As with all chiles, be sure to handle them carefully. Wash your hands thoroughly with soap and water after removing the seeds and inner ridges, where the heat from the active ingredient, capsaicin, is located. Alternatively, you can use thin latex gloves. Another tip that a student of mine shared with me is to lightly spray your hands with aerosol cooking oil before beginning to cut up chiles. Apparently, that thin coating of oil will keep the capsaicin at bay. Of course, wash your hands after to remove it.

POULTRY and RABBIT

POULTRY *and* WINE

Although squab and pheasant are certainly more flavorful than chicken, it's safe to say that most poultry has a relatively neutral flavor, which is why it's so versatile in the kitchen. This means that the choice of wine to serve with a poultry dish depends mostly on the ingredients and cooking technique you use. As you'll see by the wine recommendations accompanying the recipes in this chapter, the wines that work with chicken and other birds are as varied as the ways of preparing them. Conversely, if you have a particular bottle of wine that you're in the mood for, you can pretty much create or choose a poultry dish to suit it.

Interesting recipes to me are those that tickle as many of the senses of taste as possible. In the Western world, we've been taught that there are four senses of taste—sweet, salty, sour, and bitter. There actually are more, and if you go to other parts of the world they will talk about one, two, or even more basic senses of taste in addition to our four. If salt is a basic taste then I think pepper is certainly another, whether that pepperiness comes from different compounds in peppercorns or hot chiles. A sixth sense of taste to my mind is something we are learning more about that has best been described by the Japanese as "umami," the savory or mouthwatering quality of food coming from glutamines. The point is that delicious food will have a combination of these basic flavors. I've proposed that all recipes, whether savory or sweet, must have at least three of these basic six flavors to be of interest. This is what keeps the palate alive and interested in food. We would quickly become uninterested if only one was present. You'll have to come to one of my classes sometime to hear the whole rap and actually see how the basic tastes interact.

Wine, too, has these complex taste qualities, with the exception of salt. The most interesting wines are also those that excite as many of the taste senses as possible in a harmonious way.

CHICKEN BREASTS MARINATED IN YOGURT WITH TROPICAL FRUIT VINAIGRETTE

Serves 6

MARINADE

1 teaspoon toasted and crushed cumin seeds

½ teaspoon red pepper flakes

2 teaspoons roasted garlic (see page 264)

¼ cup minced green onion, both white and green parts

1 cup plain yogurt

1 teaspoon paprika

1 tablespoon fresh lemon juice

6 boneless, skinless chicken breast halves (6 to 8 ounces each)

VINAIGRETTE

¼ cup seasoned rice vinegar

⅓ cup olive oil

1 tablespoon honey

2 tablespoons minced green onion, both white and green parts

½ cup finely diced mango or papaya

⅓ cup finely diced firm kiwi

2 tablespoons minced fresh mint

Kosher or sea salt and freshly ground white pepper

Daikon sprouts or fresh cilantro sprigs for garnishing

RECOMMENDED WINE

The tartness of the yogurt marinade and the fruitiness of the vinaigrette call for a crisp clean **Sauvignon Blanc** or a medium-oaked **Chardonnay** that displays some tropical flavor notes.

The yogurt marinade adds an interesting flavor note to the chicken and also gives it a moist, buttery texture. Serve this on a bed of tender savory greens such as cress, arugula, frisée, or red mustard, or a combination, for a zesty lunch dish.

To make the marinade: In a large bowl, mix the cumin seeds, pepper flakes, roasted garlic, green onion, yogurt, paprika, and lemon juice. Add the chicken breasts and marinate for 4 to 6 hours, covered, in the refrigerator.

To make the vinaigrette: In a small bowl, whisk together the vinegar, olive oil, and honey, then stir in the green onion, mango, kiwi, and mint. Season to taste with salt and pepper. Allow to sit for at least 1 hour for flavors to develop.

Wipe the excess marinade off the chicken breasts and grill or broil until the chicken is just done and juicy, about 5 minutes on each side depending on the thickness. Drizzle the vinaigrette over and garnish with a sprinkling of daikon sprouts.

BREAST OF CHICKEN WITH A COAT OF MANY COLORS

When time is short or I'm at the end of a long day, I often just grill, sauté, or poach a boneless chicken breast and then top it with a tasty little "new mother sauce." Here are four of my make-ahead favorites that work equally well with other light meats such as pork or fish.

TOMATO AND GOLDEN RAISIN CHUTNEY
Makes about 2 cups

3 tablespoons olive oil

2 cups chopped onions

1 tablespoon finely chopped garlic

1½ cups peeled, seeded, and chopped fresh
    tomatoes or canned diced tomatoes, drained

1 cup dry white wine

⅔ cup white wine vinegar

3 tablespoons sugar

2 bay leaves

1 cup water

⅓ cup golden raisins

Kosher or sea salt and freshly ground pepper

In a medium saucepan, heat the olive oil and sauté the onions and garlic until soft and lightly colored. Add the tomatoes, wine, vinegar, sugar, bay leaves, and water. Bring to a boil, then reduce the heat to a simmer and continue to cook, uncovered and stirring occasionally, until the mixture is thick, about 20 minutes. Remove and discard the bay leaves and stir in the raisins. Season to taste with salt and pepper.

This can be served right away or stored, covered, in the refrigerator for up to 2 months.

OLIVE-CAPER RELISH
Makes about ¾ cup

½ cup chopped green olives

1 teaspoon roasted garlic (see page 264)

¼ cup chopped fresh parsley

2 tablespoons chopped cornichon pickles

2 tablespoons rinsed and chopped capers

½ teaspoon Dijon mustard

1 teaspoon balsamic vinegar, preferably white

2 tablespoons chopped oil-packed sun-dried
    tomatoes (optional)

2 tablespoons oil from the tomatoes (optional)

Freshly ground pepper

In a medium bowl, combine the green olives, roasted garlic, parsley, pickles, capers, mustard, vinegar, tomatoes, and tomato oil (if using), seasoning to taste with pepper. This can be served right away or stored, covered, in the refrigerator for up to 2 weeks.

SPICY SOUTHEAST ASIAN SAUCE
Makes about 1 cup

½ cup fresh lime juice

4 tablespoons Asian fish sauce

1 teaspoon minced fresh red chile, such as
   jalapeno or serrano

2 teaspoons minced garlic

1 tablespoon rice vinegar

5 tablespoons sugar

1 tablespoon coarsely chopped fresh cilantro

Combine the lime juice, fish sauce, chile, garlic, vinegar, sugar, and cilantro and stir until sugar is dissolved. Let stand for at least 30 minutes before serving for the flavors to develop. Adjust the salt, sweet, tart, and hot flavors to your taste.

JICAMA-CARROT SALSA
Makes about 2 cups

½ cup diced jicama

⅓ cup finely diced carrot

½ cup seeded and diced ripe plum tomato

¼ cup finely diced red onion

1 teaspoon minced garlic

2 tablespoons fresh lime or lemon juice

1 teaspoon seeded and chopped jalapeño chile

¼ cup coarsely chopped fresh cilantro

2 tablespoons olive oil

1 teaspoon honey

Kosher or sea salt and freshly ground pepper

In a medium bowl, combine the jicama, carrot, tomato, onion, garlic, lime juice, chile, cilantro, olive oil, and honey. Season to taste with salt and pepper. Store, covered, in the refrigerator for up to 3 days.

CHICKEN BREASTS STEAMED IN CABBAGE WITH CIDER CREAM SAUCE

Serves 4

RECOMMENDED WINE
Sweet-tart apple flavors are a classic descriptor of barrel-aged **Chardonnay**. A rich **Pinot Blanc** or an aromatic **Viognier** could also work here, as would the same **Riesling** or **Gewürztraminer** used in the recipe.

Cider Cream Sauce (facing page)

Large leaves of napa or other green cabbage

3 tablespoons unsalted butter or olive oil

2 cups peeled and thinly sliced tart apples

2 tablespoons chopped shallots

1 teaspoon good curry powder, such as Madras Curry Powder (page 97)

Kosher or sea salt and freshly ground pepper

4 boneless, skinless chicken breast halves (6 to 8 ounces each)

1 cup thinly sliced mushrooms

⅔ cup fruity white wine, such as Riesling or Gewürztraminer

This is an elegant preparation for chicken that takes a bit of time, but it's fun for a special dinner. The sauce can be made a day or two ahead, stored, covered, in the refrigerator, and then gently reheated. The chicken could be made wrapped up to 6 hours ahead and stored, covered, in the refrigerator. Wrapping the chicken breasts in cabbage keeps them moist and juicy.

Make the Cider Cream Sauce and set aside.

In a large pot of lightly salted boiling water, briefly blanch the cabbage leaves, about 15 seconds. Remove and plunge immediately into ice water to stop the cooking, then drain and set aside. In a medium sauté pan, melt 2 tablespoons of the butter and sauté the apples and shallots until tender. Add the curry powder and sauté until fragrant, about 1 to 2 minutes. Season to taste with salt and pepper.

Divide the sautéed apples among 4 of the cabbage leaves. Place a chicken breast on top of each apple mixture and fold over the cabbage leaves to completely enclose. Wrap a second cabbage leaf around the mixture. In a large sauté pan, heat the remaining tablespoon of butter over high heat and sauté the sliced mushrooms for 1 minute. Place the cabbage packets on top of the mushrooms, add the wine, cover, and steam over medium heat for 7 to 10 minutes or until the breasts are just done, but moist. Check with the point of a small knife in an unnoticeable part of the chicken.

Remove the cabbage packets and mushrooms with a slotted spoon and place on warm plates. Spoon the Cider Cream Sauce around and serve immediately.

CIDER CREAM SAUCE

3 tablespoons unsalted butter at room temperature

½ cup sliced mushrooms

½ cup minced green onions, white part only

1 cup peeled and coarsely chopped tart apples

1 tablespoon chopped fresh ginger

1 cup apple cider or ⅓ cup applejack brandy

4 cups chicken stock

1 tablespoon Dijon mustard

1 cup heavy (whipping) cream

1 tablespoon green peppercorns (see sidebar)

In a deep saucepan, melt 1 tablespoon of the butter over medium-high heat and sauté the mushrooms, green onions, apples, and ginger until just beginning to color, about 5 minutes. Add the cider, stock, and mustard and reduce by half. Add the cream and reduce to a light sauce consistency. Strain the sauce through a fine-mesh strainer. Remove from the heat and whisk in the remaining 2 tablespoons butter. Slightly crush the green peppercorns and add to the sauce, which can be kept warm in a thermos for up to 3 hours.

peppercorns

Green peppercorns are available either freeze-dried or brined. They are the immature berry of a tropical vine native to India and Indonesia. Black peppercorns are also the immature fruit, but they are dried in the sun to develop a more pungent flavor. White peppercorns are from the mature berry, left on the vine until fairly ripe and red in color. The red skin is removed by soaking and rubbing and then the peppercorns are dried. Pink peppercorns are not a true peppercorn, but rather the dried berries of the Baies rose plant, grown in Madagascar.

CHILE-RUBBED ROAST CHICKEN WITH TORTILLA-CHILE SAUCE

Serves 4

RECOMMENDED WINE
Aromatic whites like **Gewürztraminer, Riesling,** or **Viognier** provide a refreshing contrast to this Mexican-inspired dish.

Chile Rub (facing page)

One 3-pound chicken, excess fat removed

12 ounces tomatillos, husked

1 pound yellow onions, quartered

8 large garlic cloves, peeled

2 poblano chiles, seeded

2 serrano chiles, seeded

Olive oil for coating

Two 6-inch corn tortillas, lightly toasted

1½ cups rich chicken stock

½ cup fruity white wine, such as Riesling

1 cup chopped spinach

1 large bunch fresh cilantro, stemmed and chopped

Kosher or sea salt and freshly ground pepper

Fresh cilantro sprigs and toasted pumpkin seeds for garnishing (optional)

This spicy roast chicken can be done either in the "green" version, as below, or in a "red" version with the following substitutions: red onions for the yellow onions, 3 ounces seeded ancho or dried New Mexico chiles for the poblanos, and drops of fresh lime or lemon juice for seasoning. Both versions make a great party dish served with Green Chile and Cheese Rice (page 303).

Prepare the Chile Rub and coat the outside of the chicken. Set aside in a roasting pan.

Preheat the broiler. In a jelly-roll pan, lightly coat the tomatillos, onions, garlic, poblanos, and serranos with olive oil and arrange in a single layer. Broil lightly browned, about 4 minutes. Preheat the oven to 450°F. Insert half the roasted vegetables into the body cavity of the chicken. Cut the tortillas into ½-inch-wide strips and scatter them and the remaining vegetables in the bottom of the roasting pan. Truss the chicken, if you want, and place, breast-side down, in the pan. Roast for 15 minutes. Turn the chicken over and lower the oven temperature to 375°F. Roast for another 45 to 50 minutes or until the juices run clear when the joint between the leg and thigh is pierced.

Remove the vegetables from the cavity. Set the chicken aside and keep warm. In a food processor, purée, in batches if necessary, all the vegetables, tortillas, pan juices, including any browned bits, the chicken stock, wine, spinach, and cilantro. The purée should be bright green and smooth. Strain the purée through a medium-mesh strainer, pushing down on the solids. Season to taste with salt and pepper and warm in a small saucepan.

Carve the chicken into serving pieces and serve immediately with the sauce pored over or on the side. Garnish with cilantro sprigs and toasted pumpkin seeds, if using.

CHILE RUB

1 tablespoon pure chile powder, such as ancho

1 teaspoon fennel seeds

1 teaspoon coriander seeds

2 teaspoons kosher or sea salt

1 teaspoon dried Mexican oregano

½ teaspoon ground cinnamon

2 tablespoons olive oil

In a spice grinder, combine the chile powder, fennel seeds, coriander seeds, salt, oregano, and cinnamon and finely grind. Alternatively, grind by hand with a mortar and pestle. Transfer to a medium bowl and stir in the olive oil to make a smooth mixture. Store, covered, at room temperature for up to 3 days.

CORNED CHICKEN

Serves 4

RECOMMENDED WINE
A fruity **Gewürztraminer**, **Riesling**, or **Chenin Blanc** with a little residual sugar will play off the salty flavor of this chicken.

¾ cup kosher or sea salt

⅓ cup packed brown sugar

10 cups water

3 large crushed garlic cloves

10 cloves

1 teaspoon freshly grated nutmeg

1 tablespoon crushed juniper berries

One 3-pound chicken

As you may surmise by looking at the following recipe, there is no corn in "corned" chicken—or in "corned" beef either. The term comes from the old English tradition of salting meats to preserve them. For this purpose, the English used a special kind of pickling salt (not unlike kosher salt) whose large, coarse crystals resembled grain—what the English called "corn"—in size and shape. This is an example of that ancient technique, called "corning," used before refrigeration, when only cool cellars were available to preserve birds and meats.

Here, we're using chicken, but any meat could be substituted. The uncooked chicken is pickled in a brine of salt, sugar, and sweet spices in the refrigerator for 4 days; the salt is soaked out and then the chicken is roasted. Once cooked, the chicken can be used in main courses, soups, or sandwiches, in salads, or for Corned Chicken Hash (facing page)! It's certainly not a recipe you can be spontaneous about. Though it does take time, it requires little attention. I promise, you've never tasted anything like it.

In a large saucepan, combine the salt, sugar, and water and simmer until the salt dissolves. Remove from the heat and stir in the garlic, cloves, nutmeg, and juniper berries. Allow the brine to cool to room temperature.

Put the chicken in a nonreactive bowl or pot and cover with the brine, adding additional water if necessary, to barely cover the chicken. Cover the bowl or pot tightly and store in the refrigerator for 4 days, turning the chicken once a day.

Drain the chicken, rinse it well, and cover with cold water. Submerge the chicken, using a weight if necessary. Return the pot, covered, to the refrigerator for 3 hours, changing the water at least 3 times.

Preheat the oven to 375°F. Drain the chicken and pat dry. Truss and roast on a rack for 1 hour or until the juices run clear.

CORNED CHICKEN HASH WITH EGGS

Serves 4

1 pound russet potatoes, peeled and quartered

4 tablespoons olive oil

2 cups diced bell peppers, color of your choice

⅓ cup finely diced celery

1 cup chopped onion

1 tablespoon slivered garlic

3 cups cubed Corned Chicken (facing page)

2 tablespoons chopped fresh parsley

2 tablespoons chopped fresh basil

Kosher or sea salt and freshly ground pepper

3 tablespoons unsalted butter

4 large eggs

1 tablespoons white balsamic vinegar

2 tablespoons chopped fresh chives

RECOMMENDED WINE
Both eggs and vinegar can pose a bit of a problem with wine. The best bet here would be a dry sparkling white wine or **Champagne**.

If you have gone to the effort to make a corned chicken (and you should really try it sometime), here's a recipe that uses it as an ingredient. You could certainly substitute corned beef here.

In a medium saucepan of salted boiling water, cook the potatoes for 8 minutes or until slightly undercooked (still opaque in the very center). Drain, cool by running under cold water, and cut into ½-inch cubes. Set aside.

In a sauté pan, heat 2 tablespoons of the olive oil over medium heat and sauté the bell peppers, celery, onion, and garlic until crisp-tender but not brown. Remove and set aside.

Heat the remaining 2 tablespoons of olive oil over medium-high heat and sauté the diced potatoes until lightly browned. Add the vegetables, corned chicken, parsley, and basil and continue to sauté for another minute or two. Season with salt and pepper to taste. Keep warm.

In a separate sauté pan, preferably nonstick, heat 1 tablespoon of the butter and fry the eggs to your liking. Divide the hash among warm plates and top each with a fried egg. Add the remaining 2 tablespoons of butter to the egg pan and cook over medium heat until lightly browned. Whisk in the vinegar and chives and pour over the eggs. Serve immediately.

SMOKED CHICKEN BURRITOS

Serves 6

RECOMMENDED WINE
The Chipotle Mayonnaise is wonderfully spicy and smoky. A fruity, aromatic white like **Muscat**, **Riesling**, or **Gewürztraminer**, or a riper-style **Sauvignon Blanc** from California would be great.

1½ cups thinly sliced red bell peppers

1 small cucumber, peeled, seeded, and thinly sliced (1½ cups)

¾ cup peeled and thinly julienned jicama or parsnip

1 cup thinly sliced sweet red onion

Orange-Cumin Vinaigrette (facing page)

6 large (12-to-14-inch) flour tortillas

Chipotle Mayonnaise (facing page)

1¼ pounds smoked chicken, cut into medium julienne (4 cups)

¼ cup loosely packed fresh cilantro leaves

1 large ripe avocado, peeled, pitted, and sliced

Roasted White Corn Salsa for garnishing (facing page)

You can present these burritos already made or as a burrito bar and let everyone make their own. If you don't want to make the chipotle mayonnaise from scratch, simply stir a little chipotle in adobo sauce into store-bought mayo. Roasted corn salsa is an extra if you want to go whole hog, or in this case whole chicken!

In a medium bowl, toss the bell peppers, cucumber, jicama, and red onion with the Orange-Cumin Vinaigrette and set aside for at least 30 minutes.

Warm the tortillas briefly over an open flame, or cover in a damp towel and steam in a pre-heated 350°F oven, for 6 minutes until soft and pliable. Drain the bell pepper salad. Spread the Chipotle Mayonnaise on the tortillas and top each one with the bell pepper salad, chicken, cilantro, and avocado.

Fold the top and bottom of each tortilla partially over the filling. Roll the tortilla from left to right to completely enclose the filling. Serve immediately, with the Roasted White Corn Salsa.

ORANGE-CUMIN VINAIGRETTE
Makes about ½ cup

⅓ cup orange juice

2 tablespoons fresh lime or lemon juice

1 teaspoon toasted ground cumin

¼ teaspoon ground cinnamon

1 teaspoon minced fresh mint

3 tablespoons olive oil

Kosher or sea salt and freshly ground pepper

In a medium bowl, whisk together the orange juice, lime juice, cumin, cinnamon, mint, and olive oil until well combined. Season to taste with salt and pepper. Store, covered, in the refrigerator for up to 3 days.

CHIPOTLE MAYONNAISE
Makes ¾ to 1 generous cup, depending on how much oil you use

1 large egg

2 teaspoons chopped garlic

2 tablespoons chopped green onion, both white and green parts

1 teaspoon chopped chipotle in adobo sauce

2 tablespoons fresh lime juice

½ to 1 cup olive oil

Kosher or sea salt and freshly ground pepper

In a blender or food processor, combine the egg, garlic, green onion, chipotle, and lime juice and blend or process briefly. With the motor running, slowly add the olive oil to form a thick emulsion. Season to taste with salt and pepper. Store, covered, in the refrigerator for up to 5 days.

ROASTED WHITE CORN SALSA
Makes about 2 ½ cups

2 cups sweet white corn kernels (2 large ears)

¼ cup olive oil

Kosher or sea salt and freshly ground pepper

⅓ cup finely diced red bell pepper

⅓ cup finely diced red onion

⅓ cup chopped fresh cilantro or basil, or a combination

1 teaspoon seeded and minced serrano chile

1 tablespoon sherry or cider vinegar

1 teaspoon fresh lemon juice

1 teaspoon honey

Preheat the oven to 425°F. In a medium bowl, toss the corn with the olive oil and lightly season with salt and pepper. Spread out in a single layer on a baking sheet and roast in the oven until very lightly browned, about 12 minutes. Cool.

In a medium bowl, combine the corn, pepper, onion, cilantro, chile, vinegar, lemon juice, and honey. Cover and store in the refrigerator for up to 5 days.

BREAST OF CHICKEN DIANE

Serves 4

RECOMMENDED WINE
Mustard and cream are classics with a barrel-aged **Chardonnay**. Other white wines with a nice balance of oak and fruit would work too, such as **Pinot Blanc** or **Viognier**. **Sémillon**, an underappreciated grape grown fairly widely in Australia, would be worth seeking out too.

4 boneless, skinless chicken breast halves (6 to 8 ounces each)

Kosher or sea salt and freshly ground pepper

1 tablespoon olive oil

2 tablespoons unsalted butter

¼ cup finely chopped shallots or green onions, white part only

1¼ cups chicken stock (page 66), preferably low or no sodium

¼ cup brandy, apple brandy, or pear brandy

2 tablespoons Dijon mustard

2 teaspoons Worcestershire sauce, preferably white

⅔ cup heavy (whipping) cream

2 tablespoons finely chopped fresh chives

This is based on one of those old warhorses from French bistro cooking that I still think is delicious. Classically, it's done with pan-roasted beef steaks. Here, I'm using chicken breasts. The approach would work equally well with pork medallions, too. You might accompany this with quickly sautéed mushrooms and spinach.

Gently pound the chicken breasts to even them out a bit. Season liberally with salt and pepper. In a heavy-bottomed sauté pan, heat the olive oil and butter over medium-high heat and sauté the chicken breasts until golden brown and cooked through, about 4 minutes per side. Set the chicken breasts aside and keep warm under a tent of foil.

Lower the heat to medium and sauté the shallots until softened, about 2 minutes. Add the stock and brandy and bring to a boil. Scrape up the delicious browned bits from the bottom of the pan. Reduce the liquid by half and then stir in the mustard, Worcestershire sauce, and cream and reduce to a light sauce consistency. Add any juices from the chicken and season to taste with salt and pepper. Stir in the chives, pour the sauce over the chicken breasts, and serve immediately.

CHICKEN AND WHITE BEAN CHILI

Serves 6 to 8

1 pound dried small white beans, such as cannellini or navy

5 cups chicken stock (page 66)

1¼ pounds boneless, skinless chicken thighs, cut into ½-inch cubes

Kosher or sea salt and freshly ground pepper

4 tablespoons olive oil

1 cup diced onion

2 tablespoons chopped garlic

2 medium fresh poblano chiles, chopped (about 2½ cups)

1 tablespoon ground cumin

1 tablespoon dried oregano

½ teaspoon ground cinnamon

¼ teaspoon red pepper flakes

2 cups chopped fresh tomatillos

⅓ cup chopped fresh cilantro

RECOMMENDED WINE
Something fresh, fruity, and spicy would be nice here, like a chilled **Gewürztraminer**. A good white **Zinfandel** would be fun too, as would a good hand-crafted beer.

This is my wine country Super Bowl Sunday favorite. I often serve this with some finely sliced raw green cabbage, sliced radishes, chopped avocadoes, lime wedges, corn chips, and grated Pepper Jack cheese on the side for guests to add as they please.

Rinse the beans well, put in a large bowl, cover with cool water by at least 3 inches, and soak overnight. Alternatively, use the quick-soak method (see page 83). Drain the beans, put in a large pot with the chicken stock, and bring to a boil over high heat. Reduce the heat and simmer, partially covered, until the beans are tender, anywhere from 30 minutes to an hour or more depending on the bean used. Check to make sure the beans are covered with stock while cooking. Add more stock or water if needed.

Season the chicken with salt and pepper. In a large sauté pan, heat the olive oil over medium-high heat and quickly brown the chicken on all sides. Set aside. Add the onion, garlic, and chiles to the pan and sauté for 5 minutes or until the vegetables are lightly colored. Add the cumin, oregano, cinnamon, and pepper flakes and sauté for a minute or two longer. Add the chicken, onion mixture, and tomatillos to the beans. If there are any browned bits in the sauté pan, deglaze with a little white wine or water, scrape the bottom, and add to the pot.

Bring the chili to a simmer, cover, and cook until the chicken is cooked through, 8 to 10 minutes. Season to taste with salt, pepper, and additional pepper flakes, if using. Stir in the cilantro just before serving.

MY GRANDMOTHER'S FRIED CHICKEN

Serves 4

RECOMMENDED WINE
A crisp, clean white wine would offer a nice balance to this rich chicken. I'd look for a lemony **Sauvignon Blanc**, **Pinot Gris**, or unoaked or lightly oaked **Chardonnay**.

One 3½-pound chicken

1 cup sliced onion

1 tablespoon chopped garlic

2 cups buttermilk

1 cup all-purpose flour

2 teaspoons kosher or sea salt

1 teaspoon freshly ground pepper

Vegetable oil for frying

This technique of steaming and then frying the chicken is a traditional method in the South. We're using vegetable oil for frying here, but Grandmother would have used her own rendered lard, which makes for an absolutely delicious bird! It would be wonderful on a picnic with Lemony Potato Salad with Olives, Corn, and Cashews (page 52) and a great summer dessert, like Cherry and Almond Cobbler (page 321).

In a soup kettle, bring 2 inches of water to a boil. Put the chicken on a rack over (not in) the water, cover, and steam until the chicken is firm and half cooked (15 minutes).

Cool the chicken and cut into 6 or 8 serving pieces. In a medium bowl, mix together the onion, garlic, and buttermilk. Marinate the chicken in the buttermilk mixture for at least 30 minutes and up to 4 hours. In another bowl, mix together the flour, salt, and pepper. Drain the chicken and then dredge in the flour and shake off the excess.

In a heavy, deep skillet or Dutch oven, heat ½ inch vegetable oil to 365°F. Add the chicken and fry over medium heat for 8 to 10 minutes or until golden brown. Turn the chicken over and fry until brown, about 8 minutes more. Drain the chicken well and serve warm or at room temperature.

OVEN-FRIED CHICKEN WITH A CORNMEAL CRUST

Serves 4

¾ cup buttermilk

1 tablespoon grated lemon zest

¼ cup fresh lemon juice

¼ cup olive oil

2 tablespoons minced shallots

1 tablespoon chopped fresh thyme or
   1 teaspoon dried

1 tablespoon kosher or sea salt

1 tablespoon pure chile powder, such as ancho

One 3-pound chicken, cut into 8 pieces

½ cup yellow cornmeal

½ cup panko or other dry bread crumbs

⅔ cup freshly grated Parmesan or
   dry Jack cheese

3 tablespoons minced fresh parsley or basil

2 large eggs beaten with 2 tablespoons water

2 tablespoons unsalted butter, melted

RECOMMENDED WINE
The tart flavors from the buttermilk and the lemon are a natural bridge to **Sauvignon Blanc** and **Pinot Gris** or **Pinot Grigio**.

This technique gives a crisp, crunchy crust with a minimum of fat. You could also remove the skin before coating and baking, which would further reduce the fat. The marinated chicken baked without the coating is also very tasty and quick to prepare. The chicken can be served hot or at room temperature. This technique works equally well with chicken parts like breasts or thighs.

In a medium bowl, whisk together the buttermilk, 1 teaspoon of the lemon zest, the lemon juice, olive oil, shallots, thyme, 2 teaspoons of the salt, and 2 teaspoons of the chile powder. Add the chicken, turning the pieces to coat them. Marinate, covered, in the refrigerator for at least 4 hours.

In a medium bowl, combine the cornmeal, bread crumbs, Parmesan cheese, parsley, and the remaining lemon zest, salt, and chile powder. Remove the chicken from the marinade and drain briefly. Dip the pieces in the egg mixture and then dredge in the cornmeal mixture, patting to coat evenly. The chicken can be prepared up to this point 3 hours in advance and kept, uncovered, in the refrigerator.

Preheat the oven to 400°F. In a lightly oiled baking pan, arrange the chicken, skin-side up. Drizzle with the butter. Bake for 35 to 40 minutes or until crisp, golden, and cooked through. The breasts will be done a bit ahead of the legs. Remove to paper towels to absorb any excess fat. Serve warm or at room temperature.

GRILLED TAMARIND-GLAZED CHICKEN WITH SESAME SPINACH

Serves 4

RECOMMENDED WINE
A fruity, aromatic white like
Gewürztraminer, **Riesling**,
or **Viognier** would play off
the sweet-tart flavor of the
tamarind glaze.

⅔ cup firmly packed light-brown sugar

⅔ cup red wine vinegar

1 cup rich chicken stock

1 cup seeded and chopped ripe tomatoes

1 tablespoon whole mustard seeds

½ teaspoon seeded and minced serrano chile

3 tablespoons tamarind pulp or concentrate

One 3½-pound chicken

Sesame Spinach (recipe follows)

Toasted sesame seeds and fresh cilantro sprigs
  for garnishing

This simple, marvelous dish owes its unusual flavor to tamarind, a tart fruit used in Latin American and Asian cooking, which can be found in markets carrying Latin American products. The chicken improves with a good, long marinating, so don't hesitate to prepare it the day before and leave it in the refrigerator overnight.

In a saucepan, combine the sugar, vinegar, stock, tomatoes, mustard seeds, chile, and tamarind. Bring to a simmer and cook over medium heat for 10 minutes, stirring occasionally until thickened. Cool slightly, purée in a blender or food processor, and set aside.

Split the chicken in half; remove the wing tips, back, and rib bones and save to use for making stock. Coat the chicken halves with the tamarind purée and marinate, covered, in the refrigerator for 4 hours or overnight.

Prepare a charcoal fire or preheat the broiler. Grill or broil the chicken halves on both sides until crusty, rich brown, and cooked through, about 20 minutes. Cut into serving pieces and arrange on warm plates on a bed of Sesame Spinach. Garnish with a sprinkling of sesame seeds and cilantro sprigs. Serve immediately.

~~~~~~

SESAME SPINACH

1 tablespoon olive oil

1 tablespoon toasted sesame oil

2 large spinach bunches (1 pound total), washed
  and stemmed

Kosher or sea salt and freshly ground pepper

Fresh lemon juice

2 tablespoons toasted sesame seeds, both white
  and black if available

In a large pot or wok, heat the olive oil and sesame oil. Add the spinach, in batches if necessary, and sauté over high heat for 1 minute or until the spinach just begins to wilt. Season to taste with salt, pepper, and drops of lemon juice and sprinkle with the sesame seeds.

CHICKEN SCALOPPINE WITH OYSTER MUSHROOMS AND MARSALA

Serves 4

4 boneless and skinless chicken breast halves (6 to 8 ounces each)

4 fresh sage leaves

8 paper-thin slices prosciutto

4 tablespoons cold unsalted butter

2 tablespoons olive oil, plus additional as necessary

Seasoned all-purpose flour for dredging

8 to 10 ounces fresh oyster mushrooms

1 cup sweet Marsala wine

½ cup rich Chicken Stock (page 66)

Kosher or sea salt and freshly ground pepper

Crisp-fried fresh sage leaves (see page 135) for garnishing (optional)

RECOMMENDED WINE
Since **Marsala** was used in the recipe a little taste of it here might be nice. You probably wouldn't want to drink a whole glass of sweet Marsala, however. I'd suggest a soft red, or better yet a dry **rosé**.

This recipe combines chicken breast with prosciutto in a kind of saltimbocca approach usually done in Italy with veal. You could also use boneless thighs for a richer flavor. I've used Marsala wine here, which is traditional, but you could use whatever wine you like, including a sweeter-styled sherry or even a vin cotto (see Note).

Butterfly each chicken breast (or have the butcher do it for you), place between sheets of parchment or waxed paper, and with a meat mallet or the back of a small, heavy iron skillet, gently pound until about ¼ inch thick. Place a sage leaf and 2 overlapping slices of prosciutto on each chicken breast and fold over to form a sandwich, with the prosciutto on the outside. Pound gently again to an even thickness and secure with toothpicks if needed.

In a heavy skillet, melt 2 tablespoons of the butter with the olive oil over medium-high heat. Dredge the chicken breasts in seasoned flour and add to the pan. Cook until beautifully browned on both sides, about 5 minutes. Set aside and keep warm.

Add the mushrooms to the pan with a bit more olive oil if necessary and sauté until they are lightly browned and the juices have evaporated. Set aside and keep warm. Add the Marsala and stock to the pan, scraping up any browned bits. Bring to a boil and reduce by half or until the sauce has thickened lightly. Whisk in the remaining 2 tablespoons butter. Season to taste with salt and pepper. Place the chicken breasts on warm plates and top with oyster mushrooms. Spoon the sauce over and garnish with fried sage leaves, if using. Serve immediately.

Note: Vin cotto *translates to "cooked wine" in Italian. You can buy a ready-made one in fancy food stores or make your own with 5 cups hearty red wine, ½ cup honey, 2 large cinnamon sticks, and 3 cloves. Combine in a heavy saucepan and bring to a boil. Reduce the heat and simmer until reduced to 1 cup, about 20 minutes. Cool and remove the cinnamon and cloves before using.*

SOY-POACHED GAME HENS

Serves 4

RECOMMENDED WINE
A fruity white wine with a bit of residual sugar, such as **Gewürztraminer**, **Riesling**, or **Chenin Blanc**, would match up well with the sweet, aromatic poaching liquid. A crisp sparkling wine would also work.

4 cups water

¾ cup dark soy sauce

⅓ cup sugar

⅓ cup Chinese black or balsamic vinegar

4 tablespoons chopped fresh ginger

Juice and half the grated zest of 1 orange

4 large garlic cloves, bruised

¾ teaspoon fennel seeds

1 large star anise pod

One 3-inch piece cinnamon stick

¼ teaspoon red pepper flakes

2 large game hens, about 14 ounces each

Toasted sesame oil

3 cups mixed savory baby greens, such as red mustard, arugula, savoy cabbage, or mizuna

4 ounces soba noodles, cooked and cooled

Toasted sesame seeds, diagonally sliced green onions, and fresh cilantro sprigs for garnishing

This is a Chinese approach to cooking and serving poultry. The hens may be served in smaller, chopped pieces as an appetizer, or halved for a main course. This same technique also works deliciously with chicken and pork loin or tenderloin.

In a medium stockpot, heat the water, soy sauce, sugar, vinegar, ginger, orange juice, orange zest, garlic, fennel seeds, anise pod, cinnamon stick, and pepper flakes. Simmer, covered, for 5 minutes.

Add the game hens and gently simmer, covered, for 35 minutes. Remove from the heat and allow the hens to stand for 20 to 25 minutes or longer. The longer they stand the more the color and flavor of the poaching liquid will be absorbed.

Remove the hens to a cutting board, cut in half, and paint liberally with sesame oil. Strain the poaching liquid. Toss the greens and noodles gently together with a little of the liquid and arrange on plates. Top with the hen halves and garnish with sesame seeds, green onions, and cilantro.

The soy poaching liquid can be used again. Discard the fat and store, covered, in the refrigerator for up to 3 weeks, or freeze indefinitely.

GRILLED QUAIL WITH CITRUS-MUSCAT SAUCE

Serves 4

MARINADE

2 tablespoons olive oil

Grated zest and juice of 1 large orange

Grated zest and juice of 1 lime

2 teaspoons chopped fresh thyme or
   1 teaspoon dried

1 small shallot, chopped

1 teaspoon kosher or sea salt

8 partially boned quail, at least 5 ounces each

Citrus-Muscat Sauce (recipe follows)

RECOMMENDED WINE
The citrusy tang to this dish suggests a lemony **Sauvignon Blanc** or a dry but fruity **rosé**.

Farm-raised quail are delicate in flavor and benefit from marinating. Here, a citrus-based marinade and sauce complement nicely. Partially boned quail can be ordered ahead from a good butcher shop. For sources, see page 425.

In a medium bowl, mix together the olive oil, orange zest, orange juice, lime zest, lime juice, thyme, shallot, and salt. Add the quail and store, covered, in the refrigerator for 2 hours, turning occasionally. You can make the Citrus-Muscat Sauce while the quail are marinating. Remove the quail from the marinade, reserving the marinade for basting.

On a charcoal or gas grill, cook the quail, breast-side down, for 3 to 4 minutes or until well marked. Turn, baste with the reserved marinade, and grill for another 4 minutes or until cooked through but still juicy and slightly pink (not raw) inside.

Serve on warm plates, with the Citrus-Muscat sauce spooned over.

CITRUS-MUSCAT SAUCE
Makes about 2 cups

1 tablespoon olive oil

½ cup chopped carrot

¼ cup chopped celery

1 tablespoon chopped shallot or green onion,
   white part only

1 teaspoon chopped garlic

2 cups sweet Muscat wine or sweet sherry

Juice of 1 lime

½ cup fresh tangerine or orange juice

2 cups chicken stock

2 tablespoons unsalted butter

In a medium saucepan, heat the olive oil over medium-high heat and sauté the carrot, celery, shallot, and garlic until the vegetables are lightly browned. Add the wine, lime juice, and tangerine juice, and stock. Bring to a boil and reduce over high heat until lightly thickened, about 10 minutes. Remove from the heat and whisk in the butter. Keep the sauce warm.

ASIAN-MARINATED BREAST OF SQUAB

Serves 4

RECOMMENDED WINE
The dark, rich breast meat
would go wonderfully with
a lower-tannin red such as
Merlot or **Pinot Noir**.
Syrah also has a natural
gaminess to it, and so
would be another good
choice.

ASIAN MARINADE

¼ cup coarsely chopped peeled fresh ginger

2 tablespoons soy sauce

2 tablespoons fresh lime juice

1 cup olive oil

1 tablespoon Five-Spice Powder (recipe follows)

1 tablespoon toasted sesame oil

2 teaspoons freshly ground pepper

2 tablespoons finely chopped lemongrass,
   white part only, or 3 tablespoons finely grated
   lemon zest

4 whole squabs, cleaned

5 tablespoons olive oil

2 tablespoons minced shallots

8 ounces chanterelle or shiitake mushrooms,
   thickly sliced

Kosher or sea salt and freshly ground pepper

6 cups young savory sauté greens, such as
   spinach, chard, or mustard, or a combination

I love squab and don't think it's served enough. Two things about the breast: It's dark meat and it must not be overcooked. It should be pink and rosy. Cooked past that point, it quickly dries out and takes on a liver taste. This is a delicious recipe that works equally well with the breast of any bird: Quail, hen, chicken, or pheasant would all be wonderful. Adjust the cooking time as needed. You'll note that I recommend cooking the squab breast on the bone. This ensures that the breast will keep its shape. Also, cooking on the bone keeps the meat moist and adds flavor. I'm accompanying the squab here with cooked greens, but they would be equally delicious on fresh spicy greens. Try the Asian Orange Vinaigrette (page 25) on the fresh greens. Finally, you won't be able to buy just the breasts of squab. You'll have to order the whole bird, so I've tried to figure out a way to use the rest of it.

In a nonreactive medium bowl, combine the ginger, soy sauce, lime juice, olive oil, Five-Spice Powder, sesame oil, pepper, and lemongrass. Add the squabs and marinate for 4 hours or overnight in the refrigerator, turning occasionally. Remove the whole (bone-in) breast from each squab. In a sauté pan, heat 2 tablespoons of the olive oil over high heat and very quickly brown the squab breasts, about 2 minutes. Set aside. Save the remainder of the carcasses to make stock, or remove the leg and thigh portions and roast them to use as garnish.

Preheat the oven to 425°F. Put the bone-in squab breasts (and leg portions, if using) in a single layer in a roasting pan and roast for 6 to 8 minutes or until medium-rare. (If using the leg portions, cook them 5 minutes longer or until they are tender.) The flesh of the squab breasts should be pink and rosy. Set aside and keep warm.

In a sauté pan, heat 2 tablespoons of the olive oil and sauté the shallots and mushrooms until they just begin to soften. Season to taste with salt and pepper, set aside, and keep warm. Add the remaining 1 tablespoon olive oil to the pan and sauté the greens until just tender. Season to taste with salt and pepper.

Arrange the greens on warm plates. Carefully cut the squab breasts from the bone and arrange on top of the greens, with the shallots and mushrooms and the roasted leg portions alongside, if using.

FIVE-SPICE POWDER
Makes about 3 tablespoons

1 heaping tablespoon Szechuan peppercorns

½ teaspoon cloves

One 3-inch cinnamon stick

1 heaping tablespoon fennel seeds

4 star anise pods

This standard of Chinese cooking is a blend of five different aromatic spices. The choice of ingredients varies depending on the maker. Sometimes licorice root is substituted for the fennel or anise. Five-spice powder can be purchased ready-mixed, but like all ground spices it quickly loses its flavor, and I think it's best to make your own from spices that are freshly ground.

In a spice grinder, grind the spices individually, then regrind them together until the mixture is very fine. Store in the refrigerator in a jar with a tightly fitting lid for up to 3 months.

QUAIL STUFFED WITH WILD MUSHROOMS

Serves 4

1½ tablespoons unsalted butter

3 tablespoons olive oil

1 tablespoon minced shallot or green onion, white part only

3 cups wild mushrooms of your choice, cleaned and coarsely chopped

Kosher or sea salt and freshly ground pepper

2 tablespoons chicken stock or water

½ cup finely chopped leek, white and tender green parts only

8 boneless or semi-boned quail

SAUCE

½ cup dry Marsala wine

1 cup chicken stock

1 teaspoon chopped fresh thyme or ½ teaspoon dried

1 or 2 tablespoons Fig Jam (facing page)

½ teaspoon finely grated lemon zest

Kosher or sea salt and freshly ground pepper

Here's another quail and fig preparation that's simple and delicious. You can tell I like this combination, which for me says fall in the wine country. You could make your own fig jam or use a good store-bought version. I serve this with some simply sautéed greens.

In a heavy, ovenproof sauté pan, melt 1 tablespoon of the butter with 1 tablespoon of the olive oil over medium-high heat and sauté the shallot and mushrooms until the mushrooms are lightly browned and all the moisture has evaporated. Season to taste with salt and pepper and set aside. Wipe out the pan.

Preheat the oven to 400°F. In the pan, melt ½ tablespoon of the butter with the stock over medium heat and sauté the leek until tender but not browned, about 5 minutes. Season to taste with salt and pepper and add to the reserved mushrooms. Wipe out the pan again.

Stuff each quail with some of the mushroom mixture, being careful not to pack it in too tightly. Use just enough to re-form the shape of the quail. Tie the legs together with kitchen twine and season lightly. In the same pan, heat the remaining olive oil over high heat and brown the quail on all sides. Roast the quail until cooked through, about 10 minutes. Check for doneness with the point of a knife where the thigh joins the body.

To make the sauce: While the quail is cooking, combine the Marsala, stock, and thyme in a small saucepan, and reduce by half over high heat. Add the Fig Jam to taste along with the lemon zest. You should have a nice, textured sauce at this point. If not, reduce to desired consistency. Season to taste with salt and pepper.

Spoon any remaining mushroom mixture on warm plates, top with the quail, and spoon the fig sauce over.

FIG JAM

⅔ cup sugar

Grated zest and juice of 1 small lemon

1 pint fresh figs, coarsely chopped

½ cup dry white wine

In a small saucepan, combine the sugar, lemon zest, lemon juice, figs, and wine and cook over medium heat until the figs are tender and the mixture is thick. Store, covered, in the refrigerator for up to 1 month.

GRILLED QUAIL WITH PICKLED FIGS AND PROSCIUTTO

Serves 4

RECOMMENDED WINE
The sweet-tart flavors of the pickled figs are challenging for wine. However, a fruity and spicy **Gewürztraminer**, **Riesling**, or **Viognier** would be nice with this.

8 partially boned quail, at least 5 ounces each

2 tablespoons olive oil

Kosher or sea salt and freshly ground pepper

Pickled Figs (recipe follows)

12 thin slices prosciutto

Grilled quail, succulent little devils that they are, are extremely versatile. This preparation features the quail with sweet-tart pickled figs and the contrasting flavor of salty prosciutto. If you make the figs ahead, refrigerate them in their poaching liquid and return them to room temperature before serving. You get a bonus with this recipe: The leftover fig-poaching syrup is delicious on grilled meats or even ice cream. Be sure to strain it before using. The figs are served at room temperature, but the quail should be hot, right off the grill.

Prepare a charcoal fire (using mesquite charcoal, if possible) or preheat the broiler. Brush the quail with the olive oil and season to taste with salt and pepper. Grill the quail, breast-side down, for 3 to 4 minutes. Turn and continue cooking until nicely browned, 4 minutes or so. Alternatively, put the quail, skin-side up, on a baking sheet and broil until crisp on the outside, 4 minutes or so. Turn and continue broiling for another 3 minutes or until done. The quail should be slightly pink and juicy inside. Don't overcook.

Wrap each pickled fig with a slice of prosciutto and serve alongside the quail.

~~~~~~

PICKLED FIGS

1 cup sugar

1½ cups red wine vinegar

½ cup balsamic vinegar

One 3-inch cinnamon stick

6 cardamom pods, slightly crushed

2 star anise pods

6 quarter-sized coins of fresh ginger

4 slices lemon, seeded

6 peppercorns

12 firm fresh ripe figs, such as Black Mission

In a medium nonreactive pot, put the sugar, red wine vinegar, balsamic vinegar, cinnamon, cardamom, star anise, ginger, lemon, and peppercorns. Simmer, uncovered, for 10 minutes. Add the figs, cover, and continue simmering for 3 minutes. Remove from the heat and let the figs cool in the syrup. (The figs can be prepared to this point and stored in their syrup in the refrigerator for up to 2 weeks.) Using a slotted spoon, carefully remove the figs, reserving the poaching syrup for another use.

smoking foods

Smoking adds delicious flavor to many foods and, of course, is a terrific way of linking food to the smoky, toasty flavors in barrel-aged and fermented wines. Food can either be flavored with a bit of smoke and then cooked conventionally or cooked and smoked at the same time. The former method is usually called "cold smoking," in which little or no heat is used, while the latter is called "hot smoking."

There are all kinds of smokers available on the market today, including many that can be used right in the kitchen on top of the stove. These, of course, require a good ventilation system over the stove.

Any hardwood can be used for smoking, such as oak, hickory, or alder, and fruit woods, such as apple or cherry, also give great flavor. I also like to smoke with fresh herbs. Rosemary grows like a weed in the wine country, and we often throw bunches of it right on the coals to add a smoky, herbal flavor to meats, fish, or vegetables. End-of-summer herbs that are bolting, such as basil, dill, or fennel, are also great right on the coals.

A simple stove-top method to add some smoky flavor to meats or vegetables is to line a wok with heavy foil and then put hardwood shavings or sawdust in the bottom. You then put the food to be smoked on a rack and put the rack in the wok at least 2 inches above the wood. Place the wok on the stove over medium heat, and as soon as it begins to smoke, cover the top lightly with foil or a lid, or both, and allow the food to smoke for at least 3 or 4 minutes. Remove the wok from the heat, remove the lid (either with good ventilation or outside), and finish cooking the food on top of the stove or in the oven as needed.

One of my favorite quick recipes for smoked chicken or shrimp uses a marinade of Asian Orange Vinaigrette (page 25) with shrimp or boneless chicken breasts. These are marinated for at least 30 minutes and then wok-smoked as described above. Shrimp are completely cooked in 3 to 4 minutes, while boneless chicken breasts are usually done in 6 to 8 minutes.

BRINED AND SMOKED TURKEY ON THE GRILL

Serves 8 to 10

2 cups brown sugar

1 cup maple syrup

¾ cup coarse salt

3 whole heads garlic, cloves separated and crushed

6 large bay leaves

1½ cups coarsely chopped unpeeled fresh ginger

2 teaspoons red pepper flakes

1½ cups soy sauce

12 cups water

One 12-to-14-pound fresh turkey

Olive oil for coating the turkey

½ cup wood smoking chips, or as needed

The first step is to brine the turkey. Here's a more complex brine than the one used in Maple–Brined Roast Turkey (page 220). Traditional brines are made from a combination of just salt and water. I've taken the brine a step or two further with some additional flavoring ingredients. This brine is delicious with a variety of poultry or meats. The following recipe makes 4 quarts of brine, which should be plenty.

In a large enamel or stainless steel stockpot that is large enough to hold the brine and the turkey, mix together the sugar, maple syrup, salt, garlic, bay leaves, ginger, pepper flakes, soy sauce, and water. Bring to a simmer and then remove from the heat and allow to cool completely. Rinse the turkey well and remove the neck and giblets to save for stock or discard.

Put the turkey in the cooled brine and submerge it. Be sure there is enough brine to cover the bird—if not, add water to cover. Brine, covered, in the refrigerator for at least 2 days or up to 4. Turn the turkey in the brine twice a day.

Remove the turkey from the brine and pat dry. Lightly coat with olive oil and set aside. Prepare the grill by lighting 24 charcoal briquettes, preferably in a chimney starter. When hot and spotted gray, pour half the briquettes onto one side of the grate and the other half on the opposite side. Place a metal drip pan which is at least 1 inch deep in the center, with the hot coals on either side. The pan should be large enough to catch all the drips from the turkey.

Place ½ cup wood smoking chips in the center of a double layer of heavy-duty foil cut about 10 inches square. Form the foil into a bag shape, leaving the top open and put on top of one of the mounds of hot coals. (Alternatively, you can use a 6-inch cast-iron skillet to hold the wood chips.)

Put the upper rack of the grill in place and then center the turkey over the drip pan. Cover the grill and partially close the air vents to restrict the oxygen but not so much that you put out the coals. Within a few minutes, the wood chips should start smoking. Regulate the vents to keep the chips smoking and the coals slowly burning. Check every 25 minutes to make sure the coals are still hot and the chips are still smoking. Add charcoal and additional chips as needed. The internal temperature of the grill should be 275° to 325°F. I like to keep the smoke going for 1½ to 2 hours. After that, I remove any remaining wood chips and continue cooking without smoke until the turkey is done. This insures that the turkey is not going to be too smoky in flavor, but you can adjust to your own taste. The total cooking time for a 12-to-14-pound bird will be about 3 to 3½ hours. The internal temperature of the bird should be 155° to 160°F when tested at the thickest part of the thigh or breast. Make sure the thermometer is not touching bone. You can also test by cutting a little incision at the leg-thigh joint and making sure the meat is cooked and juices run clear.

Remove the turkey from the grill and allow to rest at least 15 minutes before carving. You'll have a holiday turkey you'll never forget!

turkey on the grill

One of the best turkeys you'll ever eat is one that has been slowly grilled and smoked. It's simple to do. The keys are:

Covered grill. You'll need a grill with a tight cover (we prefer a kettle style) so that you can control the amount of oxygen and heat.

Brine. To maximize flavor and moisture, start at least a day ahead and brine the bird first.

Wood chips. Select a good hardwood to use as the smoking medium. You can find various sizes, from sawdust to small chips to chunks. They all can work. Hickory and oak are probably the most commonly available, but also look for fruit woods, such as apple, pear, cherry, walnut, or pecan. Here in the wine country, I often use grapevine cuttings, with wonderful results.

Meat thermometer. I prefer the instant-read type thermometer, but use whatever you want to keep track of the temperature of the bird.

Indirect-heat method. Use the indirect method (see left), and be sure to regulate the heat so that the bird doesn't cook too quickly.

That's it!

TURKEY SALTIMBOCCA WITH LEMON EGG SAUCE AND BUTTER-BRAISED SPINACH

Serves 4

RECOMMENDED WINE
The lemon in the sauce would be a natural bridge to a lemony **Sauvignon Blanc**, or crisp **Pinot Gris** or **Pinot Grigio**. A dry sparkler would also be interesting here.

Two 12-ounce turkey tenderloins, tendon removed

2 ounces paper-thin slices prosciutto

16 large fresh sage leaves

4 ounces smoked mozzarella, sliced as thinly as possible

Butter-Braised Spinach (facing page)

Lemon Egg Sauce (facing page)

Pan-roasted cherry tomatoes and fresh sage sprigs for garnishing

The literal translation of saltimbocca *is "jump in the mouth." This is an interesting approach to the holiday turkey that can be done relatively quickly and makes a great presentation. I've poached the turkey here, but you could also slowly sauté the turkey rolls (without the plastic wrap, of course) as an alternative. The Lemon Egg Sauce is based on the Greek* avgolemono *soup. This dish was part of a menu for a class I taught called "New Wave Thanksgiving." The idea was to use traditional ingredients in a different way. It included Orange, Olive, and Fennel Salad with Cranberry Vinaigrette (page 24) and Pumpkin Crème Brûlée (page 355).*

Butterfly the tenderloins and gently pound out until about ¼ inch thick. Place even layers of prosciutto, sage leaves, and smoked mozzarella on top, leaving a border about ½ inch all around. Place the turkey on a square of plastic wrap and roll up tightly lengthwise to form a sausage shape. Twist the ends tightly and tie with kitchen twine.

Place the rolls in simmering water and poach for 20 minutes to cook the meat through (160°F on an instant-read thermometer). Remove from the water, unwrap, and cut into medallions.

Place the Butter-Braised Spinach on warm plates, arrange the medallions attractively on top, and ladle the Lemon Egg Sauce around. Garnish with cherry tomatoes and sage sprigs and serve immediately.

BUTTER-BRAISED SPINACH

1 large bunch spinach

2 tablespoons unsalted butter

1 tablespoon minced shallot or green onion, white part only

Pinch of fresh grated nutmeg

Kosher or sea salt and pepper

Wash the spinach thoroughly and remove the thick stems. In a sauté pan, melt the butter over medium heat and sauté the shallots until soft but not brown. Turn up the heat and add the spinach all at once. Stir and cook for a minute or two until the spinach is just wilted. Remove from the heat and season to taste with nutmeg, salt, and pepper.

LEMON EGG SAUCE
Makes about 1 cup

1½ cups rich chicken stock

⅓ cup dry white wine

1 teaspoon cornstarch dissolved in 2 tablespoons stock, wine, or water

2 large egg yolks

1 teaspoon finely grated lemon zest

3 tablespoons fresh lemon juice

Kosher or sea salt and freshly ground white pepper

1 tablespoon minced fresh chives

In a small saucepan, bring the stock and wine to a boil and reduce by half, about 4 minutes. In a small bowl, whisk together the corn starch, egg yolks, lemon zest, and lemon juice. Slowly whisk the reduced stock into the egg mixture, being careful not to scramble the yolks. Return the mixture to the saucepan and cook over medium heat, stirring constantly, until the sauce thickens, about 2 minutes. Immediately strain, season to taste with salt and pepper and additional lemon juice, if you want, and stir in chives just before serving.

MAPLE-BRINED ROAST TURKEY

Serves 8 to 10

RECOMMENDED WINE
This sweet and savory preparation suggests a wine with
a little residual sugar, like
our favorite aromatic whites:
Riesling, **Gewürztraminer**,
and **Muscat**. A slightly
off-dry **rosé** would also
be good, as would a dry
sparkling wine.

1¼ cups kosher salt or ¾ cup table salt

1 cup maple syrup

4 quarts cold water

One 16-pound turkey, rinsed; giblets, neck, and
tail reserved for gravy

Olive oil for coating turkey

Kosher or sea salt and freshly ground pepper

½ cup unsalted butter, melted

⅓ cup maple syrup

Brining is a great way to insure that your turkey is moist throughout, especially the breast meat, which seems to always dry out before the legs and thighs are cooked. Once you do this, I swear you'll never roast or grill a turkey (or chicken for that matter) without brining ahead.

In a large enamel or stainless steel stockpot that is large enough to hold the brine and the turkey, mix together the salt, maple syrup, and water until salt is dissolved. Add the turkey and brine, covered, in the refrigerator for 8 hours or overnight. If you don't have room in your refrigerator an alternative is to put the turkey and brine in an insulated cooler and add frozen ice packs to keep it chilled. Make sure the brine completely covers the turkey. Make more if necessary.

Preheat the oven to 475°F. Remove the turkey from the brine, rinse, and pat dry. Tie the turkey legs together, if you want, and coat with olive oil. Season lightly with salt and pepper. Place the turkey, breast-side down, on a rack in a roasting pan and roast for 25 minutes. Turn the oven down to 325°F and continue to roast for another hour. In a small bowl, mix together the butter and maple syrup and season to taste with salt and pepper. Turn the turkey breast-side up and baste frequently with the maple-butter mixture. Roast for another 2 hours or until the breast temperature reaches 165°F when an instant-read thermometer is inserted into the thickest part of the breast.

RABBIT SAUTÉED WITH MUSTARD

Serves 4

⅓ cup Dijon mustard

1 tablespoon fresh thyme (1 teaspoon dried)

5 tablespoons olive oil

One 3-to-4-pound rabbit, cut into serving pieces

Kosher or sea salt and freshly ground pepper

2½ cups rich chicken or vegetable stock

1 cup dry white wine

¾ cup heavy (whipping) cream

Drops of fresh lemon juice

2 tablespoons chopped mixed fresh herbs, such as parsley, chives, tarragon, and chervil

4 ounces pancetta or good-quality bacon, finely diced

1 cup sliced sweet red or white onion

1 cup diced mushrooms

2 cups finely sliced green cabbage

I explored the world of rabbit in great detail in my first book, American Game Cooking, *but this new recipe begged for inclusion here. I continue to be befuddled by why rabbit hasn't become more of a staple in the American kitchen, considering its great value as a lean, very low-fat meat. It's a favorite here in the wine country because it's so versatile. Because rabbit "tastes like chicken," this recipe can also be done with chicken.*

Mix the mustard, thyme, and 1 tablespoon of the olive oil together and generously brush the rabbit. Season well with salt and pepper. In a large, heavy sauté pan, heat 3 tablespoons of olive oil and brown the rabbit evenly on all sides, being careful not to burn the mustard. Add the stock and wine to the pan and simmer, covered, for 40 to 50 minutes until the rabbit is tender. Remove the rabbit and keep warm. Add the cream, bring to a boil, and reduce to a light sauce consistency. Strain carefully through a fine-mesh strainer and season to taste with salt, pepper, and drops of lemon juice. Stir in the herbs and keep warm.

While the rabbit is cooking, in a medium sauté pan, heat the last tablespoon of olive oil over medium heat and cook the pancetta until browned. Remove and drain on paper towels. Discard all but 2 tablespoons of the fat from the pan and sauté the onion and mushrooms until the vegetables just begin to color. Add the cabbage and cook until it just begins to wilt but is still crunchy. Stir in the pancetta.

Divide the onion mixture among 4 plates, top with the rabbit, and spoon the sauce over and around. Serve immediately.

BEEF, PORK, LAMB, *and* VEAL

MEAT *and* WINE

We tend to consider all meats the same when it comes to matching them with wines, but while there are good reasons for following tradition and partnering red meat with red wine, sweeter, more delicate meats—like pork, lamb, rabbit, and veal—can also match well with full-flavored white wines like Chardonnay.

It's not necessary to cook a dish with the same wine that you're going to drink with it, but if you're drinking an affordable wine, then by all means use the same one to cook with. When you choose a wine to cook with, be sure that it's a good wine and one that you'd enjoy drinking, but it doesn't have to be an expensive wine. You certainly don't want to cook with a great old priceless Cabernet any more than you want to cook with anything from the supermarket labeled "cooking wine." Thankfully, "cooking wines" have all but disappeared from the shelves. Also, don't make the mistake of using leftover wine that you may have kept in your refrigerator for weeks. After a few days, wine begins to oxidize and to become a bit vinegary, which isn't necessarily complementary to the food you're cooking.

I'm often asked two questions: (1) What does wine contribute to a dish? and (2) Does all the alcohol burn off when I cook with wine?

Wine's contribution to a dish is generally one of flavor. It adds complexity and acts as a bridge to unify individual flavors. Also, there are food flavors that are only released in the presence of a bit of alcohol.

With regard to alcohol and cooking, the conventional wisdom has always been that it burns off quickly when heated. It's true that almost all (something like 98 percent) of the alcohol in wine evaporates after only a few minutes of cooking. Be advised, though, that even after long simmering for an hour or more, a very tiny amount of alcohol does remain. If this is of concern to you or someone you are cooking for, then leave the wine or other alcohol out.

Maguelonne Toussaint-Samat's wonderful book *A History of Food* contains perhaps the best description I know of wine's role in cooking: "What part does wine play in the preparation of a dish? Apart from its gastronomic qualities of flavor, wine puts all its nutritional virtues at the service of the cooking and digestion of food. Wine contains glycerine, so it helps to bind sauces, and less fat can be used. Wine is well flavored, and allows the cook to go easy on salt or omit it altogether. Wine contains tannin, particularly when it has been cooked, and stimulates digestion. Wine contains alcohol, but very little once it has evaporated in being cooked. It stimulates the taste buds, and thus the appetite. It brings out the flavor of food and helps the system to digest fat. And it is very good for morale."

MARINATED AND GRILLED FLANK STEAK WITH LIME-CHIPOTLE SAUCE

Serves 6

3 pounds flank steak

MARINADE

2 tablespoons minced chipotle in adobo sauce

1 tablespoon minced garlic

3 tablespoons chopped fresh cilantro

⅓ cup olive oil

¾ cup hearty red wine

½ cup soy sauce

Grilled sweet red onions, grilled red and yellow bell peppers, and fresh cilantro sprigs for garnishing

Lime-Chipotle Sauce (recipe follows)

RECOMMENDED WINE
The chipotle spice and acidity are pretty intense in the sauce, and so a wine with little tannin and lots of fruit is essential. A soft fruity **Pinot Noir** could be great here, especially if it had a little chill on it. For a white wine, choose a fresh, fruity, lower-alcohol wine such as **Riesling**, **Chenin Blanc**, or **Gewürztraminer**. Off-dry sparkling wines also go well with chile spice. Beer would be great too!

This is a great outdoor summer dish since it doesn't involve any stove-top or oven cooking. The pronounced smoky, spicy heat of the chipotle chiles is delicious with the flank steak. Chipotles in adobo sauce can be found in small cans in Latino markets and the Mexican foods section of many supermarkets. When this book was originally published, chipotles were still exotic in many parts of the country. Not so today! Any leftover meat and sauce can be used in to make fajitas or a quick chili.

Carefully trim the steak of any fat.

To make the marinade: In a large bowl, mix together the chipotle, garlic, cilantro, olive oil, wine, and soy sauce. Add the steak and marinate for at least 4 hours or overnight, covered, in the refrigerator, turning occasionally.

Remove the excess marinade from the steak and grill over hot coals to the desired doneness, 4 to 5 minutes per side for medium-rare. Let the steak rest for 3 minutes.

Slice the meat thinly across the grain on an angle and arrange on warm plates topped with grilled sweet onions, peppers, and cilantro sprigs. Drizzle the Lime-Chipotle Sauce over or serve on the side.

LIME-CHIPOTLE SAUCE

½ cup honey

1 to 2 tablespoons minced chipotle in adobo sauce

3 tablespoons balsamic vinegar

2 tablespoons brown mustard

½ cup fresh lime juice

1½ tablespoons minced garlic

1 teaspoon ground cumin

½ teaspoon ground allspice

¼ cup chopped fresh cilantro

Kosher or sea salt and freshly ground pepper

In a blender, purée the honey, chipotle, vinegar, mustard, lime juice, garlic, cumin, allspice, and cilantro until smooth. Season to taste with salt and pepper.

JALAPEÑO-STUFFED STEAKS WITH POBLANO CHILE SAUCE

Serves 6

RECOMMENDED WINE
A good, hearty **Zinfandel** or **Syrah** with forward berry fruit will stand up to these lively flavors. Just be careful not to serve a wine with lots of tannin, which seems to elevate chile heat.

2 tablespoons olive oil

3 tablespoons seeded and thinly sliced jalapeño chiles

1 cup finely chopped onion

2 tablespoons chopped garlic

½ teaspoon cumin seeds

⅔ cup grated Jack or California feta

2 tablespoons chopped fresh cilantro

Six 1½-to-2-inch-thick beef tenderloin steaks

Kosher or sea salt and freshly ground pepper

Poblano Chile Sauce (recipe follows)

Cilantro sprigs for garnishing

The filling for these steaks can also be stuffed under the skin of a chicken or used to stuff pork chops. The Poblano Chile Sauce would work equally well with those meats, too. The recipe for the sauce makes more than enough to go with the steaks, so cover and refrigerate any unused sauce to garnish your next taco or tostada!

In a small skillet, heat the olive oil and sauté the chiles, onion, garlic, and cumin seeds until soft but not brown. Cool, then stir in the cheese and chopped cilantro.

Slice pockets into the steaks and stuff with the jalapeño mixture. Fasten the pockets if necessary with a skewer or tie. Season the outside to taste with the salt and pepper. Grill over hot charcoal to the desired doneness, preferably rare to medium-rare. Spoon the warm Poblano Chile Sauce onto plates and place a steak on top. Garnish with cilantro sprigs.

POBLANO CHILE SAUCE
Makes about 3 cups

1 tablespoon olive oil

1 cup chopped onion

1½ cups coarsely chopped husked tomatillos

1 tablespoon minced garlic

1 teaspoon seeded and minced serrano chile

1 pound poblano chiles, seeded and chopped

½ teaspoon toasted coriander seeds

½ teaspoon cumin seeds

1 cup rich chicken or vegetable stock

½ cup fruity white wine, such as Riesling

½ cup loosely packed fresh cilantro leaves

⅓ cup toasted almonds or pepitas, or a combination

Kosher or sea salt and freshly ground pepper

Fresh lime or lemon juice

In a sauté pan, heat the olive oil and sauté the onion, tomatillos, and garlic until lightly colored. Add the serrano chile, poblano chiles, coriander seeds, cumin seeds, stock, and wine and bring to a boil. Lower the heat and simmer for 5 to 8 minutes, uncovered, or until somewhat thickened. Cool slightly.

Place the mixture in a blender or food processor, add the cilantro and nuts, and purée. Season to taste with salt, pepper, and drops of lime juice. Thin, if you want, with additional stock Serve warm.

GRILLED RIB-EYE STEAKS WITH BLUE CHEESE BUTTER AND CRISPY ONION RINGS

Serves 6

Six 10-to-12-ounce thick-cut rib-eye steaks, well trimmed

Extra-virgin olive oil for brushing

Kosher or sea salt and freshly ground pepper

Point Reyes Original Blue Butter (recipe follows)

Crispy Onion Rings (recipe follows)

RECOMMENDED WINE
Here's a chance to drag out whatever "big boy" red wine you've been saving. Both the meat and the cheese will soften tannins in young wines like **Petite Sirah** or **Cabernet**.

You could use any good blue cheese to make the butter in this recipe, but I love Point Reyes Farmstead Original Blue (see page 421), which is made on a farm in Marin County, not too far from me. I think it's America's best blue!

Brush the steaks well with olive oil and season liberally with salt and pepper. Heat 2 heavy skillets over medium-high heat and sear steaks and cook to the desired doneness, about 4 minutes per side. Top with the Point Reyes Original Blue Butter and Crispy Onion Rings and serve immediately.

POINT REYES ORIGINAL BLUE BUTTER

2 heads roasted garlic (see page 264)

1 cup (2 sticks) unsalted butter at room temperature

½ cup crumbled Point Reyes Farmstead Original Blue cheese

2 tablespoons chopped fresh chives

Kosher or sea salt and freshly ground pepper

Squeeze the garlic from the cloves and mash in a small bowl. Mix in the butter, cheese, and chives until relatively smooth. Season to taste with salt and pepper. The butter can be wrapped in a log shape in plastic and foil and stored in the refrigerator for up to 5 days or frozen for up to 1 month.

CRISPY ONION RINGS

3 cups buttermilk

2 large sweet onions, such as Maui or Walla Walla, cut into thin rounds and separated into rings

3 cups all-purpose flour

2 tablespoons garlic powder

2 tablespoons pure chile powder, such as ancho

2 teaspoons kosher or sea salt

Vegetable oil for deep-frying

In a large bowl, put the buttermilk and onions and toss to coat. Let stand for 1 hour. In a medium bowl, mix together the flour, garlic powder, chile powder, and salt.

In a deep skillet or saucepan, heat 2 inches of the oil to 350°F. In batches, coat onions rings in the seasoned flour mixture. Fry for 2 minutes or until golden brown. Drain on paper towels and keep warm in a low oven while frying the remaining rings. Serve immediately.

SPICE-BRAISED SHORT RIBS

Serves 4

RECOMMENDED WINE
The spices in this recipe
call out for a wine that has
lots of rich, spice character.
Zinfandel and **Petite Sirah**
come to mind, and if
you are learning about
Italian varietals, as I am,
Sangiovese and **Brunello**
would be delicious too.

4 pounds beef short ribs, cut through the bone in 3-inch pieces

Kosher or sea salt and freshly ground pepper

2 cups diced onions

1 cup diced celery

½ cup diced carrot

3 tablespoons finely chopped fresh ginger

2 teaspoons Szechuan peppercorns or 1 teaspoon regular peppercorns

2 star anise pods

2 teaspoons fennel seeds

1 teaspoon crushed coriander seeds

One 2-inch cinnamon stick, broken into 4 or 5 pieces

4 cups Chicken Stock (page 66) or Beef Stock (page 68)

1 cup ruby port

1 tablespoon finely grated orange zest

1 cup orange juice

Freshly cooked aromatic rice, such as jasmine or basmati, and cilantro sprigs for garnishing

Short ribs are easy to prepare, and they fill the house with wonderful aromas. This is perfect for the cold-weather months.

Preheat the oven to 450°F. Trim the ribs of any excess fat and discard it. Generously salt and pepper the ribs. In a deep roasting pan large enough to hold them, put the ribs in a single layer, bones down. Roast in the oven until the meat is just beginning to brown, about 20 minutes. Turn the ribs and add the onions, celery, carrot, and ginger to the pan. Mix to coat the vegetables with some of the fat and then spread evenly in the pan. Roast until the vegetables are beginning to brown, 15 to 20 minutes longer.

Reduce the oven heat to 325°F and add the peppercorns, star anise, fennel seeds, coriander seeds, cinnamon, stock, port, orange zest, and orange juice to the pan. Stir gently, scraping up any browned bits. Cover the pan tightly with foil and bake until the meat is very tender when pierced, about 2½ hours.

Transfer the ribs to a serving platter and keep warm, lightly covered with foil, in a 200°F oven. Strain the pan cooking juices, pressing down on the solids to extract all the juices. Discard the solids and skim the fat from the juices. In a deep saucepan, boil the juices over high heat to concentrate and lightly thicken, about 10 minutes. You should have a generous 2 cups. Pour over the ribs and serve with aromatic rice, garnished with cilantro sprigs.

MEXICAN POT ROAST

Serves 6 to 8

3 large dried California, New Mexico, or ancho chiles, or ¼ cup pure chile powder

1¾ cups dry red wine

1¼ cups fresh orange juice

¼ cup balsamic or red wine vinegar

4 tablespoons chopped garlic

1½ tablespoons seeded and minced serrano or jalapeño chile

2 teaspoons ground cumin

¾ teaspoon ground cinnamon

1 tablespoon fresh oregano or 1½ teaspoons dried

2 teaspoons kosher or sea salt

2 pounds onions, thinly sliced

⅓ cup golden raisins or currants

3 pounds center-cut beef brisket, fat removed

Fresh tortillas, cilantro sprigs, lime wedges, sliced avocados, and crumbled queso fresco or feta cheese for garnishing

RECOMMENDED WINE
Ordinarily the chile heat would call for a fruity, lower-alcohol wine, such as a chilled **Gamay**. That would be nice, but I love this dish with a bigger but still not too tannic **Merlot**, **Syrah**, or **Pinot Noir**.

This is a south-of-the-border spin on a traditional pot roast, with sweet, spicy, and tart elements that offer a lot of flavor interest.

Remove the stems and seeds from the dried chiles (if using) and rinse. In a small saucepan, cover the chiles with water. Bring to a boil, then remove from the heat, cover, and let stand for 1 hour. Drain and set aside.

Preheat the oven to 350°F. In a blender or food processor, purée the softened chiles or chile powder with the wine, orange juice, vinegar, garlic, fresh chile, cumin, cinnamon, oregano, and salt until smooth. In a roasting pan, scatter half the onions and raisins and put the beef on top. Scatter the remaining onions and raisins over the beef and then pour on the chile mixture, spreading with a spatula to evenly coat the meat.

Cover the roasting pan tightly and bake until the brisket is very tender, about 4 hours. Shred the meat with a fork and mix with the onions and juices. Serve on warmed tortillas, garnished with cilantro, a squeeze of lime, sliced avocados, and cheese.

MY GRANDMOTHER'S POT ROAST

Serves 6 to 8

RECOMMENDED WINE
This is a hearty peasant-style dish that is a great match to big, deep reds like **Cabernet**, **Zinfandel**, or **Syrah**. A "teeth-stainer" like **Petite Sirah** would also go well.

3 pounds tri-tip (also called triangle tip or sirloin tip) or bottom round of beef

Kosher or sea salt and freshly ground pepper

4 tablespoons olive oil

4 cups sliced onions

1 cup sliced leeks

1½ cups diagonally sliced celery

1½ cups diagonally sliced carrots

¼ cup slivered garlic

¼ teaspoon red pepper flakes

3 cups hearty red wine

4 cups Beef Stock (page 68) or Chicken Stock (page 66)

2 cups canned diced tomatoes

2 large bay leaves

1 teaspoon fennel seeds

2 teaspoons minced fresh thyme or 1 teaspoon dried

2 teaspoons minced fresh sage or 1 teaspoon dried

2 teaspoons minced fresh oregano or 1 teaspoon dried

2 teaspoons cornstarch dissolved in 2 tablespoons wine or water (optional)

Roasted potatoes and sautéed shiitake or wild mushrooms for garnishing (optional)

My grandmother had a real touch for wholesome, comfort foods with tons of flavor. I don't know where her experimental side came from, but this is in memory of her. The meat is cooked until it is falling apart—stracotto, as the Italians would call it. This is my Sunday-supper favorite. As a footnote—I've done a live radio show about food in Sonoma County, California, for many years with my cohost Steve Garner. This has been the most requested recipe we've ever given out!

Preheat the oven to 375°F. Trim the beef of all visible fat and season to taste with salt and pepper. In a large, heavy-bottomed roasting pan, heat the olive oil and quickly brown the beef on all sides. Remove the beef and add the onions, leeks, celery, carrots, and garlic and cook over medium heat until the vegetables just begin to color and the onions are translucent.

Return the beef to the pan and add the red pepper flakes, wine, stock, tomatoes, bay leaves, fennel seeds, thyme, sage, and oregano. Bring to a simmer, cover, and braise in the oven for 2 to 2½ hours, or until the beef is very tender and almost falling apart.

Strain the liquid from the beef and vegetables. Allow the liquid to sit for a few minutes so that the fat will rise to the surface, then remove the fat and discard. Return the liquid to the pan, bring to a boil, and reduce over high heat by about one-third to concentrate flavors (if you want, thicken with the cornstarch mixture). Season to taste with salt and pepper.

Return the beef and braising vegetables to pan and warm through. Slice the meat and arrange in shallow bowls along with some of the braising vegetables. Generously ladle the reduced sauce around and garnish with roasted potatoes and mushrooms, if using.

SPICE-RUBBED PORK POT ROAST

Serves 8

SPICE RUB

4 teaspoons pure mild to medium chile powder, such as ancho or Chimayo

½ teaspoon ground cumin

½ teaspoon ground coriander

½ teaspoon ground ginger

¼ teaspoon Five-Spice Powder (page 211)

2 teaspoons kosher or sea salt

3 tablespoons olive oil

4 pounds boneless pork shoulder or butt roast, trimmed of excess fat

¼ cup olive oil

2 large onions, thickly sliced

6 large garlic cloves, thickly sliced

1 cup chopped fresh tomatoes or canned diced tomatoes

2 cups Chicken Stock (page 66)

1 cup orange juice

2 cups hearty red wine, such as Zinfandel

1 tablespoon brown sugar

Kosher or sea salt and freshly ground pepper

RECOMMENDED WINE
Since I'm suggesting **Zinfandel** in the recipe, why not serve the rest of the bottle with the pot roast?

This recipe combines one of my favorite all-purpose spice rubs with a slow-cooked pork roast. I keep a double or triple batch of the rub on hand for all sorts of things. Store in an airtight container for up to 2 months. You could also use the same approach below with a beef pot roast such as tri-tip (also called triangle tip or sirloin tip) or bottom round, or with pork belly (order the belly with the skin removed and the spare ribs still attached).

In a small bowl, mix together the chile powder, cumin, coriander, ginger, Five-Spice Powder, salt, and olive oil. Massage the spice rub into the roast. Marinate, covered, in the refrigerator for at least 4 hours or overnight.

Preheat the oven to 350°F. In a deep pot large enough to hold the pork comfortably, heat the olive oil over medium heat and brown the pork on all sides. Remove the pork and set aside. Pour off all but 3 tablespoons of the fat and sauté the onions and garlic over medium heat until lightly colored. Return the pork to the pot, along with any juices that may have accumulated, and the tomatoes, stock, orange juice, wine, and sugar. You should have enough liquid to barely cover the pork. If not, add equal amounts of stock, orange juice, and wine to cover.

Bring the pork to a simmer on the stove, then cover and braise in the oven for 2½ to 3 hours or until the pork is very tender and nearly falling apart. Remove the pork to a large bowl and strain the liquid through a fine-mesh strainer, pushing down on the solids. Discard the solids and briefly refrigerate the liquid so that the fat will rise to the top. Discard the fat and then add the stock mixture to a deep saucepan, bring to a boil over high heat, and reduce by at least one-third to concentrate and lightly thicken. Season with salt and pepper to taste. Return the pork to the pan and warm through. The pot roast is delicious served with roasted potatoes, polenta, or your favorite pasta.

GRILLED PORK CHOPS WITH ASIAN "GREMOLATA"

Serves 4

RECOMMENDED WINE
As with so many Asian dishes that have sweet, hot, or salty elements in them, I'd go with an aromatic white wine with forward fruit and maybe even a little residual sugar, like **Riesling**, **Gewürztraminer**, **Muscat**, or **Viognier**.

½ cup hoisin sauce

⅓ cup fresh lime juice

Eight ½-inch-thick loin pork chops, preferably bone-in

Olive oil for coating

Kosher or sea salt and freshly ground pepper

Asian "Gremolata" (recipe follows)

For this recipe, select chops that are no more than ½ inch thick. This will insure that you can get a good sear on the chop over a hot fire and also cook them through quickly. I'm including a little hoisin glaze that we'll brush on the chops in the last minute of cooking, which adds an interesting flavor note. Don't use it too early or else the sugar in the sauce will burn and become bitter. Gremolata is the classic Italian mixture of parsley, lemon zest, and garlic chopped together that I also use with Lamb Osso Buco (page 247). I'm taking some big liberties with the tradition, which is, after all, what California cooking is all about, and doing something with a bit of an Asian bent.

In a small bowl, whisk together the hoisin and lime juice and set aside. Coat the chops with olive oil and season generously with salt and pepper. Grill the chops over a hot fire for 3 to 4 minutes per side or until just done but still barely pink (not rare) in the center or along the bone. In the last minute of cooking, brush both sides generously with the hoisin mixture and grill until it just begins to brown a bit.

Arrange the chops on warm plates and sprinkle the Asian "Gremolata" over. Serve immediately, passing the remaining hoisin glaze on the side.

ASIAN "GREMOLATA"
Makes about ⅔ cup

¼ cup coarsely chopped fresh mint

¼ cup coarsely chopped fresh Thai basil or cilantro

1 tablespoon finely grated lime or lemon zest

1 teaspoon minced jalapeño or serrano chile

3 tablespoons finely chopped unsalted peanuts or macadamia nuts

In a small bowl, combine the mint, basil, zest, chile, and peanuts. Can be done an hour or two ahead.

GRILLED CALF'S LIVER WITH ONIONS AND BALSAMIC VINEGAR SAUCE

Serves 4

4 tablespoons olive oil

⅓ cup finely diced pancetta (2 ounces)

½ cup dry white wine

2 cups rich Chicken Stock (page 66) or
Beef Stock (page 68)

5 tablespoons balsamic vinegar

Kosher or sea salt and freshly ground pepper

1 tablespoon minced fresh parsley

1 tablespoon chopped fresh chives

1½ pounds ½-inch-sliced calf's liver

2 large red onions, cut into thick rings

Watercress sprigs for garnishing

RECOMMENDED WINE
A robust **Zinfandel** or **Syrah** works well with this hearty dish.

I've always liked liver if it's not overcooked—it should be pink and tender. It cooks very quickly, so be attentive! If you wish, you could whisk a tablespoon or two of softened butter into the stock and vinegar reduction to add body and richness to the sauce.

In a sauté pan, heat 1 tablespoon of the olive oil and cook the pancetta until it just begins to color. Remove and set aside. Add the wine, stock, and vinegar and cook over high heat until reduced to a light sauce consistency. Season to taste with salt and pepper, stir in the parsley and chives, and keep warm.

Prepare a charcoal fire or preheat a stove-top grill pan. With the remaining 3 tablespoons olive oil, liberally coat the liver and onions and season taste with salt and pepper. Grill both over hot coals until the onions begin to soften and brown and the liver is medium-rare, about 3 to 4 minutes per side.

Serve the liver on the onions, drizzled with the warm sauce and sprinkled with the reserved pancetta. Garnish with watercress sprigs.

STICKY RICE "TAMALES" WITH STAR ANISE BEEF OR PORK

Makes 8 tamales

RECOMMENDED WINE
The spicy Asian flavors suggest a soft, aromatic white wine such as **Gewürztraminer** or **Viognier** or a low-tannin red like **Gamay** for contrast.

FILLING

1 tablespoon peanut or olive oil

1 pound lean pot roast, preferably tri-tip (also called triangle tip or sirloin tip)

1 cup water

3 tablespoons dark soy sauce

½ cup dry white wine or vermouth

1 tablespoon brown sugar

2 star anise pods

¼ teaspoon red pepper flakes

One 2-inch piece cinnamon stick

½ teaspoon dried orange peel

2 green onions, both white and green parts, sliced diagonally into 2-inch lengths

2 large garlic cloves, smashed

One 2-inch piece fresh ginger, peeled and cut into coins

TAMALES

½ ounce (2 large) dried shiitake mushrooms

1 cup white or black short-grain sticky rice

2 cups cold water

2 tablespoons peanut or olive oil

1 teaspoon kosher or sea salt

2 teaspoons Thai red curry paste

3 tablespoons chopped fresh basil

8 or more large iceberg or romaine lettuce leaves, blanched briefly in boiling water to soften

Fresh cilantro sprigs and toasted black sesame seeds for garnishing

The Thai red curry paste called for in the recipe is available in Asian markets. If you can't find it, substitute ¼ teaspoon cayenne pepper. The recipe calls for using lettuce leaf wraps. Alternatively, you could use bottled grape leaves that are well rinsed. I love the star anise beef filling, and if you don't feel like rolling and steaming the tamales, the filling is delicious just spooned onto cold lettuce leaves.

To make the filling: In a heavy skillet, heat the peanut oil and quickly brown the beef. In a large saucepan, combine the beef, water, soy sauce, wine, brown sugar, star anise, pepper flakes, cinnamon stick, orange peel, green onions, garlic, and ginger. Bring to a boil, then reduce the heat to a simmer, cover, and cook until the beef is very tender, about 1½ hours. Remove the star anise, cinnamon stick, and ginger. Cool the beef in the liquid, then remove and shred.

To make the tamales: In a small bowl, soak the mushrooms in 2 cups of warm water for 30 minutes to rehydrate. Drain well, mince, and reserve.

In a saucepan, combine the rice, cold water, 1 tablespoon of the peanut oil, salt, and curry paste. Bring to a simmer, whisking to dissolve the curry paste. Cover and simmer over very low heat for 15 to 20 minutes, until the liquid is absorbed. Let stand, covered, for another 10 minutes. Transfer to a medium bowl and fold in the remaining 1 tablespoon of the peanut oil, the rehydrated mushrooms, and the basil. Spread the rice onto the lettuce leaves in a uniform layer, leaving about a ½-inch border. Spoon about 1 heaping tablespoon of the beef filling down the center of the rice, then roll to enclose the filled rice completely. You may need to use more than one leaf to make a tamale. Tie with kitchen twine, if you want. In a steamer over boiling water, steam the tamales for 30 to 40 minutes. Remove the twine, put the tamales on a plate, and serve hot, garnished with cilantro sprigs and sesame seeds.

BEEF OR PORK WITH A COAT OF MANY COLORS

Here are some wine country ideas for saucing or topping a simple grilled or pan-sautéed piece of beef or pork.

AVOCADO SALSA
Makes about 2 cups

1 large, firm ripe Hass avocado, peeled, pitted, and cut into small dice

½ cup seeded and diced ripe yellow or red tomato

2 tablespoons finely chopped red or green onion, both white and green parts

½ teaspoon seeded and minced serrano chile

½ teaspoon minced garlic

1 tablespoon fresh lime or lemon juice

2 tablespoons chopped fresh cilantro

Big pinch of sugar

Kosher or sea salt and freshly ground white pepper

This is a simple salsa that is delicious with many things. For instance, I've suggested it as a garnish for Smoked Chicken Burritos (page 200).

In a medium bowl, gently combine the avocado, tomato, onion, chile, garlic, lime juice, cilantro, and sugar. Season to taste with salt and pepper. Store, covered, in the refrigerator if not serving immediately. Best used the day it is made.

BLACKBERRY SAGE SAUCE
Makes about 1½ cups

1 tablespoon olive oil

⅓ cup chopped shallots or green onions, white part only

1 cup chopped cremini mushrooms

2 cups hearty red wine

½ cup sweet port

5 cups rich Chicken Stock (page 66) or Beef Stock (page 68)

2 cups fresh or frozen blackberries

¼ cup coarsely chopped fresh sage

1 tablespoon honey

Kosher or sea salt and freshly ground pepper

In the summer, wild blackberries are everywhere in the wine country. They are a little seedy, but their flavor is fantastic. I love this sauce with grilled meats and game birds. Since the sauce takes a while to reduce, I'd double the recipe and store some frozen for a quick, elegant meal later.

In a saucepan, heat the olive oil and sauté the shallots and mushrooms until lightly browned. Add the wine, port, stock, blackberries, and sage and reduce, uncovered, over high heat until the sauce has thickened lightly and coats the back of a spoon. This could take 40 minutes or so. Strain through a fine-mesh strainer, pressing on the solids. Season to taste with honey, salt, and pepper. The sauce may be made ahead and stored, covered, in the refrigerator for up to 5 days or frozen for up to 6 months.

ARTICHOKE PESTO
Makes about 2 cups

One 6½-ounce jar marinated artichoke hearts, drained and coarsely chopped

⅓ cup diced red bell pepper

⅓ cup chopped green or black olives, or preferably a combination

⅓ cup chopped lightly toasted walnuts

½ cup loosely packed fresh basil leaves, chopped

1 tablespoon chopped roasted garlic (see page 264)

¾ cup extra-virgin olive oil or Basil Oil (page 80)

⅓ cup coarsely grated pecorino or Parmesan cheese

1 teaspoon finely grated lemon zest

Drops of fresh lemon juice

Kosher or sea salt and freshly ground pepper

This is not a traditional pesto, in that the ingredients are left chunky. The flavors are marvelous, however, and improve after sitting for a day or two. I often make a big batch of this to use not only on grilled meats but also on pasta, rice, or a slice of good toasted peasant-style bread.

In a medium bowl, combine the artichoke hearts, bell pepper, olives, walnuts, basil, roasted garlic, olive oil, cheese, and lemon zest. Season to taste with lemon juice, salt and pepper. Store, covered, in the refrigerator for up to 3 days.

PEPPERED BRANDY-CREAM SAUCE
Makes about 1½ cups

2 tablespoons unsalted butter

⅓ cup chopped shallots or green onions, white part only

2 teaspoons chopped garlic

⅓ cup finely chopped cremini or shiitake mushrooms

¾ cup brandy or Cognac

4 cups rich Beef Stock (page 68) or Chicken Stock (page 66)

2 teaspoons green peppercorns

1 teaspoon cracked peppercorns

½ teaspoon fennel seeds

2 tablespoons Dijon mustard

1¼ cups heavy (whipping) cream

Kosher or sea salt and freshly ground pepper

2 teaspoons chopped fresh parsley

1 teaspoon chopped fresh tarragon

Every once in a while, I get a craving for a little tenderloin done with this classic sinful sauce.

Melt the butter in a sauté pan over medium-high heat and sauté the shallots, garlic, and mushrooms until just beginning to brown. Raise the heat to high and add the brandy, stock, peppercorns, fennel seeds, and mustard and reduce by half. Add the cream and reduce to desired consistency. Strain or not as you desire. Season to taste with salt and pepper and stir in the parsley and tarragon just before serving. The sauce can be made ahead and stored, covered, in the refrigerator for up to 3 days. Gently reheat it before serving.

PORK AND PEPPER STEW WITH ORANGES

Serves 6 to 8

RECOMMENDED WINE
A chilled barrel-fermented and aged **Chardonnay** goes well with this stew. On the red side, a fruity, berry-tinged **Zinfandel** with its peppery complexity is a nice alternative.

2½ pounds boneless pork shoulder or butt, cut into 2-inch cubes

Kosher or sea salt and freshly ground pepper

4 tablespoons olive oil

2 pounds onions, halved and thickly sliced

4 tablespoons thickly sliced garlic

1 cup diagonally sliced celery

2 seeded and thickly sliced large poblano chiles

1 teaspoon minced jalapeño chile

1 cup thinly sliced red bell pepper

¾ teaspoon whole fennel seeds

2 teaspoons dried Mexican oregano

2 cups canned diced tomatoes, including juice

2½ cups rich Chicken Stock (page 66) or Mushroom Stock (page 70)

½ cup dry white wine

3 tablespoons pure California or New Mexico chile powder

1 teaspoon dried shrimp powder (optional)

⅓ cup golden raisins

3 tablespoons chopped fresh cilantro

1½ cups fresh orange segments

Orange-Cinnamon Rice (facing page)

Orange segments and fresh cilantro sprigs for garnishing

This stew brings together spice and sweet fruit flavors in a delicious way. Like all stews, it's even better the next day, and it freezes well if you want to make a big batch. Almost any other meat will work here, too, such as beef, veal, or chicken. Don't let the long list of ingredients scare you off. It's really a pretty easy recipe once you get everything together.

Liberally season the pork with salt and pepper. In a heavy pot, heat 2 tablespoons of the olive oil and quickly brown the pork. Remove and set aside.

Add the remaining 2 tablespoons of the olive oil to the pot and heat. Sauté the onions, garlic, celery, poblano chiles, jalapeño chile, and red bell pepper until they just begin to color. Add the fennel seeds, oregano, tomatoes, stock, wine, chile powder, and shrimp powder (if using), and bring to a boil. Add the pork and raisins. Reduce the heat, cover, and simmer until the pork is tender, about 35 to 40 minutes. Remove from the heat. Using a spoon, skim any fat from the top.

Stir in the cilantro and 1½ cups orange segments. Ladle the stew onto warm plates and serve with the Orange-Cinnamon Rice. Garnish with orange segments and cilantro sprigs.

ORANGE-CINNAMON RICE

1 tablespoon olive oil or unsalted butter

⅓ cup minced onion

1 cup basmati or other long-grain rice

2 teaspoons grated orange zest

One 4-inch cinnamon stick

1¼ cups water

½ cup fresh orange juice

½ teaspoon kosher or sea salt

In a medium saucepan, heat the olive oil over medium heat and sauté the onion until soft but not brown. Add the rice and sauté 2 minutes longer, stirring occasionally. Add the orange zest, cinnamon stick, water, orange juice, and salt and bring to a boil, stirring once or twice.

Reduce the heat to a simmer, cover, and cook for 15 minutes or until all the liquid is absorbed. Remove the cinnamon stick. Let stand for 5 minutes, partially covered, before serving.

PORK CHOPS BRAISED WITH DRIED FRUITS AND ALMONDS

Serves 6

RECOMMENDED WINE
The sweet dried fruits and the spices in this dish are a great match for the **Gewürztraminer** that is also recommended for the cooking wine.

Six 1¼-inch-thick center-cut pork chops, trimmed of fat

Kosher or sea salt and freshly ground pepper

¼ cup olive oil

1½ cups chopped red onions

2 teaspoons minced garlic

2 teaspoons orange zest

4 cups fresh orange juice

1 cup fruity white wine like, Gewürztraminer

2 cups rich Chicken Stock (page 66)

1 tablespoon seeded and minced serrano chile

1 cup Oven-Dried Apple Slices (page 179)

1 cup dried figs or prunes, halved

3 tablespoons peeled and chopped fresh ginger

One 2-inch piece cinnamon stick

1 teaspoon ground allspice

Kosher or sea salt and freshly ground pepper

Toasted slivered almonds for garnishing

I entered this recipe in a contest sponsored by the Pork Council many years ago. I didn't win, but I still prepare this wonderful casserole in the winter, when I'm craving rich, comforting foods. These chops are delicious served with Moroccan-Inspired Cinnamon Couscous with Sweet Spice Vegetables (page 282).

Preheat the oven to 325°F. Season the chops to taste with salt and pepper. In a heavy, flame-proof casserole or Dutch oven, heat 2 tablespoons of the olive oil and quickly brown the pork chops on both sides. If necessary, do this in batches to avoid crowding. Remove and set aside. Heat the remaining olive oil in the casserole over medium heat and sauté the onions and garlic until lightly colored. Return the chops to the casserole and add the orange zest, orange juice, wine, stock, chile, Oven-Dried Apple Slices, figs, ginger, cinnamon, and allspice. Cover and bring to a simmer. Braise in the oven for 1 hour or until the chops are tender.

Remove the chops and fruits to plates and keep warm. Discard the cinnamon stick. Reduce the juices to a light sauce consistency and season to taste with salt and pepper. Serve the pork chops with the sauce and garnish with toasted almonds.

GRILLED PORK TENDERLOIN WITH BERRIES AND NECTARINES

Serves 4

1 cup red wine vinegar

1 cup hearty red wine

¾ cup sugar

3 tablespoons olive oil

1 teaspoon finely grated lemon zest

One 2-inch piece cinnamon stick, broken

Kosher or sea salt and freshly ground pepper

3 cups fresh or frozen blackberries or raspberries

Two 12-ounce trimmed pork tenderloins

2 cups Chicken Stock (page 66), low salt or unsalted

2 large, firm ripe nectarines, pitted and halved

This simple recipe uses a fresh berry marinade that works equally well with duck breasts. The nectarines need to be full of flavor for this to work. Alternatively, you could use mango or pineapple if flavorful nectarines aren't available.

Combine the vinegar, wine, sugar, 1 tablespoon of the olive oil, lemon zest, cinnamon stick, 1 teaspoon salt, ½ teaspoon pepper, and the berries in a saucepan and bring to a boil. Remove from the heat, cool, and store, covered, in the refrigerator if not using immediately.

Place the pork in the cooled berry mixture and marinate for 2 to 4 hours, covered, in the refrigerator. Remove the pork from the marinade and reserve the marinade for the sauce.

In a saucepan, combine 2 cups of the reserved marinade with the stock. Bring to a boil and reduce by half or to a light sauce consistency. Strain through a fine-mesh strainer and discard the solids. Season to taste with salt and pepper and keep warm.

Brush the pork and nectarines with the remaining olive oil and season the pork to taste with salt and pepper. Grill or broil the pork and nectarines until just done. The pork should be slightly pink in the center and juicy. The nectarines should retain their shape.

Spoon the sauce onto warm plates. Slice the pork on the bias and arrange on top of the sauce. Slice and arrange the nectarines attractively around. Serve immediately.

HONEY-MUSTARD APRICOT GLAZE FOR PORK

Makes about 2 cups

RECOMMENDED WINE
As I've noted with other recipes, a natural bridge between food and the wine served with it is to use the same wine in both places. A **Riesling** or **Gewürztraminer** with just a little residual sugar would be a nice choice here. If you wanted something "redder," then I'd select an off-dry **rosé** or lower-tannin red such as **Gamay**.

5 ounces dried California apricots

1½ cups fruity white wine, such as Riesling or Gewürztraminer, or water

2 tablespoons unsalted butter

¼ cup minced shallots

⅔ cup white wine vinegar

¼ cup Dijon mustard

½ cup honey

Kosher or sea salt and freshly ground white pepper

I can't resist including this glaze, which is delicious on pork tenderloins or chops. Make up the glaze and marinate the pork in a cup of it in the refrigerator for a few hours, or overnight if you have time. Wipe off the excess glaze, then grill or broil the pork until it's nicely browned, and brush with the remaining glaze in the last few minutes so that it doesn't burn. This recipe makes enough for 3 pounds of pork.

In a heavy saucepan, combine the apricots and wine. Bring to a boil, reduce the heat, and simmer, uncovered, for 12 to 15 minutes or until the apricots are tender and the liquid is reduced by half. In a sauté pan, melt the butter and sauté the shallots until softened but not brown.

Transfer the apricot mixture and the shallots to a food processor along with the vinegar, mustard, and honey. Season to taste with salt and white pepper and purée until smooth. Return the mixture to the saucepan and bring to a simmer. Simmer, uncovered, for 8 to 10 minutes or until thickened.

Cool and store, covered, in the refrigerator for up to 3 weeks.

SPICY BRAISED EGGPLANT WITH PRUNES AND PORK

Serves 4 to 6

½ cup vegetable oil

1 pound lean pork, diced

1 tablespoon toasted sesame oil

1 pound eggplant, peeled or unpeeled, diced

1 tablespoon minced garlic

1 tablespoon minced fresh ginger

½ cup thinly sliced green onions, both white and pale green parts

1 cup rich Chicken Stock (page 66) or Vegetable Stock (page 69)

2 tablespoons dark soy sauce

⅓ cup thinly sliced prunes

1½ tablespoons Chinese hot bean paste

2 teaspoons cornstarch

Lots of fresh cilantro sprigs and fine julienne of red bell pepper for garnishing

RECOMMENDED WINE

A clean, slightly sweet **Gewürztraminer** or **Chenin Blanc** would be the best choice among wines. More often than not, I have jasmine tea with this dish.

At one point in my cooking career, I did a lot of cooking with a Chinese friend, who taught me a great deal about quick cooking and Asian flavors. This recipe comes from that time, and I still cook it at home. Substitute chicken or shrimp or, for a nonmeat version, shiitake mushrooms. The hot bean paste called for in the recipe is generally available at Asian markets. If you can't find it, use ½ teaspoon seeded and minced serrano chile.

In a heavy-bottomed sauté pan, skillet, or wok, heat 2 tablespoons of the vegetable oil. Quickly sauté the pork until lightly browned and cooked through. Drain and set aside.

Add the remaining vegetable oil and sesame oil to the pan and quickly sauté the eggplant until lightly browned (about 4 minutes). Add the garlic, ginger, and green onions and cook for 2 to 3 minutes, until the eggplant is just tender but not mushy.

Add ½ cup of the stock, the soy sauce, prunes, and bean paste and simmer for 3 minutes. In a small bowl, dissolve the cornstarch in the remaining ½ cup of stock and add to the pan. Raise the heat to high and cook for 2 minutes longer or until the sauce thickens lightly. Stir in the cooked pork.

Garnish with cilantro sprigs and red bell pepper.

CHINESE-STYLE RIBS WITH SPICY CABBAGE SALAD

Serves 6 to 8 as an appetizer, 3 to 4 as a main course

RECOMMENDED WINE
The sweet, smoky flavors of the ribs are nicely contrasted by a soft, fruity **Gamay** or **Pinot Noir**, served chilled. For white wine, choose a fruity **Riesling**, **Gewürztraminer**, or **Viognier**. An ice-cold Bud (or a local brew such as Red Tail Ale if you're in Northern California) is not bad in a pinch either!

5 pounds pork spareribs

⅓ cup seasoned rice vinegar

½ cup soy sauce

⅓ cup honey or maple syrup

⅓ cup hoisin sauce

2 teaspoons toasted sesame oil

2 tablespoons minced garlic

½ teaspoon Five-Spice Powder (page 211)

2 tablespoons minced fresh ginger

1½ teaspoons Asian chile sauce
   or ½ teaspoon red pepper flakes

1 tablespoon grated orange zest

½ cup fresh orange juice

Spicy Cabbage Salad (facing page)

There are probably as many variations of barbecued ribs as there are cooks who do them. This is one of my favorites, with some decidedly Chinese flavors at work here. Many cooks parboil the ribs before they marinate and grill them. I've never particularly liked this method. I think they taste better cooked low and slow on the grill. For even more flavor, you could use some hardwood chips to add a bit of smoke. If I'm grilling, I simply put the chips in the middle of a square of heavy foil and then fold up the sides to make an open bag. I put this on the coals and cover the grill to restrict the oxygen, and the resulting smoke adds even more interest. I prefer sweet woods like apple or alder to mesquite or hickory, which can quickly overpower the food.

Remove the white membrane from the underside of the spareribs, along with any excess fat, if you want. In a small bowl, mix together the vinegar, soy sauce, honey, hoisin sauce, sesame oil, garlic, Five-Spice Powder, ginger, chile sauce, orange zest, and orange juice. Reserve 1 cup and pour the remainder over the ribs to coat. Marinate for 4 hours, covered, in the refrigerator or overnight, turning occasionally.

To cook in the oven: Preheat the oven to 350°F and put the ribs on a rack in a roasting pan in a single layer. Roast for about 1¼ hours or until the meat is tender, basting occasionally with the marinade.

To grill: Use the indirect-heat method, with charcoal on both sides of the grill and a drip pan that has been filled with water and put underneath (see page 217). Grill for 1 hour or until the meat is tender, basting occasionally with the reserved marinade.

Serve warm, with Spicy Cabbage Salad.

SPICY CABBAGE SALAD

6 cups finely shredded red or green cabbage, or a combination

2 cups finely julienned or shredded carrots

1 red bell pepper, seeded and finely julienned

1 cup julienned snow peas

¼ cup seasoned rice wine vinegar

⅓ cup fresh lime or lemon juice

2 tablespoons Asian fish sauce or soy sauce

2 tablespoons olive or peanut oil

1 tablespoon sugar

2 teaspoons minced fresh ginger

1 teaspoon seeded and minced serrano or bird chile

⅓ cup chopped fresh cilantro

Kosher or sea salt and freshly ground pepper

In a large bowl, mix together the cabbage, carrots, bell pepper, and snow peas and refrigerate. In a small bowl, whisk together the vinegar, lime juice, fish sauce, olive oil, sugar, ginger, and chile and allow to sit for at least an hour before using. Stir into the cabbage mixture along with the cilantro. Season to taste with salt and pepper and serve.

HAM GLAZED WITH MAPLE AND ORANGE

Serves 8 or so

RECOMMENDED WINE
A **Gewürztraminer** with
its citrusy-tropical fruit flavors or a chilled, fruity
Gamay would be terrific
choices here. The salt in
ham requires a fresh, fruity,
lower-alcohol wine.

One 6-to-8-pound cooked ham,
   preferably bone-in

1½ cups dark brown sugar

3 tablespoons grated orange zest

1½ cups orange juice

¾ cup maple syrup

18 cloves

3 cups dry white wine

Kosher or sea salt and freshly ground pepper

2 tablespoons chopped fresh parsley

The quality of hams varies widely, as we all know. I always look for one that has no water added and with the bone in. Although not made in California, I've always loved the hams and bacon from Nueske's (see page 425) in Wisconsin, a mail-order company. Although the bone makes it a little harder to carve, it contributes mightily to the flavor and texture of the ham. It also is a good indicator that you're not getting something that has been formed or otherwise constructed.

Preheat the oven to 325°F. Trim the ham of excess fat and lightly score the surface.

In a small saucepan, combine the sugar, orange zest, ¾ cup of the orange juice, and the maple syrup and bring to a boil. Reduce the heat and simmer for 10 minutes or until the glaze is fairly thick.

Spread the glaze evenly over the surface of the ham. Press the cloves into the ham and put on a rack in a roasting pan. Add the wine and remaining orange juice to the bottom of the pan and roast for about 10 minutes per pound or until the ham is richly browned.

Remove the ham to serving platter and keep warm. Degrease the pan juices, season to taste with salt and pepper, and stir in the parsley. Slice the ham and serve with the pan juices.

LAMB OSSO BUCO WITH TOMATOES, OLIVES, AND HERBS

Serves 8

16 center-cut 2-inch-thick meaty lamb
hind shanks (5 to 6 pounds)

All-purpose flour for dredging

Kosher or sea salt and freshly ground pepper

3 tablespoons olive oil

4 cups sliced yellow onions

4 tablespoons chopped garlic

2 cups diced celery

2 cups diced carrots

3 cups diced plum tomatoes

5 cups rich Lamb Stock (page 68) or Chicken
Stock (page 66)

2½ cups dry red wine

1 cup pitted whole Niçoise, Kalamata, or other
oil-cured black olives

2 teaspoons fennel seeds

2 tablespoons minced fresh oregano or
2 teaspoons dried

2 teaspoons minced fresh thyme
or 1 teaspoon dried

1 tablespoon seeded and chopped serrano chile
or ½ teaspoon red pepper flakes

Gremolata (page 86)

Fresh herb sprigs for garnishing

RECOMMENDED WINE
The robust flavors in this
dish are perfect for a
Zinfandel, Petite Sirah, or
Rhone-style wine, such as
Syrah or **Mourvèdre.**

*Braising tougher cuts of meat in liquid and seasonings at a lower temperature adds an incredible
amount of flavor and helps tenderize the meat by slowly melting the collagen and softening the tough
connective fibers of the meat. Classic osso buco is made with veal shanks, but I like lamb even better. Ask
for lamb shanks cut osso buco style, 2 inches thick.*

Preheat the oven to 350°F. Dredge the lamb shanks in flour and shake off the excess. Season to
taste with salt and pepper. In a deep flameproof casserole or Dutch oven, heat 2 tablespoons of
the oil and brown the shanks on all sides. Remove the shanks, wipe the casserole clean, and heat
the remaining 1 tablespoon oil. Sauté the onions, garlic, celery, and carrots until lightly browned.
Add the tomatoes, stock, wine, olives, fennel seeds, oregano, thyme, and chile. Return the shanks
to the casserole and scoop some of the vegetable mixture on top of them.

Cover the casserole and braise for 2 hours. Uncover and cook for 30 minutes more or until the
lamb is very tender. Remove the shanks and set aside. Strain the braising liquid and reserve the
vegetables. Remove the fat from the braising liquid and return it to the casserole. Over high
heat, cook the liquid until reduced to a light sauce consistency. Return the meat and vegetables
to the casserole and heat through. Season to taste with salt and pepper.

Serve the lamb shanks in wide-rimmed soup bowls and ladle the hot braising liquid around.
Sprinkle with the gremolata and garnish with herb sprigs.

LAMB AND EGGPLANT ROLLS WITH SAVORY TOMATO SAUCE

Serves 6

RECOMMENDED WINE
I like this dish best with a fruity **Cabernet** that is relatively low in tannin. Cabernet often has hints of mint in it, which would reflect the flavors of the filling well. If you prefer a white, an herbal **Fumé Blanc** or **Sauvignon Blanc** also goes nicely.

COATING MIXTURE

¾ cup finely toasted and chopped almonds

⅓ cup freshly grated dry Jack or Parmesan cheese

2 teaspoons minced fresh oregano or 1 teaspoon dried

½ teaspoon kosher or sea salt

2 large globe eggplants (about 3 pounds)

1 tablespoon extra-virgin olive oil, plus additional for brushing

Kosher or sea salt and freshly ground pepper

½ cup finely chopped red onion

1 tablespoon finely chopped garlic

1 pound ground lamb

3 tablespoons dry couscous or fine bulgur wheat

⅓ cup plain yogurt

2 teaspoons Madras Curry Powder (page 97)

3 tablespoons minced sun-dried tomatoes

½ cup blanched, squeezed, and chopped spinach or Swiss chard

2 teaspoons chopped fresh mint

2 teaspoons grated orange zest

¼ teaspoon red pepper flakes

1 cup buttermilk

Savory Tomato Sauce (facing page)

Fresh mint sprigs for garnishing

This Eastern Mediterranean–inspired dish looks a little daunting, but it is easy to make once you get into it. The filled eggplant rolls can be made a day ahead and stored covered in the refrigerator, as can the sauce. As a final garnish you could also drizzle a little Mint Oil (see page 80) around the plate for added interest.

To make the coating mixture: In a small bowl, combine the almonds, dry Jack, oregano, and salt and set aside.

Preheat the oven to 375°F. Slice the eggplant lengthwise into twelve ½-inch slices. Brush them liberally with olive oil on both sides and season with salt and pepper. Lay the eggplant in a single layer on a baking sheet and bake for 15 minutes or until the eggplant is lightly browned and softened. Set aside.

In a small sauté pan, heat the 1 tablespoon olive oil over medium heat and sauté the onion and garlic until softened. In a medium bowl, combine the onion mixture, the lamb, couscous, yogurt, Madras Curry Powder, sun-dried tomatoes, spinach, mint, orange zest, and pepper flakes. Mix thoroughly. Place even amounts of filling down the center of each eggplant slice. Roll up the slices. Carefully dip the rolls in the buttermilk and then gently roll in the coating mixture. Place the rolls, seam-side down, on a lightly oiled baking sheet. Bake for 20 to 25 minutes or until cooked through.

Serve the eggplant rolls on pools of the warm Savory Tomato Sauce, garnished with mint sprigs.

SAVORY TOMATO SAUCE

1 tablespoon olive oil

½ cup finely chopped red onion

2 teaspoons minced garlic

½ cup chopped carrot

3 pounds tomatoes, peeled, seeded, and chopped

½ cup rich Vegetable Stock (page 69) or Chicken Stock (page 66)

¼ cup hearty red wine

1 tablespoon minced mixed fresh herbs, such as rosemary, savory, and oregano

⅛ teaspoon red pepper flakes

Kosher or sea salt and freshly ground pepper

1 tablespoon minced fresh mint

In a medium saucepan, heat the oil and sauté the onion, garlic, and carrot until soft and just beginning to color. Stir in the tomatoes and cook until they begin to release their juice. Add the stock, wine, herbs, and pepper flakes, bring to a simmer, and cook, uncovered, for 15 minutes. Cool slightly. Transfer the mixture to a blender or food processor and purée. Return to the pan and season to taste with salt and pepper. Stir in the mint and keep warm.

GRILLED LEG OF LAMB WITH CURRANT–BELL PEPPER CHUTNEY

Serves 4

RECOMMENDED WINE
Bell peppers accent the herbal dimension often found in both **Cabernet Sauvignon** and **Merlot**. Cassis and currants help bring out the classic varietal fruit flavors of these wines.

MARINADE

1½ cups dry red wine

1 tablespoon Madras Curry Powder (page 97)

1 tablespoon chopped fresh rosemary
  or ½ tablespoon dried

1 tablespoon chopped fresh thyme
  or ½ tablespoon dried

2 garlic cloves, minced

⅛ teaspoon red pepper flakes

½ leg of lamb (4 pounds), boned and butterflied
  (ask your butcher to do this for you)

Kosher or sea salt and freshly ground pepper

Currant–Bell Pepper Chutney (recipe follows)

Here is another great treatment for lamb. Lots of lamb is raised in the Northern California wine country, and the savory and sweet flavors in this recipe are reminiscent of many preparations I've encountered here. The chutney, which blends sweet, tart, and spicy flavors, can be used with a wide variety of broiled or grilled meats.

To make the marinade: In a medium bowl, mix together the red wine, Madras Curry Powder, rosemary, thyme, garlic, and pepper flakes.

Transfer to a sealable plastic bag, add the lamb, and marinate in the refrigerator for at least 4 or up to 8 hours. Remove the lamb from the marinade and pat dry. Season liberally with salt and pepper.

Grill the lamb over a mesquite or charcoal fire for 8 to 10 minutes per side, or until the lamb is medium-rare and juicy inside, 125°F on an instant-read thermometer. Set the lamb aside to rest for 5 minutes, tented with foil to keep it warm.

Slice the lamb across the grain and top with Currant–Bell Pepper Chutney.

CURRANT–BELL PEPPER CHUTNEY

¾ cup dried currants

2 tablespoons olive oil

1 cup chopped onion

1½ cups chopped red bell peppers

1 cup Chicken Stock (page 66)

⅓ cup port or cassis

2 tablespoons sherry vinegar

1 tablespoon chopped fresh mint

Kosher or sea salt and freshly ground pepper

In a small bowl, soak the currants in warm water for 30 minutes. Drain.

In a large sauté pan, heat the olive oil over medium-high heat and sauté the onion and bell peppers for 3 minutes, or until the onion is just beginning to soften and brown. Add the stock, port, vinegar, and softened currants. Cook, uncovered, over medium-high heat until most of the liquid has evaporated, about 10 to 15 minutes. Cool and stir in the mint and season to taste with salt and pepper.

RACK OF LAMB WITH HOT-SWEET MUSTARD

Serves 4

Two 8-bone racks of lamb (1½ pounds each)

Kosher or sea salt and freshly ground pepper

2 tablespoons olive oil

2 tablespoons chopped garlic

2 tablespoons chopped shallots or green onion, white part only

1 cup hot-sweet mustard (see Note)

¼ cup chopped fresh mint

1 tablespoon dry sherry (optional)

½ teaspoon freshly ground white pepper

RECOMMENDED WINE

Mustard has a natural affinity for **Pinot Noir**. Classically, they both come from the same region in France and just seem to do a wonderful dance together.

A particularly tasty hot-sweet mustard called Mendocino Mustard, which is made in Northern California, inspired this dish, but any hot-sweet mustard will do. A simple accompaniment would be some quickly sautéed greens.

Preheat the oven to 425°F. Remove and discard the fat covering, known as the cap, from the racks. French-trim the bones of any additional fat, scraping them as clean as possible. Ask your butcher to do this or to show you how it is done. Season the racks well with salt and pepper. In a heavy-bottomed skillet, heat the olive oil and quickly sear the racks on all sides until nicely browned. Set aside.

In a food processor or blender, combine the garlic, shallots, mustard, mint, sherry, and white pepper. Process briefly to combine the ingredients—the mixture should be quite thick. Put the lamb in a shallow roasting pan on a rack, meat-side up. Liberally coat the top and sides of the racks with the mustard mixture.

Roast the lamb for 12 to 15 minutes for medium-rare (125°F on an instant-read thermometer). Allow the racks to rest for 5 minutes before cutting. Serve the racks cut into double chops.

Note: Commercially prepared hot-sweet mustards are widely available now. If you can't find one, you can make your own by taking any hot mustard and adding a bit of brown sugar to it. The goal is to have both the hot and the sweet come through equally.

LEG OF LAMB STUFFED WITH WILD MUSHROOMS AND FIGS

Serves 8 to 10

3 tablespoons olive oil, plus additional for coating

½ cup finely chopped shallots or green onions, white parts only

½ cup finely chopped carrot

¼ cup finely chopped celery

2 tablespoons finely chopped garlic

1 cup coarsely chopped cremini mushrooms

½ cup lightly toasted pine nuts

⅓ cup chopped dried figs

⅓ cup bulgur wheat

¼ cup loosely packed fresh mint, chopped

1 teaspoon chopped fresh thyme

1 teaspoon chopped fresh rosemary

2 teaspoons grated lemon zest

1¼ pounds ground lamb

1 large egg, lightly beaten

Kosher or sea salt and freshly ground pepper

One 8-to-9-pound leg of lamb, boned

RED WINE DEGLAZING SAUCE

⅔ cup diced onion

⅔ cup diced carrot

⅔ cup diced celery

3 garlic cloves, diced

1 cup hearty red wine

3 cups rich Chicken Stock (page 66) or Mushroom Stock (page 70)

Kosher or sea salt and freshly ground pepper

2 tablespoons finely chopped fresh parsley

You can stuff a large leg of lamb with any savory stuffing. Here's one I really like. The sauce is a classic one; it is quickly made and is a good technique for any roasted meat. Make sure you have a friendly butcher who will bone the leg for you.

Position a rack in the middle of the oven and preheat to 500°F. In a medium sauté pan, heat the 3 tablespoons olive oil and sauté the shallots, carrot, celery, garlic, and mushrooms until lightly colored. Remove from the heat and transfer to a medium bowl. Stir in the pine nuts, figs, bulgur, mint, thyme, rosemary, and lemon zest. Allow the mixture to cool completely, then mix in the ground lamb and egg. Season to taste with salt and pepper. (It's a good idea to sauté a teaspoon to taste for seasoning, since this filling can't be tasted raw.)

Season the cavity of the leg of lamb with freshly ground pepper. Sew the small end of the leg with a trussing needle and twine or use a skewer to close. Spoon the stuffing into the cavity and sew or skewer the opening to enclose the stuffing completely. With kitchen twine, tie the leg securely at 2-inch intervals. Coat the lamb generously with olive oil and season well with salt and pepper.

Place the lamb on a rack in a roasting pan in the middle of the oven and roast for 10 minutes. Reduce the heat to 375°F and roast for another 30 minutes. At this time, scatter the vegetables for the red wine deglazing sauce—onion, carrot, celery, and garlic cloves—in the bottom of the pan, then roast another 45 minutes until medium-rare, or until an instant-read thermometer registers 125°F in the thickest part of the leg. When the meat is done, transfer the lamb to a serving platter and cover very loosely with foil to keep warm.

To make the red wine deglazing sauce: Put the roasting pan over high heat and add the wine and stock. Boil for 6 to 8 minutes to reduce, scraping up any browned bits from the bottom of the pan. Carefully strain and degrease the sauce and season to with salt and pepper. Stir in the chopped parsley.

Serve the lamb cut into ½-inch-thick slices, with the sauce spooned around.

RACK OF LAMB WITH SUN-DRIED CHERRY SAUCE AND PARSNIP CHIPS

Serves 8

RECOMMENDED WINE
As mentioned, **Merlot** or **Pinot Noir** would work nicely. If you wanted to use **Zinfandel**, the addition of freshly ground pepper to the marinade and sauce would help make that connection. With **Cabernet**, be careful of getting the sauce too sweet.

1 cup olive oil

½ cup dry white wine

1 tablespoon minced garlic

2 teaspoons minced fresh rosemary or 1 teaspoon dried

2 teaspoons minced fresh thyme or 1 teaspoon dried

1 teaspoon kosher or sea salt

1 teaspoon freshly ground pepper

Four 8-bone lamb racks, Frenched

Sun-Dried Cherry Sauce (facing page)

Butter-braised Swiss chard, deep-fried parsnip chips cut lengthwise, and fresh thyme or rosemary sprigs for garnishing (optional)

Sun-dried cherries are one of my favorite ingredients since they mirror the flavor of many red wines, particularly Merlot and Pinot Noir. For the sauce, note that the amount of stock used in the reduction will depend on the richness and body of the stock. If it's weak, you may need to use more. You don't have to do the parsnip chips, but they are very good and make for an interesting presentation. Besides, we should all be eating more parsnips! "Frenched" lamb racks mean, that the fat covering has been removed, along with all the excess fat on the rib bones. You'll often find them this way in markets, or ask a butcher to do it for you.

In a medium bowl, whisk together the olive oil, wine, garlic, rosemary, thyme, salt, and pepper and marinate the racks for 6 hours or overnight, covered, in the refrigerator. Turn occasionally. Remove the racks and pat dry.

Preheat the oven to 425°F. Prepare the Sun-Dried Cherry Sauce and keep warm. First, sear the racks in a large sauté pan over medium-high heat until nicely browned on all sides, about 5 minutes. You can do this an hour or so ahead of time and keep the racks at room temperature. When ready to serve, roast the racks in the oven until rare to medium-rare (120° to 125°F), 12 to 15 minutes, depending on the size of the rack. Allow the racks to rest for 5 minutes before slicing.

Cut the racks into double chops and arrange on warm plates with the Swiss chard, if using. Spoon the Sun-Dried Cherry Sauce around the chops and arrange the parsnip chips over. Garnish with thyme sprigs, if using, and serve immediately.

SUN-DRIED CHERRY SAUCE

3 tablespoons olive oil

¼ cup chopped shallots

1½ cups chopped shiitake or cremini mushrooms

7 cups rich brown chicken or lamb stock

1½ cups hearty red wine

1 cup sun-dried cherries

1 teaspoon grated orange zest

½ cup fresh orange juice

2 teaspoons chopped fresh thyme

½ cup port

Kosher or sea salt and freshly ground pepper

In a sauté pan, heat the olive oil and sauté the shallots and mushrooms until very lightly browned. Add the stock and wine and reduce by half. Add half the cherries, the orange zest, orange juice, thyme, and port and reduce to a light sauce consistency. Strain and add the remaining cherries. Season to taste with salt and pepper. Remove the fat from the sauce and keep warm.

why roasted meat should rest before carving

Ever wonder why recipes call for allowing roasted meat to sit for a few minutes after you take it out of the oven or off the grill? The reason for this is that the meat near the surface contains less juice just off the heat than it did when you started to cook it. During cooking, the juices near the surface evaporate from the heat or are driven toward the center. If you carve immediately after cooking, while these juices are still unevenly distributed, the meat toward the edges will be dry. Also, you'll lose juices because the meat in the center can't hold all the accumulated juices that collected there during cooking.

A few minutes' rest gives the juices a chance to redistribute themselves, through osmosis, throughout the meat. So give chickens or thick steaks at least 3 to 5 minutes before cutting, and large roasts, such as prime rib of beef or leg of lamb, at least 15 minutes.

SPICY LAMB STEW WITH CRACKED GREEN OLIVES AND ORANGE RICE

Serves 6

RECOMMENDED WINE
A hearty **Zinfandel**, **Syrah**, or **Petite Sirah** would be a nice spicy bridge to this stew.

3 pounds trimmed boneless lamb shoulder, cut into 2-inch cubes

Kosher or sea salt and freshly ground pepper

3 tablespoons olive oil

6 rinsed and chopped anchovy fillets

½ teaspoon red pepper flakes

3 tablespoons finely slivered garlic

2 cups chopped yellow onions

1 teaspoon crushed coriander seeds

½ teaspoon crushed cumin seeds

1 tablespoon fresh oregano or 2 teaspoons dried

3 cups rich Lamb Stock (page 68) or Chicken Stock (page 66)

1¼ cups dry white wine

2 cups cracked green olives, well rinsed and pitted (see Note)

½ cup coarsely chopped fresh parsley

Red wine vinegar

Orange Rice (facing page)

Frizzled Onions (facing page)

Fresh mint sprigs for garnishing (optional)

All cooks should have a good lamb stew as part of their repertoire, and here's one of my favorites. Like all stews, this is even better the second day.

Lightly season the lamb with salt and pepper. In a casserole or Dutch oven, heat the olive oil and brown the lamb well on all sides. Remove the lamb with a slotted spoon and set aside. Remove all but 2 tablespoons of fat from the pan and add the anchovies, pepper flakes, garlic, onions, coriander seeds, and cumin seeds and sauté until just beginning to color, about 2 minutes. Add the oregano, stock, and wine and return the meat to the pan. Simmer, covered, for 1½ hours or until the meat is very tender. Allow the stew to rest off the heat for at least 30 minutes for the fat to rise to the surface. Skim the fat off and discard.

At serving time, add the olives to the stew and bring to a simmer. Stir in the parsley and season to taste with salt, pepper, and drops of vinegar. Serve with the Orange Rice and Frizzled Onions and garnish with mint sprigs, if using.

Note: "Cracked" refers to olives in which the meat has been split before curing to allow the curing brine to penetrate better. You can take uncracked green olives and smack them with the flat side of a chef's knife to create a similar effect. Cracked green olives are generally available in bulk in good delicatessens. Any good black or green olive can be used for this recipe, however, such as Cerignola, Lucques, Niçoise, Kalamata, and Picholine.

ORANGE RICE

1 tablespoon unsalted butter or vegetable oil

½ cup finely chopped onion

1 cup basmati rice or other long-grain rice

1¼ cups rich Chicken Stock (page 66)
   or Vegetable Stock (page 69)

1 teaspoon grated orange zest

½ cup fresh orange juice

2 teaspoons minced fresh ginger

2 tablespoons coarsely chopped golden raisins

Kosher or sea salt and freshly ground pepper

In a sauté pan, melt the butter over medium heat and sauté the onion until soft but not brown. Add the rice and continue to sauté and stir for 3 minutes longer. Add the stock, orange zest, orange juice, ginger, and raisins and stir in. Lightly season with salt and pepper, reduce the heat to a simmer, and cover. Cook for 15 minutes or until all the liquid is absorbed. Allow to rest off the heat for 5 minutes. Fluff with a fork and serve warm.

FRIZZLED ONIONS

¾ cup all-purpose flour

2 teaspoons kosher or sea salt

½ teaspoon ground pepper, preferably white

Canola or olive oil for frying

2 onions, thinly sliced and separated into rounds

In a medium bowl, mix together the flour, salt, pepper. Heat 1 inch of oil in a deep saucepan to 350°F on an instant-read thermometer. Dredge the onion rings in the seasoned flour and shake off the excess. Fry in batches in the hot oil until crisp and brown. Drain on paper towels. Can be prepared up to an hour ahead.

GRILLED VEAL CHOPS WITH CABERNET AND WILD MUSHROOM SAUCE

Serves 6

RECOMMENDED WINE
With **Cabernet Sauvignon** being used in the sauce, it's only natural to use it on the table as well. California Cabernet often has a mint flavor note to it, hence the addition of a little fresh mint to the sauce as a bridge ingredient.

Six 1¼-inch-thick loin veal chops, 10 to 12 ounces each

Herb Marinade (facing page)

12 ounces wild or cultivated exotic mushrooms, such as chanterelle, oyster, or portobello

Extra-virgin olive oil for coating

Kosher or sea salt and freshly ground pepper

Cabernet and Mushroom Sauce (facing page)

Fresh herb sprigs of your choice for garnishing (optional)

Veal has come into some disfavor because of the way that it was traditionally raised for the commercial market. There are now a number of ethical veal producers who raise their animals in a kind and humane way. Be sure to ask your butcher or meat department what the source of the veal is. Veal is a sweet, delicious meat that I love grilled. Note that the Cabernet and Wild Mushroom Sauce used here needs to be made ahead. It can be made up to 5 days ahead of time, stored, covered, in the refrigerator, and reheated when it comes time to serve the dish.

In a large bowl, cover the veal chops with the Herb Marinade and store, covered, in the refrigerator for a minimum or 4 hours or up to overnight. Turn occasionally.

In a medium bowl, toss the mushrooms with the olive oil, season to taste with salt and pepper, and cook on a hot grill until just done. Set aside and keep warm. Remove the chops from the marinade and grill or broil until just done, about 5 minutes per side. The meat should be rosy in the center and juicy.

Place the veal chops on warm plates, surround with the Cabernet and Wild Mushroom Sauce, and top with the grilled mushrooms and herb sprigs, if using.

HERB MARINADE
Makes about 1 cup

½ cup chopped onion

2 tablespoons minced garlic

3 tablespoons minced fresh basil

1 tablespoon minced fresh mint

⅓ cup dry white wine

1 teaspoon kosher or sea salt

1 teaspoon cracked pepper

⅓ cup olive oil

In a blender or food processor, combine the onion, garlic, basil, mint, wine, salt, and pepper and blend or process with 3 or 4 short bursts. Transfer to a medium bowl and whisk in the olive oil.

CABERNET AND WILD MUSHROOM SAUCE
Makes about 1¼ cups

½ ounce dried porcini mushrooms, soaked in 1 cup warm water for 20 minutes

2 tablespoons olive oil

½ cup sliced shallots or green onions, white part only

2 cups chopped shiitake or cremini mushrooms

1 tablespoon chopped garlic

1 cup chopped fresh or canned tomatoes

6 cups rich Beef Stock (page 68) or Chicken Stock (page 66), low-salt or no-salt

2 cups hearty red wine, such as Cabernet Sauvignon

2 bay leaves

2 teaspoons fresh thyme or 1 teaspoon dried

1 tablespoon Dijon mustard

2 teaspoons minced fresh mint

Kosher or sea salt and freshly ground pepper

Strain the porcini, reserving the soaking liquid, and chop. In a deep saucepan, heat the olive oil over medium-high heat and sauté the porcini, shallots, shiitakes, and garlic until lightly browned. Add the tomatoes, stock, wine, bay leaves, thyme, and mustard and bring to a boil. Continue to boil until the mixture is reduced to a light sauce consistency, about 25 minutes. Strain through a fine-mesh strainer, pressing down on the solids, and discard the solids. Add the mint and season to taste with salt and pepper.

VEGETARIAN MAIN COURSES *and* SPECIAL SIDES

VEGETABLES *and* WINE

Until recently, no one thought much about the relationship between vegetables and wine except to occasionally pronounce that they don't go together. Not going together meant either that the vegetables would ruin the wine (asparagus and artichokes being two famous wine ruiners), or that the wine would overpower the vegetables, which were too delicate to hold their own. But as we've expanded our choices of vegetables and ways to prepare them, we've discovered that vegetable-based dishes and even individual vegetables can go wonderfully with many wines. I am a great enthusiast of roasting and grilling vegetables. Both of these methods develop a complexity and depth of flavor in the vegetable that can match up to even a rich red wine. Try roasted young beets with a good California Pinot Noir or Merlot — delicious together!

Many of the recipes in this section are full-bodied dishes, designed for the center of the plate. You'll note that some contain a fair amount of cheese, but you can certainly use less cheese if you are concerned about fat. Thank goodness, though, cheese has returned to the American menu after being bashed by the fat police, which was the case when the original edition of this book was published. This is not, strictly speaking, a "vegetable" chapter, because in this book, as in wine country cuisine, vegetables are everywhere, not segregated to the side of the plate. Look to the "Salads," "Soups," and "Pastas, Gnocchis, Pizzas, and Risottos" chapters for more vegetable and vegetarian ideas.

ROASTING AND GRILLING VEGETABLES

The simplest way to bring out the flavor of vegetables, other than eating them fresh and raw, is to grill or roast them. Traditionally, most of us were taught to use water to cook vegetables, through boiling, blanching, or steaming. The trouble is that when you cook with water, flavor drains away from the vegetables into the water, and as a result, you have to add flavor back to the poor depleted things through the use of rich sauces or other toppings. Steaming does the least damage, but it also contributes nothing to flavor. I rarely use water or steam to cook vegetables anymore.

In grilling and roasting, you don't lose flavor to water. In fact, these dry-heat methods actually concentrate flavor by evaporating water in the vegetables. This also concentrates the natural sugar in the vegetables, which caramelizes and browns, yielding a golden exterior that is full of flavor. Because of the rich flavors and textures that result, grilled and roasted vegetables can certainly compete with meat for the center of the plate.

ROASTED GARLIC, TOASTED GARLIC, AND POACHED GARLIC

ROASTED GARLIC

Roasted garlic is a staple in my kitchen and appears in many recipes throughout the book. I consider it to be part of the basic larder of ingredients everyone should have on hand — almost up there with salt and pepper. I keep several heads of roasted garlic on hand at all times to add to soups, sauces, marinades, dressings, and pasta. When garlic is roasted, it changes from the bold, sharp pungent flavor we associate with raw garlic to something subtle, sweet, and buttery soft. And since it's roasted whole in the husk, you can easily squeeze out just what you need.

Preheat the oven to 375°F. Cut off the top ¼ inch of the garlic head to reveal the cloves. Drizzle a little olive oil over and season lightly with salt and pepper. Wrap loosely in aluminum foil and roast in the oven for 30 to 40 minutes or until the garlic is very soft when squeezed. You can also open up the foil for the last 10 minutes to allow the garlic to caramelize a bit, which adds another interesting flavor note. Cool and store roasted garlic in the refrigerator in a sealed container for up to 3 weeks or freeze it if you have a bumper crop from your garden.

TOASTED GARLIC

Separate the cloves and put them unpeeled in a dry sauté pan over medium heat. Shake and turn them occasionally until the cloves develop toasty brown spots on the skin. Remove and cool and the skin will easily slip off. The additional benefit of this method is that you've added a lovely toasty flavor to the garlic.

POACHED GARLIC

Separate the cloves but don't peel. Put in a small saucepan and cover with at least ½ inch cold water. Place over high heat and bring to a boil. As soon as the water boils, drain and repeat the process one more time. Rinse to cool off the garlic. Peel the poached garlic and store, covered, in the refrigerator for up to 2 weeks.

ROASTED VEGETABLES

The most commonly roasted vegetables are root vegetables—carrots, onions, beets, parsnips, potatoes, and the like—but many other vegetables are also wonderful roasted, such as cauliflower, artichokes, broccoli, and especially garlic, which has become a staple in my kitchen.

The technique I use is very simple: Preheat the oven to 400°F. Coat the vegetables by tossing with a little olive oil and season lightly with salt and freshly ground pepper. Put them whole (or halved or quartered if they're really huge) in a single layer in a baking pan and cover with aluminum foil. Roast in the oven until the vegetables are half cooked and just beginning to soften. Uncover the pan and finish cooking, allowing the vegetables to brown lightly and develop their sweet, wonderful flavor. Cooking times will vary depending on size and the particular vegetable. I start them covered in order to allow the internal water to steam and soften the vegetables a bit; then they won't dry out too much. The goal is to have soft, luscious interiors and browned exteriors without too much shriveling.

ROASTING PEPPERS TO REMOVE THE SKIN

Peppers are roasted, or charred, to remove the skin, but in the process something wonderful happens to the flavor. Once you've tasted fresh roasted peppers with their sweet, smoky flavor you'll never again be satisfied with their poor canned cousins, like pimientos.

To roast peppers, use a long-handled fork and char them over an open flame until they are blackened all over. Or you can halve them and broil, skin-side up, about 4 inches from the heat until they are browned and their skin begins to bubble. Put the peppers in a bowl, cover with plastic wrap, and let them steam for a few minutes. With your fingers or the point of a knife, remove the skin. Do not wash the peppers—this washes away much of that lovely toasty, roasted flavor you've developed from the charring and browning.

Discard the stem and seeds. Roasted peppers freeze well indefinitely and are also delicious stored in olive oil in the refrigerator for up to 3 weeks.

Use rubber gloves if you're roasting and peeling chiles.

ROASTING TOMATOES FOR STOCKS AND SAUCES

Especially in the winter, store-bought tomatoes often lack flavor and appeal. For a sauce or soup, I think canned tomatoes are often a better choice, because they have a bit more flavor than fresh. One way of developing flavor in fresh tomatoes is to roast them. To roast tomatoes, preheat the oven to 375°F. Stem the tomatoes and put them in a crowded single layer on a lightly oiled baking sheet with sides (a jelly-roll pan is ideal). If the tomatoes are large, cut them in half and put cut-side down. There's no need to oil them. Roast in the oven until the tomatoes are beginning to brown. The tomatoes will collapse and look a little abused, but that's okay. Depending on the tomatoes, it can take 30 minutes for the tomatoes to brown. Be sure not to burn them. Transfer the tomatoes to a food processor, making sure to scrape all the browned bits and pieces out of the pan, and pulse a few times to make a chunky sauce. The browning, or caramelization, has heightened the tomato flavor.

GRILLED VEGETABLES WITH THREE MARINADES

My favorite vegetables on the grill are thick slices of red onion, eggplant, summer squash, and tomatoes. The simplest and most straightforward way to season vegetables for the grill is to toss them with a little olive oil, a drop or two of balsamic vinegar, and a sprinkling of kosher salt and freshly ground pepper. As with other cooking techniques, if you are preparing more than one kind, make sure they are of a variety and size that will cook in the same time. (And if you're cutting them, be sure to leave them large enough so they don't fall through the grill!) Grill vegetables over hot coals so they will cook quickly and retain their texture.

For more complex flavors, here are three marinades I especially like with vegetables. These may be made a day ahead and stored covered in the refrigerator.

MUSTARD MARINADE
Makes 2½ cups

¾ cup olive oil

⅓ cup minced green onion, both white and pale green parts

½ cup dry white wine

4 tablespoons roasted garlic (see page 264)

1 cup Dijon mustard

1½ tablespoons sugar

Kosher or sea salt and freshly ground pepper

In a medium bowl, whisk together the olive oil, green onion, wine, roasted garlic, mustard, and sugar until combined. Transfer to a bowl and season to taste with salt and pepper.

BASIL-PARMESAN MARINADE
Makes 2½ cups

2 cups loosely packed fresh basil leaves, chopped

1⅓ cup olive oil

½ cup white wine vinegar

2 tablespoons minced garlic

⅔ cup freshly grated Parmesan cheese

Kosher or sea salt and freshly ground pepper

Place the basil, olive oil, vinegar, garlic, and Parmesan cheese in a food processor or blender and pulse in short bursts until just combined. Transfer to a bowl and season to taste with salt and pepper. The marinade should have a bit of texture. This marinade is especially good with grilled tomatoes and onions.

THAI-STYLE MARINADE
Makes 2½ cups

6 tablespoons Thai fish sauce

¼ cup firmly packed light-brown sugar

¼ cup soy sauce

1 cup unsweetened coconut milk

¾ teaspoon red pepper flakes

2 tablespoons curry powder, such as Madras Curry Powder (page 97)

6 tablespoons fresh lime juice

6 tablespoons chopped fresh cilantro

Place the fish sauce, sugar, soy sauce, coconut milk, pepper flakes, curry powder, lime juice, and cilantro in a food processor or blender and process in short bursts until smooth. This marinade goes especially well with eggplant and bell peppers.

SOFT CORN POLENTA WITH TOMATO SALAD AND EGGS

Serves 4

3 tablespoons unsalted butter or 2 tablespoons olive oil

3 cups chicken or vegetable stock or water

1 cup coarse polenta

1 cup fresh corn kernels (1 large ear) or frozen corn kernels

4 large eggs

½ cup freshly grated Parmesan or Asiago cheese, plus more for garnishing

Kosher or sea salt and freshly ground pepper

Tomato Salad (recipe follows)

RECOMMENDED WINE
Eggs can be a bit of a problem with wine. I'd serve a dry sparkling wine here or a citrusy **Sauvignon Blanc**.

This is a quick, delicious brunch, lunch, or supper dish. You could add some sautéed spinach to the recipe, too, and substitute roasted or grilled mushrooms for the eggs.

In a medium saucepan, combine the butter and stock and bring to a boil over medium-high heat. Whisk in the polenta slowly to prevent lumps and stir until the mixture returns to a boil. Stir in the corn. Reduce the heat and simmer, stirring occasionally, for 8 to 10 minutes or until the mixture is smooth and cooked to your liking. If you prefer a softer texture, cook for a few minutes more, adding a bit more stock and being sure to stir to prevent sticking and burning. Remove from the heat, cover, and keep warm.

Poach or fry the eggs. Stir the grated cheese into the polenta and season to taste with salt and pepper. Divide the polenta into 4 shallow soup plates. Top with the Tomato Salad and then the eggs. Garnish with shaved cheese and serve immediately.

TOMATO SALAD

3 tablespoons extra-virgin olive oil

1 tablespoon thinly sliced garlic

1 quart cherry tomatoes, halved

¼ cup coarsely chopped mixed fresh herbs, such as chives, parsley, basil, and tarragon

Kosher or sea salt and freshly ground pepper

In a small sauté pan, heat the olive oil over medium heat and sauté the garlic until softened and just beginning to brown. Add the tomatoes and stir for 1 minute more or until they just barely begin to soften. Remove from the heat, cool slightly, and stir in the herbs. Season to taste with salt and pepper.

CREAMY GARLIC POLENTA WITH WILD MUSHROOMS AND TOMATO-FENNEL BROTH

Serves 6 to 8

RECOMMENDED WINE
An Italian **Chianti** or California **Sangiovese** would be good with this, as would a bolder-style California **Pinot Noir** which will bridge to the earthy mushrooms.

½ ounce dried porcini mushrooms, soaked in 1 cup warm water for 20 minutes

2 tablespoons olive oil

1 cup finely chopped yellow onion

½ cup coarsely chopped mushrooms

1 tablespoon finely chopped garlic

2 tablespoons finely chopped fresh basil

4 cups rich Vegetable Stock (page 69) or Chicken Stock (page 66)

1 cup coarse polenta

Kosher or sea salt and freshly ground white pepper

½ cup heavy (whipping) cream

⅓ cup finely grated aged Asiago or dry Jack cheese

Tomato-Fennel Broth (recipe follows)

Sautéed fresh wild mushrooms and deep-fried basil sprigs (page 135) for garnishing (optional)

Creamy polenta is a wonderful dish for a chilly fall or winter evening. I've surrounded this one with a Tomato-Fennel Broth. You could just as easily use any good fresh vegetable stock or broth.

Drain the porcini and chop. In a large saucepan, heat the olive oil and sauté the porcini, onion, mushrooms, and garlic until very lightly colored. Add the basil and stock and bring to a boil.

Whisk in the polenta slowly to prevent lumps and stir until the mixture returns to a boil. Reduce the heat and simmer for 10 to 15 minutes, stirring occasionally. The polenta should be thick and creamy. Add more stock if necessary. Season to taste with salt and pepper and keep warm.

Just before serving, add the cream and cheese and stir vigorously. Spoon onto warm plates, ladle a ring of warm Tomato-Fennel Broth around, and garnish with sautéed wild mushrooms and basil sprigs, if using. Save any remaining Tomato-Fennel Broth for another use.

~~~~~~

TOMATO-FENNEL BROTH
Makes about 2 cups

1 tablespoon olive oil

1 cup chopped onion

½ cup chopped mushrooms

1 teaspoon chopped garlic

1 cup chopped fresh fennel

1 teaspoon fennel seeds

½ cup dry white wine

1 cup Vegetable Stock (page 69) or Chicken Stock (page 66)

¾ cup fresh fennel juice

¾ cup fresh tomato juice

Kosher or sea salt and freshly ground pepper

In a medium saucepan, heat the olive oil and sauté the onion, mushrooms, garlic, fennel, and fennel seeds until just beginning to color. Add the wine and stock, bring to a boil, and simmer, uncovered, for 10 minutes. Remove from the heat and strain though a fine-mesh strainer, pushing down on the solids. Return to the pan, add the fennel juice and tomato juice, gently warm, and season to your taste with salt and pepper.

WILD MUSHROOM POT PIE

Serves 6

½ ounce dried porcini mushrooms, soaked in
1 cup warm water for 20 minutes

2 tablespoons unsalted butter

2 tablespoons olive oil

½ cup chopped shallots or green onions, white
part only

1 tablespoon minced garlic

8 cups mixed fresh wild mushrooms, tough stems
removed, thickly sliced or quartered

½ cup dry white wine

1½ cups rich Chicken Stock (page 66)
or Vegetable Stock (page 69)

2 tablespoons dry sherry or brandy

2 tablespoons Dijon mustard

1½ cups heavy (whipping) cream

2 teaspoons chopped fresh thyme or
1 teaspoon dried

Kosher or sea salt and freshly ground pepper

Herbed Bread Crumbs (recipe follows)

RECOMMENDED WINE
Mushrooms and **Pinot Noir**
are a great match. A rich,
full-on buttery **Chardonnay**
would also work nicely.

This is a simple but delicious recipe that can be made a day or two ahead. Any combination of mushrooms can be used. I always like to include some dried mushrooms such as shiitake or porcini because they have a much more intense flavor than their fresh counterparts. Save the soaking water to make soup or stocks.

Preheat the oven to 400°F. Drain the porcini mushrooms and chop. In a large sauté pan, melt the butter with the oil over medium heat and sauté the shallots and garlic until softened but not brown. Add the porcini and wild mushrooms in batches, increase the heat, and sauté until lightly colored. Remove the mushrooms and set aside. Add the wine, stock, sherry, mustard, cream, and thyme to the pan along with any mushroom juices, bring to a boil, and reduce by half, about 6 minutes.

Stir the mushrooms back into the sauce and season to taste with salt and pepper. Divide the mixture among 6 lightly buttered 8-ounce ovenproof dishes or use a single large ceramic casserole dish. Sprinkle the Herbed Bread Crumbs on top of each and bake until the mushrooms are bubbling and the topping is lightly browned. Serve immediately.

Note: If making ahead, be sure to refrigerate the pot pies and add the crumb mixture just before baking.

HERBED BREAD CRUMBS

1 cup coarse white bread crumbs, preferably
panko

1 cup freshly grated dry Jack or Parmesan cheese

¼ cup chopped fresh parsley

3 tablespoons finely chopped fresh chives

2 teaspoons finely grated lemon zest

Drops of olive oil

In a medium bowl, combine the bread crumbs, cheese, parsley, chives, and lemon zest with a few drops of olive oil to very lightly coat. Set aside until ready to use.

EGGPLANT SANDWICHES ON BABY GREENS WITH SHERRY-SHALLOT VINAIGRETTE

Serves 6

RECOMMENDED WINE
Try a grassy, herbal **Sauvignon Blanc** if you want a white, or for a red, a softer-style **Cabernet** or one of the new **Cabernet Francs** from California. Cabernet Franc has traditionally been used as a blending grape for Bordeaux-style red wines, but a few producers in California are doing an outstanding job of making Cabernet Franc varietals.

2 medium eggplants, cut into twelve 1-inch-thick slices, ends discarded

¼ cup olive oil

Kosher or sea salt and freshly ground pepper

6 ounces fresh mozzarella cheese, drained

½ cup loosely packed fresh basil leaves

12 anchovy fillets, rinsed and patted dry

1½ cups dry bread crumbs, preferably panko

½ cup finely chopped walnuts

All-purpose flour for dredging

2 large eggs, beaten with 1 tablespoon water

Olive oil for frying

3 cups mixed savory baby greens, such as arugula, frisée, red mustard, and spinach

Sherry-Shallot Vinaigrette (recipe follows)

Fried capers (page 33) and fresh rosemary for garnishing (optional)

This is an interesting presentation that makes a delicious main course. The sandwiches can also be cut into wedges and served as a fun appetizer. I've suggested garnishing the dish with fried capers and rosemary leaves. If you've not tasted these before you're in for an interesting treat. The sharp flavors of both are reduced to a pleasant crispy garnish. To prepare them, simply follow the recipe for Fried Capers, adding rosemary leaves. This can be done a couple of hours ahead of time. For a completely vegetarian version of this dish, delete the anchovies and substitute chopped oil–cured olives, or use dulse flakes to taste. Dulse is a very nutritious seaweed that has a salty flavor reminiscent of anchovy. You'll find it in natural foods stores.

Preheat the oven to 400°F. Lightly brush the eggplant slices with the olive oil and season to taste with salt and pepper. Put in a single layer on baking sheets and bake in the oven until lightly browned and tender, about 15 minutes.

Slice the cheese into ⅛-inch slices and arrange on 6 of the eggplant slices. Coarsely chop the basil and anchovies together and sprinkle over the cheese slices. Top with a matching eggplant slice to form a sandwich.

In a small bowl, stir together the bread crumbs and walnuts. Dredge the sandwiches in flour and shake off the excess. Dip in the egg mixture and then in the bread crumb mixture. Can be prepared ahead to this point and stored, uncovered, in the refrigerator for up to 2 hours before finishing.

Heat ½ inch olive oil in a skillet to 350°F. Cook the sandwiches in a single layer, in batches if necessary, turning once, until golden brown on both sides. Drain on paper towels and keep warm while frying the remaining sandwiches (can be cooked ahead and reheated in a 300°F oven at serving time).

Toss the greens with a little Sherry-Shallot Vinaigrette and arrange attractively on plates. Put the eggplant sandwiches on top, scatter fried capers and rosemary around (if using), and serve immediately.

SHERRY-SHALLOT VINAIGRETTE
Makes ¾ cup

2 tablespoons minced shallots

1 teaspoon Dijon mustard

1 teaspoon fresh lemon juice

2 tablespoons sherry vinegar

2 teaspoons dry sherry

½ cup olive oil

Kosher or sea salt and freshly ground pepper

In a small bowl, whisk together the shallots, mustard, lemon juice, vinegar, and sherry. Continue whisking and slowly incorporate the olive oil in a steady stream. Season to taste with salt and pepper.

PARMESAN SOUFFLÉ ROLLED WITH GREENS AND LEEKS WITH A RED BELL PEPPER SAUCE

Serves 8

RECOMMENDED WINE
A crisp, grassy "green" white like **Sauvignon Blanc**, or **Pinot Gris** or **Pinot Grigio**, would be a good choice, or a crisp sparkler.

FILLING

3 tablespoons olive oil

2 cups chopped red onions

1 tablespoon minced garlic

1 cup thinly sliced leeks, white and tender green parts only

¾ cup dry white wine

1 pound young braising greens, such as spinach, kale, or chard, chopped

2 cups grated Swiss or Gouda cheese

1½ cups grated dry Jack or Asiago cheese

2 tablespoons chopped fresh basil

Kosher or sea salt and freshly ground pepper

SOUFFLÉ

6 large eggs, separated

1½ cups half-and-half

4 tablespoons unsalted butter, plus additional for the baking sheet

5 tablespoons all-purpose flour, plus additional for the baking sheet

1½ teaspoons kosher or sea salt, plus additional for the egg whites

½ teaspoon white pepper

¼ teaspoon freshly grated nutmeg

½ cup freshly grated dry Jack or Parmesan cheese

Red Bell Pepper Sauce (recipe follows)

This dish has a lot of elements, but don't let that scare you off. It's a very pretty dish for a special occasion. The filling and the Red Bell Pepper Sauce can be prepared a day ahead. The soufflé layer can be prepared an hour ahead. You'll need no more than 15 minutes before serving time to assemble the elements and heat them up. This also demonstrates that soufflés can be made in a number of different ways.

To make the filling: In a sauté pan, heat the olive oil and sauté the onions, garlic, and leeks until they are just beginning to color. Pour in the wine, add the greens, and cook until the liquid is evaporated and the greens are tender. Cool and gently squeeze to remove excess moisture. Chop the greens into pieces no more than ¼ inch in size. Transfer to a medium bowl and toss with the Swiss cheese, dry Jack cheese, and basil. Season to taste with salt and pepper.

To make the soufflé: In a medium bowl, lightly beat the egg yolks and set aside. In a small saucepan, heat the half-and-half to scalding. In another saucepan, make a roux by melting the 4 tablespoons butter over low heat, stirring in the flour, and cooking for 3 minutes, stirring constantly with a wooden spoon, without browning. Whisk in the half-and-half and cook, stirring constantly, for another 3 minutes until thick. Remove from the heat and stir in the salt, pepper, and nutmeg. Gradually whisk the white sauce into the egg yolks and set aside.

Beat the egg whites until they form stiff peaks. Stir a quarter of the beaten whites along with half the cheese into the white sauce to lighten it. Gently fold in the rest of the whites.

Preheat the oven to 400°F. Butter a 10-by-15-inch baking sheet and line with parchment. Lightly butter the parchment and dust with flour. Pour the soufflé mixture onto the sheet, spread it evenly to the corners, and sprinkle the remaining cheese over. Bake in the oven for 15 minutes until the top is browned and puffed. Remove from the oven and cool. The soufflé is now ready to fill and roll.

Reduce the oven temperature to 350°F. Spread the filling evenly over the soufflé layer. Starting with the long edge, carefully and as tightly as possible roll the soufflé jelly-roll style using the parchment to help the process. Discard the parchment. Put the roll on a baking sheet and bake for 8 to 10 minutes or until heated through and the cheese is just beginning to melt.

Spoon the warm Red Bell Pepper Sauce into the center of warm plates. Slice the rolled soufflé into 8 thick rounds and arrange on top of the sauce. Serve immediately.

RED BELL PEPPER SAUCE

3 tablespoons unsalted butter

1 cup minced yellow onion

4 cups chopped red bell peppers (2 large peppers)

½ cup dry white wine

1 cup rich vegetable or chicken stock

2 teaspoons honey

Drops of hot pepper sauce

Kosher or sea salt and freshly ground white pepper

In a medium saucepan, melt the butter and slowly sauté the onion and peppers until very soft but not brown. Add the wine and stock and over medium heat reduce the liquid by half. Transfer to a blender or a food processor and purée. Strain through a fine-mesh strainer, pushing down on the solids. Season to taste with the honey, hot pepper sauce, and salt and pepper. Thin, if you want, with additional stock. Keep warm. For a richer-tasting sauce, try roasting the peppers first and substituting a ½ teaspoon chopped chipotle in adobo sauce in place of the hot sauce.

EGGPLANT TORTA WITH SMOKED TOMATO SAUCE

Serves 8 to 10

4 eggplants (4 pounds), cut lengthwise into ⅓-inch-thick slices

Extra-virgin olive oil for brushing, plus 2 tablespoons

Kosher or sea salt and freshly ground pepper

3 tablespoons minced garlic

2½ pounds fresh ripe tomatoes, peeled, seeded, and chopped

1 cup loosely packed fresh basil leaves, coarsely chopped

1 teaspoon crushed fennel seeds

⅓ cup dry white wine

¾ cup freshly grated Parmesan cheese, plus additional for topping

6 ounces mozzarella or Monterey Jack cheese, coarsely grated

3 large eggs, beaten until light with 2 tablespoons water

Smoked Tomato Sauce (recipe follows)

You'll need a 9-inch springform cake pan for this recipe. In the filling, you can add or substitute any other vegetable that you like, such as sautéed mushrooms or sautéed zucchini. You'll have more than enough Smoked Tomato Sauce for this recipe. Save the remainder to toss with pasta for a quick meal. If you don't want to go to the effort of making the Smoked Tomato Sauce, simply buzz up some good canned tomatoes and add smoked paprika to taste. You can find smoked paprika at gourmet foodstores (see page 424).

Preheat the oven to 400°F. Lightly brush the eggplant slices with some olive oil and season to taste with salt and pepper. In two batches if necessary, put the eggplant on baking sheets in a single layer and bake for 20 minutes or until lightly brown and soft. Remove and cool. Lower the oven temperature to 350°F.

Meanwhile, in a medium saucepan, heat the 2 tablespoons olive oil and sauté the garlic for 2 minutes. Add the tomatoes, basil, fennel seeds, and wine. Simmer until thick, about 20 minutes. Season to taste with salt and pepper.

Lightly oil the bottom and sides of a 9-by 2-inch springform pan. Line the bottom and sides of the pan with a layer of the eggplant slices; the eggplant should hang over the rim by at least 3 inches. Spoon in one-third of the tomato sauce. Top with one-third of the Parmesan cheese and mozzarella. Add another layer of eggplant, trimming to fit snugly. Add the second third of the tomato sauce, followed by a second third of the cheeses. Add a third layer of the eggplant, followed by the remaining tomato sauce and cheeses. Top with the remaining eggplant. Using a sharp knife or metal skewer, poke holes down through the layers. Pour the egg mixture over the top so that it soaks in evenly. Fold the overlapping edges of eggplant over the top and sprinkle with a little Parmesan cheese.

Bake the eggplant torta on a baking sheet at 350°F for 35 to 40 minutes. Remove and let stand for at least 10 minutes before serving. Run a knife around the edge of the pan before releasing the spring.

Serve the torta cut into wedges and surrounded by the Smoked Tomato Sauce. The torta may be served warm or at room temperature.

~~~~~~

SMOKED TOMATO SAUCE
Makes about 2½ cups

2 pounds ripe tomatoes, halved and seeded

2 tablespoons extra-virgin olive oil

1 cup diced red onion

1 tablespoon chopped garlic

1 tablespoon chopped fresh oregano
   or 1 teaspoon dried

½ cup dry white wine

Kosher or sea salt and freshly ground pepper

Drops of balsamic vinegar

Place the tomatoes in a single layer in a roasting pan. In a smoker or grill that can be enclosed, on the hot coals put green fruit wood or wood chips that have been soaked in water for 3 to 4 hours. Replace the grill rack. Set the roasting pan of tomatoes on the grill.

Cover the grill, leaving a vent open to keep the coals burning. Smoke the tomatoes for at least 20 minutes to develop the flavor. Let cool enough to handle, and chop the tomatoes.

In a sauté pan, heat the olive oil and sauté the onion, garlic, and oregano until the onion is soft but not brown. Add the wine. Increase the heat and cook, stirring, until the liquid has mostly evaporated. Add the smoked tomatoes to the pan. Simmer, uncovered, for 3 to 4 minutes. Transfer the mixture to a blender or food processor and purée. Press though a medium-mesh strainer and return the sauce to the pan. Season to taste with salt and pepper and drops of balsamic vinegar. Thin, if you want, with stock or water.

fresh tomato paste

During the summer, when tomatoes are at their peak, I like to make my own fresh tomato paste. It doesn't have the strongly cooked flavor of canned paste, and I much prefer it. Here's what to do:

Peel and seed dead-ripe tomatoes and purée them with a food mill or in a food processor. Pour the purée into a cotton jelly bag (generally available wherever canning supplies are sold) and hang it up over a bowl; let the clear liquid drip off for several hours or overnight. Save the drippings for stock and freeze the paste in ice cube trays. When frozen, pop out the tomato cubes and store in airtight bags in the freezer. You'll have about 2 tablespoons of paste per cube.

MEDITERRANEAN POLENTA TAMALES WITH RATATOUILLE FILLING AND PEPPER-CORN CREAM SAUCE

Serves 4 to 5

RECOMMENDED WINE
A number of wines can work here. A buttery **Chardonnay** goes wonderfully with the sweet corn and cream in the sauce. A grassy-herbal **Sauvignon Blanc** would highlight those flavors of the filling.

POLENTA DOUGH

2 cups water

½ cup yellow cornmeal

½ cup coarse polenta

¼ cup freshly grated Parmesan cheese

2 tablespoons minced red bell pepper

¼ cup unsalted butter

Kosher or sea salt and freshly ground pepper

RATATOUILLE FILLING

2 tablespoons olive oil

½ cup ¼-inch diced eggplant

1 cup ¼-inch diced zucchini or yellow squash, or a combination

1 cup ¼-inch diced red onion

1 cup chopped mushrooms of your choice

½ cup red or yellow pear tomatoes, halved

1 tablespoon minced fresh basil

1 teaspoon minced shallot or green onions, white part only

Kosher or sea salt and freshly ground pepper

8 large dried corn husks, soaked for 2 hours in warm water

Pepper-Corn Cream Sauce (recipe follows)

This is another of the "Here today, gone tamale" explorations from the global tamale book I never wrote. (I did teach a class on tamales once. The final course was a dessert tamale, chocolate-mocha with a raspberry sauce, which is not included in this book!) You can explore tamales on your own. Although this recipe looks complicated, it's really an outline with total flexibility. In place of the ratatouille filling, try any cooked vegetable mixture; leftover Roasted Eggplant Caponata (page 294) would be a great substitution. And there are numerous sauces throughout the book that you could use in place of the Pepper-Corn Cream Sauce, such as Roasted Tomatillo and Avocado Sauce (page 173) or Smoked Tomato Sauce (page 275). Have fun!

To make the polenta dough: In a medium saucepan, bring the water to a boil. Slowly pour in the cornmeal and polenta, stirring constantly. Lower the heat and continue stirring until very thick, about 5 minutes. Fold in the Parmesan cheese, bell pepper, and butter. Stir and cook until the butter melts. Season to taste with salt and pepper. Let the dough cool a little.

To make the ratatouille filling: In a large sauté pan, heat the olive oil over medium-high heat and sauté the eggplant, zucchini, onion, and mushrooms until lightly colored but still holding their shape. Transfer to a medium bowl and toss with the tomatoes, basil, and shallot and season to taste with salt and pepper.

Remove the husks from the water, drain, and pat dry. Spread out the corn husks on a dry work surface. Pinch off an egg-sized piece of the polenta dough mixture. Pat it onto the corn husk, flattening the dough to about 4 inches square and ¼ inch thick, leaving a border of husk at least ½ inch wide around the perimeter of the dough. Spread a tablespoon of the ratatouille filling lengthwise in the center of the dough. Fold the husk together until the edges overlap and the polenta and its filling are completely enclosed by the husk.

Gently flatten the top and bottom of the husk and fold the ends up to enclose. Place the tamales, folded-side down, in a steamer over boiling water and steam for 30 minutes. Remove and cool for 10 minutes for the dough to set up. To serve, open the husks to reveal the tamales and spoon on some of the Pepper-Corn Cream Sauce.

PEPPER-CORN CREAM SAUCE

1 tablespoon olive oil

¼ cup minced shallots

1 teaspoon seeded and minced serrano chile

1 cup dry white wine

2½ cups rich Vegetable Stock (page 69)
    or Chicken Stock (page 66)

1 cup heavy (whipping) cream

¼ cup finely diced red, yellow, or poblano chiles,
    or a combination

½ cup fresh sweet corn kernels (1 medium ear),
    or frozen corn kernels

Kosher or sea salt and freshly ground pepper

Drops of fresh lemon or lime juice

In a medium saucepan, heat the olive oil and sauté the shallots and chile until soft but not brown. Add the wine and stock, bring to a boil, and reduce the liquid by half. Add the cream and continue to boil until reduced to a light sauce consistency. Stir in the diced chiles and corn. Season to taste with salt, pepper, and drops of lemon juice. Keep warm.

BEGGAR'S PURSES WITH GREENS AND WARM LEMON SAUCE

Serves 8

RECOMMENDED WINE
As often is the case with vegetable dishes, a crisp, lemon-tinged **Sauvignon Blanc** would match the herbal, citrus flavors in this dish.

2 tablespoons olive oil

2 cups chopped red onions

2½ cups diced fresh shiitake or cremini mushrooms

1½ pounds fresh spinach or chard leaves, washed well and stemmed

¼ teaspoon freshly grated nutmeg

4 tablespoons minced fresh basil or 2 tablespoons dried

⅔ cup grated dry Jack or Gruyère cheese, or a combination

Kosher or sea salt and freshly ground pepper

Basil Crêpes (facing page)

Whole fresh chives or leek strips for tying purses

Warm Lemon Sauce (facing page)

Fresh herb sprigs for garnishing

This is a very pretty dish that requires a bit of work but is worth it for a special dinner. The filling can be made a day ahead and stored covered in the refrigerator. The Basil Crêpes can be made ahead and stored refrigerated for a couple of days or frozen for up to 2 months. I suggest putting a sheet of waxed paper in between each crêpe before freezing to insure that you'll be able to get them apart after thawing. The Warm Lemon Sauce should be made no more than a couple of hours before serving; keep it warm in a thermos. I love this sauce as an accompaniment to almost every green vegetable. First-of-the-season crisp-cooked asparagus in a pool of the Warm Lemon Sauce is sublime!

In a sauté pan, heat 1 tablespoon of the olive oil over medium heat and sauté the onions for 2 minutes. Do not brown. Add the mushrooms and continue cooking until the onions are soft and translucent. Transfer to a medium bowl.

Add the remaining olive oil to the pan and over high heat very quickly wilt the spinach. Cool immediately and blot dry with paper towels. Coarsely chop the spinach and combine with the onion mixture. Stir in nutmeg, basil, and cheese. Season to taste with salt and pepper.

Place a dollop of filling in the center of each of the Basil Crêpes. Gather the crêpes together just above the filling and tie each one very gently with a chive to form a purse. Place 2 purses on each plate and surround with the Warm Lemon Sauce and a garnish of herb sprigs. The purses can be served warm (reheat in the oven or microwave) or at room temperature.

BASIL CRÊPES
Makes sixteen 8-inch crêpes

1 cup water

1 cup whole milk

1½ cups all-purpose flour

4 large eggs

3 tablespoons olive oil, plus additional
    for the pan

¾ teaspoon kosher or sea salt

5 tablespoons minced fresh basil

In a blender or food processor, combine the water, milk, flour, eggs, 3 tablespoons olive oil, and salt and blend or process until smooth, about 15 seconds. Add the basil and mix in with a short burst. Cover and let sit for at least 30 minutes.

Lightly oil a 10-inch crêpe pan or nonstick skillet and put over medium heat. When hot, pour in a scant ¼ cup batter and tilt in all directions to just cover the bottom of the pan. Pour out any excess. Cook for about 1 minute or until the center of the crêpe is dry and the bottom lightly browned. Turn and cook the other side for 30 seconds or so. Cool on a rack. Repeat for the remaining crêpes. Can be made ahead, wrapped in plastic wrap, and stored, covered, in the refrigerator for 2 days or in the freezer for up to 2 months.

WARM LEMON SAUCE
Makes about 1½ cups

2 tablespoons unsalted butter

¼ cup slivered shallots or green onions, white
    part only

2 cups rich Chicken Stock (page 66)
    or Vegetable Stock (page 69)

½ cup dry white wine

2 teaspoons cornstarch

3 large egg yolks

¼ cup fresh lemon juice

2 tablespoons finely chopped fresh dill

2 teaspoons finely grated lemon zest

Kosher or sea salt and freshly ground pepper

In a deep saucepan, melt the butter and sauté the shallots for a minute or two or until they just begin to soften. Add the stock and wine and boil over high heat until the mixture is reduced by half, about 5 minutes. In a medium bowl, whisk together the cornstarch, egg yolks, and lemon juice until just combined. Slowly whisk the shallot mixture into the egg yolks to temper them. Return to the saucepan and, over medium heat, continue to stir until the sauce thickens, about 2 minutes. Be careful not to overcook or the eggs will scramble. If they begin to curdle, immediately strain and add a little cold stock or water to cool down the mixture. Stir in the dill and lemon zest and season to taste with salt and pepper.

basil

One of the most popular of all herbs, basil is a member of the mint family. *Basil* comes from the Greek word for "king," which gives you some idea of how important it has been to the kitchen throughout the centuries. The varieties of basil are endless, ranging from the tiny piccolo fino verde (considered the connoisseur's basil) to the pungent cinnamon, lemon, and licorice basils that can be grown easily in a small herb garden.

Basil appears in almost as many cuisines as cilantro does, with a special prominence in Mediterranean, Indian, and Southeast Asian cooking. During my time as culinary director for Fetzer Vineyards Valley Oaks Food and Wine Center, we'd grow at least two dozen different basils every year, and it always seemed to be the crop most remembered by those who visited.

RICOTTA CHEESE–LEMON THYME TART WITH SWEET CORNMEAL CRUST

Serves 8 to 12

RECOMMENDED WINE
I originally developed this recipe to go with our old friend **Sauvignon Blanc**.

CRUST

½ cup unsalted butter at room temperature

2 tablespoons sugar

1 cup yellow cornmeal

2 large eggs at room temperature

1 teaspoon kosher or sea salt

1½ cups all-purpose flour

FILLING

1 tablespoon unsalted butter

4 tablespoons minced shallots or green onions, white part only

⅔ cup heavy (whipping) cream

½ cup white wine

½ teaspoon kosher or sea salt

¼ teaspoon ground white pepper

12 ounces fresh whole-milk ricotta cheese

3 large eggs, beaten

1½ tablespoons chopped fresh lemon thyme or other fresh herbs, such as chives, parsley, or basil

I love the crust on this tart because even a novice baker can make it. It's almost impossible to screw up! The key to this simple recipe is to get good ricotta. My favorite is one made by Bellwether Farms (see page 421) in Sonoma County where I live. They make both a cow and a sheep's milk version. This makes a nice first course, or you can cut it into smaller wedges and serve as an appetizer.

To make the crust: Preheat the oven to 350°F. Using an electric mixer fitted with the paddle attachment, or by hand with a wooden spoon, in a large bowl beat the butter and the sugar until light and fluffy. Add the cornmeal, eggs, and salt and beat until well combined. Add the flour and mix until the dough forms a ball. The mixture should be soft and moist. Wrap in plastic wrap and refrigerate for 1 hour or overnight. Lightly butter a 9-inch tart pan with a removable bottom and dust with cornmeal. On a lightly floured work surface, roll the dough into a circle 11 inches in diameter. Roll the dough up onto the rolling pin and transfer to the tart pan, evenly pressing the dough into the sides. Trim the excess dough. Prick with a fork several times and bake for 8 minutes until just lightly brown. (Wrap and save any leftover dough in the freezer. Leftover dough is good for making biscuits.)

To make the filling: Preheat the oven to 350°F. In a small saucepan, melt the butter and sauté the shallots until soft but not brown. Add the cream, wine, salt, and white pepper and cook over medium heat until reduced by half. Cool. Add the ricotta cheese, eggs, and thyme and beat until smooth. Pour into the prepared tart shell.

Bake in the oven for 35 to 40 minutes or until the filling is just set and lightly browned. Serve warm or at room temperature.

SERRANO CHILE AND GARLIC JACK CHEESE SOUFFLÉ

Serves 4

3 tablespoons unsalted butter

3 tablespoons minced shallots

3 tablespoons seeded and minced serrano chiles

3 tablespoons all-purpose flour

1¼ cups half-and-half

4 large eggs, separated

2 cups freshly grated garlic Jack cheese

⅓ cup freshly grated Parmesan cheese

4 tablespoons minced fresh cilantro

4 tablespoons finely diced red bell pepper

Kosher or sea salt and freshly ground pepper

Salsa Cruda (page 173) for garnishing

RECOMMENDED WINE
Chile heat goes well with an aromatic white wine with just a little residual sugar in it, which describes many **Rieslings**, **Gewürztraminers**, and **Muscats**.

Making soufflés is really very easy. I don't know why many cooks are so intimidated by them. This one, served with a fresh green salad, would make a perfect light supper. Garlic Jack cheese, which was originally made in the wine country, has bits of fresh garlic and parsley incorporated into it. You could also substitute Cheddar cheese or a soft goat cheese. One other note: Serrano chiles can vary in their heat. The only way I know to determine the heat of an individual serrano is to taste a tiny piece. You may want to adjust the amount of chiles you use accordingly (see page 21 for a discussion of chile heat).

Preheat the oven to 350°F. Butter a 1½-quart soufflé dish. In a medium saucepan, melt the butter over medium heat and sauté the shallots and chiles until just softened, about 2 minutes. Add the flour and continue to cook and stir to make a roux, about 3 minutes—do not brown. Add the half-and-half in a slow stream, whisking constantly. Bring just to a boil. Lower the heat and simmer for 2 minutes to cook the flour and make a thick sauce, whisking continuously. Remove from the heat, cool slightly, and whisk in the egg yolks, one at a time. Stir in the garlic Jack cheese, Parmesan cheese, cilantro, and bell pepper. Season to taste with salt and pepper.

In a medium bowl, beat the egg whites until stiff but not dry. Stir one-quarter of the egg whites into the cheese mixture to lighten it. Carefully but thoroughly fold in the remaining whites. Gently pour the mixture into the prepared dish. Bake for 25 to 30 minutes or until the soufflé is puffed and golden.

Serve with Salsa Cruda on the side.

MOROCCAN-INSPIRED CINNAMON COUSCOUS WITH SWEET SPICE VEGETABLES

Serves 8

RECOMMENDED WINE
The spice of this dish goes well with spicy whites such as **Gewürztraminer** or bright lemony wines with good acidity like **Riesling** and **Sauvignon Blanc**.

¼ cup olive oil

2 cups ½-inch diagonally sliced red onions

2 tablespoons chopped fresh ginger

1 cup diagonally sliced carrots

1 cup thickly sliced parsnips

2 cups ½-inch-diced sweet potatoes

2 cups canned diced tomatoes, including juice

2 teaspoons ground cinnamon

½ teaspoon ground allspice

¼ teaspoon cayenne pepper

2 cups rich Vegetable Stock (page 69) or Chicken Stock (page 66)

1 cup cooked garbanzo beans

½ cup raisins, preferably golden

1 teaspoon honey

Kosher or sea salt and freshly ground pepper

Cinnamon Couscous (facing page)

Red Pepper Chutney (facing page)

Toasted slivered almonds and fresh mint sprigs for garnishing (optional)

Don't be put off by the list of ingredients here. This is a delicious and very satisfying recipe and helps make the point that vegetables can provide a meal as hearty as one that is based on meat. Use whatever combination of vegetables you want. The sweet spices used here are reminiscent of those used in Morocco. The Red Pepper Chutney is a takeoff on the Moroccan condiment called harissa. You can certainly substitute prepared harissa if you like or leave it out entirely, but a little bit helps enliven the dish.

In a large skillet, heat the olive oil over medium heat and sauté the onions and ginger until just beginning to soften and brown. Add the carrots, parsnips, and sweet potatoes and lightly brown, about 3 minutes. Add the tomatoes, cinnamon, allspice, cayenne pepper, stock, garbanzos, raisins, and honey. Season to taste with salt and pepper. Simmer, uncovered, for a few minutes to combine the flavors. Be careful not to overcook; the vegetables should be cooked through but have texture.

Serve in warm soup bowls with Cinnamon Couscous and a dollop of Red Pepper Chutney. Garnish with almonds and mint sprigs, if using.

CINNAMON COUSCOUS
Makes about 3 cups

1¼ cups rich Vegetable Stock (page 69)
   or Chicken Stock (page 66)

¼ teaspoon saffron threads (optional)

1 teaspoon ground cinnamon

¼ teaspoon freshly grated nutmeg

1 tablespoon olive oil

1 cup couscous

In a medium saucepan, simmer the stock and saffron together for 3 minutes. Add the cinnamon, nutmeg, and olive oil and pour through a fine-mesh strainer over the couscous in a medium bowl. Cover and let stand for 5 minutes, then fluff with a fork.

RED PEPPER CHUTNEY
Makes ½ cup

½ cup finely chopped roasted red bell pepper

2 teaspoons minced garlic

1 teaspoon crushed toasted cumin seeds

¼ cup chopped fresh mint

¼ cup finely chopped Kalamata olives

2 tablespoons rinsed and chopped capers
   (optional)

1 teaspoon minced jalapeño chile or ¼ teaspoon
   cayenne pepper

Kosher or sea salt and freshly ground pepper

In a small bowl, stir together the bell pepper, garlic, cumin seeds, mint, olives, capers (if using), and chile. Season to taste with salt and pepper. Store, covered, in the refrigerator for up to 5 days.

TOMATO AND CHEESE FONDUE

Serves 8 to 10

RECOMMENDED WINE
The tomato base with the cheese suggests a bright white like **Sauvignon Blanc** or a softer-tannin red like **Pinot Noir**, **Syrah**, or an Italian **Chianti**.

2 tablespoons olive oil

¼ cup finely chopped shallots or green onions, white part only

2 tablespoons finely chopped garlic

One 28-ounce can crushed tomatoes with basil

1 cup hearty red wine

1 tablespoon finely grated orange zest

1 tablespoon finely chopped fresh basil

Kosher or sea salt and freshly ground pepper

8 ounces fresh mozzarella, drained

Crusty French bread cut into cubes for serving

I've always loved fondues, but they can be a little rich. Here's a version that cuts down on the fat but still provides lots of flavor. I'm using fresh mozzarella here, but you could use any good melting cheese that you like, such as Jack or Gruyère. Serve with good crusty peasant-style bread, which you can use to dip and scoop up the cheesy mixture. If you have a fondue pot, by all means use it. The cheese may take a little longer to melt, but it'll be a great conversation piece.

In a large skillet, heat the olive oil over medium heat and sauté the shallots and garlic until soft but not brown. Add the tomatoes and wine and simmer, uncovered, for 5 to 10 minutes until the mixture reduces to a light sauce consistency. Stir in the orange zest and basil and season to taste with salt and pepper.

Preheat the oven to 325°F. Pour the mixture into an attractive 6-cup ovenproof baking dish. Put the cheese in the middle and bake in the oven for 15 minutes or until the cheese is softened.

Serve immediately, with lots of crusty French bread.

Often referred to in the South as "a mess of greens," the earthy, soul-satisfying, slightly bitter taste of mustard and turnip greens, collards, kale, and Swiss chard is a favorite that appears on Southern tables with great regularity. Served on New Year's Day with black-eyed peas and ham, they symbolize good luck and monetary gain. More contemporary uses call for greens in pastas and in pizzas with herbs and sausage, or with black-eyed peas and tomatoes in comforting winter soups. Nutritionally, greens are very high in vitamin A, calcium, and potassium, and they are very low in calories.

Greens should be used as soon after purchasing them as possible, and they should always be thoroughly washed. Most dishes made with greens match nicely with a crisp, herbal-tinged Fumé Blanc.

Mustard greens: The slightly frilly, bright-green oval leaves have a sharp, mustardy tang with a hint of hot radish. They make a wonderful addition to salads and stir-fries.

Turnip greens: The leafy green tops to the turnip plant are said to do everything from curing hangovers to awakening slumbering sexual desires. Turnip greens find their contemporary place in soups and stir-fries, where their slightly bitter, chewy edge can be toned down with other flavors.

Kale: The ruffled, green-purple leaves of kale are quite dramatic and are often used ornamentally, as well as in soups, stews, and sautés.

The Dutch, British, Germans, and Scots all prize this humble member of the cabbage family and value its mystical properties. Today, you'll find many varieties on the market. I love the Lacinato, or black kale, with which I make Grilled Kale Salad (page 16).

Collards: Legendary in the South, hearty collards, a relative to cabbage, originated in Africa. Collard leaves should be separated from the tougher stems and ribs and simmered in seasoned stock for a few hours, or for 15 to 30 minutes if a crunchier texture is what you want. They also blend beautifully with pork and ham hocks and other smoky, salty, and spicy flavors.

Swiss chard: This member of the beet family is a mainstay of southern French cooking and is infinitely versatile. Green and red (or rhubarb) chard are the most common varieties. You'll find chard with stems in a rainbow of colors at farmers' markets. Chard is used as an excellent flavor and textural addition to pastas, salads, sausage, and soups, particularly when combined with olive oil, pine nuts, mushrooms, garlic, and currants or raisins.

Dandelion greens: Long a staple in the South, where they are traditionally braised or sautéed with pork, the notched leaves of this bitter delicacy are now more commonly found in contemporary salads. Dandelion greens adapt well to hot dressings with oil, balsamic vinegar, bacon bits, hot pepper sauce, and perhaps cheese or croutons. Dandelion greens need to be cooked for only a short time.

VEGETARIAN RED CHILI WITH PEPITAS

Serves 8 to 10

RECOMMENDED WINE
The red chile spiciness
calls for a chilled fruity
white like **Riesling** or
Gewürztraminer, or
maybe a nice ice-cold
beer!

2 cups dried heirloom beans, such as annelino, painted desert, scarlet runner, calico lima, or appaloosa

Vegetarian Red Chile Stock to cover (facing page)

2 tablespoons olive oil

1½ cups diced white onions

½ cup peeled and finely chopped carrots

2 tablespoons thinly sliced garlic

½ cup diagonally cut celery

2 teaspoons cumin seeds

2 teaspoons coriander seeds

2 teaspoons dried oregano, preferably Mexican

2 cups hearty red wine

2 cups diced zucchini

1 cup diced fennel bulb

1 large poblano chile, diced (1½ cups)

3 cups canned diced tomatoes, including juice

Kosher or sea salt and freshly ground pepper

Fresh lime or lemon juice

⅔ cup chopped fresh cilantro

Toasted pepitas (pumpkin seeds) and queso fresco (Mexican fresh cheese) for garnishing (optional)

There are hundreds, if not thousands, of varieties of dried beans grown around the world, in every shape, color, and size imaginable. They truly are the jewels of the plant kingdom. With the advent of the food pyramid, there has come a whole new interest in beans as part of a healthful diet. The Vegetarian Red Chile Stock included here is delicious for use in other recipes that call for a richly flavored vegetable stock. Don't let the rather long list of ingredients scare you off. They each have a flavor purpose, and actually the recipe is pretty easy to do.

Soak the beans overnight with water to cover by at least 3 inches or use the quick-soak method (see page 83). Drain the beans. In a deep saucepan, combine the beans and enough Vegetarian Red Chile Stock to cover by at least 1 inch. Bring to a boil, then reduce the heat, and simmer, covered, until just cooked through (varies depending on the type of bean).

Meanwhile, in a stockpot, heat the olive oil over medium heat and sauté the onions, carrots, garlic, and celery until beginning to color. Add the cumin seeds, coriander seeds, and oregano and sauté for an additional 5 minutes. Add the red wine and beans along with their cooking liquid. Add additional stock as needed to cover. Bring to a boil, reduce the heat, and simmer for 5 to 10 minutes.

Add the zucchini, fennel, chile, and tomatoes. Bring to a simmer and cook an additional 5 to 10 minutes, stirring occasionally and adding stock as needed. The vegetables should still have texture. Season to taste with salt, pepper, and drops of fresh lime juice.

Just before serving, stir in the cilantro. Ladle into warm serving bowls and garnish with pepitas and queso fresco, if using.

VEGETARIAN RED CHILE STOCK
Makes 4 quarts

6 ounces dried ancho chiles, lightly toasted
   (4 large chiles)

¼ cup olive oil

4 cups coarsely chopped onions

1 cup chopped carrots

1 cup chopped celery

2 cups chopped mushrooms

1 tablespoon coriander seeds

1 teaspoon fennel seeds

2 teaspoons cumin seeds

3 large bay leaves

2 teaspoons dried oregano

6 cups fresh or canned tomatoes, including juice

2 cups hearty red wine

4 quarts water

Kosher or sea salt and freshly ground pepper

Cover the chiles with warm water and allow to soften for 1 hour.

In a large stockpot, heat the olive oil and sauté the onions, carrots, celery, and mushrooms until just beginning to color. Drain the chiles, seed and stem them, and add to the stockpot along with the coriander seeds, fennel seeds, cumin seeds, bay leaves, oregano, tomatoes, wine, and water and bring to a boil.

Reduce the heat and simmer, partially covered, for 1 hour. Season to taste with salt and pepper and strain through a fine-mesh strainer, pushing on the solids to extract all their juice. Store, covered, in the refrigerator for up to a week or freeze for 3 months.

SPICY TOMATO AND GARLIC STEW WITH EGGS

Serves 6

1 tablespoon olive oil

1 cup very finely diced white onion

6 cups clear rich Chicken Stock (page 66) or Vegetable Stock (page 69)

2 tablespoons chile-garlic sauce

2½ cups peeled, seeded, and diced ripe tomatoes or canned diced tomatoes, drained

Kosher or sea salt and freshly ground pepper

3 cups lightly packed baby spinach or other tender greens

1 tablespoon finely grated lemon zest

6 Croûtes (recipe follows)

6 large eggs, poached or gently fried

2 tablespoons finely chopped mixed fresh herbs, such as chives, parsley, and cilantro

This is a very simple dish that lends itself to all kinds of additions. For me, it's comfort food—something I can fix when I don't feel like cooking. The chile-garlic sauce is available in Asian markets and in many supermarkets. I like Lee Kum Kee brand from Hong Kong, which is widely distributed.

In a deep saucepan, heat the olive oil over medium heat and sauté the onion until softened but not brown. Add the stock, chile-garlic sauce, and tomatoes and simmer for a few minutes to heat through. Season to taste with salt and pepper.

Place a small handful of spinach in the center of each warm bowl. Sprinkle with the lemon zest and ladle the soup around. Top the spinach with a Croûte and a poached or gently fried egg (the yolk should still be runny). Sprinkle with herbs and instruct everyone to stir the egg into the soup!

CROÛTES

3 tablespoons olive oil

1 teaspoon pressed garlic

1 teaspoon sweet or smoked paprika

Six ½-inch-thick slices peasant-style bread, crusts removed and trimmed to fit the bowls to be used for serving

Preheat the oven to 350°F. In a small bowl, combine the olive oil, garlic, and paprika and paint the bread on both sides. Bake in the oven until golden brown and nearly crisp but still soft in the center, 6 minutes or so.

VEGGIE BURGER

Serves 6

4 tablespoons olive oil

1 cup finely chopped onion

1 tablespoon minced garlic

1 cup finely diced carrots

½ teaspoon seeded and minced serrano chile

½ teaspoon ground ginger

1 teaspoon ground cumin

1 cup chopped unpeeled roasted eggplant

1 cup chopped firm-cooked unpeeled red potatoes

1 cup coarsely grated zucchini, squeezed dry

3 tablespoons chopped fresh cilantro

2 tablespoons whole-wheat flour

1 large egg, lightly beaten

1 cup soft whole-wheat bread crumbs

Kosher or sea salt and freshly ground pepper

RECOMMENDED WINE

A number of wines could work, depending on what you serve with the burger. If I were serving a lemony salad, I'd go toward a **Sauvignon Blanc**. With the addition of a full-flavored cheese, try a barrel-aged **Chardonnay** or even a peppery **Zinfandel**.

I ask — how could you have a cookbook from California without including at least one squeaky-clean veggie-burger kind of recipe! I like to top the burger with a nice cheese and a dollop of Salsa Cruda (page 173) and serve the burger with a little salad on the side, perhaps savory greens dressed with a lemony vinaigrette. Add or substitute any vegetables or even nuts that you like.

In a large sauté pan, heat 2 tablespoons of the olive oil over medium heat and sauté the onion and garlic until they just begin to color. Add the carrots, chile, ginger, and cumin and continue to cook until the carrots just begin to soften. Stir in the eggplant, potatoes, zucchini, and cilantro and cook for 2 to 3 minutes, stirring occasionally. Remove from the heat.

When cool enough to handle, gently mix in the flour, egg, and bread crumbs. Season to taste with salt and pepper and shape into patties. Sauté the patties in the remaining 2 tablespoons olive oil until golden brown on both sides.

cooking dried beans

There are hundreds of varieties of dried beans, and if you add the rest of the legume family, including lentils and peas, there are well over two thousand varieties that we know of. There has been an amazing resurgence of interest in beans in recent years. We've come to understand not only how good they are for us (being the most inexpensive and most healthful source for protein, since they contain no associated fat), but also how they have myriad other positive health benefits. With their abundance of dietary fiber, they seem to help prevent a number of cancers as well as alleviate blood glucose problems.

Beyond health, however, beans are beautiful and delicious! They are poetic, with names like painted pony, Jacob's cattle, European soldier, yin-yang, scarlet runner, and rattlesnake. They come in every shape, size, and color imaginable. Flavor and texture also vary dramatically. The exotic varieties beyond the usual navy, pinto, lima, and black beans are now widely available. Two good sources for unusual bean varieties are Phipps Country Store and Farm and Purcell Mountain Farms (see page 424).

TO COOK BEANS

Most recipes call for soaking dried beans overnight, which is fine if you've thought ahead. An alternative quick-soak method also works very well (see page 83).

Whether you soak beans conventionally or use the quick-soak method, to finish cooking make sure the beans are covered by at least 2 inches of fresh water, not the soaking water.

Most cooks advise against adding salt to beans until they are tender. You can, however, add ½ teaspoon salt per cup of dried beans and any herbs or other seasonings you like. Do not add tomatoes or other acidic ingredients until the beans are almost done, otherwise the beans will be tough. My grandmother used to add a pinch of baking soda for each cup of dried beans, which apparently raises the pH of the water, making it less acidic, which in turn makes the beans more soluble and quicker cooking. This does, however, destroy some nutrients, so even though my grandmother did it — don't!

Bring the beans to a simmer, cover, and simmer gently until done. Covering helps insure that the beans will cook evenly. Check the liquid from time to time to make sure the beans are covered. That's all there is to it!

One cup of dried beans will yield 2 to 3 cups of cooked beans. Cooked beans freeze wonderfully in their liquid, so be sure to cook up an extra batch for freezing and quick use later on. Also, save any bean-cooking liquid. It makes a tasty alternative vegetable stock to substitute for or use with meat stock.

OKRA, PEPPERS, AND BEANS WITH LEMON RICE SALAD

Serves 8

3 tablespoons olive oil

1 pound white onions, quartered

1 large poblano chile (4 to 5 ounces), seeded and sliced

2 red bell peppers, seeded and cut into large triangles

1 teaspoon chopped serrano chile

3 tablespoons slivered garlic

2 cups ripe diced tomatoes or canned diced tomatoes, drained

½ teaspoon lightly toasted fennel seeds, slightly crushed

½ teaspoon lightly toasted cumin seeds, slightly crushed

2 teaspoons chopped fresh oregano, preferably Mexican

¼ teaspoon ground cinnamon

½ cup dry white wine

2½ cups rich Vegetable Stock (page 69) or Chicken Stock (page 66)

8 ounces fresh okra, halved lengthwise, or tender young green beans

2 cups cooked heirloom beans, such as gigante, cannellini, or appaloosa

⅓ cup roughly chopped fresh cilantro

Kosher or sea salt and freshly ground pepper

Lemon Rice Salad (page 53)

RECOMMENDED WINE
If you decide to do all the parts of this recipe, there will obviously be lots of flavors happening here. I'd suggest a richer white, maybe with a little oak influence like **Chardonnay** or **Pinot Blanc**. For a red, go with a lighter style like **Pinot Noir** or **Syrah**, which has some nice earthy tones.

This is basically a rich stew of vegetables topped, just before serving, with a bright rice salad. The idea is to serve the stew hot and the salad cold, which adds the seductive dimension of differing temperatures. The Lemon Rice Salad recipe makes more then you'll need for the stew. You'll have enough left over for tomorrow!

In a sauté pan, heat the olive oil and sauté the onions, poblano chile, bell peppers, serrano chile, and garlic until just beginning to color and become crisp-tender. Add the tomatoes, fennel seeds, cumin seeds, oregano, cinnamon, wine, and stock and simmer for 3 to 4 minutes. Don't over-cook; the vegetables should still have texture. Add the okra and continue cooking for 2 to 3 minutes or until the okra is barely tender (when overcooked, okra becomes slimy). Stir in the beans and chopped cilantro and warm through. Season to taste with salt and pepper.

Ladle the vegetables into warm soup plates and top with a heaping tablespoon or two of the Lemon Rice Salad.

SPICY GINGER HUMMUS

Makes about 2 ½ cups

RECOMMENDED WINE
Since you are probably not going to make your whole meal out of hummus, I'd pick a wine that would go with the other components of the menu. On the other hand, if this is just a snack, the heat from the chile-garlic sauce would suggest a fresh, fruity, unoaked aromatic white such as **Riesling**, **Gewürztraminer**, **Viognier**, or **Muscat**.

2 teaspoons chopped garlic

1 tablespoon peeled and finely chopped fresh ginger

2 cups canned garbanzo beans (from two 15-ounce cans), drained and rinsed

¼ cup cashew or peanut butter

1 tablespoon soy sauce

1 teaspoon chile-garlic sauce, such as sriracha (see Note)

¼ teaspoon ground cumin

⅓ cup Vegetable Stock (page 69) or water

¼ cup fresh lemon juice

¼ cup chopped fresh cilantro

1 green onion, chopped, both white and green parts

Classic hummus is made with garbanzos and tahini (sesame butter). I've changed the mix a bit, as you'll note. It's very simple to make and delicious as a dip for raw vegetables or as a spread for grilled vegetable sandwiches.

In a food processor, combine the garlic, ginger, beans, cashew butter, soy sauce, chile-garlic sauce, and cumin and pulse to chop. Add the stock and lemon juice and process until nearly smooth but still with a little texture. Add the cilantro and green onion and pulse a couple of times to just combine. Store, covered, in the refrigerator for up to a week.

Note: Chile-garlic sauce is available in the Asian foods section of many supermarkets and at Asian markets.

BAKED OLIVES AND VEGETABLE CRUDITÉS WITH WARM GARLIC DIPPING SAUCE

Serves 8

BAKED OLIVES

2 cups mixed olives, such as Kalamata and Sicilian green, rinsed and drained

½ cup dry white wine

⅓ cup extra-virgin olive oil

1 tablespoon slivered garlic

3 tablespoons minced fresh parsley

2 tablespoons minced mixed fresh herbs, such as basil, oregano, thyme, and chervil, or 2 teaspoons dried

¼ teaspoon red pepper flakes

Freshly ground pepper

WARM GARLIC DIPPING SAUCE

4 tablespoons unsalted butter

10 garlic cloves, finely slivered

10 anchovy fillets, well rinsed and chopped

1 cup olive oil

2 tablespoons sherry vinegar

3 tablespoons chopped fresh parsley

CRUDITÉS

6 cups mixed crisp vegetables, such as carrots, celery, green onions, parsnips, jicama, and red bell pepper, peeled and cut into thick strips

Crusty French bread for serving

RECOMMENDED WINE
Given this dish's Italian roots, I'd go for a rich Italian varietal, like **Sangiovese, Barbera, Brunello**, or even a **Zinfandel**.

This is really two appetizers in one: the olives, and the raw vegetables with the dipping sauce. The latter is reminiscent of the classic Italian dish bagna cauda. It makes a great starter for a big family meal or as an hors d'oeuvre for entertaining. Baking the olives softens their briny flavors.

To prepare the baked olives: Preheat the oven to 375°F. In a baking dish, arrange the olives in a single layer. Add the wine and 2 tablespoons of the olive oil. Cover tightly with foil and bake for 30 minutes. Most of the liquid should be absorbed; the olives should be tender and plump.

Meanwhile, using a mortar and pestle, combine the garlic, parsley, herbs, pepper flakes, and the remaining olive oil. Mash to form a paste. (This may also be done in a food processor, although the texture will not be the same.) When the olives are out of the oven and still hot, combine with the garlic paste, tossing thoroughly to mix. Season to taste with pepper. Let the olives marinate for several hours or overnight before serving. The olives may be stored, covered, in the refrigerator for several weeks. Bring to room temperature before serving.

To make the warm garlic dipping sauce: In a small saucepan, melt the butter and sauté the garlic until soft but not brown. Stir in the anchovies, olive oil, vinegar, and parsley and heat through. Keep warm.

Arrange the crudités and olives on a platter or on individual plates around a ramekin filled with the warm garlic dipping sauce. Serve immediately, with lots of crusty French bread.

ROASTED EGGPLANT CAPONATA

Serves 6 to 8

RECOMMENDED WINE
A crisp **Sauvignon Blanc**, or soft red like **Gamay**, or a **rosé** made from Grenache is a nice contrast to the sweet-tart flavors of this summery dish.

peeling garlic

Most cooks have heard about smashing a clove of garlic with the side of a chef's knife to loosen the surrounding papery husk. The problem, however, is that unless you hit it just right, some of the husk gets driven into the meat of the clove. Then you get garlic-smelling fingers and cutting board. Also, the smashing and breaking of the clove means that the fresh garlic flavor and aroma will start to oxidize and change.

I've found two easy alternative ways to peel garlic and keep the clove whole: Soak the whole head overnight in cold water. In the morning you can easily remove the husk. Or, dry-roast cloves in a sauté pan over medium heat for 3 or 4 minutes, which also adds an interesting toasted flavor to the garlic. Again, the husk will slip off very easily.

Once peeled, store garlic cloves in a sealed container in your refrigerator for up to 10 days. I prefer storing them in olive oil. The oil then is infused with garlic flavor, which is useful in making dressings and sautéing.

2 pounds eggplant, any variety, peeled or not as you please, sliced lengthwise ¼ inch thick

3 tablespoons olive oil

1 cup chopped yellow onion

5 cloves roasted garlic (see page 264)

½ cup diced celery

1½ cups seeded and chopped tomatoes, fresh or canned

2 tablespoons rinsed capers

3 tablespoons toasted pine nuts

2 tablespoons golden raisins or currants

⅓ cup chopped Kalamata olives

2 tablespoons light brown sugar

⅓ cup red wine vinegar

Kosher or sea salt and red pepper flakes

This is a dish that is better made ahead to allow the flavors to marry. It's perfect for a picnic or as part of a summer buffet and can be the basis for a tasty eggplant and pasta salad. As with many wine country dishes (even those appropriated from other cultures!), there is a mix of sweet and savory flavors happening here. Caponata is a good accompaniment for grilled meats, poultry, and seafood; it's also terrific spread on grilled bread.

Preheat the oven to 400°F. Lay the eggplant slices on a baking sheet in a single layer. Roast for 15 to 20 minutes or until tender and lightly browned. Remove, coarsely chop, and reserve.

In a large sauté pan, heat the olive oil over medium heat and sauté the onion, roasted garlic, and celery until softened but not brown, stirring occasionally. Add the tomatoes and cook for 2 to 3 minutes. Add the capers, pine nuts, raisins, olives, brown sugar, and vinegar. Over medium heat, cook for 6 to 8 minutes, stirring frequently. Add the eggplant and season to your taste with salt and pepper flakes. Serve at room temperature. Can be stored, covered, in the refrigerator for up to 5 days.

the world of eggplant

If you need another reason to be glad you live in the twenty-first century, consider what people used to think about eggplant. "Doubtless these apples have a mischievous quality," wrote Englishman John Gerard in his 1597 *Herball*. "Eat at your own risk," he warned.

And he wasn't alone. The French suspected the curvaceous eggplant of causing epilepsy and fevers and disdained it until the nineteenth century. And although the ever-curious Thomas Jefferson grew eggplant at Monticello, Americans didn't really embrace it until the modern wave of immigrants—southern Italians, Chinese, Middle Easterners, and Indians—showed us irresistible ways to prepare it.

Thank goodness for progress. Today's cookbooks overflow with ideas for this versatile vegetable, and farmers offer every size, shape, and color imaginable. From the small egg-shaped white varieties that gave the eggplant its name to the shiny purple globe eggplants best known to American shoppers, all are eminently worth eating.

In farmers' markets and Asian markets, look for the cherry-sized eggplants that Southeast Asians prize for pickling. Italian, Chinese, and Japanese cooks prefer the long, slender varieties that are now commonplace in many markets; ranging from lavender to deep purple, they usually have a more tender skin, milder flavor, and firmer flesh than their large counterparts do. Halve and grill them, brushed with olive oil. Cut them in chunks and braise them with tomatoes, bell peppers, and zucchini to make a ratatouille. Or steam them, shred them, and season with soy sauce and a little sesame oil.

The familiar plump globe eggplants are perfect for making large round slices for eggplant parmigiana, or for stuffing and rolling. Be wary of overripe ones; they can be seedy and bitter. Unsure? Try the touch test: If the flesh stays indented after you press it gently, the eggplant is overripe.

For adventuresome cooks, eggplant is the chameleon of the kitchen: It adopts the flavor and style of whatever you put with it. Give it a Mediterranean influence with capers, olives, and tomatoes; or veer toward Turkey with garlic, mint, and yogurt; or dress it Indian-style with fresh coriander, spicy chiles, and tomato. As vegetarians around the world know, eggplant is a satisfying and low-calorie meat substitute.

MEDITERRANEAN SWEET AND SOUR EGGPLANT

Serves 6 to 8

RECOMMENDED WINE
Because of the sweet and sour contrast, the same wines suggested for the Roasted Eggplant Caponata (page 294) would be appropriate here—a crisp **Sauvignon Blanc**, or a soft red like **Gamay**, or a **rosé** made from Grenache.

2 eggplants (2 pounds), ends removed and sliced about ½ inch thick

½ cup extra-virgin olive oil

Kosher or sea salt and freshly ground pepper

1 large white onion (12 ounces), cut into large dice

2 tablespoons slivered garlic

One 15-ounce can diced tomatoes, including juice (about 2 cups)

3 tablespoons sherry vinegar

2 tablespoons sugar

2 tablespoons coarsely chopped fresh mint

2 tablespoons coarsely chopped fresh parsley

Spicy baby greens, such as arugula, and toasted pine nuts for garnishing (optional)

This is a great picnic or alfresco dish that is also delicious served on crostini and as a topping for almost any grilled or crisply fried fish or meat. I also love to toss this with cooked pasta, either hot or cold. I'm oven-roasting the eggplant here, but you could also grill it, which would add a nice smoky flavor. I'm using canned tomatoes, because frankly most of the fresh tomatoes we get in the market are pretty tasteless. If you grow tomatoes or have a farmers' market near you, by all means use fragrant, ripe tomatoes in place of the canned.

Preheat the oven to 425°F. Brush the eggplant slices liberally on both sides with 4 tablespoons of the olive oil. Season to taste with salt and pepper and put in a single layer on 2 baking sheets. Roast in the oven for 18 to 20 minutes or until lightly browned and just cooked through. Chop into ¾-inch chunks and set aside.

In a large sauté pan, heat the remaining olive oil and cook the onion and garlic until softened and just beginning to color, about 6 minutes. Stir in the tomatoes with their juice, vinegar, and sugar and simmer for 5 minutes or so. Stir in the eggplant, mint, and parsley and season to taste with salt and pepper. Cool, cover, and allow to sit for an hour for the flavors to marry. Can be made ahead and stored, covered, in the refrigerator for up to 3 days. Serve at room temperature, with a garnish of spicy baby greens and a scattering of pine nuts, if using.

RADICCHIO BAKED WITH CREAM AND DRY JACK CHEESE

Serves 4

4 heads radicchio

3 tablespoons unsalted butter

Kosher or sea salt and freshly ground pepper

¾ cup heavy (whipping) cream

½ cup freshly grated dry Jack
  or Parmesan cheese

In this recipe, the bitterness of radicchio contrasts with the sweet cream and slightly salty cheese. This is rich food, but great as an accompaniment for simple roasted poultry or meats, or as an intriguing first course when there isn't much other cream, butter, or cheese on the menu.

Preheat the oven to 400°F. Cut the radicchio heads in half lengthwise through the core. In a saucepan of lightly salted boiling water, in batches if necessary, blanch the radicchio halves for 1 minute. Drain and gently squeeze to remove any excess water. Put the radicchio on several layers of paper towels to drain further.

In a large sauté pan, melt the butter over low heat. Add the radicchio in one layer, season to taste with salt and pepper, and sauté for 4 to 5 minutes, turning frequently and gently.

Lightly butter a baking dish large enough to hold the radicchio in one layer. Arrange the radicchio halves cut-side down. Pour the cream over. Sprinkle with the grated cheese. Bake for 20 minutes or until the cream thickens and begins to bubble and the top is lightly browned.

radicchio

In recent years, this member of the chicory family has become widely available. When this book was originally written, radicchio was pretty exotic and, because of its bitter taste, not universally accepted. In Italy, the home of radicchio, varieties are named after towns or regions where it is grown—such as radicchio di Verona or radicchio di Treviso. Many varieties of radicchio are now grown in California, and although we always tend to think of it as a red, compact-headed plant, there are also green and golden varieties that look much like romaine lettuce. Radicchio has a distinctive flavor that is mellowed when cooked. A favorite preparation for radicchio is to halve it, lightly oil it, season it with salt and pepper, and grill it. Served warm with a few drops of a good balsamic vinegar and a shaving or two of Parmesan or dry Jack cheese, it makes a perfect course on its own.

CORN PUDDING

Serves 6 to 8 as a side dish

RECOMMENDED WINE
Barrel-aged **Chardonnay** and sweet summer corn are one of the great wine-food combinations.

2 tablespoons unsalted butter

1 cup finely chopped yellow onion

⅓ cup finely chopped red bell pepper

½ teaspoon dry mustard

¼ teaspoon freshly grated nutmeg

2½ cups fresh raw corn kernels (3 large ears)

1¼ cups half-and-half

4 teaspoons cornstarch dissolved in 2 tablespoons white wine or water

3 large eggs, separated

Kosher or sea salt and freshly ground pepper

This is a quick and simple side dish that could be baked right along with a roast chicken. I've also served this as a main dish, accompanied by Smoked Tomato Sauce (page 275).

Preheat the oven to 375°F. Butter a 1½-quart baking dish. In a medium sauté pan, melt the butter and sauté the onion and bell pepper until soft but not brown. Add the mustard, nutmeg, corn, half-and-half, and cornstarch mixture and bring just to a simmer. Transfer to a large bowl to cool. Beat the egg yolks until light and stir into the corn mixture. Season to taste with salt and pepper.

In a large bowl, beat the egg whites until they hold stiff peaks. Fold carefully into the corn mixture. Pour into the prepared baking dish. Bake for 30 minutes or until lightly browned and puffed. Serve immediately.

Note: The pudding may also be baked in individual ramekins; for 8-ounce servings, reduce the cooking time to 15 to 20 minutes or until lightly browned and puffed.

CHILE CORN CAKES

Serves 4 to 6 as a side dish

2 tablespoons olive oil

1 tablespoon unsalted butter

¾ cup finely chopped red bell pepper

2 cups fresh raw corn kernels (2 large ears)

¾ cup finely chopped onion

2 teaspoons pure chile powder, such as ancho

½ teaspoon ground cumin

¼ cup rich chicken stock

¾ cup all-purpose flour

1 teaspoon baking powder

½ cup yellow cornmeal

1 large egg, lightly beaten

½ cup milk

2 tablespoons chopped fresh cilantro

Kosher or sea salt and freshly ground pepper

Vegetable oil for frying

Sour cream, lime wedges, and fresh cilantro
   sprigs for garnishing (optional)

RECOMMENDED WINE
A sweeter-style **Chardonnay** would be lovely here, as would a ripe **Viognier** or **Pinot Blanc**.

These spicy corn cakes, or fritters, are an excellent accompaniment to poultry and meat dishes.

In a large saucepan, heat the olive oil and butter over medium-high heat and sauté the pepper, corn, and onion until the onion begins to soften but not brown, about 3 minutes. Add the chile powder and cumin and cook for 2 minutes, stirring constantly. Add the chicken stock and stir, scraping up any browned bits from the bottom of the pan. Continue cooking until most of the liquid has evaporated. Remove from the heat and set aside.

Into a medium bowl, sift together the flour and baking powder. Add the cornmeal, egg, and milk. Stir until very smooth. Add the corn mixture and cilantro. Season to taste with salt and pepper.

In a large sauté pan, heat ¼ inch vegetable oil over medium-high heat. In large dollops, add the corn batter and sauté until golden brown, 3 to 4 minutes on each side. Transfer to paper towels to drain. Cook in batches, adding additional oil as necessary. Serve warm, with a dollop of sour cream, squeeze of lime, and cilantro sprigs, if using.

DEEP-DISH POTATO AND OLIVE CAKE

Serves 8 as a side dish

RECOMMENDED WINE
A crisp dry white wine such as **Sauvignon Blanc** would seem to be the choice here, but I also love this dish with a rich, mellow **Merlot** or **Syrah**, which often has olive-herbal flavors.

how to store potatoes

Ideally, potatoes should be stored in a dry root cellar at about 50°F. Since almost no one has root cellars anymore, we need to find another cool, dry place in the kitchen. Do not store potatoes in the refrigerator. Anything below 45°F causes the starch to turn to sugar, giving the potato an undesirable sweet flavor. Also, don't store onions and potatoes together. Onions give off gases that cause potatoes to deteriorate faster.

2 pounds baking potatoes, such as russets

5 tablespoons extra-virgin olive oil

¾ cup finely chopped red onion

½ teaspoon ground fennel

¼ cup coarsely chopped mixed fresh herbs, such as parsley, chives, tarragon, mint, and chervil

Kosher or sea salt and freshly ground pepper

4 tablespoons finely chopped black olives

This crisp potato cake is excellent with roasted meats, or topped with a fresh salsa or herbed mayonnaise and served as a first course. The secret to achieving crispness is using a glass pie plate. You could also substitute thinly sliced sweet potato for some of the regular potatoes.

Preheat the oven to 375°F. Slice the unpeeled potatoes very thinly lengthwise. A mandoline is very helpful here. Rinse well in cold running water and pat dry with paper towels.

In a sauté pan, heat 2 tablespoons of the olive oil and sauté the onion until soft but not brown. Set aside. In a small bowl, mix together the fennel and herbs and set aside.

Lightly oil a 9-inch deep-dish glass pie plate with 1 tablespoon olive oil. Arrange one-third of the potatoes in an overlapping layer on the bottom of the plate and lightly season with salt and pepper. Layer with half the onion mixture, half the herbs, and half the olives. Top with an overlapping layer of the second one-third of the potatoes and lightly season. Then layer with the remaining onions, herbs, and olives. Finish with the remaining potatoes. Drizzle with the remaining 2 tablespoons olive oil and season again with salt and pepper. Firmly press on the potatoes to form a compact cake.

Bake the cake in the oven for 40 minutes, pressing occasionally with a spatula to make it compact. Raise the oven temperature to 450°F and bake for another 10 minutes or until the potatoes are tender and the top is golden brown and crisp.

Cool for a few minutes, then cut into wedges and serve warm or at room temperature.

FRIED GREEN TOMATOES WITH CAPER-HERB AIOLI

Serves 4 to 6 as a side dish

1 cup all-purpose flour

2 large eggs, lightly beaten with 1 tablespoon water

1 cup coarse dry bread crumbs, preferably panko

⅔ cup freshly grated dry Jack or Parmesan cheese

2 teaspoons finely chopped fresh chives

Big pinch cayenne pepper

1½ pounds large, firm green (unripe) tomatoes

Olive oil for frying

Kosher or sea salt and freshly ground pepper

Caper-Herb Aioli (recipe follows)

RECOMMENDED WINE
The Caper-Herb Aioli and tart green tomatoes are ideal flavor foils for a crisp **Fumé Blanc** or **Sauvignon Blanc**, or a **Pinot Gris** or **Pinot Grigio**.

This is a great way to utilize underripe tomatoes with delicious results. These tomatoes are great as part of an appetizer plate, which the Italians would call "fritto misto." Traditionally, aioli (basically a garlic mayonnaise) is made in a mortar and pestle with the eggs and garlic mashed together and the oil slowly added. The texture is indescribable and worth trying when you have the time.

Place the flour and eggs in separate small bowls. In a third small bowl, mix together the bread crumbs, cheese, chives, and cayenne pepper.

Slice the tomatoes ⅓ inch thick. One slice at a time, dredge the tomatoes in the flour, then the eggs, and then the bread crumb mixture. In a heavy-bottomed skillet, heat ¼ inch oil and sauté the tomato slices on both sides until golden brown. Drain briefly on paper towels and serve warm, seasoned to taste with salt and pepper and a dollop of Caper-Herb Aioli.

~~~~~~

CAPER-HERB AIOLI
Makes about 1 cup

2 tablespoons roasted garlic (see page 264)

1 teaspoon chopped fresh garlic

1 large egg yolk (see Note)

2 teaspoons fresh lemon juice

½ cup olive oil

2 tablespoons finely chopped mixed fresh herbs, such as chives, basil, parsley, chervil, and tarragon

2 teaspoons chopped rinsed capers

Kosher or sea salt and freshly ground pepper

In a blender or food processor, combine the roasted garlic, chopped garlic, egg yolk, and lemon juice and process for a few seconds to blend. With the machine running, slowly add the olive oil to form a thick emulsion. When most of the olive oil has been added and the mixture is thick, add the herbs and capers and pulse briefly just to combine. Season to taste with salt and pepper. Cover and refrigerate for at least 1 hour before using to allow the flavors to marry. Store, covered, in the refrigerator for up to 3 days.

Note: If raw egg is of concern, substitute 2 hard-boiled egg yolks.

THE BEST "STEWED" TOMATOES

Serves 4 to 6

RECOMMENDED WINE
Tomatoes and red wines that are fruity and fresh without too much tannin are terrific together. Try a **Gamay**, **Syrah**, or young red **Zinfandel** that isn't too high in alcohol.

½ cup chopped fresh parsley

½ cup chopped fresh basil

2 teaspoons minced fresh rosemary

2 tablespoons minced garlic

½ cup panko or other dry bread crumbs

¾ cup freshly grated Parmesan or
dry Jack cheese

2 tablespoons chopped anchovies that
have been rinsed and dried

Extra-virgin olive oil for the herb mixture

3 pounds ripe tomatoes, peeled and cored
(see Note)

¼ cup dry white wine simmered with
2 tablespoons unsalted butter

Kosher or sea salt and freshly ground pepper

When good tomatoes are abundant, this simple dish is hard to beat. It's a great addition to a picnic buffet. Chop it coarsely to make a wonderful sauce for pasta or a topping for grilled meats and fishes. For those uses, don't peel the tomatoes. For a completely vegetarian dish, substitute rinsed and chopped capers or olives for the anchovies.

Preheat the oven to 425°F. In a medium bowl, combine the parsley, basil, rosemary, garlic, bread crumbs, cheese, and anchovies. Toss with a few drops of olive oil until lightly coated and loose but not soggy. Oil a baking dish just large enough to hold the tomatoes in a crowded single layer and arrange the tomatoes in the dish. Drizzle the warm wine-butter mixture over them. Season to taste with salt and pepper and top with the herb mixture. Bake for 15 minutes. Lower the heat to 350°F and bake for 15 to 20 minutes longer or until the topping is browned and the tomatoes are very soft. Remove from the oven and serve warm or at room temperature.

Note: To peel tomatoes, cut a small "X" in the opposite or flower end. Plunge them into lightly salted boiling water and submerge for 15 to 20 seconds. Remove and plunge immediately into ice water. The skin should split and loosen and easily peel off. If not, repeat the process.

GREEN CHILE AND CHEESE RICE

Serves 4

2 tablespoons unsalted butter or olive oil

½ cup finely chopped onion

1 tablespoon finely chopped garlic

1 cup basmati or other long-grain rice

1 teaspoon dried oregano

½ teaspoon fennel seeds

2 cups Chicken Stock (page 66), Corn Stock (page 69), or Rich Vegetable Stock (page 69)

1 medium roasted and peeled poblano chile (see page 265)

¼ cup chopped fresh cilantro

6 ounces dry Jack cheese, cut into ½-inch dice

RECOMMENDED WINE
If the rice is being served alone, I would choose a simple, crisp unoaked **Chardonnay**. If the rice is being offered as part of a larger meal with a lot of additional chile heat, then I'd recommend a fruity, off-dry wine, such as **Riesling**, **Gewürztraminer**, or **Chenin Blanc**.

This rice makes a delicious accompaniment to almost anything. I love the idea of burying little cheese "presents" in the rice to discover as you serve. For a simple meatless meal, serve the rice with some grilled or roasted tomatoes and a salad of savory greens.

In a medium saucepan, melt the butter over medium heat and sauté the onion and garlic until soft but not brown. Add the rice, oregano, and fennel seeds. Continue to sauté for 2 minutes more, stirring occasionally.

Add the stock and bring to a boil. Lower the heat to a simmer, cover, and cook for 10 minutes; the stock will be mostly absorbed but still visible. Stir in the chile and cilantro and gently poke the cheese into the rice in various spots. Replace the cover and continue to cook for 5 minutes or until all the stock is absorbed. Remove from the heat and let stand, uncovered, for 3 to 5 minutes before serving.

ROASTED GARLIC-TARRAGON CUSTARDS

Serves 6

RECOMMENDED WINE
Tarragon goes well with very crisp white wines that have a bit of a green note to them. **Sauvignon Blanc** is classically described this way.

3 tablespoons chopped fresh tarragon

3 large eggs

4 tablespoons roasted garlic (see page 264)

1 teaspoon kosher or sea salt

½ teaspoon freshly ground pepper

1 cup half-and-half or whole milk

¾ cup Rich Vegetable Stock (page 69) or Chicken Stock (page 66)

Unsalted butter or olive oil for coating ramekins

12 whole fresh tarragon leaves

These savory custards can either be featured as a first course on a bed of baby greens or served as a side dish with grilled meats and poultry.

Blanch the chopped tarragon in boiling salted water for 5 seconds. Drain and plunge into ice water to set the color, then drain again.

Preheat the oven to 350°F. In a blender or food processor, combine the chopped tarragon, eggs, roasted garlic, salt, and pepper. Process in short bursts until smooth and the garlic is fully incorporated. Stir in the cream and stock.

Lightly butter or oil six 4-ounce ovenproof ramekins and divide the custard mixture among them. Place 2 whole tarragon leaves on top of each. Put the ramekins in a baking pan just large enough to hold them and fill the pan with boiling water to come three-fourths of the way up the sides of the ramekins.

Place in the oven and bake for 30 to 35 minutes or until the centers of the custards are just set and lightly browned. Remove the ramekins from the water bath and let sit for 5 minutes.

Run a sharp knife around the side of each custard and unmold. Carefully turn the custard over so that the browned top is up. Serve warm.

FRIED STUFFED SQUASH BLOSSOMS

Serves 8

FILLING

3 tablespoons golden raisins, softened in ½ cup warm water or white wine for 20 minutes

2 tablespoons olive oil

¼ cup chopped shiitake mushrooms

1 cup whole-milk ricotta cheese

3 tablespoons chopped oil-packed sun-dried tomatoes

3 tablespoons chopped fresh basil

2 tablespoons grated Parmesan cheese

¾ teaspoon minced lemon zest

2 tablespoons toasted pine nuts

1 teaspoon minced garlic

2 teaspoons chopped fresh parsley

16 squash blossoms with baby squash attached

BEER BATTER

1 cup beer

1 cup all-purpose flour

1 teaspoon kosher or sea salt

1 ½ teaspoons sweet paprika

Pinch of cayenne pepper

Vegetable oil for frying

RECOMMENDED WINE
An herbal-tinged **Fumé Blanc** or **Sauvignon Blanc** plays nicely off the savory stuffing.

Many people have never experimented with stuffing the beautiful blossoms of baby squash. If this technique seems a little daunting, try the recipe with the vegetable itself: Preheat the oven to 375°F. Scoop out the insides of baby summer squash or zucchini, stuff with the filling, and bake for 6 to 8 minutes in the oven. They are delicious plain, but if you wanted to put a little sauce on top, choose something simple and light, such as a fresh tomato sauce. And now for the blossoms . . .

To make the filling: Drain and chop the raisins. In a skillet, heat the olive oil and sauté the mushrooms. In a medium bowl, mix together the raisins, mushrooms, ricotta cheese, tomatoes, basil, Parmesan cheese, lemon zest, pine nuts, garlic, and parsley.

Gently open the squash blossoms and place a heaping tablespoon of filling inside each one. Gently twist the end of each blossom together to completely enclose the filling.

To make the beer batter: In a medium bowl, mix together the beer, flour, salt, paprika, and cayenne pepper.

In a large deep saucepan, pour the vegetable oil to a depth of 2 inches. Heat to 360°F. Dip each stuffed blossom into the beer batter, allowing the excess batter to drip off. Place in the hot oil and fry for 3 to 4 minutes or until golden brown. Transfer to paper towels to drain thoroughly. Keep warm while frying the remaining blossoms.

DESSERTS

DESSERTS *and* WINE

Matching wine to a sweet dessert can be a real challenge. Champagne or a California sparkling wine (true Champagne is produced in the Champagne region of France) is often suggested as a dessert accompaniment, but I find most rich desserts overwhelm the lovely delicacy of a good sparkler. The real issue is the residual sugar in the wine. If the sugar or sweetness in the dessert isn't in the same ballpark and in balance, the wine will be stripped of its fruit and all you are left with on the palate is acid and alcohol—hardly what you want to have with dessert. Sweet wines such as late-harvest Rieslings, ports, late-harvest Zinfandels, and Sauternes can work with desserts, but these wines are so wonderful they are often dessert themselves!

When I'm lucky enough to get one of these great sweet wines, I typically either enjoy it on its own or contrast it with a savory cheese. Some of the traditional matches are wonderful: port with English Stilton, and late-harvest Rieslings or Sauternes with creamy blues such as Roquefort or Point Reyes Farmstead Original Blue or Maytag Blue from Iowa. But other than these traditional matches, dessert is often better enjoyed on its own. If you want to give it a go, however, as noted above make the sweetness in the dessert the same level as it is in the wine.

BLUEBERRIES AND CREAM

Serves 6

2 pints fresh blueberries

¼ cup sugar

1 teaspoon grated lemon zest

One 3-inch cinnamon stick or 1 star anise pod

¼ cup dry red wine

1 teaspoon minced fresh mint

FRENCH CREAM

1½ teaspoons unflavored gelatin

1 cup heavy (whipping) cream

½ cup sugar

1 cup sour cream

1 teaspoon vanilla extract

1 teaspoon grated lemon zest

Fresh mint sprigs for garnishing (optional)

The cream part of this recipe is my grandmother's. I've seen variations of it referred to as Russian or French cream—to me, it's Grandma's cream. I love to serve this with Almond-Orange Biscotti (page 392).

In a small saucepan, combine 1 pint of the blueberries, the sugar, lemon zest, cinnamon stick, and wine and simmer over medium heat, uncovered, for 5 minutes or until the mixture is syrupy. Remove from the heat and cool. Stir in the remaining blueberries and mint. Remove and discard the cinnamon stick. Store, covered, in the refrigerator for up to 5 days.

To make the French cream: In a small saucepan, heat the gelatin, cream, and sugar over medium heat. With a rubber spatula or wooden spoon, stir until the sugar is dissolved. In a medium bowl, combine the sour cream, vanilla, and lemon zest. Gradually add the hot cream mixture, stirring just until the mixture is smooth.

Rinse a 2½-cup metal mold with cold water (or use individual ramekins). Shake out but do not dry. Pour the cream mixture into the wet mold. Refrigerate for 4 hours or longer until the mixture is set and firm.

Unmold the cream by placing the mold in a warm-water bath for a few seconds to loosen the cream. Turn over onto a cutting board. Slice the cream into serving pieces and, with a spatula, place on chilled plates. Spoon the remaining blueberries around and garnish with mint sprigs, if using.

BAKED APPLES WITH SHERRY CUSTARD SAUCE AND AMARETTI SNOW

Serves 8

8 medium-tart baking apples, such as Fuji or Newton Pippin

⅓ cup golden raisins

1¼ cups fruity, slightly sweet wine, such as Riesling or Gewürztraminer

½ cup toasted pine nuts

⅓ cup melted unsalted butter

¾ cup brown sugar

1 teaspoon grated lemon zest

½ teaspoon freshly grated nutmeg or ground mace

Sherry Custard Sauce (facing page)

8 Amaretti Cookies, crushed (facing page)

8 large fresh mint sprigs for garnishing (optional)

This is a bit of an upscale version of that old standard, baked apples. The Sherry Custard Sauce and amaretti cookies should be made ahead. The custard sauce uses the same technique as the Ginger Custard Sauce on page 327. If you'd rather not make your own amaretti, then store-bought are fine. The recipe included makes more than you'll need for the baked apples.

Peel and core the apples and put in a baking dish just large enough to hold them. In a small saucepan, bring the raisins and wine to a simmer and then set aside for 15 minutes to allow the raisins to plump.

Preheat the oven to 375°F. Drain the raisins, reserving the liquid. In a small bowl, combine the raisins with the pine nuts and stuff the apples. In a small saucepan, combine the butter, brown sugar, reserved raisin liquid, lemon zest, and nutmeg and heat gently to melt the sugar (about 2 minutes). Drizzle the mixture over the apples and bake in the oven for 25 to 30 minutes or until the apples are tender when pierced with a toothpick. Baste the apples occasionally with the juices.

Put the warm apples in shallow wide-rim bowls. Spoon the Sherry Custard Sauce around. Crush 6 of the cookies and sprinkle over the apples before serving. Garnish with mint sprigs on top of the apples to suggest stems, if using.

SHERRY CUSTARD SAUCE

3 large egg yolks

¼ cup sugar

1¼ cups half-and-half

2 tablespoons dry sherry, such as fino

Drops of fresh lemon juice

In a medium bowl, whisk together the egg yolks and sugar until lightly colored. In a small saucepan, heat the half-and-half to steaming but do not boil. Slowly pour into the egg yolk mixture, whisking constantly to prevent the egg yolks from scrambling. Pour the mixture back into the saucepan and cook over medium-low heat, stirring constantly with a spatula, until the sauce thickens lightly. Remove from the heat, strain immediately into a metal bowl, and put the bowl in a larger bowl filled with ice water, or refrigerate. Stir occasionally to speed cooling. When cool, stir in the sherry and season to taste with drops of the lemon juice. Store, covered, in the refrigerator for up to 5 days.

AMARETTI COOKIES
Makes about 24 cookies

1¼ cups lightly toasted blanched almonds

¾ cup confectioners' sugar

2 teaspoons all-purpose flour

2 large egg whites

⅓ cup granulated sugar

1 teaspoon grated lemon zest

1 teaspoon almond extract

Preheat the oven to 275°F. Line 2 baking sheets with parchment and lightly butter. In a food processor, grind the almonds to a powder by pulsing off and on to keep the powder loose. In a small bowl, mix the almonds with the confectioners' sugar and flour. In a large bowl, beat the egg whites to soft peaks. Gradually beat in the granulated sugar until stiff. Fold in the almond flour, lemon zest, and almond extract.

Pipe the mixture onto the prepared baking sheets in 1½-inch rounds. Bake for 1 hour or until set but not brown. Turn off the oven and let the amaretti dry out for an additional hour. The cookies should be very crisp. Store in an airtight container.

BRAISED APRICOTS WITH HONEY AND YOGURT

Serves 6

Grated zest and juice of 1 large lemon

1¾ cups light brown or turbinado sugar

1 cup dry white wine

1 cup water

1½ pounds firm ripe apricots (8 or 9)

¼ cup loosely packed fresh mint leaves (optional)

1 cup whole-milk yogurt

1 tablespoon confectioners' sugar

Pinch of kosher or sea salt

3 tablespoons fragrant honey

½ cup slivered blanched almonds, lightly toasted

Fresh mint sprigs for garnishing

Apricots are one of Mother Nature's great gifts to us and are my favorite stone fruit. Like many things in nature, there are a number of varieties that differ in size, from as small as a cherry to as large as a peach, and color, including white, black, grey, and pink. The eastern Mediterranean area around Turkey is the home of many of these exotic varieties.

In America, only a few varieties are grown commercially, mostly in California. The orange-colored Blenheim is the one we usually see in the market, and it can be very good. The little problem with apricots, however, is that they will acquire their orange color before they are fully ripe, and if picked at this stage they never develop their intense flavor and aroma. This is generally what happens commercially, because at this stage they are very firm (read hard*) and as a result are easier to ship. But, like tomatoes and other fruits picked unripe, they are just a shadow of what they could be if only they were allowed to fully ripen before being picked. The growth in farmers' markets where fruits are sold ripe is helping many people understand the intoxicating sweetness and perfume that tree-ripened apricots offer.*

Here's one of my favorite recipes using apricots, which I hope will become a favorite of yours, too. You could substitute peaches or nectarines. It's also an example of something that I don't think we do enough of, and that is to bring cold and warm elements together on the same plate. It can be very seductive! Be sure to get a good yogurt for this—it'll make all the difference. I'm especially fond of Greek-style yogurts, which are very thick. I love the goat's-milk yogurt from Redwood Hill Farms (see page 421) near where I live in Sonoma County, California. Seek out a good honey, too, one that has distinctive flavor and aroma, such as lavender, heather, fireweed, or orange blossom.

Preheat the oven to 350°F. In a small saucepan, combine the lemon zest, lemon juice, brown sugar, wine, and water. Bring to a boil and stir to dissolve the sugar. Reduce the heat and simmer until the mixture thickens slightly, about 5 minutes.

Halve and pit the apricots and place them in a single layer, cut-side down, in a cake pan or ovenproof dish. They should fit snugly. Strain the hot syrup over them, cover with foil, and braise in the oven for 5 minutes. Uncover, carefully turn the apricots over, re-cover with the foil, and braise for another 3 to 5 minutes or until the fruit is tender but not mushy. Remove from the oven, turn the apricots again, and cool. Cover the fruit and braising liquid with plastic wrap and store in the refrigerator for 2 hours or overnight.

Remove the apricots from the syrup and drain on paper towels. Pour the syrup into a small saucepan and add the mint leaves, if using. Over high heat, bring to a boil and reduce until lightly thickened, 6 to 8 minutes. In a small bowl, stir together the yogurt, confectioners' sugar, and salt until smooth. Strain the warm syrup onto plates or flat pasta bowls, discarding the mint, and top with the apricot halves, cut-side up. Spoon the yogurt mixture into the center of each apricot, then drizzle with the honey and a sprinkling of almonds, and serve immediately with a garnish of mint sprigs.

COFFEE-POACHED PEARS WITH CINNAMON TWISTS

Serves 8

2 large oranges

6 cups strong coffee

2½ cups dark-brown sugar

4 quarter-size slices fresh ginger

One 3-inch cinnamon stick

8 small, firm ripe pears, peeled, halved, and cored

¾ teaspoon cornstarch

Fresh orange segments and fresh mint sprigs for garnishing

Cinnamon Twists (facing page)

The idea for this recipe came from my frugal Scottish–German grandmother, who never wasted anything. With my eye on the leftover coffee I always seem to have around, I developed this poaching liquid for pears. Classically, red wine is used to poach fruits and, as I thought about it, I realized that coffee has many of the same qualities as wine: acidity, tannin, and rich flavor. The Cinnamon Twists, which I find irresistible, came later.

Strip the zest from and juice the oranges and reserve ¼ cup of the juice. In a large, wide nonreactive saucepan, combine the coffee, brown sugar, orange zest, all but the ¼ cup orange juice, ginger, and cinnamon stick and bring to a boil. Lower the heat and simmer for 4 minutes. Add the pears and return to the simmer. Gently simmer until the pears are cooked through and tender when tested with a toothpick. The cooking time will vary greatly depending on the type, size, and ripeness of the pears. When tender, remove from the heat. Strain 1 cup of the poaching liquid into a small saucepan. Leave the pears in their liquid while making the sauce.

In a small bowl, put the cornstarch and stir in the reserved ¼ cup orange juice until a paste forms and the cornstarch is completely dissolved. Add to the small saucepan containing the poaching liquid. Bring to a simmer and cook for 2 minutes until lightly thickened. Remove from the heat and set aside to cool.

Serve the pears sliced and fanned in shallow bowls or on plates. Spoon some of the sauce over and around the slices; garnish with 2 or 3 orange segments and mint sprigs. Serve the Cinnamon Twists on the side.

CINNAMON TWISTS
Makes 24 twists

1½ cups all-purpose flour

1 cup (2 sticks) cold unsalted butter, cut into bits

½ cup sour cream

½ cup finely chopped almonds

½ cup sugar

1½ tablespoons ground cinnamon

In a food processor or by hand, combine the flour and butter. Pulse 2 or 3 times or cut in until the mixture resembles very coarse cornmeal. Add the sour cream and pulse briefly or stir until the dough just begins to come together. Do not overmix. Form into a disk, wrap in plastic wrap, and refrigerate for 4 hours or overnight.

Preheat the oven to 400°F. Line a baking sheet with aluminum foil or parchment. In a medium bowl, combine the almonds, sugar, and cinnamon. Sprinkle the almond-sugar mixture over a work surface, put the disk of dough on top, and roll into a 9-by-12-inch rectangle about ⅛ inch thick, encrusting the underside of the dough with the almond-sugar mixture. Trim the edges and cut into 24 even strips, 9 inches long by ½ inch wide.

Gently pick up the ends of the strips and twist 2 or 3 times to form corkscrews and place on the baking sheet. Bake the twists for about 15 minutes or until they're brown and crisp. Remove to a rack and allow to cool. Store in an airtight container. Best eaten the same day they are baked.

COMPOTE OF FRESH AND DRIED FRUITS

Serves 8 to 10

drying foods

The most ancient technique for preserving food is drying. Over the centuries different cultures devised all kinds of clever ways to dry foods. In the Middle East, fruits were wrapped in dried palm leaves and then buried in hot sand to dry out. In the Mediterranean, tomatoes and other fruits and vegetables were sliced, liberally salted to discourage spoilage and bugs, and then dried in the hot summer sun.

All kinds of machines are available now for drying foods at home. Additionally, your home oven (especially if it's a convection oven) can be used to dry almost anything. The only appliance I cannot make work successfully for drying is the microwave oven. Despite the claims of manufacturers, food dried in the microwave always seems to turn out overcooked and tough. A good book on drying foods at home is Mary Bell's *Complete Dehydrator Cookbook*, published by Morrow way back in 1994.

Two 750-ml bottles dry white wine

¼ cup fresh lemon juice

1 cup sugar

Two 4-inch cinnamon sticks

2 large bay leaves

1 tablespoon coriander seeds, slightly crushed

2 teaspoons peppercorns

1 pound mixed dried fruits, such as figs, pears, and peaches

¼ cup dry sherry

1 tablespoon chopped candied ginger

2 pounds firm ripe pears or apples, or a combination, peeled, cored, and cut into thick wedges

2 teaspoons finely grated lemon zest

1½ cups fresh or frozen blueberries, raspberries, or cherries, or a combination

Vanilla Bean Ice Cream (page 369) or Yogurt Cheese (facing page) and fresh mint sprigs for garnishing (optional)

The idea here is to have a sparkling combination of fruits that keep their identity and are not overcooked. You can add whatever fresh fruits you like in addition to the berries; for example, a slice or two of mango, papaya, or kiwi makes a nice addition at serving time. The compote can be warmed to order in a microwave or on the stovetop. I've suggested a dollop of Vanilla Bean Ice Cream here, but you could substitute mascarpone, yogurt, Yogurt Cheese, or sour cream if you want.

In a nonaluminum pot, combine the wine, lemon juice, sugar, cinnamon sticks, bay leaves, coriander seeds, and peppercorns and bring to a simmer. Cover and simmer for 10 minutes. Remove from the heat and strain.

Return the liquid to the pan and add the dried fruits, sherry, and candied ginger and simmer, covered, for 8 minutes more. Add the fresh pears and lemon zest and simmer until the pears are just tender, 3 to 5 minutes. Remove from the heat and cool or refrigerate. Add the berries and store, covered, in the refrigerator for up to 10 days.

Spoon into bowls and top with a dollop of Vanilla Bean Ice Cream or Yogurt Cheese, and mint sprigs, if using.

YOGURT CHEESE

This is a simple, relatively low-fat cheese (depending on the type of yogurt used) that is easily made. I recommend using a plain whole-milk yogurt that is not too tart. Start with twice as much yogurt as you'd like to end up with. In other words, use 4 cups yogurt to make 2 cups yogurt cheese.

Line a strainer with a double thickness of cheesecloth that has been well rinsed. Set in a bowl so that the strainer is suspended. Scoop the yogurt into the strainer, cover lightly, and refrigerate overnight or up to 2 days, depending on how thick you'd like the yogurt cheese to be. When the cheese stops dripping, transfer it to a suitable container and store, covered, in the refrigerator.

The cheese can be used as is or it can be flavored. To make a dessert cheese, add a little sugar and vanilla or finely grated citrus zest. For a savory cheese, mix in some chopped fresh herbs, salt, and pepper.

SWEET ROSEMARY SYRUP
Makes about 1 cup

½ cup sugar

½ cup dry white wine

¼ cup water

2 tablespoons whole fresh rosemary leaves

1 large bay leaf

One 1-inch strip lemon zest

½ teaspoon peppercorns

2 tablespoons balsamic vinegar

This herb-infused syrup for serving with fresh fruits is a magic elixir. Try other herbs, such as lemon thyme, lavender, or sage, in place of the rosemary. I love a combination of fresh figs, pears, and raspberries served with a slice of fresh young goat cheese and drizzled with a few tablespoons of the syrup. Hazelnut Biscotti (page 391) are a perfect complement.

In a saucepan, combine the sugar, wine, water, rosemary, bay leaf, lemon zest, peppercorns, and vinegar. Bring to a boil and cook for 3 minutes. Cool, strain, and store, covered, in the refrigerator, indefinitely.

SOUP OF FRUITS WITH MUSCAT SABAYON AND COCONUT SHORTBREADS

Serves 6 to 8

Fresh fruits of choice, cut attractively into various shapes

Muscat Sabayon (recipe follows)

Coconut Shortbreads (facing page)

Fresh mint sprigs and confectioners' sugar for dusting

Not really a soup at all, this interesting dessert depends on finding the best available fresh fruits. I like to use a combination of fresh kiwi and berries, and tropical fruits such as mango, miniature banana, passion fruit, papaya, and star fruit. For the Muscat Sabayon, I've suggested sweet Muscat wine, but any balanced, sweet white wine such as a late-harvest Riesling could be used. Of course, that's the wine you'd also want to serve!

Arrange the fruits attractively in shallow, wide-rim soup plates (saving any small berries to scatter on at the last moment). Prepare the Muscat Sabayon and spoon around the fruits. Scatter any berries over the top. Place a wedge of Coconut Shortbread on the side of each plate and garnish with mint sprigs and a dusting of sugar.

For an interesting alternative presentation, quickly brown the Muscat Sabayon with a propane torch before adding the berries and mint. Serve immediately.

~~~~~~

MUSCAT SABAYON

7 large egg yolks

½ cup sugar

Pinch of kosher or sea salt

¾ cup Muscat wine

2 tablespoons kirsch or orange-flavored liqueur, such as Grand Marnier (optional)

In a heatproof bowl, beat the egg yolks, sugar, and salt until light. Put the bowl over a saucepan of simmering water (not touching the water) and whisk in the Muscat and kirsch. Continue whisking and turning the bowl until the mixture mounds and quadruples in volume. There should be no liquid visible and the mixture should be thick and the consistency of whipped cream. Serve immediately.

COCONUT SHORTBREADS
Makes 32 cookies

8 ounces cold unsalted butter, cut into ¼-inch bits, plus additional for the tart pans

2 cups all-purpose flour

⅔ cup sugar

¼ teaspoon kosher or sea salt

4 cups shredded unsweetened coconut

1 large egg yolk

2 teaspoons finely grated lemon zest

2 tablespoons fresh lemon juice

1½ teaspoons vanilla extract

Cold water as needed

Preheat the oven to 350°F. Lightly butter two 9-inch tart pans with removable bottoms. Using an electric mixer fitted with the paddle attachment, or by hand with a wooden spoon in a large bowl, combine the butter, flour, sugar, salt, coconut, egg yolk, lemon zest, lemon juice, and vanilla and mix until the dough just comes together and can be formed into a ball. You will need to add enough water so that the dough will hold together when pinched. Be careful not to get it too wet.

Divide the dough in half and press each half evenly into one of the prepared tart pans. Refrigerate for 30 minutes, then bake for 35 to 40 minutes or until lightly browned.

Cool for 2 minutes, then cut into wedges while still warm. Let cool and refrigerate before removing the shortbreads from the pans. If the shortbreads seem too moist or soft, put them back in the oven and bake for 3 to 5 minutes longer until crisp. Store in an airtight container in the refrigerator or freezer.

BANANA-MANGO FRITTERS

Serves 4

32 wonton wrappers

2 large bananas, diced

2 large mangoes, diced

Vegetable oil for deep-frying

Confectioners' sugar for dusting

Orange Caramel Dipping Sauce (recipe follows)

This was a recipe created out of panic one day when we didn't have a dessert to serve for unexpected guests. We had wonton wrappers left over from one of our guest chefs who had made scallop ravioli, so using wontons to make dessert seemed a perfect idea. I've served it several times, varying the dipping sauces. It's best made for a small group, so you can serve the fritters just as hot and crisp as possible.

Lay 16 wonton wrappers on a work surface and put a small amount of the bananas and mangoes on each, being sure to leave a border all around. Lightly paint the border with a little water and place the remaining 16 wrappers on top of the fruit. Gently but firmly seal the edges of the wontons with the tines of a fork. Put the fritters on a baking sheet lined with waxed paper. They can be stored, uncovered, in the refrigerator until ready to fry.

Just before serving time, in a large pan pour vegetable oil to a depth of 2 inches and heat to 360°F. Carefully drop the fritters into the hot oil and fry until golden brown on both sides, 30 to 40 seconds per side. Dust with the sugar and serve immediately with Orange Caramel Dipping Sauce.

ORANGE CARAMEL DIPPING SAUCE
Makes 1½ cups

½ cup heavy (whipping) cream

¾ cup fresh orange juice

1¼ cups sugar

¾ cup water

5 tablespoons cold unsalted butter, cut into small bits

1 teaspoon vanilla extract

⅛ teaspoon kosher or sea salt

2 tablespoons brandy or bourbon

1 teaspoon grated orange zest

In a saucepan, combine the cream and orange juice and heat until just beginning to simmer. Remove from the heat and keep warm.

In a deep saucepan, combine the sugar and water. Bring to a boil, then reduce the heat to a simmer, washing down any sugar crystals clinging to the side of the pan with a pastry brush dipped in water. Swirl the pan occasionally until the syrup turns golden brown.

Remove from the heat and carefully whisk the cream mixture into the caramelized sugar. The caramel sauce will bubble dramatically, so be careful. Whisk in the butter in small increments until completely combined. Stir in the vanilla, salt, brandy, and orange zest.

CHERRY AND ALMOND COBBLER

Serves 8

5 cups pitted, fresh Bing cherries or Royal Ann cherries

¾ cup sugar

2½ tablespoons fresh lemon juice

3 tablespoons arrowroot or cornstarch

¼ teaspoon almond extract

1 teaspoon grated lemon zest

½ teaspoon ground cinnamon

1 cup all-purpose flour

1½ teaspoons baking powder

½ teaspoon kosher or sea salt

¼ cup (½ stick) cold unsalted butter, cut into small bits

½ cup half-and-half or milk

1 large egg

½ teaspoon vanilla extract

⅓ cup blanched and coarsely chopped almonds

Lightly sweetened whipped cream or Vanilla Bean Ice Cream (page 369) for garnishing

In California, the cherry season is very short, just a few weeks during midsummer. This cobbler and the flan are two ways to take advantage of cherries' short stay. IQF (individually quick-frozen without sugar) cherries are occasionally available in the market and can be substituted, but of course they are not as good as fresh ones.

Preheat the oven to 400°F. Lightly butter a 2-quart baking dish. In a medium saucepan, combine the cherries, ½ cup of the sugar, the lemon juice, arrowroot, almond extract, grated lemon zest, and cinnamon. Cook over low heat, stirring occasionally, and bring to a simmer, about 4 to 5 minutes. Pour into the prepared baking dish.

In a food processor or by hand, combine the flour, the remaining ¼ cup sugar, the baking powder, and salt and pulse 2 or 3 times or stir to mix. Add the butter and pulse or cut in until the mixture is just combined but still crumbly. Add the half-and-half, egg, and vanilla and pulse or stir again to form a smooth batter.

Drop the batter by heaping teaspoons on top of the cherry mixture, leaving some space in between them. Scatter the almonds over. Bake for 20 minutes or until the top is lightly browned and the cherry mixture is bubbling.

Serve warm or at room temperature with lightly sweetened whipped cream or Vanilla Bean Ice Cream.

BLACKBERRY GRUNT

Serves 6 to 8

BLACKBERRIES

8 cups fresh or IQF frozen blackberries

¾ cup sugar

½ cup red wine or water

1 tablespoon finely grated lemon zest

DUMPLING DOUGH

1 cup all-purpose flour

2 tablespoons sugar

1 teaspoon baking powder

½ teaspoon baking soda

⅛ teaspoon kosher or sea salt

2 tablespoons unsalted butter, melted

⅔ cup buttermilk (or a mixture of plain yogurt and skim milk or water) plus more to make a soft dough

2 tablespoons sugar mixed with 1 teaspoon ground cinnamon

Whipped cream, Vanilla Bean Ice Cream (page 369), or sweetened yogurt

Grunts are one of those great "Grandma" desserts that trace their history back to Colonial times. They are in the large family of desserts that includes crisps, cobblers, betties, pandowdies, and slumps, which consist of fruit cooked in combination with some sort of crust (on top, on the bottom, or both) or dumpling.

Although there is a great debate as to what makes a "grunt," the consensus seems to be that both grunts and slumps are simmered on top of the stove rather than baked in the oven like crisps, cobblers, and the like. The most famous slump, no doubt, is the apple slump that Louisa May Alcott, author of Little Women, *prepared in her home in Concord, Massachusetts. The fruit was cooked and then pieces of yeasted dough were placed on top. It was then covered and cooked until the dough was done. The name* slump *came from the fact that when spooned out onto the plate this dish "slumps" and has no recognizable shape. Grunts are very similar. They usually are made with berries and topped with a baking powder dumpling. The name supposedly comes from the sound the berries make as they simmer in the pot!*

My favorite grunt is one my grandmother made using blackberries. She would make it in the summer when the wild berries were plentiful. However, you can make and enjoy this year-round, since most markets carry IQF (individually quick frozen without sugar) berries. These are often better than fresh in most markets because they are picked and frozen when they are fully ripe and at the peak of flavor. The price is usually very good too. Too often the fresh berries we see have been picked underripe so that they'll travel better.

To prepare the blackberries: In a heavy, deep casserole, combine the berries, sugar, wine, and lemon zest and bring to a simmer over medium heat.

To make the dumpling dough: While the berries are cooking, in a medium bowl stir together the flour, sugar, baking powder, baking soda, and salt. Stir in the melted butter. Add enough of the buttermilk to form a soft dough. It should be wetter than a biscuit dough.

Using a soup spoon, put heaping spoonfuls of the dumpling dough on top of the fruit. Make sure you have at least one per person. Sprinkle the dumplings with the cinnamon sugar. Tightly cover with a lid or a sheet of foil and cook the mixture over medium-low heat so that the fruit just barely simmers. Keep covered until the dumplings are puffed and set and the surface is firm when touched with a fingertip. This will take about 12 minutes or so.

Spoon the warm grunt into serving bowls and spoon on whipped cream, Vanilla Bean Ice Cream, or sweetened yogurt.

OLD-FASHIONED FRESH FRUIT CRISP

Serves 8 to 10

6 to 8 cups peeled and sliced fresh fruit, such as apples, peaches, blackberries, figs, strawberries, or plums, or a combination

1½ cups dark brown sugar

1½ cups old-fashioned rolled oats (not instant)

¾ cup all-purpose flour

¾ cup freshly grated Asiago or Parmesan cheese

1 teaspoon kosher or sea salt

1 teaspoon finely grated lemon zest

1 cup (2 sticks) unsalted cold butter, cut into ¼-inch bits

Crisps are classic comfort food and so easy to make out of any available fruit. I love to serve this warm with ice cream, unsweetened whipped cream, or a nice custard sauce. You could make Ginger Custard Sauce (page 327) or Sherry Custard Sauce (page 311), with or without the special flavorings.

Preheat the oven to 375°F. Lightly butter a 9-by-12-inch glass or enamel baking dish and place the fruit in the bottom.

In a medium bowl, mix together the sugar, oats, flour, cheese, salt, and lemon zest. With an electric mixer, in a food processor, or with your fingertips, quickly mix the butter bits into the sugar mixture to form a coarse meal. The mixture should be loose and crumbly, so work quickly to avoid melting the butter.

Sprinkle the topping mixture over the fruit and bake in the oven until the top is lightly browned and the fruit is bubbling, about 35 minutes depending on the fruit.

PEACHES AND DUMPLINGS

Serves 4 to 6

1 cup all-purpose flour

2 teaspoons plus ¾ cup sugar

1½ teaspoons baking powder

½ teaspoon baking soda

¼ teaspoon kosher or sea salt

1 large egg, separated

½ cup buttermilk, plus additional as needed

1 tablespoon unsalted butter, melted

1¼ cups fruity white wine or water

¼ teaspoon ground cinnamon

½ teaspoon ground ginger

4 cups peeled and sliced ripe peaches

1 cup fresh blackberries or blueberries

Crème Fraîche (page 37), or whipped cream, and fresh mint sprigs for garnishing (optional)

If it seems like many of my desserts are old-fashioned Grandma kinds of preparations, you're right! I think those are the kind of desserts that show off seasonal fruits the best. This recipe is best eaten when the dumplings are just cooked. You can, however, hold the dish, covered, for up to an hour before serving.

In a medium bowl, sift together the flour, the 2 teaspoons sugar, the baking powder, baking soda, and salt. In another medium bowl, mix together the egg yolk, the ½ cup buttermilk, and the butter. Quickly stir into the flour mixture just to combine. Add more buttermilk if the batter seems too dry. Beat the egg white to soft peaks and fold into the batter. Set aside.

In a 4-quart Dutch oven or other nonreactive pan with a lid, combine the wine, the ¾ cup sugar, the cinnamon, and ginger and bring to a boil. Add the peaches and blackberries and simmer for 3 minutes. Do not overcook the fruit.

Drop the dumpling batter by spoonfuls onto the simmering fruit. Cover and cook for 8 to 10 minutes until the dumplings are firm. Serve warm, with a dollop of Crème Fraîche and a sprig of mint, if using.

APPLE-JACK TART WITH GINGER CUSTARD SAUCE

Serves 8

CRUST

6 tablespoons (¾ stick) cold unsalted butter

1 cup all-purpose flour

1 tablespoon granulated sugar

Big pinch of kosher or sea salt

½ teaspoon grated lemon zest

1 large egg yolk, beaten

FILLING

5 cups peeled and sliced tart green apples

2 tablespoons fresh lemon juice

½ teaspoon freshly ground white pepper

½ cup brown sugar

1 tablespoon all-purpose flour

2 teaspoons ground cinnamon

½ teaspoon freshly grated nutmeg

⅓ cup golden raisins, soaked in brandy or Grand Marnier (optional)

TOPPING

⅓ cup granulated sugar

⅓ cup all-purpose flour

6 tablespoons (¾ stick) cold unsalted butter, cut into small bits

⅔ cup freshly shredded dry Jack, Parmesan, or sharp Cheddar cheese

3 tablespoons finely chopped toasted almonds

Ginger Custard Sauce (recipe follows)

This is a delicious tart with an interesting flavor note of dry Jack (or Parmesan) cheese added to the streusel topping. The idea is based on the classic New England and Midwest tradition of serving warm apple pie with a slice of sharp Cheddar cheese on top. In this recipe I haven't blind-baked the shell, but you could do so, especially if you were going to make the tart ahead to serve later. Prebaking the shell would help keep it from getting too soggy. If you don't have time to make the crust, the dessert works equally well made as a crisp without the crust: Simply turn the filling into an 8-inch-square baking dish or a 9-inch deep-dish pie plate and proceed with the directions for assembling the tart. For peeling the apples, I like to use the old fashioned peeler-corer that also slices the apple in a continuous connected ribbon that gives the apple an interesting appearance for this recipe.

To make the crust: Cut the butter into ¼-inch bits. In a food processor or by hand, pulse or cut the butter into the flour, sugar, salt, and lemon zest until it resembles coarse cornmeal. Add the egg yolk and mix quickly until just combined. Add drops of water if needed. Gather the dough and gently press together into a flattened cake. Wrap in plastic wrap and refrigerate until firm, 1 hour or overnight. Lightly butter and flour a 9-inch tart pan with a removable bottom. On a lightly floured work surface, roll the dough into a circle 11 inches in diameter. Roll the dough up onto the rolling pin and transfer to the tart pan, evenly pressing the dough into the sides. Trim the excess dough.

To make the filling: In a large bowl, mix together the apples, lemon juice, pepper, brown sugar, flour, cinnamon, nutmeg, and raisins, if using.

To make the topping: In a food processor, combine the sugar, flour, butter, cheese, and almonds and pulse 2 or 3 times until it forms a coarse crumbly mixture. It should be loose.

Preheat the oven to 375°F. Fill the prepared tart shell with the apple filling, pressing down gently to fill all the spaces. It will be heaping. Scatter the topping evenly over the apples and bake for 45 minutes or until the top is golden and the apples tender when pierced with the point of a knife.

The tart can be served warm or at room temperature. Cut a wedge and spoon the Ginger Custard Sauce around.

~~~~~~

GINGER CUSTARD SAUCE
Makes about 2 cups

3 tablespoons roughly chopped fresh ginger

⅓ cup sugar

¼ cup water

1½ cups half-and-half

1 teaspoon vanilla extract

4 large egg yolks

This sauce is based on the famous French dessert sauce called crème anglaise ("English cream"). It's something everyone should know how to make, with or without the ginger. Once cooled, it makes not only a delicious sweet sauce but is the basis for the very best ice cream you'll ever eat. Simply put it in an ice-cream maker and freeze according to the manufacturer's directions. I'm cooking the ginger in a sugar syrup here to inactivate the enzymes that can cause the cream to curdle. If not using ginger you can omit this step but use extra caution in adding the hot cream mixture to the egg yolks.

In a small saucepan, put the ginger, sugar, and water and simmer for about 6 minutes. The syrup should be thick but not brown. Remove from the heat and let stand for 30 minutes for the flavor to develop. Heat again, add the half-and-half and vanilla, and bring just to the simmer.

In a medium bowl, beat the egg yolks until slightly thickened. Stir in the hot cream mixture slowly to avoid scrambling the eggs. Return the entire mixture to the saucepan and cook over medium-low heat until the sauce begins to thicken (180°F). Immediately strain and refrigerate. To prevent a skin from forming, press a piece of plastic wrap right down on the surface of the sauce, then cover and refrigerate. Can be made ahead and stored, covered, in the refrigerator for up to 3 days.

apples

Ever since Eve took her fateful bite of apple, the glorious fruit has been immortalized as a symbol of temptation and seduction. The apple tree is native to Europe and western Asia and started rapidly gaining popularity in North America in the seventeenth century. Dwarf apple trees are the best choice for the home gardener since they can be more easily maintained than standard apple trees and will bear fruit within two to three years, as opposed to five or six.

At the Valley Oaks garden, we organically grew over 85 different apple varieties to explore their different color, shape, texture, and taste. There are over 7,000 varieties known, but only about 100 are grown commercially.

Apples have the ability to act as a ripening agent for other foods by emitting ethylene gas. To speed the ripening of tomatoes, put them in a paper bag with an apple or two and they'll ripen quickly. This can also have a downside. Storing a number of apples in the refrigerator can cause lettuce to brown, carrots to become bitter, and cucumbers to turn yellow.

Of the varieties commercially available, here are my favorites:

Golden Delicious: Originated in West Virginia in the early 1900s. Green yellow to bright yellow skin, firm flesh, juicy, crisp, and sweet. A midseason ripener. A good keeper and an excellent all-around apple for eating out of hand or cooking.

Gravenstein: Originated in the early 1800s in Germany and Sweden. Favored now in Northern California. Greenish yellow to orange-yellow with light-red stripes. Aromatic, crisp, juicy flesh. An early ripener. They are good eaten out of hand when just picked but don't hold up to storage. Gravensteins make wonderful applesauce and cider, and they're a favorite in the wine country.

Northern Spy: Originated in New York, supposedly from an errant seed sprouted near Canandaigua around 1800. Red-and-yellow skin. Firm, tender, crisp, and juicy. It stores well and is one of the best apples for pie.

Empire: Developed in the 1960s in New York. A Red Delicious–McIntosh cross with lovely aromatic qualities. Dark red-and-yellow skin. An excellent eating apple for kids. Crisp, juicy flesh. Also known as the Royal Empire, it stores well and makes a great cider.

Granny Smith: Originated in Australia, supposedly sprouting from a pile of apples tossed out by a southeastern Australian named Mrs. Smith in 1868. Grass-green skinned. Requires a long season to ripen. A good keeper with crisp, tart, simple flavor. Not nearly as interesting as Newtown Pippin.

Newtown Pippin: Originated on Long Island in the early 1700s. It is the oldest commercially grown variety in America. The first American apple to gain popularity in Europe. Green or yellow skin with pinkish blush at the base. Juicy, with fine-grained flesh. Late-season ripener and a good keeper, it is a great cooking apple.

McIntosh: A Canadian variety from the 1800s. Green-red skin. Tender and aromatic. Excellent for eating, making applesauce, and especially making cider. A midseason ripener, this variety turns mealy if stored too long.

Jonagold: A cross between Jonathan and Golden Delicious, first released in 1968. It has become the leading variety grown in the Pacific Northwest. It is an excellent sweet-tart dessert apple that makes a great pie.

Fuji: Developed from American parents, Ralls Janet and Red Delicious, it is now the most popular apple in China and Japan. It is the best keeper of all the sweet apples and will last up to a year if kept refrigerated.

Gala: A strikingly beautiful red-and-yellow apple that was originally developed in New Zealand by crossing Golden Delicious and Kidd's Orange Red. Great eaten out of hand, it also makes great sauce and cider.

Winesap: With a pungent sweet-sour flavor with fine aroma, this important late-season apple does equally well in sauces, pies, and cider.

JACK DANIEL'S SUN-DRIED CHERRY TART

Serves 12

FILLING

2 cups coarsely chopped dried cherries

¾ cup Jack Daniel's whiskey

GLAZE

½ cup Jack Daniel's whiskey

3 tablespoons sugar

One 3-inch strip orange zest

CRUST

¾ cup all-purpose flour

2 tablespoons cocoa powder

½ teaspoon ground cinnamon

¼ teaspoon baking powder

½ cup (1 stick) plus 2 tablespoons unsalted butter at room temperature

½ cup plus 2 tablespoons sugar

1 large egg yolk

½ teaspoon almond extract

2 cups finely ground almonds (do this in a food processor with the metal blade)

I believe I developed this recipe for a contest sponsored by (you guessed it) Jack Daniel's. I didn't win, but I still like the tart. The approach is similar to the traditional linzer torte: a fruit filling cooked until almost jammy, baked in a textured, nutty dough. Use any fruit you'd like, including dried apricots or pears, or golden raisins.

To make the filling: In a small saucepan, simmer the cherries and the Jack Daniel's until the whiskey is absorbed and the cherries are soft. Remove from the heat and cool.

To make the glaze: In a small saucepan, combine the whiskey, sugar, and orange zest. Bring to a boil and reduce by half. Remove the orange zest.

To make the crust: In a medium bowl, sift together the flour, cocoa powder, cinnamon, and baking powder. In another medium bowl, cream the butter and sugar together, then add the egg yolk and almond extract and mix well. Mix in the flour mixture and then the almonds.

Preheat the oven to 350°F. Divide the dough in half. Press half the dough onto the bottom and one-third the way up the sides of a 10-inch springform pan. Divide the remaining dough into 8 pieces and roll into 10-inch-long ropes for use on top of the tart. Pour the filling into the tart shell and arrange the ropes of dough in a lattice design on top of the tart.

Place the tart on a baking sheet and bake for 30 minutes or until the edges start to brown and the dough is set. Cool the tart on a wire rack for 5 to 10 minutes. Paint the entire top of the tart evenly with the glaze. Gently run a knife around the edges to loosen and remove the sides of the springform pan. Serve warm or at room temperature.

GRAPEFRUIT-BANANA BRÛLÉE TART

Serves 12

CRUST

1 cup all-purpose flour

Pinch of kosher or sea salt

1 tablespoon sugar

¼ cup toasted, skinned, and chopped hazelnuts

½ cup (1 stick) cold unsalted butter, cut into small bits, plus additional for the tart pan

½ teaspoon vanilla extract

2 tablespoons ice water

FILLING

2 small, firm ripe bananas

½ cup fresh grapefruit juice

2 teaspoons grated lemon zest

½ cup sugar, plus ⅓ cup for the top of the tart

½ teaspoon cornstarch

2 large eggs

3 large egg yolks

Pinch of kosher or sea salt

⅓ cup unsalted butter, melted

Fresh raspberry purée and fresh mint sprigs for garnishing (optional)

The combination of the tart grapefruit and the sweet banana in this recipe is very intriguing. I'm a great fan of grapefruit and think we don't use them nearly enough. This tart needs to be started well ahead of serving—the dough needs to be chilled before rolling, then frozen before filling, and the filling should chill several hours before going under the broiler or torch. The final step (caramelizing the sugar) takes just a few seconds. For a really simple grapefruit dessert, try putting a good layer of either light- or dark-brown sugar on a cold grapefruit half and then caramelizing it quickly under the broiler or with a torch. The tart/sweet and cold/hot taste sensation is wonderful.

To make the crust: In a food processor, combine the flour, salt, sugar, and hazelnuts. Pulse 2 or 3 times to combine. Add the butter and pulse until the dough resembles very coarse cornmeal. Add the vanilla and water and pulse until the dough just begins to come together. Remove the dough and flatten it into a disk. Wrap in plastic wrap and refrigerate for at least 2 hours.

Lightly butter a 9-inch tart pan with a removable bottom. Roll the dough into a circle 11 inches in diameter. Roll the dough onto the rolling pin and transfer to the prepared tart pan, pressing the dough into the bottom and sides. Trim off any excess and prick the bottom with a fork. Freeze the shell for at least 1 hour before baking.

Preheat the oven to 375°F. Line the shell with heavy-duty aluminum foil and fill with dried beans to weight down. Bake for 6 to 8 minutes. Carefully remove the foil and the beans and bake for 4 minutes longer or until very lightly browned. Cool in the pan and set aside.

To make the filling: Slice the bananas and arrange evenly over the bottom of the prepared tart shell. In a stainless-steel bowl, whisk together the grapefruit juice, lemon zest, sugar, cornstarch, eggs, egg yolks, salt, and melted butter. Transfer to the top of a double boiler over simmering water and whisk until thick. Pour over the bananas in the tart shell. Refrigerate for at least 3 hours or until firm.

Just before serving, lightly but evenly coat the top of the tart with the remaining ⅓ cup sugar. Put under a hot broiler and broil until the sugar caramelizes to a dark brown. Or hold a propane torch 3 inches from the tart and flame the sugar. It takes about a minute. Cut into wedges. Serve with raspberry purée and garnish with mint strips, if using.

CARAMEL, CHOCOLATE, AND MACADAMIA NUT TART

Serves 8 to 12

CRUST

⅓ cup cold unsalted butter, cut into small bits, plus additional for the tart pan

1½ cups all-purpose flour

½ teaspoon kosher or sea salt

1 large egg yolk, lightly beaten

2 tablespoons ice water

CARAMEL FILLING

½ cup sugar

1¼ cups heavy (whipping) cream

½ cup dark corn syrup

¼ cup (½ stick) unsalted butter

1½ cups lightly toasted unsalted macadamia nuts

CHOCOLATE GLAZE

3 ounces bittersweet chocolate, chopped

⅓ cup heavy (whipping) cream

3 tablespoons sugar

This dessert was one of the favorites in the early days of my namesake restaurant, John Ash & Company. Every time we tried to take it off the menu, we'd be bombarded with groans and moans. So it stayed. This tart keeps very well in the refrigerator, but allow it to come to room temperature before serving; otherwise, the caramel is too hard.

To make the crust: Using an electric mixer fitted with the paddle attachment or by hand, in a large bowl beat or cut the butter into the flour and salt very quickly to resemble coarse cornmeal. Add the egg yolk and 1 tablespoon of the water and mix until the dough just comes together. If too dry, add a little more cold water. This may also be made in a food processor using the plastic or metal blade. Wrap the dough in plastic wrap and chill for at least 2 hours or overnight. This dough freezes well.

Preheat the oven to 375°F. Lightly butter the bottom and sides of a 9-inch tart pan with a removable bottom. On a lightly floured work surface, roll the dough to a diameter of 11 inches. Roll the dough onto the rolling pin and transfer to the tart pan. Gently press the dough into the bottom and sides of the pan. Trim off any excess and prick the dough with a fork. Line the dough with heavy foil and fill with dried beans to weight the dough. Bake for 5 to 7 minutes or until the dough is partially cooked but not brown. Carefully remove the foil and the beans; continue to bake for 3 to 4 minutes longer until lightly brown. Remove and set aside to cool.

To make the caramel filling: In a heavy saucepan over medium-high heat, combine the sugar, ½ cup of the cream, the corn syrup, and butter. Bring the mixture to a boil, stirring occasionally, and cook until it reaches 240°F on a candy thermometer, the soft-ball stage. Slowly, because it will bubble up, add the remaining ¾ cup cream. Return the mixture to the boil and cook until it reaches 220°F. Remove from the heat and cool slightly. Arrange the nuts evenly in the baked tart shell and pour the warm caramel over. Cool and refrigerate until firm.

To make the chocolate glaze: Combine the chocolate, cream, and sugar in a double boiler and cook over medium low heat just until the chocolate melts. Remove from the heat and whisk until smooth.

Quickly pour the chocolate glaze over the top of the chilled tart. Rotate and tilt the tart to spread evenly. Chill again to firm the chocolate. Return the tart to room temperature before serving.

FRESH PEACH AND ALMOND TART

Serves 8 to 10

CRUST

⅓ cup cold unsalted butter, cut into small bits, plus additional for the tart pan

2 tablespoons cold vegetable shortening

1½ cups all-purpose flour

1 tablespoon granulated sugar

Pinch of kosher or sea salt

⅓ cup ice water

PEACHES

4 large or 6 small, firm ripe peaches

3½ cups dry white wine

1 cup water

1½ cups granulated sugar

Two 3-inch strips lemon zest

One 3-inch piece vanilla bean, split lengthwise

3 cloves

1 teaspoon peppercorns

FILLING

½ cup (1 stick) unsalted butter

½ cup confectioners' sugar

⅓ cup all-purpose flour

½ cup almond paste

2 teaspoons grated lemon zest

¼ cup ground almonds (do this in a food processor)

2 large egg whites

This is one of my favorite summer desserts, and it works equally well with nectarines or apricots. The tart is best eaten the day it's made, so plan ahead, because the dough needs to chill for 2 hours before being rolled and then for another hour before being filled. You can prepare the peaches while the dough is in the refrigerator, but make the filling just before baking. The dough makes a really wonderful crust and it keeps well in the freezer, so you might want to make a double batch and roll it and freeze it, unbaked, for another use. Another bonus of this recipe is the peach–poaching liquid, which should be saved. It's delicious drizzled on fruit or pancakes and can be used again to poach more fruit.

To make the crust: In a food processor or by hand, pulse or cut the butter and shortening into the flour, sugar, and salt. Add the ice water and pulse briefly; the dough should just pull together.

Transfer the dough to a lightly floured work surface. Gather the dough into a ball (it will seem slightly dry) and knead it briefly with the heel of your hand. If the dough seems too dry, add a few more drops of ice water. Form the dough into a disk, wrap with plastic wrap, and refrigerate for at least 2 hours before using.

Lightly butter a 9-inch tart pan. Roll the dough into a circle 11 inches in diameter. Then roll it up onto the rolling pin and transfer to the prepared tart pan. Gently press the dough into the bottom and sides of the pan, trimming off the excess. Prick the dough with a fork and return to the refrigerator for at least 1 hour.

Preheat the oven to 350°F. Line the tart shell with heavy-duty aluminum foil and fill with dried beans to weight down the dough. Bake for 5 minutes. Carefully remove the foil and beans and bake the tart shell for 3 minutes longer or until the dough is set and lightly browned.

To prepare the peaches: Halve and pit the peaches. In a medium saucepan, combine the wine, water, sugar, lemon zest, vanilla bean, cloves, and peppercorns. Bring to a boil and reduce the heat. Add the peaches and simmer for 4 to 5 minutes or until just barely tender. Remove the peaches with a slotted spoon. Peel and set aside.

To make the filling: Preheat the oven to 375°F. In a medium bowl, combine the butter, sugar, flour, almond paste, lemon zest, and ground almonds and beat until smooth. In a small bowl, beat the egg whites until foamy and quickly stir into the filling. Spread the filling evenly in the bottom of the prepared tart shell.

Arrange the poached peach halves in a circle, cut-side down, on top of the filling. Bake the tart for 25 to 30 minutes or until the filling is set and lightly colored. Remove and allow to cool before cutting into wedges.

RICOTTA, HONEY, AND FIG TART

Serves 8 to 10

1½ cups Hazelnut Biscotti (page 391) crumbs or other cookie crumbs

¼ cup (½ stick) unsalted butter, melted

2 cups whole-milk ricotta cheese (facing page)

⅓ cup honey

Pinch of kosher or sea salt

1 tablespoon grated lemon zest

½ cup heavy (whipping) cream

2 teaspoons unflavored gelatin

2 pounds ripe figs

Bittersweet chocolate shavings for garnishing

This is a very simple dessert that requires exceptionally good ricotta and honey. You can make your own ricotta, or buy some from a good delicatessen or cheese shop. Regular supermarket ricotta just doesn't have enough flavor. My favorite ricotta is a sheep's milk version made by Cynthia Callahan at Bellwether Farms (see page 421). Good honey is also essential. I prefer honey made from flowers such as orange, star thistle, or heather.

Preheat the oven to 375°F. In a medium bowl, mix the biscotti crumbs with the butter. Press into an 8-inch tart pan with a removable bottom. Put the tart pan on a baking sheet and bake for 8 to 10 minutes or until the crust is set and lightly browned. Remove and allow to cool. Set aside.

In a food processor, combine the ricotta, honey, salt, and lemon zest. Process until the mixture is smooth, about 60 seconds. Scoop the mixture into a medium bowl. In a small saucepan, place the cream and sprinkle the gelatin on top. Allow the gelatin to soften for 3 minutes. Over low heat, stir until the gelatin is dissolved. Then whisk the cream-gelatin mixture into the ricotta mixture and pour into the prepared shell. Chill for at least 2 hours or until firm.

Remove the tart from the pan and place on a serving plate. Slice the figs, 2 or 3 length-wise slices each, and arrange on the tart. Garnish with chocolate shavings.

RICOTTA CHEESE
Makes 3 to 4 cups

4 quarts whole milk

6 tablespoons fresh lemon juice

Kosher or sea salt

There are many different recipes for making your own ricotta cheese. One of the simplest and best that I know is the version from Deborah Madison's book The Savory Way. *It's a magical process to participate in and the result is wonderful. A thermometer is helpful here. My bet is that once you make your own ricotta you'll never again buy the little white tubs in the supermarket.*

In a nonreactive saucepan over very low heat, combine the milk and lemon juice. Gradually bring the milk up to 180°F; it should take 25 to 30 minutes. A fine skin will form and there will be tiny bubbles all around the edge of the milk. When the milk reaches 180°F, remove the pan from the heat, cover, and leave it in a warm spot (an oven with the pilot light on is perfect) for 6 hours. The curds will have formed and separated from the whey.

Line a strainer or colander with a well-rinsed double layer of cheesecloth and set it over a larger bowl. Ladle the curds into the strainer and season lightly with salt. Refrigerate overnight until the cheese is well drained. For a thicker, firmer cheese, you can tie the filled cheesecloth into a pouch and hang it from a refrigerator shelf with a bowl underneath for up to 1 day. Remove the cheese from the cloth, put it in a covered container, and store in the refrigerator for up to 1 week. The whey that has been drained off can be used in baking (my grandmother used to add it to her pancake batter).

LEMON TARTLETS WITH FRESH BERRIES, FRESH PLUM SAUCE, AND ORANGE-GINGER STAR COOKIES

Serves 10

LEMON CURD

¾ cup (1½ sticks) unsalted butter

1 cup fresh lemon juice

1¼ cups sugar

1 teaspoon cornstarch

4 large eggs

6 large egg yolks

½ teaspoon kosher or sea salt

2 tablespoons grated lemon zest

FRESH PLUM SAUCE

1½ pounds Santa Rosa or other plums, halved and pitted

3 tablespoons sugar

2 teaspoons grated lemon zest

¼ cup slightly sweet white wine, such as Riesling or Gewürztraminer

DOUGH FOR TARTLETS AND STAR COOKIES

½ cup plus 1 tablespoon sugar

2 tablespoons minced candied ginger

¾ cup (1½ sticks) unsalted butter at room temperature

1 teaspoon vanilla extract

½ teaspoon kosher or sea salt

2 teaspoons grated orange zest

1½ cups all-purpose flour

Fresh raspberries and blackberries and fresh mint sprigs for garnishing

I fell in love with lemon curd years ago while staying at bed and breakfast inns in England. It seemed there was always a jar of curd at the breakfast table to spread on warm scones. In this dessert, I've taken lemon curd and put it in a flavorful shortbread shell and served it along with a scattering of fresh berries. Yum! I've given directions for a very elegant presentation, but the components are very simple to make and all can be prepared ahead.

To make the lemon curd: In a double boiler over simmering water, melt the butter. Add the lemon juice, sugar, cornstarch, eggs, egg yolks, salt, and lemon zest, whisking until thick. Remove from the heat and cool. Chill the curd, covered, for 4 hours or overnight until set. Store any leftover curd, tightly covered, in the refrigerator for up to 1 month.

To make the fresh plum sauce: In a saucepan, combine the plums, sugar, lemon zest, and wine and simmer, uncovered, until thick. Transfer to a food processor and purée. Strain through a medium-mesh strainer. Store, covered, in the refrigerator.

To make the dough for the tartlet shells and the Orange-Ginger Star Cookies: In a food processor, combine the sugar and candied ginger and process until the ginger is pulverized. Using an electric mixer fitted with the paddle attachment, or by hand with a wooden spoon, cream the sugar mixture and butter until light and fluffy. Beat in the vanilla, salt, and orange zest. Add the flour and mix until well blended.

Divide the dough in half. Take one portion and divide it into 10 walnut-sized balls. Make the tartlet shells by pressing each ball into a cup in a tartlet tin; chill for at least 30 minutes. Roll the remaining dough and, using a small, star-shaped cutter, cut out stars. Place them on a lightly buttered baking sheet. Chill for 30 minutes.

Preheat the oven to 350°F. Bake the star cookies for 8 to 10 minutes and the tartlets for 12 to 15 minutes or until lightly browned. Remove and cool. Store in an airtight container.

Use a pastry bag to pipe the curd into the prepared shells or simply spoon it in. Place 1 or 2 tartlets on a plate. Drizzle the Fresh Plum Sauce around and garnish with a scattering of berries, an Orange-Ginger Star Cookie, and a mint sprig.

WALNUT-ORANGE TART

Serves 8 to 10

CRUST

1 cup all-purpose flour

½ cup (1 stick) cold unsalted butter, cut into bits

1 teaspoon vanilla extract

1 to 2 tablespoons ice water (if needed)

FILLING

¾ cup heavy (whipping) cream

⅔ cup sugar

1 tablespoon grated orange zest

½ teaspoon vanilla extract

Big pinch of kosher or sea salt

2 tablespoons Grand Marnier or other orange liqueur

2¼ cups lightly toasted walnut halves

Fresh berries or sliced mango for garnishing

This is a simple tart to make and it keeps very well. You can use any kind of nut you want—a combination of walnuts, pecans, and hazelnuts is great!

To make the crust: In a food processor or by hand, combine the flour, butter, and vanilla. Pulse or cut until the dough resembles coarse oatmeal. If the dough is too dry, add a little ice water. Gather the dough into a ball and wrap well with plastic wrap. Refrigerate for at least 30 minutes.

Preheat the oven to 350°F. Lightly butter a 9-inch tart pan with a removable bottom. On a lightly floured work surface, roll the dough to 11 inches in diameter. Then roll the dough up onto the rolling pin and transfer it to the prepared tart pan, trimming any excess. Gently press it into the bottom and sides of the pan. Prick the dough with a fork. Line the tart shell with heavy-duty aluminum foil and fill with dried beans to weight down the dough. Bake for 5 minutes. Carefully remove the foil and beans and bake the tart shell for 3 minutes longer or until the dough is set and lightly browned. Remove and allow to cool.

To make the filling: In a saucepan, combine the cream and sugar. Heat, stirring, until it just simmers and the sugar dissolves. Stir in the orange zest, vanilla, salt, and Grand Marnier. Remove from the heat.

Place the walnut halves in an even layer on the bottom of the prepared crust. Pour the cream mixture over the nuts. Put the tart on a baking sheet and bake for 30 to 35 minutes. The tart should be lightly browned on top; it will bubble as it bakes. Remove and cool briefly. Do not refrigerate.

Serve the tart warm or at room temperature. Garnish with berries or mango, if using.

CHESS PIE

My good friend Steve Garner, with whom I have cohosted a radio show in Northern California for the past eighteen years, is one of the best cooks I know. Born and raised in Kentucky, he is a real expert on the traditional cooking of the South. A while back we somehow got on the subject of chess pie, one of the great traditional desserts of the South. There are several stories about where the word chess comes from, but the one that I've heard most often is that it basically was a poor man's cheesecake and took advantage of three ingredients that almost every Southern farm household had on hand: flour or cornmeal, eggs, and milk or buttermilk. The combination of these three things, along with a little sugar or honey, when baked in a crust yielded a delicious pie or tart that was easy to make, kept well without refrigeration, and was the perfect foil for any fresh seasonal fruit.

Well, to continue the story about my buddy Steve, we were comparing notes on our favorite chess pie recipe. I had one that my Grandmother gave me that I thought was the best I'd ever tasted. He had his favorite — one from The Old Talbert Tavern (no longer open) in Kentucky. Steve also collected a number of other authentic recipes from sources such as church and Junior League cookbooks, old copies of Southern Living, *and even the recently revised* Joy of Cooking. *Being the wild man that he is, he prepared eight different versions, and we had a taste-off to determine which we felt was the best. Each had a different proportion and combination of ingredients. One used crushed soda crackers in place of the flour or cornmeal, a couple added raisins or other dried fruit, one used vinegar to curdle the milk in place of using buttermilk, and on and on. Well, after all that work we decided that, at least to our taste, my grandmother's version and The Old Talbert Tavern version were equally good. We declared them both winners. So here they are to enjoy.*

MY GRANDMOTHER'S LEMON CHESS PIE
Serves 8 to 10

Dough for a 9-inch pie or tart shell (page 340)

3 large eggs

1 cup sugar

2 tablespoons yellow cornmeal

2 teaspoons grated lemon zest

1½ tablespoons fresh lemon juice

½ cup (1 stick) unsalted butter, melted

2 teaspoons vanilla extract or 1½ tablespoons dark rum

3 tablespoons golden raisins, plumped in warm water or bourbon and drained

Lightly whipped unsweetened cream for garnishing

Preheat the oven to 425°F. With a fork, prick the prepared pie shell all over and then line with heavy foil, gently pressing evenly into the shell. Fill with dried beans to weight down the dough. Bake for 5 minutes, then carefully remove the foil and bake for 4 to 5 minutes more or until the shell is set and very lightly browned. Remove from the oven and cool. Reduce the oven heat to 350°F.

In a medium bowl, beat the eggs until blended. Add the sugar, cornmeal, lemon zest, and lemon juice and beat until well combined. Stir in the butter, vanilla, and raisins and pour into the pie shell. Bake for 40 minutes or until the filling is set and lightly browned. The pie will puff up, then sink as it cools. Serve warm or at room temperature (not cold) with lightly whipped unsweetened cream.

OLD TALBERT TAVERN'S CHESS PIE
Serves 8 to 10

Dough for a 9-inch pie or tart shell (page 340)

¼ cup (½ stick) unsalted butter at room temperature

1¼ cups sugar

1 tablespoon self-rising flour

Pinch of kosher or sea salt

2 large eggs

1 teaspoon vanilla extract

½ cup whole milk

Slightly sweetened and crushed blackberries or blueberries for garnishing

Preheat the oven to 375°F. Line a pie plate with your favorite dough. You can blind-bake the shell if you prefer, or set it aside in the refrigerator and use unbaked.

Using an electric mixer fitted with the paddle attachment, or by hand with a wooden spoon, cream the butter and sugar together until light and fluffy (4 to 5 minutes in a mixer). Gradually add the flour and salt, then the eggs one at a time, making sure the mixture is smooth before each addition. Stir in the vanilla and milk until just mixed. Pour into the prepared shell and bake for 10 to 15 minutes or until the center is just set. Reduce the heat to 350°F and bake for an additional 25 to 30 minutes or until the filling is firm. Remove, cool, and serve warm or at room temperature with blackberries.

CALIFORNIA FOUR-NUT TORTE

Serves 8

CRUST

⅓ cup unsalted cold butter, cut into ¼-inch bits, plus additional for the cake pan

½ cup coarsely ground almonds

½ cup coarsely ground hazelnuts (filberts)

3 tablespoons all-purpose flour

2 tablespoons sugar

FILLING

1 cup brown sugar

2 tablespoons brandy or orange liqueur

3 large eggs

1 teaspoon baking powder

½ cup all-purpose flour

½ cup chopped pine nuts

1 cup chopped walnuts

1 cup shredded coconut

This cake is rich and delicious and a good keeper because of its moisture. I usually serve it with some ripe berries, or a combination of fruit, such as blueberries and peaches, and a dusting of confectioners' sugar. It really doesn't need anything more. The shredded coconut called for in the filling can be either sweetened or unsweetened, depending on how sweet a cake you want. I usually use sweetened.

To make the crust: Butter an 8-inch cake pan. With an electric mixer or by hand, quickly beat the butter, almonds, hazelnuts, flour, and sugar until combined and no large lumps of butter are visible. You'll need to work quickly so that the butter does not melt. The mixture should be somewhat crumbly. Press the mixture evenly onto the bottom and sides of the cake pan, reaching about two-thirds of the way up the sides. Set aside in the refrigerator.

To make the filling: Preheat the oven to 350°F. Using an electric mixer fitted with the paddle attachment, or by hand with a wooden spoon, in a large bowl beat the sugar, brandy, eggs, and baking powder until smooth. Beat in the flour and then stir in the pine nuts, walnuts, and coconut.

Pour the filling into the prepared crust and bake for about 25 minutes. Do not overbake. The cake should be soft and like caramel in the center. Cool on a rack before removing the cake from the pan. The cake can be made in advance and stored, well wrapped in plastic wrap, in the refrigerator for up to 3 days or in the freezer for up to 1 month.

CHOCOLATE TRUFFLE TORTE

Serves 10 to 12

½ cup (1¼ sticks) unsalted butter, plus additional for the pan

10 ounces bittersweet chocolate, finely chopped

1 tablespoon instant espresso or 2 tablespoons dark rum (optional)

8 large eggs, separated

½ cup sugar

Pinch of kosher or sea salt

2 teaspoons grated orange zest

Unsweetened cocoa powder, confectioners' sugar, and blackberry sauce for garnishing (optional)

So, this is my "death by chocolate" contribution to the world of cooking, a loving send off to life itself, and a heck of a way to go, at that! A little slice is all you need. I love serving this with some very slightly sweetened blackberry sauce or barely sweetened whipped cream to help balance some of the richness.

Preheat the oven to 350°F. Very lightly butter a 9-inch springform pan and place a circle of parchment or waxed paper on the bottom. In a small saucepan over low heat, melt the ½ cup butter until just melted but not hot. Add the chocolate and espresso powder (if using), and whisk until melted. Cool slightly. In a medium bowl, beat the egg yolks and half the sugar together until light in color. Add the warm chocolate mixture and mix together.

In an electric mixer fitted with the whisk attachment, beat the egg whites with the salt and orange zest, and add the remaining sugar gradually just until the egg whites hold stiff peaks. Stir one-quarter of the beaten egg whites into the chocolate mixture to lighten it. Carefully fold in the remaining whites.

Pour the batter into the pan and bake for 45 minutes. Cool and store in the refrigerator if not serving the same day. Note that the cake will have a "cracked" top surface, which is part of its charm!

Slice the cake into small wedges and dust alternately with good unsweetened cocoa powder and confectioners' sugar and add a tablespoon or two of blackberry sauce to the plate, if using.

CALIFORNIA ALMOND CAKE WITH BALSAMIC STRAWBERRIES AND ORANGE MASCARPONE

Serves 8

½ cup (1 stick) unsalted butter at room temperature, plus additional for the cake pan

¼ cup all-purpose flour, plus additional for the cake pan

8 ounces almond paste

¾ cup granulated sugar

3 large eggs

2 teaspoons grated lemon zest

2 tablespoons Grand Marnier or other orange liqueur

½ teaspoon baking powder

Balsamic Strawberries (recipe follows)

Confectioners' sugar for garnishing

Orange Mascarpone (recipe follows)

This almond cake is very moist and can certainly be made in advance. It is a great cake to freeze and have on hand for unexpected company. Dressing strawberries with balsamic vinegar and pepper is an old Italian tradition.

Preheat the oven to 350°F. Lightly butter and flour an 8-inch round cake pan. Using an electric mixer fitted with the paddle attachment, or by hand with a wooden spoon, beat the almond paste, butter, and granulated sugar until pale and fluffy. One at a time, beat in the eggs, followed by the lemon zest and Grand Marnier. In a small bowl, sift together flour and baking powder. Beat the flour mixture into the almond-egg mixture until just combined. Pour the batter into the prepared pan and bake for 35 to 40 minutes. A toothpick inserted in the center should come out clean. Cool on a rack before removing the cake from the pan.

Serve a wedge of the cake with a scoop of the Balsamic Strawberries. Dust with a sprinkling of confectioners' sugar and pipe a small rosette of the Orange Mascarpone from a pastry bag or simply put a dollop on the cake.

BALSAMIC STRAWBERRIES

2 pints ripe strawberries, stemmed and halved

¼ cup balsamic vinegar, preferably white

2 tablespoons honey

½ teaspoon freshly ground pepper

1 teaspoon rinsed and dried green peppercorns, slightly crushed

In a medium bowl, gently combine the strawberries, vinegar, honey, pepper, and green peppercorns. Allow to stand, covered, in the refrigerator for at least 1 hour before serving.

ORANGE MASCARPONE

3 ounces mascarpone cheese

1 teaspoon grated orange zest

1 teaspoon Grand Marnier or other orange liqueur

In a medium bowl, combine the mascarpone cheese, orange zest, and Grand Marnier and beat well.

FLOURLESS WALNUT CAKE

Serves 12

Butter and flour for the cake pan

4 large eggs, separated

1 cup plus 1 tablespoon granulated sugar

2 teaspoons grated lemon zest

12 ounces walnuts, finely ground (pulse a few times in a food processor)

Confectioners' sugar, cocoa powder, and fresh berries for garnishing

This is a very simple recipe that depends entirely on the quality of the walnuts. If you suspect your walnuts have been in storage for a while, lightly toast them on a baking sheet in a preheated 375°F oven for 3 to 4 minutes to refresh their flavor. This is a great cake to serve with a late-harvest Riesling or sweet orange Muscat wine. Be sure the chopped walnuts are loose and that you haven't turned them into walnut butter.

Preheat the oven to 375°F. Lightly butter and flour an 8-inch round cake pan. Using an electric mixer fitted with the paddle attachment, or by hand with a wooden spoon, beat the egg yolks and granulated sugar together until light and fluffy, about 4 minutes. Stir in the lemon zest.

In another bowl, using the whisk attachment, beat the egg whites until they hold stiff peaks. Fold one-quarter of the whites into the egg-yolk mixture to lighten it. Add the ground walnuts, stirring until thoroughly blended. Carefully fold in the remaining egg whites to maintain a light texture.

Pour the batter into the prepared pan and bake for 55 to 60 minutes or until firm and golden brown. Cool on a rack before removing the cake from the pan.

Cut into wedges and serve garnished with confectioners' sugar, cocoa powder, and fresh berries.

NECTARINE UPSIDE-DOWN CAKE IN A SKILLET

Serves 8 to 10

1 cup sugar

2 tablespoons water

6 large, firm ripe nectarines (2 pounds), each pitted and cut into 8 wedges

6 tablespoons (¾ stick) unsalted butter at room temperature

¼ cup maple syrup

¼ cup heavy (whipping) cream

2 large eggs, separated

1 teaspoon ground ginger

2 teaspoons baking powder

1 cup all-purpose flour

1 teaspoon ground cinnamon

1 teaspoon grated lemon zest

Lightly whipped unsweetened cream for garnishing

This is a cake I don't remember my grandmother making, but it sure seems like a Grandma cake. It's best eaten the day it's made, but that shouldn't be a problem because it's so good. Make sure your cast–iron skillet is well seasoned. If not, scrub it well with a nonmetallic scrubber, dry it, and lightly coat the interior with vegetable oil. Put the skillet in a 350°F oven for 3 to 4 hours. Cool and wipe clean, and you should end up with a smooth, shiny surface that's essentially nonstick. Wash with soap and water only and coat with oil after every use, and you'll have a pan that you'll use often because cast iron is such a wonderful heat conductor.

Preheat the oven to 350°F. In a 9-inch cast-iron skillet, dissolve ¾ cup of the sugar in the water and cook until the sugar caramelizes to a medium gold. Turn off the heat and carefully place the nectarine slices in a circular pattern, being careful not to touch the hot sugar with your hands. Set the skillet aside. Using an electric mixer fitted with the paddle attachment, or by hand with a wooden spoon, beat the butter until soft. Beat in the remaining ¼ cup sugar, maple syrup, and cream until smooth. Beat in the egg yolks one at a time.

In a medium bowl, sift the ginger, baking powder, flour, and cinnamon together and fold into the batter along with the lemon zest until well combined. In a large bowl, beat the egg whites until stiff but not dry. Mix one-quarter of the whites into the batter to lighten it and then carefully fold in the remaining whites. Spread over the top of the nectarines and bake in the oven for 20 to 25 minutes or until the cake is golden brown and springy to the touch.

Let cool for 10 minutes, then run a knife around the edge of the skillet to loosen the cake. Place a serving platter over top of the skillet and invert the cake quickly onto the platter. Serve warm or at room temperature, with the whipped cream.

LEMON-GLAZED PERSIMMON BARS

Makes 8 to 12 bars

½ cup vegetable oil, plus additional for the jelly-roll pan

1¾ cups sifted all-purpose flour, plus additional for the jelly-roll pan

1 cup Hachiya persimmon pulp

1 large egg

1 cup sugar

1 teaspoon kosher or sea salt

½ teaspoon ground cloves or ground ginger, or a combination

1 teaspoon ground cinnamon

½ teaspoon freshly grated nutmeg

¾ cup chopped walnuts, almonds, or other nuts

¾ cup coarsely chopped dates or raisins

Lemon Glaze (recipe follows)

In the fall, when persimmons are ripe, this is one of my favorite desserts. I often serve the bars warm, with a scoop of homemade ice cream.

Preheat the oven to 350°F. Lightly oil and flour a jelly-roll pan.

In a medium bowl, mix the persimmon pulp with a beater or whisk until smooth. In another medium bowl, beat the egg lightly. Add the sugar and ½ cup vegetable oil and mix well. Add this mixture to the persimmon mixture.

In a large bowl, combine the flour, salt, cloves, cinnamon, and nutmeg; then stir in the persimmon mixture, walnuts, and dates. Spread the mixture in the pan. Bake for 25 minutes or until golden brown.

Glaze while hot with the Lemon Glaze. Cut into 8 to 12 bars.

LEMON GLAZE

1 cup confectioners' sugar, sifted

3 tablespoons fresh lemon juice

In a small saucepan, combine the sugar and lemon juice. Bring to a simmer and stir until the sugar is melted. Remove from the heat and set aside.

persimmons

Native to China and Japan, persimmons are grown widely in California as well as around the Mediterranean. There are hundreds of varieties of persimmons, but the best known and most frequently grown is the variety called Hachiya. When firm it can be quite tart and astringent, but as it softens and ripens, it becomes very sweet and honeylike. Its pulp is delicious in breads, puddings, sauces, and similar recipes. Since persimmons on the tree tend to ripen simultaneously, there often is a glut of fruit all at once in the late fall. A trick that local growers use is to cut off the very tip of the persimmon to allow for expansion and then wrap and freeze the fruit. Then they partially defrost it and eat it like a frozen mousse or ice. You can use the pulp from a frozen persimmon exactly as you would use the pulp from a fresh one.

In recent years, another variety of persimmon called Fuyu has made its way into the market. This persimmon is different from Hachiya in that it is best eaten firm, almost like an apple. It is sweet when firm with no astringency and perfect in salads or desserts in its raw form.

LEMON POLENTA CAKE WITH WARM SPICED APRICOT SAUCE

Serves 8 to 10

¼ cup vegetable oil, plus additional for the pan

1 cup stone-ground cornmeal, or ¾ cup cornmeal plus ¼ cup polenta

½ cup all-purpose flour

1½ teaspoons baking powder

¼ teaspoon kosher or sea salt

1 cup sugar

2 large eggs

2 large egg whites

2 tablespoons unsalted butter at room temperature

½ cup plain yogurt

1½ tablespoons grated lemon zest

2 tablespoons fresh lemon juice

Warm Spiced Apricot Sauce (facing page)

Yogurt Cheese (page 317) or Crème Fraîche (page 37), and fresh mint sprigs for garnishing (optional)

This is a rustic, peasant-style cake. Polenta, or ground cornmeal, is a staple in the Northern Italian kitchen. The polenta found in American markets is often of a coarser texture than the true Italian polenta, so in this recipe I've used stone-ground cornmeal. If you can't find stone-ground then go ahead and use a bit of coarse polenta with regular cornmeal. By itself, regular cornmeal is too fine. The crunch of the polenta meal adds an interesting texture that I like. The Warm Spiced Apricot Sauce seems to make this a perfect dessert for fall and winter.

Preheat the oven to 350°F. Line the bottom of an 8-inch cake pan with lightly oiled waxed paper. In a medium bowl, sift together the cornmeal, flour, baking powder, and salt. Set aside. In another medium bowl, beat the sugar, eggs, and egg whites until creamy. Add the vegetable oil, butter, yogurt, lemon zest, and lemon juice and beat until smooth. Fold in the dry ingredients until combined. Do not overmix.

Pour the batter into the prepared pan and smooth the top with a spatula. Put in the oven and bake for 40 minutes or until a toothpick inserted in the center of the cake comes out clean. Cool for 15 minutes on a rack. Invert and peel off the paper. Cool completely before serving.

Slice the cake and place the slices on plates. Spoon the Warm Spiced Apricot Sauce over. Garnish with a dollop of Yogurt Cheese and mint sprigs, if using.

WARM SPICED APRICOT SAUCE

One 3-inch cinnamon stick, broken into 3 or 4 pieces

6 cloves

1½ cups dry white wine

1 cup diced dried apricots

3 tablespoons honey

2 tablespoons brandy

2 tablespoons dried currants

1 teaspoon grated lemon zest

Place the cinnamon sticks and cloves on a square of cheesecloth and tie loosely to form a bag. In a small saucepan, combine the spice bag, wine, apricots, and honey. Bring to a boil, reduce heat, and simmer uncovered for 10 to 15 minutes or until slightly thickened, stirring often.

Remove the spice bag and discard. Add the brandy, currants, and lemon zest and simmer for 2 minutes longer. Allow to cool. Store covered in the refrigerator for up to 2 months. Serve warm.

BANANA BREAD PUDDING

Serves 8 to 10

Unsalted butter for buttering bread and baking dish

12 slices (½ inch) challah or other egg bread, crusts removed, or 6 large croissants

3 cups half-and-half

2 teaspoons vanilla extract

1 tablespoon finely grated lemon zest

½ teaspoon kosher or sea salt

½ teaspoon ground cinnamon

4 large eggs

⅔ cup brown sugar, plus 2 tablespoons for topping

2 large ripe bananas

2 teaspoons fresh lemon juice

Burnt Almond Caramel Sauce (page 369) or lightly whipped cream for garnishing (optional)

Bread puddings are very easy to make and a great way to use up leftover bread or croissants. You can flavor them any way that you like. The key to a good bread pudding to my mind is to let the bread soak in the custard mixture for at least 30 minutes before baking. When we made them at the restaurant, we'd let them soak overnight in the refrigerator before baking them in the morning. This insured a moist, custardy pudding.

Preheat the oven to 375°F. Butter a shallow 2-quart baking dish. Lightly butter the bread on both sides, put the bread on a large baking sheet, and bake in the oven, turning once, until lightly toasted on both sides. (If using croissants, you can omit this step.) In a small saucepan, whisk together the half-and-half, vanilla, lemon zest, salt, and cinnamon. Heat the mixture over medium heat until just about to simmer. In a medium bowl, whisk together the eggs and ⅓ cup of the brown sugar until smooth. Slowly pour in the warm cream mixture, whisking all the time. This tempers the egg yolks and makes for a more custardy pudding

Cut the bread into 1-inch squares and put in a large bowl. Pour the cream (custard) mixture over and stir gently. Allow to soak for at least 30 minutes and up to overnight in the refrigerator. Into a medium bowl, slice the bananas and toss with the remaining ⅓ cup brown sugar and the lemon juice. Stir this into the bread and custard mixture and pour into the prepared baking dish, making sure that the ingredients are evenly distributed. Sprinkle the remaining 2 tablespoons brown sugar over the top of the pudding.

Place the baking dish in a larger pan in the oven and add enough boiling water to the pan to reach halfway up the sides of the dish. Bake for 50 to 55 minutes or until the custard is mostly set. It will still be a little jiggly in the center but will set up as the pudding cools. Serve warm or at room temperature with Burnt Almond Caramel Sauce or whipped cream, if using.

HONEY RICE PUDDING

Serves 8

1 ¼ cups water

¾ cup short- or medium-grain white rice

Unsalted butter or vegetable oil for the cake pan

2½ cups whole milk

3 large eggs

3 large egg yolks

½ cup honey

1 teaspoon vanilla extract

2 teaspoons finely grated lemon zest

¼ teaspoon kosher or sea salt

¼ teaspoon freshly grated nutmeg

¼ cup golden raisins, plumped in water or rum for 30 minutes

¼ cup superfine sugar

As a kid, I loved rice and tapioca puddings. In this version I've prepared the pudding in a cake pan so that it can be presented a little more elegantly. It's still just homey old rice pudding, however.

Preheat the oven to 300°F. In a small saucepan, bring the water to a boil, add the rice, and reduce to a simmer. Cover and cook for 8 to 10 minutes or until the water is absorbed. Transfer the rice to a medium bowl and cool.

Butter an 8-inch (1-quart capacity) cake pan and set aside. In a small saucepan, heat the milk to scalding. In a medium bowl, beat the eggs, egg yolks, honey, vanilla, lemon zest, salt, and nutmeg together until smooth. Add the hot milk in a slow stream, stirring to prevent curdling. Drain the raisins and stir into the egg mixture along with the cooled rice. Pour into the prepared cake pan and put in a larger baking pan. Add enough hot water to the baking pan to come two-thirds of the way up the side of the cake pan and bake the pudding for 1 hour and 10 minutes or until the custard is just set. Transfer to a rack and let cool, then cover and refrigerate for at least 4 hours. Cut into wedges and serve on chilled plates.

Variations: For an interesting brûlée presentation, sprinkle superfine sugar over the top of the pudding and with a propane torch, cook the sugar until it caramelizes and is golden brown. The pudding can also be baked in individual ramekins. The baking time will be about 45 minutes.

FRESH CHERRY FLAN

Serves 6 to 8

Butter for the baking dish

3½ cups sweet ripe cherries, any variety

½ cup granulated sugar

2 large egg yolks

1 large egg

⅓ cup unsalted butter, melted

1 cup all-purpose flour

3 tablespoons dark rum

1 teaspoon grated lemon zest

1 cup milk

Confectioners' sugar and Crème Fraîche
(page 37) for garnishing

This version of the classic French clafouti works equally well with any other fresh, ripe fruit, such as blackberries, apricots, and peaches—but I love cherries.

Carefully pit the cherries, leaving them whole.

Preheat the oven to 400°F. Butter a 9-inch baking dish. In a large bowl, combine the granulated sugar, egg yolks, and egg and mix until smooth. Beat in the melted butter, followed by the flour, rum, lemon zest, and milk. The batter should be very smooth. Alternatively, the batter may be quickly made in a blender or food processor.

Arrange the cherries in the bottom of the prepared dish and pour the batter on top. Bake for 35 to 40 minutes or until golden brown and lightly puffed and set.

Serve warm, with a dusting of confectioners' sugar and a dollop or two of Crème Fraîche.

PUMPKIN CRÈME BRÛLÉE

Serves 8

4 cups heavy (whipping) cream

1 teaspoon vanilla extract

8 large egg yolks

¾ cup granulated sugar, plus 4 tablespoons

⅔ cup puréed pumpkin or other sweet winter squash, such as Kabocha or Sweet Dumpling

2 teaspoons minced candied ginger

¼ teaspoon ground cloves

4 tablespoons brown sugar

Mint sprigs and raspberries for garnishing, if available

Here's a brûlée that I think is great for the holiday season. Use it as an alternative for traditional pumpkin pie. Although you can use canned pumpkin, the flavor of fresh baked pumpkin is marvelous and it's really worth the extra time. Caramelize the sugar under a hot broiler or use a propane torch, which I think is easier.

Preheat oven to 350°F. Heat the cream and vanilla in a saucepan to scalding. In a medium bowl, beat the egg yolks and the ¾ cup granulated sugar together until light in color. Slowly add the hot cream, stirring constantly to melt the sugar. Gently stir in the pumpkin, ginger, and cloves until well mixed.

Divide the mixture among eight 6-ounce ramekins and place in a roasting pan. Fill the pan with boiling water to reach halfway up the sides of the ramekins. Cover loosely with foil and bake for 1 hour and 15 minutes until the custards are firm at the edges. Remove, cool, and store covered in the refrigerator for at least 3 hours or overnight.

Preheat the broiler. In a small bowl, mix together the 4 tablespoons granulated sugar and the brown sugar. Sprinkle 1 tablespoon mixed sugar evenly over the surface of each custard. Broil until the sugar is caramelized. Alternatively, use a propane torch. Garnish with mint sprigs and fresh berries, if using. Serve within an hour to maintain the crisp sugar topping.

MANGO CRÈME BRÛLÉE

Serves 8

4 cups heavy (whipping) cream	1 cup ¼-inch diced fresh mango
One 4-inch piece vanilla bean, split lengthwise	4 tablespoons superfine sugar
⅛ teaspoon kosher or sea salt	4 tablespoons brown sugar
8 large egg yolks	Fresh mint sprigs and fresh berries for garnishing (optional)
¾ cup granulated sugar	

Mangoes are not a native California fruit, but we do see a great number of them, beginning in January, imported from Mexico and Central America. As a result, I always think of mangoes as one of the wintertime fruits — perfect for this brûlée.

Preheat the oven to 300°F. In a small saucepan, heat the cream, vanilla bean, and salt to scalding. Remove the vanilla bean from the hot cream. Scrape the tiny seeds back into the cream. In a medium bowl, beat the egg yolks and the granulated sugar until well mixed and light in color. Slowly add the hot cream mixture, stirring constantly to melt the sugar. Strain and skim off any bubbles.

Divide the cream mixture among eight 6-ounce ramekins and distribute the mango evenly among them. Put the ramekins in a baking pan just large enough to hold the them. Fill the pan with boiling water to reach halfway up the sides of the ramekins. Cover loosely with foil and bake for 1 hour and 15 minutes in the oven or until the custard is firm at the edges.

Remove from the oven and cool. Refrigerate, covered, for at least 3 hours or overnight. In a small bowl, combine the superfine and brown sugars. Preheat the broiler and sprinkle 1 tablespoon of the mixed sugars evenly over the surface of each custard. Broil until the sugar is caramelized. Alternately, you can caramelize the sugar with a propane torch. Serve within an hour to maintain the crisp sugar topping.

Garnish with the mint sprigs and fresh berries, if using.

CHOCOLATE SOUFFLÉ

Serves 8

1 tablespoon unsalted butter, plus additional for the soufflé dishes

¼ cup granulated sugar, plus additional for the soufflé dishes

5 ounces bittersweet chocolate, finely chopped

1 tablespoon all-purpose flour

⅓ cup milk

1 teaspoon vanilla extract

4 large eggs, separated

2 teaspoons finely grated orange zest

⅛ teaspoon cream of tartar

Confectioners' sugar and a fresh purée of strained, lightly sweetened raspberries for garnishing (optional)

This soufflé is a little denser than traditional versions. Its great attribute, however, is that it can be made ahead and held in the refrigerator for up to a day before baking. Allow a little longer baking time if you are taking it straight from the refrigerator.

Preheat the oven to 375°F. Lightly butter 8 individual soufflé dishes (4 to 6 ounces) or one 6-cup soufflé dish and sprinkle with sugar, turning the dishes to coat evenly. Set in the refrigerator to chill while making the soufflé mixture.

In a double boiler, melt the chocolate, stirring occasionally. (Alternatively, you can melt it in the microwave. Put the chocolate in a glass bowl and heat for 1 minute at half power. If necessary, give it 10-second doses at half power until just beginning to melt).

In a small saucepan, melt the butter over low heat, add the flour, and cook and stir for 3 minutes. Add the milk and whisk until the mixture is smooth and lightly thickened. Continue to cook for 5 minutes until the mixture thickens nicely. Remove from the heat and gently stir in the melted chocolate, vanilla, egg yolks, and orange zest until thoroughly combined. Set aside and cool to room temperature.

In a large bowl, beat the egg whites with cream of tartar until they hold soft peaks. Gradually sprinkle in the granulated sugar and continue to beat until the whites are stiff but not dry. Stir one-fourth of the whites into the chocolate mixture to lighten it and then carefully fold in the remaining whites. Pour the mixture into the prepared soufflé dishes and put on a baking sheet.

Bake individual soufflés for 12 to 14 minutes or one large soufflé for 30 to 35 minutes, or until a wooden skewer tests moist but not gooey. The soufflés will puff and crack before they are done. Remove from the oven, dust with confectioners' sugar, and garnish with a spoonful or two of berry purée, if using.

WINE AND FRESH FRUIT ICE

Makes about 1 quart

1¼ cups red or white wine

¾ cup sugar

2 cups puréed, unsweetened fresh fruit
   (strained, if you want)

1 tablespoon fresh lemon juice

Dark rum to taste (optional)

This is a basic recipe to make any kind of fresh fruit ice. You can make the finished product more like a sorbet by folding a lightly whipped (until frothy) egg white into the other ingredients just before they go into the ice-cream freezer. The wine choice is up to you, but I'd use a white wine for light-colored fruits, such as peaches, melons, and apples, and a red wine for dark fruits, such as blueberries, blackberries, and the like. Do experiment! A pinch of ground cinnamon or cloves is also a nice addition with most fruits.

In a small saucepan, heat the wine and sugar over medium heat and cook, stirring, until the sugar is dissolved. Stir the hot syrup into the fruit purée and add the lemon juice and rum, if using. Refrigerate or set over a bowl of ice until very cold. Freeze in an ice-cream maker according to the manufacturer's directions.

ROASTED BANANA ICE

Makes about 2 quarts

2 pounds ripe bananas	⅓ cup fresh orange juice
1½ cups sugar	2 tablespoons fresh lime or lemon juice
3 cups water	2 tablespoons dark rum

Originally, I made this with regular fresh bananas but then tried roasting them first. I loved the result. This creamy ice is a wonderfully refreshing finish to a spicy meal. You can try substituting coconut milk for part of the water and adding a pinch of nutmeg or cinnamon to the mix.

Preheat the oven to 375°F. On a baking sheet, put the whole, unpeeled bananas and roast them for 15 minutes or until their skin is black and just beginning to split. Remove from the oven and, when cool enough to handle, discard the skin. You should have 2 cups of banana pulp.

While the bananas are roasting, in a medium saucepan over medium heat, stir the sugar with the water and simmer, stirring, until the sugar is completely dissolved. Remove from the heat and cool.

In a medium bowl, combine the banana pulp, cooled sugar syrup, orange juice, lime juice, and rum. Refrigerate the mixture for 2 hours or until very cold. Freeze in an ice-cream maker according to the manufacturer's directions. Transfer to a storage container and put in the freezer for a few hours to allow the flavors to mellow. This ice is best served within 2 days.

MEYER LEMON SORBET

Makes 1½ quarts

2 tablespoons grated Meyer lemon zest

1 cup fresh Meyer lemon juice

1¼ cups sugar

⅛ teaspoon kosher or sea salt

4 cups half-and-half

Meyer lemons are a special fruit in the wine country. Thought to be a cross between an orange and a lemon, they have a yellow-orange flesh that is very aromatic and not as tart as that of ordinary Eureka lemons. They prefer the colder climate of the wine country to those hot areas where lemons are ordinarily grown. Most of the crop comes from backyard gardeners, although some Meyers are now being grown commercially, so they are increasingly available in markets around the country. You can use Eureka lemons to make this sorbet, but it won't be quite the same. I'd suggest substituting one-third fresh orange juice for the regular lemon juice to better approximate the distinctive Meyer lemon taste.

In a medium bowl, mix together the lemon zest, lemon juice, sugar, salt, and half-and-half and pour into an ice-cream maker; the cream will look curdled but will smooth out when frozen. Freeze according to the manufacturer's directions. Allow the sorbet to soften slightly before serving.

LYCHEE SORBET WITH FRESH FRUITS

Serves 4

One 15-ounce can lychees in syrup

½ tablespoon unflavored gelatin

½ cup sugar

¼ cup water

4 servings of whatever fresh fruits and berries
   are at their seasonal best

The lychee is an Asian fruit with a distinctive flavor. You usually see lychees canned in syrup, but in the summer you can find them fresh in Asian markets and some farmers' markets. Also look for their hairy cousin, rambutan.

Drain off ½ cup of the lychee syrup and transfer to a small bowl. Sprinkle the gelatin over the syrup and set aside 1 minute.

Meanwhile, heat the sugar and water in a saucepan over medium-high heat until the sugar melts, then remove from the heat. Whisk in the gelatin mixture and set aside.

Put the lychees and remaining syrup in a food processor (remove the seeds if they are still in the fruit) and purée. Add the gelatin mixture and process for 15 seconds or until very smooth. Freeze in an ice-cream maker according to the manufacturer's directions. Or, pour into a shallow container and freeze for 24 hours, stirring often to keep crystals from forming. Serve with fresh fruit — you can certainly include a tropical fruit or two, such as mango or pineapple.

COFFEE GRANITA

Makes about 1 quart

granitas

In Italy, granitas are a staple in cafés, especially during warm-weather months. The word *granita* comes from the Italian *grano*, meaning "kernel," or "grain." Granitas were first sold from vending carts in village squares in the early to mid-1800s in Italy. Initially, the coffee or fruit mixtures were partially frozen in a copper cylinder similar to a modern ice-cream maker. Each mixture was then transferred to a container in the cart, and it's thought that the jolting motion of the carts moving over cobblestone roads created the pebblelike texture.

¾ cup water

⅔ cup sugar

2½ cups strongly brewed espresso coffee

2 tablespoons dark rum or orange liqueur

Lightly whipped, barely sweetened heavy (whipping) cream and chocolate covered espresso beans for garnishing

In a small saucepan, place the water and sugar and bring to a boil to dissolve the sugar. Add the coffee and rum and remove from the heat. Transfer the syrup to a nonreactive bowl or pan and put in the freezer. After an hour, as the mixture begins to freeze, stir the ice from around the edges of the container into the syrup. About every 30 minutes, continue to stir to incorporate the frozen portion back into the syrup. As the mixture freezes, it will have a slushy appearance. As it becomes more solid, scrape a tablespoon across the granita to break it up. Repeat scraping every 30 minutes until the mixture is solid, about 4 hours.

Alternatively, you can stir every 30 minutes until the granita reaches the slushy stage. Let it freeze solid at this point and then remove, chop into small pieces, and pulse in a food processor until granita texture is achieved. Return to the freezer for 30 minutes before serving.

Scoop the granita into chilled glasses and top with whipped cream and a scattering of chocolate espresso beans. Serve immediately.

GREEN APPLE GRANITA

Makes about 1 quart

2 pounds tart Gravenstein or Pippin apples

1¼ cups unsweetened apple juice

1¼ cups granulated sugar

2 tablespoons fresh lemon juice

2 tablespoons Calvados, applejack, or dark rum

Peel, core, and slice the apples. Put in a heavy saucepan with the apple juice and sugar. Bring to a boil, cover, and cook over medium heat until very tender (about 15 minutes).

Process the apple mixture in a food processor until very smooth. Strain through a fine-mesh strainer, pushing down on the solids to extract as much of the purée as possible. Stir in the lemon juice and Calvados. Cool. Follow the directions for making Coffee Granita, as above.

LEMON TEA GRANITA

Makes about 1 quart

2½ cups strong brewed tea

⅔ cup sugar

½ cup fresh lemon juice

½ teaspoon finely grated lemon zest

Candied Lemon Zest (recipe follows) for garnishing

Any flavorful tea will work here. For something unusual, try genmai green tea or a smoked tea such as Lapchang Souchong.

In a nonreactive saucepan, bring the tea, sugar, and lemon juice to a boil. Reduce the heat and simmer for 2 to 3 minutes. Add the grated lemon zest and transfer to a nonreactive bowl or pan and follow the directions for Coffee Granita (facing page). When serving, garnish with Candied Lemon Zest.

CANDIED LEMON ZEST

Zest from 2 large lemons, cut into julienne

1 cup sugar, plus additional for rolling cooked zest

⅓ cup light corn syrup

½ cup dry white wine or sake

In a small saucepan, put the lemon zest and cover with water. Bring to a boil, reduce heat, and simmer for 5 minutes. Drain and set aside. Add the 1 cup sugar, corn syrup, and wine to the pan and bring to a boil. Remove from the heat and stir in the drained zest. Let stand for 1 hour. Drain again (reserving the syrup for other uses) and transfer the zest in a single layer to a wire rack. After an hour, as the zest begins to dry, roll it in additional sugar. Store in an airtight container in the freezer for up to a month.

WATERMELON GRANITA

Makes about 1½ quarts

5 cups seeded and diced watermelon pulp (about a 6-pound melon)

⅓ cup sugar

2 teaspoons grated lime zest

¼ cup fresh lime juice

¼ cup sweet white wine, such as Riesling

In a food processor, purée the watermelon (you might have to do this in batches) until smooth and set aside. Transfer to a large bowl.

In a small saucepan, combine the sugar, lime zest, lime juice, and wine. Simmer, stirring, until the sugar dissolves. Remove from the heat, cool, and add to the puréed watermelon. Pour the mixture into ice cube trays and freeze until solid.

Put the frozen cubes in a single layer in the bowl of a food processor and pulse 9 or 10 times until very finely chopped but still frozen. Serve immediately in chilled stemmed glasses.

FRESH BLACKBERRY ICE CREAM AND WALNUT SHORTBREADS

Makes 1½ quarts

2 cups half-and-half

2 cups heavy (whipping) cream

6 large egg yolks

1¼ cups sugar

1 tablespoon grated lemon zest

4 cups ripe wild blackberries, puréed and
   strained of seeds

Sliced nectarines and edible flower petals (see
   page 418) for garnishing (optional)

Walnut Shortbreads (recipe follows)

Wild blackberries grow all over the wine country, and their flavor, when ripe, is like nothing else in the world. The Walnut Shortbreads that accompany this recipe are equally good made with pecans or almonds.

In a medium saucepan, combine the half-and-half and heavy cream. Heat just to a simmer. Remove from the heat and set aside.

In a medium bowl, beat the egg yolks, sugar, and lemon zest together until lightly colored. Slowly beat in the hot cream mixture, being careful not to scramble the eggs. Return the mixture to the saucepan and cook over medium-low heat, stirring constantly, until the mixture thickens (180°F). Remove from the heat and stir in the blackberry purée. Cool the mixture, then freeze in an ice-cream maker according to the manufacturer's directions. Transfer to a storage container and freeze until firm.

Serve a scoop of the Blackberry Ice Cream on top of some sliced nectarines and scatter the flower petals, if using. Accompany with 1 or 2 Walnut Shortbreads.

WALNUT SHORTBREADS
Makes 16 shortbreads

1 cup all-purpose flour

½ cup granulated sugar

½ cup (1 stick) cold, unsalted butter, cut into
   8 pieces

1¼ cups lightly toasted walnuts or pecans

2 teaspoons grated orange zest

1 tablespoon coarse or decorating sugar

Preheat the oven to 350°F. In a food processor, combine the flour, granulated sugar, and butter. Pulse 8 to 10 times or until the mixture resembles coarse cornmeal. Be careful not to overmix. Add the walnuts and orange zest and continue to pulse until the walnuts are coarsely chopped.

Evenly press the mixture into the bottom of a 9-inch tart pan with a removable bottom and sprinkle with the coarse sugar. Bake for 25 to 30 minutes or until golden brown. Immediately remove the sides of the pan and cut the shortbread into 16 wedges.

berries

Picking and eating wild berries in midsummer is one of our simplest and greatest culinary pleasures. According to American Indian legend, berries grow by the heavenly road—a wonderfully stained and thorny road it must be!

In addition to the profusion of wild berries available in many regions, a growing number of supermarkets and produce stores carry a wider array of specialty berries during the height of the season.

The best way to store berries is unwashed, in an open or perforated basket in the refrigerator, where they can breathe, to prevent molding. While the obvious use of berries is in pies, cobblers, ice creams, sherbets, and mousses, they can also be used in relishes and sauces for meat and game to add a sweet-tart tang to the dish. When used this way, berries marry beautifully with Cabernet Sauvignon, Zinfandel, and Pinot Noir.

Blackberries: There are many local varieties of blackberries in each region. Most are medium sized to large, with a deep maroon or purple black color, and are usually found in large clusters on the vine.

Blueberries: Indigenous to North America, this small, blue-black-skinned fruit invites instant eating and is a favorite fruit for pies, jams, and tarts.

Boysenberries: A hybrid of raspberry, blackberry, and loganberry, boysenberries are popular in pies and pastries.

Currants: Red and black currants are more available than in years past. These semitransparent berries are quite tart and are best combined with sweeter berries to offset their pungent burst of flavor. Currants are an excellent accent to game meats and can replace vinegar or lemon juice in many recipes.

Huckleberries: The small huckleberry is virtually indistinguishable from wild blueberries. Known for their intense tangy flavor and crunchy edible seeds, huckleberries must be gathered in the wild. Favored in sauces and pies, they are also irresistible by themselves and as garnishes for other foods.

Loganberries: Loganberries are considered by some to be a variety of the western dewberry (a trailing vine blackberry), by others a hybrid dewberry-raspberry. Whatever they are, they display a purplish dark-red color, and their flavor is slightly tart and very distinctive, which makes them desirable for preserves, desserts, winemaking, cordials, and liqueurs.

Marionberries: Often difficult to find, marionberries are a real treasure. These luscious, dark, blue-black berries have a ravishing aroma, lovely texture, and superb acid balance.

Raspberries: Nearly 90 percent of the nation's supply of raspberries is raised in the Pacific Northwest and is widely available from mid-June to mid-August. Black raspberries are relished for their intensely concentrated sweetness, while the red and golden varieties have a mildly citric, sweet character. Especially rich in pectin, all raspberries are well suited for jams, jellies, and preserves.

FRESH PEACH ICE CREAM WITH BLUEBERRY AND THYME SAUCE

Makes 2 quarts

2 cups half-and-half

2 cups heavy (whipping) cream

9 large egg yolks

1½ cups sugar

2½ cups peeled and finely chopped ripe peaches, tossed with 2 tablespoons fresh lemon juice

Blueberry-Thyme Sauce (recipe follows)

Fresh thyme sprigs for garnishing

The combination of thyme and blueberries in the sauce and fresh, ripe peaches in the ice cream makes this a wonderfully aromatic dessert.

In a medium saucepan, combine the half-and-half and heavy cream. Heat just to a simmer. Remove from the heat and set aside.

In a medium bowl, beat the egg yolks and sugar together until light and thickened. Slowly beat in the hot cream. Return the mixture to the saucepan and cook over medium-low heat, stirring constantly, until the mixture thickens (180°F). Remove from the heat and stir in the chopped peaches. Cool the mixture, then freeze in an ice-cream maker according to the manufacturer's directions. If not using immediately, transfer to a container and store in the freezer.

Allow the ice cream to soften at room temperature for 10 to 15 minutes before serving. Scoop into chilled bowls and spoon the Blueberry-Thyme Sauce around. Garnish with thyme sprigs.

BLUEBERRY-THYME SAUCE
Makes 3 cups

3 cups fresh blueberries

⅓ cup dry red wine

1 tablespoon fresh thyme leaves, preferably lemon thyme

One 2-inch piece vanilla bean, split lengthwise

2 tablespoons honey

1 teaspoon grated lemon zest

In a saucepan, combine the blueberries, wine, thyme, vanilla bean, honey, and lemon zest and simmer for 4 to 5 minutes. Remove from the heat and allow to cool to room temperature. Remove the vanilla bean.

The sauce may be used as is or strained through a coarse strainer for a smoother consistency. Store, covered, in the refrigerator for up to 2 weeks. Serve warm or at room temperature.

LEMON VERBENA ICE CREAM

Makes 1½ quarts

1½ cups whole milk

1½ cups heavy (whipping) cream

½ cup coarsely chopped fresh lemon verbena
leaves

6 large egg yolks

⅔ cup honey

Finely chopped fresh lemon verbena leaves
for garnishing

The distinct lemon taste and aroma of lemon verbena is really intriguing. Try this same ice cream substituting other lemon-scented herbs, such as lemon thyme, lemon basil, or lemon geranium.

A shrub native to Chile and Argentina, lemon verbena was brought to Europe by the Spanish explorers. It has a very distinctive and pungent lemon flavor and aroma. Lemon verbena is used in a variety of ways, most often as a tea, which is said to aid digestion. It's a good substitute for lemongrass in Southeast Asian dishes. It's very easy to grow and quite attractive. Lemon verbena is very sensitive to frost, so most gardeners grow it indoors in containers.

In a medium saucepan, combine the milk, cream, and coarsely chopped lemon verbena and bring to a simmer. Remove from the heat.

In a medium bowl, beat the egg yolks and honey together until light. Whisk in the hot milk mixture and return to the saucepan. Cook over medium-low heat, stirring constantly, until the mixture begins to thicken (180°F). Remove from the heat and immediately strain and cool.

Freeze in an ice-cream maker according to the manufacturer's directions. Transfer to a container and freeze until firm. Allow the ice cream to soften for a few minutes before serving. Garnish with finely chopped fresh lemon verbena.

VANILLA BEAN ICE CREAM WITH
BURNT ALMOND CARAMEL SAUCE

Makes 2 quarts

4 cups whole milk

Two 3-inch pieces vanilla bean, split lengthwise

10 large egg yolks

1¼ cups sugar

2 cups heavy (whipping) cream, whipped to soft peaks

Burnt Almond Caramel Sauce (recipe follows)

This is my favorite recipe for vanilla ice cream. Other flavorings, such as coffee or chocolate, can be added.

In a medium saucepan, combine the milk and vanilla beans over medium heat until the milk just begins to simmer. In a medium bowl, beat the egg yolks with the sugar until light and thick. Slowly, in a thin stream, whisk the hot milk into the egg mixture. Return to the saucepan and heat gently over medium heat until the mixture just begins to thicken (180°F).

Remove the mixture at once from the heat and strain into a medium bowl. Cool the mixture, then freeze in an ice-cream maker according to the manufacturer's directions. When the ice cream is partially frozen, add the whipped cream and continue freezing until the ice cream is firm. Transfer the ice cream to a storage container and keep in the freezer.

Allow the ice cream to soften slightly before serving it. Scoop out into chilled bowls and pour warm Burnt Almond Caramel Sauce on top.

BURNT ALMOND CARAMEL SAUCE

1 cup slivered almonds

5 tablespoons unsalted butter

¾ cup dark-brown sugar

3 tablespoons hot water

Pinch of cream of tartar

Kosher or sea salt

½ cup Gewürztraminer wine

1 cup heavy (whipping) cream

1 tablespoon instant espresso powder

1 teaspoon vanilla extract

Preheat the oven to 350°F. Spread the almonds on a baking sheet and toast for 10 minutes or until golden, then remove them and turn off the oven. Dot the almonds with 2 tablespoons of the butter and return to the oven for another 10 minutes.

In a medium saucepan, combine the brown sugar, the remaining 3 tablespoons butter, the hot water, cream of tartar, and a pinch of salt. Cook the mixture over medium heat until a candy thermometer reads 230°F. Add the wine, cream, espresso powder, vanilla, and almonds very carefully, since the caramel sauce will boil up. Stir over low heat until combined and smooth. Increase the heat and simmer for 5 minutes. Remove from the heat and allow to cool. Store, covered, in the refrigerator. Serve warm or at room temperature.

FRESH CORN ICE CREAM WITH ALMOND LACE COOKIE FANS

Makes 2 quarts

3 cups fresh, sweet raw corn kernels (2 to 3 ears), cobs reserved and broken into 3-inch lengths

4 cups half-and-half

One 3-inch piece vanilla bean

8 large egg yolks

½ cup sugar

½ cup light honey

1 teaspoon grated lemon zest

1 teaspoon seeded and minced serrano chile (optional)

Almond Lace Cookie Fans (facing page)

Fresh mint sprigs for garnishing

Corn ice cream may sound a little strange, but it's quite delicious. The recipe requires fresh sweet corn; frozen or canned just doesn't make it. To extract even more flavor, run the point of the knife down the center of each row of kernels before scraping them off the cob to release the milk and then scrape the cobs well to extract every bit of the sweet corn milk. I've included an optional addition of chile for the adventurous. Also, try the ice cream with a little toasted curry powder or ground ginger in place of the chile.

In a blender or food processor, combine the corn and 1 cup of the half-and-half and process in short bursts to purée the corn. Transfer the mixture to a large saucepan and add the remaining 3 cups half-and-half, the corn cobs, and the vanilla bean. Simmer over medium heat for 1 to 2 minutes or until the corn is tender. Remove from the heat.

In a medium bowl, combine the egg yolks, sugar, honey, lemon zest, and chile (if using), and mix well. Remove and discard the cobs from the corn-cream mixture. Also remove the vanilla bean, split it, and scrape the seeds into the mixture. In a slow, steady stream, whisk the hot corn-cream mixture into the egg yolk mixture.

Return the mixture to the saucepan and cook over low heat, stirring constantly, until it just begins to thicken (about 180°F). Be careful not to boil it or the mixture will curdle. Strain through a fine-meshed strainer and cool. Freeze in an ice cream maker according to the manufacturer's directions. If not using immediately, transfer to a storage container and put in the freezer.

Serve in chilled bowls with Almond Lace Cookie Fans and mint sprigs.

ALMOND LACE COOKIE FANS
Makes 16 to 20 cookies

½ cup (1 stick) unsalted butter at room temperature, plus additional for the baking sheets

1 tablespoon all-purpose flour, plus additional for the baking sheets

¾ cup ground almonds (do this in a food processor)

½ cup sugar

2 tablespoons milk

1 teaspoon grated orange zest

Preheat the oven to 350°F. Lightly butter and flour at least 2 baking sheets. In a large sauté pan, combine the almonds, sugar, butter, flour, milk, and orange zest. Stir over low heat with a wooden spoon until the butter melts and the ingredients are well mixed. Remove from the heat.

On a baking sheet, place heaping teaspoons of the batter about 5 inches apart. (The batter will spread during baking.) Bake for 8 to 10 minutes or until evenly browned. Remove from the oven. Using a wide spatula, remove the cookies from the baking sheet and immediately shape as you want, into tightly rolled cigarettes, or fans, or allow to cool and serve flat.

Store in airtight containers for 2 days or in the freezer for up to a month.

FROZEN ORANGE SOUFFLÉS

Serves 8

8 oranges

⅔ cup sugar

2 teaspoons grated lemon zest

6 large egg yolks

2 teaspoons minced fresh mint

2¼ cups heavy (whipping) cream, whipped to firm peaks

6 tablespoons Grand Marnier or other orange-flavored liqueur

Cocoa powder for garnishing

This simple dessert always seems to capture people's attention. It can be made a day ahead.

Cut one-third of the top off each orange and scoop out all the flesh, reserving it and any juice. Strain the flesh, firmly pressing down to extract as much juice as possible. In a small saucepan, combine the juice, sugar, and lemon zest and reduce by half over high heat, stirring to help the sugar melt. Set aside and cool.

In a medium bowl, beat the egg yolks and juice mixture together until light and thick. Carefully fold in the mint, whipped cream, and Grand Marnier. Using a pastry bag or a spoon, pipe the mixture into the orange shells. Freeze for at least 3 hours or until the mixture is firm. Serve garnished with a dusting of cocoa powder on top.

GINGER, FIG, AND CRANBERRY SEMIFREDDO

Makes one 2-quart terrine

2¾ cups heavy (whipping) cream

8 large egg yolks

⅔ cup sugar

¼ cup minced candied ginger

⅓ cup coarsely chopped dried figs

⅓ cup coarsely chopped dried cranberries or cherries

2 tablespoons grated orange zest

Fresh blackberry purée, fresh mint springs, and Hazelnut Biscotti (page 391) for garnishing

Semifreddo, which translates to "half frozen" in Italian, is very easy to make and keep. This is one I like to do in the winter. You could substitute whatever dried fruits you like in the semifreddo. For the purée, use IQF (individually quick frozen without sugar) blackberries—simply thaw and purée them, strain, and flavor to taste with drops of lemon juice and honey.

Using an electric mixer fitted with the whisk attachment, or by hand with a wooden spoon, beat the cream until stiff and set aside. With the paddle attachment or by hand, using another bowl, beat the egg yolks until light. Gradually beat the sugar into the egg yolks and continue beating for several minutes until light and fluffy. Gently fold the whipped cream into the egg mixture. Fold in the ginger, figs, cranberries, and zest.

Line a 2-quart terrine with plastic wrap and fill with the mixture. Cover the top with plastic wrap and freeze for at least 6 hours or overnight.

Unmold the semifreddo, cut it into slices, and surround each serving with fresh blackberry purée, mint sprigs, and a few biscotti.

BREADS, OTHER BAKED GOODS, *and* SPREADS

BREADS

In many of the bread recipes following, I call for the use of an electric mixer. I find that a good, heavy-duty mixer, such as that made by Hobart, to be one of the indispensable pieces of equipment in my kitchen (no, I don't own any Hobart stock!). Though expensive, they last a lifetime and are ideal for mixing and kneading yeast doughs. If you don't have a mixer, you can also make any of the breads entirely by hand. The mixing and kneading will take longer to get to the satiny look and feel of the dough described in the recipes.

FOCACCIA

There is really no difference between focaccia and pizza. Carol Field, in her wonderful book The Italian Baker, *points out that both are flat, round breads seasoned with oil and cooked in the oven or over embers and are called pizza in the south and focaccia in the north. Here are two of my favorite focaccia recipes, which I've made as rectangles.*

BASIC FOCACCIA

Makes one 12-by-17-inch focaccia

1 tablespoon plus ½ teaspoon active dry yeast

1½ cups warm water (100°F)

½ cup fruity olive oil, plus additional for the bowl and the jelly-roll pan

3¾ cups unbleached all-purpose flour

2½ teaspoons kosher or sea salt

1 to 2 tablespoons chopped fresh herbs (optional)

Optional toppings: thinly sliced red onions, seeded slivered tomatoes, grated cheese

In a large bowl, stir the yeast into the warm water and let stand about 10 minutes. Stir in ¼ cup of the olive oil, then the flour, salt, and herbs, if using. Turn the dough out onto a lightly floured work surface and knead until smooth and elastic, 8 to 10 minutes. Lightly oil a large clean bowl and add the dough, turning to coat it. Cover the bowl tightly with plastic wrap and let the dough rise until doubled, 1 to 1½ hours.

Lightly oil a 12-by-17-inch jelly-roll pan. Flatten and stretch the dough to cover as much of the pan as possible, then dimple the top quite vigorously with your fingertips to stretch it some more. Cover with a towel and let it rest 10 minutes.

Dimple and stretch the dough again to completely cover the pan. Cover with a towel and let it rest another 30 minutes. Preheat the oven to 425°F.

Brush the dough with the remaining ¼ cup olive oil and bake on the upper rack of the oven until it just starts to turn golden, 12 to 15 minutes. Scatter whatever toppings you desire over the top and continue to bake until golden brown, about 10 to 15 minutes longer. If you'd like, remove the focaccia from the pan at this point and finish cooking it directly on the oven shelf for a crisp bottom crust.

GRILLED FLAT BREAD

Makes six 10-inch breads

2½ cups warm water (100°F)

1 package active dry yeast

1 teaspoon honey

1½ cups whole-wheat flour

2 teaspoons kosher or sea salt, plus additional
    for sprinkling

1½ cups plus 2 tablespoons extra-virgin olive oil,
    plus additional for oiling the bowl

3½ to 4½ cups all-purpose flour

1½ cups chopped mixed fresh herbs, such as
    basil, parsley, chives, and savory

This is a fun bread to do right after you've grilled vegetables or meats. You can also add tomatoes, cheeses, and herbs after the first turn and have a savory, smoky pizza that is as good or better as anything done in an oven, in my opinion!

In a small bowl, make a sponge by mixing together the warm water, yeast, and honey and let stand until mixture is foamy, about 10 minutes. Stir in the whole-wheat flour, cover with plastic wrap, and let stand at room temperature for 1 to 4 hours.

Put the sponge in the bowl of an electric mixer fitted with a dough hook and add the salt, 2 tablespoons of the olive oil, and 3½ cups of the flour and beat for 3 to 5 minutes or until the dough is smooth. The dough should be soft but not sticky. If sticky, beat in additional flour, ¼ cup at a time, until the dough is soft.

Place the dough in a large oiled bowl, turn to coat evenly, and cover with a damp towel and allow to rise in a warm place until doubled, 1 to 2 hours. (Can be refrigerated overnight at this point.) Punch the dough down and form into 6 equal balls.

Working with one piece of dough at a time, keeping the remaining pieces covered, roll each ball on a lightly floured board into a circle 8 to 10 inches in diameter. Brush with 2 tablespoons of the olive oil and sprinkle 2 tablespoons of the chopped herbs evenly over and gently press in. Turn the bread over and similarly coat with olive oil and herbs. Sprinkle coarse salt over both sides to taste. Set aside and shape and season the remaining balls.

Allow the breads to rest for 15 to 20 minutes covered with a damp towel and then grill the breads on both sides over medium coals until lightly colored, puffed and speckled brown, and cooked through. Cooking time will be about 6 to 8 minutes total.

Serve warm or at room temperature.

GARDEN HERB AND CHEESE BREAD

Makes 3 loaves

3 tablespoons active dry yeast

3 cups warm water (100°F)

6 to 7 cups unbleached all-purpose flour

3 tablespoons olive oil, plus additional for the bowl

½ cup chopped mixed fresh herbs, such as chives, tarragon, and basil

1⅓ cups coarsely grated cheese, such as Asiago, fontina, or Gruyère

1½ tablespoons kosher or sea salt

2 teaspoons freshly ground pepper

3 tablespoons coarse cornmeal

1 large egg beaten with 1 tablespoon water

This is a bread for taking advantage of the herbs in the summer garden. It's delicious as a sandwich bread, and it's also nice grilled for bruschetta. (The dough is also wonderful made into individual rolls.) You can certainly follow this recipe to the letter, but if you have an interest in exploring the subtleties of bread baking, you can try a slow-rise method by placing the dough in the refrigerator overnight before forming it into loaves. The slow rise intensifies the flavor of the herbs and, I think, gives the bread a better texture.

Using an electric mixer fitted with the paddle attachment, or by hand with a wooden spoon, in a large bowl place the yeast and water and stir. Mix in 2 cups of the flour and let sit undisturbed until bubbly, about 15 minutes.

Add the 3 tablespoons olive oil, the herbs, cheese, salt, and pepper, and the remaining flour 1 cup at a time with the machine running. Continue adding flour until the dough pulls away from the sides of the bowl. Depending on the flour and humidity, more or less flour may be needed.

Using a dough hook or by hand, knead the bread for 5 to 7 minutes until the dough is satiny and smooth. Coat a clean bowl with olive oil and add the dough, turning to coat. Cover with a damp towel or plastic wrap and let the dough rise in a warm spot until doubled, 1 to 1½ hours. Punch down, knead briefly, and form into 3 individual loaves.

Preheat the oven to 375°F. Put the loaves on a baking sheet that has been lightly coated with cornmeal. Cover lightly and let the loaves rise until doubled, about 30 minutes. Carefully paint the top of the loaves with the egg wash. Bake in the lower third of the oven for 30 to 35 minutes or until the loaves are golden brown and the bottoms sound hollow when thumped. Put the loaves on racks and allow to cool before slicing.

BROWN SODA BREAD

Makes 1 large loaf

1½ cups unbleached all-purpose flour

1½ cups whole-wheat flour

6 tablespoons kibbled or cracked wheat

6 tablespoons wheat bran

1 teaspoon kosher or sea salt

1 teaspoon baking soda

2 tablespoons cold unsalted butter, cut into small pieces

1 large egg

1½ cups buttermilk

This is a delicious Old World–style bread that I learned to make from a wonderful Irish neighbor.

Preheat the oven to 450°F. In a large bowl, mix together the all-purpose flour, whole-wheat flour, kibbled wheat, wheat bran, salt, and baking soda. With your fingers, mix and turn it for 2 to 3 minutes to lighten the mixture and trap air into it. With your fingers or with a mixer, quickly rub in the butter so that no large lumps appear. In a small bowl, whisk together the egg and buttermilk. Make a well in the center of the flour mixture and pour in the buttermilk mixture. With your fingers, quickly mix in a circle to form a loose dough. This shouldn't take more than a minute or two. You want to be careful not to overmix.

Dust the top of the dough with a little whole-wheat flour, turn out the dough onto a lightly floured work surface, and tidy gently around the edges. The dough will be soft. Flip the loaf over onto a baking sheet and flatten slightly with your fingers. The loaf should be about 2 inches thick. With a sharp knife, cut a cross on top of the loaf about ½ inch deep and poke a hole in each quarter of the cross (this is to let the fairies out!). Put the loaf in the oven and bake for 15 minutes. Reduce the temperature to 400°F and bake for another 18 to 20 minutes. To check if the bread is done, tap the bottom—it should sound hollow. Cool on a rack.

WINTER SQUASH BREAD

Makes two 10-inch round loaves or 20 to 22 small rolls

1½ cups warm water (100°F)

1 package active dry yeast

¼ cup light-brown sugar

2 large eggs

1 cup winter squash or pumpkin purée, canned or homemade (see Note)

1 tablespoon kosher or sea salt

½ cup yellow cornmeal, plus additional for sprinkling

5½ to 6 cups unbleached all-purpose flour

Olive oil for bowl and baking sheet

Here's a bread to make in the winter. It really is worth the little bit of extra effort to use freshly baked squash or pumpkin instead of canned. Always allow bread to cool thoroughly. This is a nice bread for toast, too.

In a large bowl, add the water and sprinkle the yeast and a pinch of brown sugar over. Stir to combine and let stand until foamy, about 10 minutes.

With a whisk, beat the eggs and squash purée into the yeast mixture. Add the remaining brown sugar, salt, cornmeal, and 2 cups of the flour. Beat hard with a whisk until smooth, about 3 minutes. Add the flour ½ cup at a time and beat with a wooden spoon until a soft dough is formed.

Turn the dough out onto a lightly floured work surface and knead vigorously for about 5 minutes to create a soft, smooth, and elastic dough. Add enough flour for the dough to hold its own shape. Oil a clean bowl and add the dough, turning to coat. Cover with plastic wrap and let the dough rise at room temperature until doubled, 1 to 1½ hours.

Preheat the oven to 450°F. Lightly oil a baking sheet or line with parchment and sprinkle with cornmeal. Gently deflate the dough and turn out onto a lightly floured work surface. Form the dough into 2 large round loaves and put on the prepared baking sheet. Cover the loaves loosely with plastic wrap and let them rise for 30 minutes, or until doubled. If available, heat a baking stone in the oven while the loaves are rising. Dust the tops of the loaves with flour.

Slash the loaves decoratively with a serrated knife, then slide them onto the stone, if using. Put the loaves on the middle rack in the oven, then immediately reduce the temperature to 375°F and bake for 45 to 50 minutes or until the loaves are lightly browned. Cool on a rack.

Note: To make squash purée, preheat the oven to 375°F. Use pumpkin or any kind of squash, such as delicata, acorn, butternut, or Hubbard. Cut the squash in half and scoop out and discard the seeds. Put the squash in a baking dish, cut-side up. Brush with a little butter or olive oil, season with salt and pepper, and bake in the oven for 45 minutes or until tender. Scoop out the flesh and mash or purée until smooth in a blender or food processor.

BRIOCHE

Makes 2 medium loaves or about 20 rolls

¾ cup whole milk

¼ cup sugar

3 packages active dry yeast

6 large eggs plus 3 large egg yolks at room temperature, lightly beaten

2 teaspoons kosher or sea salt

4 to 5 cups unbleached all-purpose flour

1 cup (2 sticks) unsalted butter at room temperature, plus additional for the pans

Vegetable oil for the bowl

1 large egg beaten with 1 tablespoon milk

Buttery brioche is one of life's great pleasures. It can be shaped into the familiar rolls with a topknot or baked in a loaf pan. It's delicious toasted and is the basis for the very best bread puddings. For a savory treat, try baking brioche rolls with a little square of creamy goat cheese or Camembert placed in the center of the dough. Brioche also makes the most wonderful toast to eat as is or to use as the base of a simple winter dish of creamed mushrooms and leeks. My grandmother used to do a variation of this by adding sliced hard-boiled eggs and a little sherry to the cream sauce.

In a small saucepan, heat the milk and sugar, stirring, so that it is just warm to the touch (120°F). Pour the mixture into the bowl of an electric mixer or a large bowl and sprinkle the yeast on top. Stir briefly to dissolve and let the mixture sit for 5 to 10 minutes until it begins to foam. Add the beaten eggs and yolks, salt, and 3 cups of the flour to the bowl and beat with the electric mixer fitted with the paddle attachment, or by hand with a wooden spoon, until the mixture is smooth. Add the butter a tablespoon or two at a time and beat into the dough. Add the remaining flour ½ cup at a time, beating continuously until the dough is shiny and no longer sticky, about 5 minutes.

Transfer the dough to a large, lightly oiled bowl, and turn to coat it. Cover the bowl with a towel and let the dough rise until doubled, about 1 hour. Butter 2 medium loaf pans or 20 individual brioche molds. Punch down and knead briefly. Divide the dough among the prepared pans or molds. Let it rise until doubled, about 1 hour.

Preheat the oven to 400°F. Brush the tops of the brioche with the beaten egg-milk glaze. Bake on the center rack for about 25 minutes for loaves and 12 to 14 minutes for rolls. Check periodically—the brioche should be a rich golden brown and firm to the touch. Remove from the oven and cool slightly before turning out from the pan.

BISCUITS

While bread baking has become a high art, we forget how easy and tasty good biscuits can be. The secret of producing light, delicate biscuits is to work or knead the dough as little as possible. Mix just enough to combine the ingredients. They can and should look a little "lumpy" before baking. The one exception is when you use whole-wheat flour, as in Parmesan–Tomato Biscuits (page 385). Here, you need to knead a little more, just enough to make a smooth dough.

POTATO BISCUITS
Makes about 16 biscuits

8 ounces waxy or boiling potatoes, peeled, cooked, and mashed (¾ cup)

¼ cup (½ stick) unsalted butter, melted

1⅓ cups all-purpose flour, plus additional for dusting

1 tablespoon baking powder

1 teaspoon baking soda

1 teaspoon kosher or sea salt

1 teaspoon sugar

2 tablespoons chopped fresh chives

⅓ cup buttermilk

1 large egg white beaten with 1 teaspoon water

Position a rack in the middle of the oven and preheat to 425°F. In a large bowl, mix the mashed potatoes and butter together until combined. Sift the flour, baking powder, baking soda, salt, and sugar into the bowl and add the chives. Scoop and lift until well combined. The objective is to keep the mixture light and crumbly and not turn it into a paste.

Add the buttermilk and stir until the dough just comes together. On a lightly floured work surface, roll the dough ½ inch thick, cut out rounds with a 2-inch cutter, and transfer to an ungreased baking sheet. Reroll the scraps and cut more rounds, utilizing all the dough.

Brush the tops lightly with the egg white wash and bake in the middle of the oven for 15 minutes or until the biscuits are puffed and golden. Serve warm or at room temperature.

HERB DROP BISCUITS

Makes about 16 biscuits

1 cup unbleached all-purpose flour

1 cup cake flour

2 teaspoons baking powder

½ teaspoon baking soda

1 teaspoon sugar

½ teaspoon kosher or sea salt

1 cup heavy (whipping) cream, whipped to hold soft peaks

2 large eggs, lightly beaten

3 tablespoons chopped mixed fresh herbs, such as chives, basil, and savory

Position a rack in the middle of the oven and preheat to 425°F. In a medium bowl, sift together the all-purpose flour, cake flour, baking powder, baking soda, sugar, and salt. Carefully fold the cream, eggs, and herbs into the flour mixture until just combined.

Drop by heaping tablespoons onto an ungreased baking sheet, 3 to 4 inches apart. Bake in the middle of the oven for 12 to 15 minutes or until lightly browned. Serve warm.

POPPY SEED–BUTTERMILK BISCUITS

Makes about 20 biscuits

2 cups unbleached all-purpose flour

2½ teaspoons baking powder

1½ teaspoons sugar

1 teaspoon kosher or sea salt

⅓ cup cold unsalted butter, cut into tiny bits

⅔ cup buttermilk

2 tablespoons unsalted butter, melted

3 tablespoons poppy seeds

Position a rack in the middle of the oven and preheat to 450°F. In a medium bowl, sift together the flour, baking powder, sugar, and salt. Add the butter and blend quickly with a fork (or in a food processor) until it resembles coarse cornmeal. Add the buttermilk and mix and knead until the dough just comes together, 20 to 30 seconds.

On a lightly floured work surface, roll the dough ½ inch thick, cut out rounds with a 2-inch cutter, and transfer to an ungreased baking sheet. Reroll the scraps and cut more rounds, utilizing all the dough. Brush the tops of the biscuits with the melted butter and generously top with poppy seeds. Bake the biscuits in the middle of the oven for 12 to 15 minutes or until puffed and golden. Serve warm.

PARMESAN-TOMATO BISCUITS

Makes 12 to 14 biscuits

1 cup unbleached all-purpose flour

¾ cup whole-wheat flour

1 tablespoon baking powder

1 teaspoon kosher or sea salt

½ cup freshly grated Parmesan cheese

1 teaspoon minced fresh oregano

1 teaspoon minced fresh basil

⅔ cup tomato juice, preferably fresh

2 tablespoons minced sun-dried tomato (optional)

½ cup (1 stick) unsalted butter, melted

This recipe can also be made into scones. Instead of cutting the rolled dough into biscuits, form a whole cake, about 1 inch thick, cut into 8 wedges leaving the cake intact, and bake as directed.

Preheat the oven to 450°F. In a medium bowl, sift together the all-purpose flour, whole-wheat flour, baking powder, and salt. Stir in the Parmesan cheese, oregano, basil, tomato juice, sun-dried tomato if using, and all but 2 tablespoons of the melted butter. Mix until the dough comes together.

On a lightly floured work surface, knead the dough briefly to make a fairly smooth dough. Roll the dough ½ inch thick, cut out rounds with a 2-inch cutter, and transfer to an ungreased baking sheet. Reroll the scraps and cut more rounds, utilizing all the dough.

Brush the tops of the biscuits with the remaining 2 tablespoons melted butter. Bake in the upper third of the oven for 10 to 12 minutes or until the biscuits are puffed and lightly browned. Serve warm.

baking powder and baking soda

There are two ways of leavening, or causing doughs or batters to rise during baking. We can use active dry yeast, but it will work only in doughs in which the gluten has been kneaded and developed and made elastic enough to capture the bubbles of carbon dioxide the yeast slowly releases, akin to a balloon bumping up to the ceiling.

The other way of leavening dough is to use chemical leaveners, such as baking powder or baking soda, which release carbon dioxide much more quickly. Both work as a result of the action between two opposing forces — acid and alkaline. The alkaline component in the leavening process is almost always baking soda, or sodium bicarbonate. (Potassium bicarbonate is available for those on severely sodium-restricted diets, but it tends to absorb moisture readily, it reacts prematurely, and it sometimes has a bitter taste.)

You can use baking soda alone if the dough or batter has enough acid in it from other ingredients, such as yogurt or sour milk, that contain lactic acid. (Sweet milk can be soured by adding 2 teaspoons of lemon juice or vinegar to each cup of milk.)

Commercial baking powders contain both the alkaline soda and an acid, usually sodium aluminum sulfate or phosphate, and often some inert starch to absorb moisture from the air and prevent premature reaction. This combination produces "double-acting" powder, which means that some carbon dioxide is produced when the powder is mixed with a liquid in a batter and then a second charge of gas occurs in response to the heat of the oven.

Aluminum-based ingredients are of concern to some people; in response, commercial baking powders have become available that use monosodium phosphates instead of aluminum. Rumford is the best-known brand in the United States.

You can make a perfectly acceptable non-aluminum "simple-acting" baking powder at home by mixing ¼ teaspoon baking soda with ½ teaspoon cream of tartar. This mixture is equivalent to 1 teaspoon baking powder in a recipe. My grandmother always made her own because she felt commercial baking powders had a chemical taste.

FAVORITE CORN MUFFINS

I love corn muffins of all kinds, and following are my favorites, which are a little different from the standard.

SAGE-CORN MUFFINS
Makes 12 muffins

¼ cup (½ stick) unsalted butter, plus additional for the muffin pan

1½ cups unbleached all-purpose flour

⅔ cup yellow cornmeal

1½ tablespoons sugar

1 tablespoon baking powder

½ teaspoon baking soda

1 teaspoon kosher or sea salt

¼ cup minced green onions, both white and pale green parts

2 large eggs, beaten

1 cup buttermilk

1 tablespoon minced fresh sage or 1 teaspoon dried

1 cup fresh, sweet, raw corn kernels (1 large ear)

1 teaspoon seeded and minced serrano chile (optional)

This recipe works best with fresh sage and corn, but it's also good with dried sage and frozen corn. Try other fresh herbs, such as savory, oregano, and rosemary, in place of the sage—and add more chile if you like!

Position a rack in the middle of the oven and preheat to 375°F. Lightly butter a muffin pan. In a medium bowl, sift together the flour, cornmeal, sugar, baking powder, baking soda, and salt. In a small sauté pan, melt the butter and sauté the green onions slowly until softened but not browned and add to the flour mixture. Add the eggs, buttermilk, sage, corn, and chile (if using), and stir just to combine.

Divide the batter among 12 muffin cups (fill two-thirds full) and bake on the middle rack of the oven for 25 to 30 minutes or until the muffins are puffed and golden. Serve warm.

CRAB-CORN MUFFINS

Makes 10 muffins

¼ cup (½ stick) unsalted butter, plus additional for the muffin pan

1 cup all-purpose flour

1 cup yellow cornmeal

1 teaspoon sugar

2 teaspoons baking powder

1 teaspoon baking soda

½ teaspoon kosher or sea salt

½ cup finely diced yellow onion

¼ cup finely diced red bell pepper

¼ cup finely diced poblano or Anaheim chile

1 large egg, beaten

1½ cups buttermilk

¼ cup chopped fresh chives or green onions, both white and green parts

2 tablespoons chopped fresh parsley

1 cup Dungeness crabmeat, shredded and picked over to remove any pieces of shell

We love Dungeness crab in Northern California. It's sweet and meaty, and I think the best-tasting crab there is (although I get lots of arguments from crab lovers in other parts of the country). Use whatever crab is available to you.

A salad of savory greens served along with these hearty muffins makes a perfect summer meal for me. You could also make mini corn-crab muffins, split them, and layer them with some thinly sliced cucumbers, sweet red onion, and smoked salmon for a dynamite hors d'oeuvre or first course.

Preheat the oven to 375°F. Generously butter 10 cups of a muffin pan. Sift the flour, cornmeal, sugar, baking powder, baking soda, and salt together in a medium bowl and set aside.

In a sauté pan, melt the ¼ cup butter and sauté the onion, bell pepper, and poblano chile until soft but not brown. Cool and add to the flour mixture. Add the egg, buttermilk, chives, parsley, and crab and stir just to combine.

Divide the batter among the prepared muffin cups (fill two-thirds full) and bake in the oven for 25 to 30 minutes or until the muffins are puffed and browned. These are best served warm but are also good at room temperature.

FLOUR TORTILLAS

Makes sixteen 8-inch tortillas

⅓ cup cold vegetable shortening

3 cups unbleached all-purpose flour, plus additional for dusting

2 teaspoons kosher or sea salt

2 teaspoons baking powder

1 cup warm water (100°F)

While flour tortillas are generally available in supermarkets, fresh homemade tortillas are demonstrably better and worth making. Traditionally, the fat used in tortilla making is lard, and although we've called for vegetable shortening here, you might try substituting part lard for some of the shortening to get a sense of the authentic flavor. A detailed discussion of tortilla making can be found in Rick Bayless's wonderful book of several years ago called Authentic Mexican.

In a food processor or by hand, pulse or cut the shortening into the flour, salt, and baking powder until the mixture resembles coarse cornmeal. Add the water in a steady stream and process until the dough just comes together. Turn out onto a lightly floured work surface and knead for 4 to 5 minutes or until the dough is smooth and silky.

Divide the dough into 4 equal pieces and then divide each of those into 4 pieces, forming them into 16 balls. Shape each ball into a flat, round circle, pulling the dough from the center to form a somewhat thick mushroom-cap shape about 3 inches in diameter. Cover both balls and rounds with a damp towel to keep them from drying out. After all the balls are shaped into rounds, let them rest, covered, for 15 minutes. On a lightly floured work surface, roll each round about ¹⁄₁₆ inch thick and 8 inches in diameter. Repeat with the remaining dough, keeping the tortillas covered with the damp towel.

Heat an ungreased griddle or cast-iron skillet over medium-high heat until a drop of water sizzles on contact. Cook a tortilla until one side is a lightly speckled brown and small bubbles appear on top, about 30 seconds. Turn and cook the other side until speckled. Transfer to a plate and cook the remaining tortillas. Wrap in a dry towel and serve.

To heat the tortillas, wrap in aluminum foil and put in a preheated 325°F oven for 4 minutes. The tortillas can be frozen but are best eaten soon after being made.

CREAM CHEESE STRAWS

Makes about 4 dozen straws

1 cup (2 sticks) unsalted butter at room
  temperature

1 cup cream cheese, preferably natural,
  without emulsifiers and thickeners, at
  room temperature

⅓ cup grated Parmesan cheese

⅓ cup heavy (whipping) cream

2 ½ cups unbleached all-purpose flour, plus
  additional for dusting

1½ teaspoons kosher or sea salt

⅛ teaspoon cayenne pepper

I love these very simple little straws as an appetizer all by themselves or served alongside a savory salad or antipasto plate of cold meats. The addition to the dough of chopped fresh herbs, such as chives or tarragon, or both, is a tasty variation.

Using an electric mixer fitted with the paddle attachment, or by hand with a wooden spoon, in a large bowl beat the butter, cream cheese, and Parmesan cheese until smooth. Beat in the cream and then gradually beat in the flour, salt, and pepper. Gather up the dough, dust it lightly with flour, and wrap in plastic wrap. Refrigerate for at least 2 hours.

Position a rack in the middle of the oven and preheat to 350°F. Roll the dough to ⅓-inch thickness and cut it into pencil-thin strips about 4 inches long. Put them on ungreased baking sheets and bake in the middle of the oven for 10 to 12 minutes or until very lightly browned. Cool and store in an airtight container for up to 5 days.

POPPY SEED STRAWS

Beat ¾ cup poppy seeds into the dough along with the flour and proceed as above.

SALT STRAWS

Roll and cut the dough as directed above. Beat 1 large egg yolk with 2 teaspoons milk and brush the straws with the mixture. Carefully roll the straws in an equal mixture of kosher or sea salt and caraway seeds and bake as above.

BISCOTTI

Biscotti are a rather ancient cookie, or cracker. In Italy, where they originated, they were a staple of sailors or travelers who went to sea for months at a time. As their name indicates, they are twice baked, bis cotto, to make them very dry, so they'll last a long time and not mold or otherwise deteriorate.

Because they are crisp and crunchy, they are ideal with fresh fruits and ice creams. I also love (as the Italians do) dunking them in good coffee or a tumbler of young robust red wine.

HAZELNUT BISCOTTI
Makes about 24 biscotti

1 cup lightly toasted and skinned hazelnuts

1 cup sugar

½ cup (1 stick) unsalted butter, melted

4 tablespoons hazelnut liqueur or brandy

3 large eggs

3 cups unbleached all-purpose flour

2 teaspoons baking powder

¼ teaspoon kosher or sea salt

Position a rack in the middle of the oven and preheat to 350°F. Coarsely chop the hazelnuts. In a medium bowl, combine the hazelnuts, sugar, butter, liqueur, and eggs and mix well. Stir in the flour, baking powder, and salt. Turn the dough out onto a lightly floured work surface and knead briefly, then form into a long loaf about 2 inches in diameter. Put the loaf on a parchment-lined or lightly oiled baking sheet and bake in the middle of the oven for 25 minutes or until firm. The loaf will have a cakelike texture. Remove from the oven and cool.

Cut the loaf diagonally into ½-inch slices and put the slices on a baking sheet. Bake for 20 minutes more, turning them once, until both sides are lightly browned and toasted. Cool and store in an airtight container.

ALMOND-ORANGE BISCOTTI

Makes about 36 biscotti

3 large eggs, separated

1½ cups sugar

⅓ cup unsalted butter, melted and cooled

1 cup lightly toasted and coarsely chopped almonds

2 tablespoons Grand Marnier or other orange-flavored liqueur

2 tablespoons chopped candied orange peel or 3 tablespoons finely grated orange zest

3½ cups unbleached all-purpose flour

1½ teaspoons baking powder

Preheat the oven to 325°F. Butter a baking sheet or line it with parchment. Using an electric mixer fitted with the paddle attachment, or by hand with a wooden spoon, in a large bowl beat the egg yolks with ¾ cup of the sugar until light and the sugar is dissolved. Stir in the melted butter, the almonds, Grand Marnier, and orange zest. In another bowl, using the whisk attachment, beat the egg whites until they just begin to form peaks and gradually beat in the remaining ¾ cup sugar until the whites form stiff peaks.

In a medium bowl, sift together the flour and baking powder. Fold one-third of the flour into the egg yolks, then fold one-third of the egg whites in. Repeat, alternating, until well combined. The dough will be firm and slightly sticky. If the dough is too soft, add more flour. With floured hands, divide the dough into two logs about 2 inches in diameter. Arrange the logs on the prepared baking sheet and bake for 20 to 25 minutes or until they are lightly brown and firm to the touch. Remove from the oven and set the baking sheet on a rack for 10 minutes. On a cutting board, cut the logs diagonally into slices ½ inch wide. Put the slices on the baking sheet and bake for 5 to 7 minutes on each side or until the biscotti are very lightly browned and crisp. Cool on racks and store airtight.

CHOCOLATE-MINT BISCOTTI

Omit the almonds, Grand Marnier, and orange peel. Add 6 ounces bittersweet chocolate melted with 1 tablespoon cocoa powder, and ¼ cup finely chopped fresh mint.

ALMOND-RAISIN BISCOTTI

Add ½ cup golden raisins that have been plumped in ⅔ cup fruity white wine, such as Riesling or Gewürztraminer. Drain them first. Omit the Grand Marnier.

ROSEMARY-WALNUT BISCOTTI

Substitute lightly toasted and coarsely chopped walnuts for the almonds. Omit the Grand Marnier and orange peel. Add 1 teaspoon vanilla extract and 2 tablespoons finely chopped fresh rosemary.

WHOLE-WHEAT AND PEAR BISCOTTI

Makes about 32 biscotti

1 cup whole-wheat flour

1½ cups unbleached all-purpose flour

1 cup sugar

1 teaspoon baking soda

¼ teaspoon kosher or sea salt

½ teaspoon ground cinnamon

3 large eggs

2 tablespoons dry red wine

1 cup coarsely chopped dried pears

1 cup lightly toasted and coarsely
   chopped walnuts

This is a recipe I've adapted from Carol Field that I've come to like a lot. She is an extraordinary baker, and I can't recommend her books highly enough.

Preheat the oven to 325°F. Lightly oil a baking sheet or line it with parchment. Using an electric mixer fitted with the paddle attachment, or by hand with a wooden spoon, in a large bowl beat the whole-wheat flour, all-purpose flour, sugar, baking soda, salt, cinnamon, eggs, and wine together until a smooth dough is formed. Stir in the pears and walnuts. Turn the dough out onto a lightly floured board and knead it briefly.

With floured hands, divide the dough in half and form into logs about 2 inches in diameter. Arrange the logs on the prepared baking sheet and bake for 25 to 30 minutes or until the logs are lightly browned and firm to the touch. Cool on the baking sheet on a rack for 10 minutes and then cut the logs crosswise diagonally into ¾-inch slices. Put the biscotti on the baking sheet and bake them for 5 minutes on each side or until they are very lightly browned.

SPREADS

HERB BUTTER
Makes about 2 cups

2 cups (4 sticks) unsalted butter at room temperature

1 cup minced shallots or green onions, both white and green parts, that have been slowly sautéed in butter and a splash of white wine until very soft but not brown

3 tablespoons small edible flower petals, such as bachelor's button, calendula, or herb flowers (see page 418)

⅓ cup chopped tender young herbs, such as chives, tarragon, dill, parsley, or a combination

Kosher or sea salt and freshly ground white pepper

This is really more a method than a hard-and-fast recipe. You can make the spread for current use or roll into logs, wrap tightly with foil and freeze for later use.

In a bowl, mix all the ingredients together well. Roll into 4 logs, wrap with plastic, and refrigerate until firm. To serve, cut the butter into thick rounds and place on a butter plate on top of a nasturtium leaf or grape leaf, if you'd like.

CURRIED RED LENTIL SPREAD
Makes about 1½ cups

2 tablespoons olive oil

2 tablespoons minced shallots

1 tablespoon minced garlic

1 teaspoon good curry powder, such as Madras Curry Powder (page 97)

2 teaspoons black mustard seeds

½ teaspoon minced fresh serrano chile

2 cups cooked red lentils, liquid reserved

¼ cup chopped fresh cilantro

Kosher or sea salt and freshly ground pepper

This simple spread is delicious on crisp pita triangles. Add more or less chile as your taste dictates.

In a sauté pan, heat the olive oil over medium heat and sauté the shallots, garlic, curry powder, mustard seeds, and chile until fragrant and the shallots are softened, about 3 minutes. Add to a food processor along with lentils, cilantro, and enough cooking liquid to make a spreadable mixture. Season to taste with salt and pepper. Store, covered, in the refrigerator for up to 5 days.

BLACK BEAN SPREAD

Makes about 2½ cups

1 cup dried black beans

1 tablespoon olive oil

1 pound red onions, chopped

2 tablespoons minced garlic

1½ teaspoons seeded and minced serrano chile

½ teaspoon fennel seeds, crushed

½ teaspoon ground cumin

½ teaspoon ground cinnamon

2 tablespoons tomato paste

1 teaspoon sauce from chipotle in adobo sauce

1 tablespoon sherry vinegar

1½ tablespoons minced fresh cilantro

Kosher or sea salt and drops of Tabasco sauce

Sort the beans, rinse them well, and soak overnight in lots of cold water. Change the water several times if possible. In a large, shallow pan, cover the beans with fresh water and cook over medium heat until very tender, about 1 hour.

While the beans are cooking, in a medium saucepan, heat the olive oil, and add the onions, garlic, chile, fennel seeds, cumin, and cinnamon. Cover and cook until very tender, about 10 minutes. Purée the onion mixture and transfer to a medium bowl.

Drain the beans, saving the cooking liquid. Mash the beans, or purée them in a food processor, until very smooth, adding a tablespoon or two of cooking liquid if necessary. (For a very smooth spread, press the mixture through a strainer to remove bean skins.) Add the beans to the onion purée. Stir in the tomato paste, adobo sauce, sherry vinegar, and cilantro. Season to taste with salt and drops of Tabasco sauce. Store, covered, in the refrigerator for up to 10 days.

WHITE BEAN AND OLIVE SPREAD

Makes about 2½ cups

1 cup dried Great Northern or navy beans

1 tablespoon olive oil

1 pound yellow onions, chopped

2 teaspoons roasted garlic (see page 264)

1½ tablespoons minced Kalamata or other oil-cured olives

1½ tablespoons drained and minced oil-packed sun-dried tomatoes

2 teaspoons minced fresh tarragon

1 tablespoon minced fresh chives

1 teaspoon white-wine Worcestershire sauce

1 teaspoon grated lemon zest

1 teaspoon rinsed and minced capers

Drops of fresh lemon juice

Kosher or sea salt and freshly ground white pepper

Sort the beans, rinse them well, and soak overnight in lots of cold water, changing it several times if possible. In a large, shallow pan, cover the beans with fresh water and cook over medium heat until very tender.

While the beans are cooking, in a covered pan, heat the olive oil and slowly sauté the onions and garlic until very tender. Do not let the onions brown. Purée the onion mixture and transfer to a medium bowl.

Drain the beans, reserving the cooking liquid. Mash the beans or purée them in a food processor until very smooth, adding a tablespoon or two of cooking liquid if necessary. (For a very smooth spread, press through a strainer to remove the bean skins.) Add the mashed beans to the onion purée. Stir in the olives, sun-dried tomatoes, tarragon, chives, Worcestershire sauce, lemon zest, and capers. Season to taste with lemon juice, salt, and pepper. Store covered in the refrigerator up to 5 days. Best served warm or at room temperature.

EGGPLANT–ROASTED GARLIC SPREAD

Makes about 2 cups

1 large eggplant (2½ pounds)

Olive oil for brushing the eggplant

Kosher or sea salt and freshly ground pepper

1 large head roasted garlic (see page 264)

2 tablespoons sherry vinegar

1 cup loosely packed fresh basil leaves, chopped

Preheat the oven to 400°F. Cut off the stem from the eggplant and discard. Cut the eggplant into 1-inch-thick rounds, brush both sides liberally with olive oil, and season to taste with salt and pepper. Roast in the oven until soft and lightly browned, about 25 minutes.

In a food processor, combine the eggplant, garlic, vinegar, and basil and purée until smooth. Season to taste with salt, pepper, and additional vinegar.

Can be stored, covered, in the refrigerator for up to 5 days.

ROASTED RED PEPPER AND ALMOND SPREAD

Makes about 2 cups

3 large red bell peppers (1¼ pounds)

2 tablespoons olive oil

½ cup chopped white onion

2 teaspoons minced garlic

⅔ cup blanched almonds, lightly toasted

3 tablespoons chopped fresh basil or other favorite fresh leafy herbs, such as mint or cilantro

1 slice white sandwich bread, crust removed

Fresh lemon juice, white balsamic vinegar, or sherry vinegar

Kosher or sea salt and freshly ground pepper

I've specified almonds here, but you could certainly use other nuts, like walnuts, in their place. Walnuts have tannins, which give a little bite to the mixture, while almonds are sweeter. This is great as a spread or dip, as an accompaniment to rice or potatoes, and as a stuffing, for baked zucchini or chicken breasts, for example.

Char the peppers over a gas flame or under a hot broiler. Put in a medium bowl, cover with plastic wrap, and allow to sweat for 5 minutes. Remove, scrape off charred skin (do not wash), and remove and discard the stems and seeds. Set aside. In a sauté pan, heat the olive oil and sauté the onion and garlic until soft but not brown. In a food processor, combine the onion mixture, bell peppers, almonds, basil, bread, and lemon juice and process until fairly smooth but still a little textured. Season to taste with salt and pepper. Store, covered, in the refrigerator for up to 3 days.

DRINKS

APPLE–ROSE HIP ICED TEA

Makes 2 drinks

½ cup apple juice or white grape juice

2 teaspoons dried rose hips or 4 rose hip or hibiscus tea bags

Finely crushed ice

¼ cup ginger ale

1 teaspoon fresh lemon juice

Fresh mint sprigs and slices of your favorite apple for garnishing

Rose hips are available at health food stores and are very rich in vitamin C. They also add a rosy hue to the drink.

Heat the apple juice and rose hips and simmer for 3 minutes. Remove from the heat and allow to cool. Strain and chill.

Fill 2 tall glasses half full of crushed ice and pour in the juice mixture, ginger ale, and lemon juice. Garnish each glass with a mint sprig and an apple slice.

FIRE AND ICE

Serves 6 to 8

⅔ cup sugar

½ cup water

2 teaspoons seeded and minced serrano or jalapeño chile

2 tablespoons minced red bell pepper

2 tablespoons minced fresh mint

½ cup fresh lime or lemon juice

2 cups sparkling mineral water

4 cups apple juice or Gewürztraminer or another fruity white wine

This is an amusing takeoff on Fire and Ice Melon Salad with Figs and Prosciutto (page 21). I often garnish this drink with a spear or two of fresh melon.

In a small saucepan, bring the sugar and water to a boil and cook, stirring, until the sugar is dissolved, about 2 minutes. Remove from the heat, stir in the chile and bell pepper and cool.

Combine the syrup with the mint, lemon juice, mineral water, and apple juice and pour over ice in wineglasses.

GINGER-MINT TEA

Serves 4

¾ cup thinly sliced fresh ginger

One 3-inch strip orange zest

One 3-inch strip lemon zest

One 3-inch cinnamon stick, broken into 3 pieces

2 tablespoons honey

1 cup fruity white wine, such as Riesling or Gewürztraminer

4 cups water

⅓ cup loosely packed fresh mint leaves

This can be made with or without the wine, as you choose. Both ginger and mint have extraordinary abilities to soothe the stomach and aid digestion. Ginger is also touted as a natural alternative to medicines for motion sickness. I just know that this tea makes me feel very good.

In a medium saucepan, combine the ginger, orange zest, lemon zest, cinnamon pieces, honey, wine, and water and bring to a simmer. Let the mixture steep over very low heat for 10 minutes. Add the mint leaves and steep for 10 minutes more. Strain carefully and serve hot or iced.

HONEYDEW LEMONADE

Makes 8 cups

Zest of 2 lemons, cut into strips

1 cup fresh lemon juice

¾ cup sugar

1 honeydew melon (about 3 pounds), seeds and rind removed and cut into 1-inch cubes

2 cups sparkling or still water

Thin lemon slices and fresh mint sprigs for garnishing

This is a simple drink to make, and any sweet, ripe melon can be used. The idea for drinks of this kind comes from the drink called agua fresca, found in Mexico.

In a small saucepan, combine the lemon zest, lemon juice, and sugar and bring to a boil. Simmer, stirring occasionally, for 5 minutes or until the sugar dissolves. Strain the syrup and cool it.

In a food processor, purée the honeydew, then force the purée through a fine-mesh strainer, if you want. In a pitcher, combine the purée and cooled syrup and mix well. Chill. Just before serving, add water and serve over ice. Garnish with lemon slices and mint.

HOT BEAU

Makes six 6-ounce drinks

1 small orange or tangerine, scrubbed if not organic

12 cloves

One 750-ml bottle Gamay Beaujolais

1 cup fresh orange or tangerine juice

½ cup orange-flower honey

Ten 3-inch cinnamon sticks

¼ teaspoon freshly grated nutmeg

6 whole allspice berries (optional)

Thinly sliced peeled oranges or tangerines for garnishing

"Beau" is short for Beaujolais, that amiable, fruity red wine. This is a spin on hot mulled wine that's perfect for the holidays, or with a "hot beau" if you so choose. The drink was developed by one of our talented culinary students at Valley Oaks, Jim Mitchell, who also does a mean Elvis impression.

Preheat the oven to 325°F. Stud the orange with the cloves. Put the orange in a baking dish and roast it until it becomes soft, 30 to 45 minutes. In a nonreactive saucepan, combine the roasted orange, Gamay Beaujolais, orange juice, honey, 4 of the cinnamon sticks, the nutmeg, and allspice berries, if using. Heat the mixture over medium-high heat, stirring frequently, until the honey dissolves and the liquid almost comes to a boil. Strain and divide the drink among 6 cups or coffee glasses. Garnish each with a cinnamon stick and an orange slice.

ORANGE-GEWÜRZTRAMINER LIFT

Serves 4 to 6

One 750-ml bottle Gewürztraminer

½ cup fresh orange juice

6 cinnamon sticks

2 cloves

½ teaspoon minced lime zest

½ teaspoon minced lemon zest

½ teaspoon minced orange zest

Fresh long mint sprigs and orange slices for garnishing

I enjoy inventing new drinks that use wine in them. This is a refreshing warm or cold drink featuring spicy, fruity, floral Gewürztraminer.

In a saucepan, combine the wine, orange juice, cinnamon sticks, and cloves. Bring to a boil and simmer for 2 minutes. Remove the cinnamon sticks and cloves. Add the lime, lemon and orange zest. Serve hot or chilled over ice. Garnish with mint sprigs and an orange slice on the rim of the glass.

PEACH–OPAL BASIL LEMONADE

Serves 4

2 cups fruity white wine, such as Riesling

2 cups water

1 cup loosely packed fresh opal basil leaves

1½ cups peeled and chopped ripe peaches

⅔ cup fragrant honey, such as orange blossom

¾ cup fresh lemon juice

Fresh opal basil sprigs and ripe peach slices for garnishing

Opal, or purple, basil is one of the dozens of basil varieties. It gives this drink a beautiful pink cast. You can use regular basil if opal is not available.

In a medium saucepan, combine the wine, water, basil, chopped peaches, and honey and bring to a boil. Lower the heat, cover, and simmer for 5 minutes or until the peaches are very soft. Remove from the heat and let the mixture cool. Strain through a very fine-mesh strainer, pressing down on the solids. Stir in the lemon juice, adjusting the sweetness level with more honey, if you want, and chill. To serve, pour over ice cubes and garnish with basil sprigs and slices of fresh peach.

STRAWBERRY SUNSET

Serves 4

2 cups sliced ripe strawberries

2 cups fresh orange juice

2 tablespoons honey

3 tablespoons balsamic vinegar

⅓ cup yogurt

¾ cup crushed ice

Fresh mint sprigs for garnishing

When strawberries are at their peak in summer, this is a tasty drink with which to watch the sun go down. The recipe will serve eight if you fill the glasses only halfway and top off with a chilled crisp California sparkling wine (in which case omit the yogurt).

In a blender, purée the strawberries, orange juice, honey, and vinegar. Add the yogurt and crushed ice and blend briefly to combine. Pour into tall glasses and garnish with mint sprigs.

TAMARIND TEA WITH SCENTED GERANIUM

Serves 4

scented geraniums

Scented geraniums are simple to grow, especially in pots. One good mail-order source for seedlings is Mountain Valley Growers (see page 426). Besides tea, scented geraniums make an interesting base for sorbet, and they can be substituted for mint in any recipe that calls for it. They can also be used to flavor oils and vinegars.

2½ tablespoons tamarind pulp or concentrate

2 tablespoons honey

2½ cups dry white wine, water, or apple juice

3 to 4 large lemon scented geranium leaves or the zest from 1 small lemon

One of the most flavorful herbal teas I know is one made from scented geranium (not common garden geraniums). Scented geraniums are easy to grow and come in a wide variety of scents, including nutmeg, cinnamon, and rose. My favorite for tea is an heirloom variety of lemon geranium called Mabel Grey. To make scented geranium tea, simply steep the leaves of scented geraniums in hot water until the flavor develops. Strain and serve hot or cold. In this recipe I've added tamarind pulp, which gives an added flavor dimension. Tamarind pulp is available both in Latino and Southeast Asian markets; it is used extensively in those cuisines.

In a medium saucepan, put the tamarind, honey, wine, and geranium leaves and bring to a simmer. Partially cover and simmer slowly for 3 minutes. Remove from the heat and allow the mixture to steep and cool. Strain and serve hot or cold over ice cubes.

ZINFANDEL SANGRÍA

Serves 6

One 750-ml bottle Zinfandel

Juice of 4 large oranges, strained (1¼ cups)

Juice of 4 large limes, strained (about ⅓ cup)

⅓ cup sugar, preferably superfine

1 small orange, thinly sliced

1 small red apple, cored and cut into wedges

½ cup raspberries or blackberries, or a combination

This is a grown-up summer fruit salad in a glass! Be sure to give the fruit time to macerate and flavor the drink.

In a large pitcher, combine the wine, orange juice, lime juice, and sugar and stir vigorously to dissolve the sugar.

Add the orange slices, apple wedges, and berries and refrigerate the sangria for 6 hours or overnight to let the flavors develop. Serve in tall glasses over ice cubes with some of the macerated fruit for garnish.

MATCHING FOOD *with* WINE

"Cuisine is when things taste like themselves," wrote Curnonsky many years ago. In California's wine country, this observation defines the essence of our cuisine. Clean, vivid flavors are artfully created by integrating superb fresh ingredients with classic yet simple cooking techniques. Not surprisingly, it is wine itself that seems to most enhance the food of the wine country. Over the years, considerable discussion has taken place about the marriage of food and wine. Almost scientifically, we in the wine industry have scrutinized the intricacies of which wine should go with which dish, partly because wine is not as deeply imbedded in America's culture and table as it is in Europe. In treating wine intellectually, we've created unnecessary impediments for people to make wine more a part of their daily lives. This complication translates, unfortunately, into intimidation about wine for some people who might otherwise enjoy it more often.

Whether it's the confusion of making the proper varietal or brand selection, the ritualistic act of opening the bottle using a corkscrew, or the proper pouring of the wine with the requisite smelling and sniffing ritual, there is a certain mystique about wine for many Americans. But, it's really very simple! And this guide will, I hope, explain the basics.

I'm also reminded that no matter how much we might talk about the principles of matching food and wine, when the two are enjoyed within the company of good friends and loved ones, a far deeper, more spiritual connection takes place that makes almost any food and wine combination work wonders.

TASTING AND APPRECIATING WINE IN FIVE EASY STEPS

Wine appreciation is developed almost completely from experience and memory. More often than not, this skill is nurtured by tasting alongside more experienced wine tasters who can articulate their impressions and help develop a point of reference for less-experienced tasters. Therefore, it is highly recommended that anyone interested in learning more seek out information through local tasting groups. A good wine store might be a source for information about such groups, and often such stores have these kinds of tastings themselves.

To help further understanding about wine tasting, I'm going to try to demystify some of the older rituals about wine and hopefully lead you to more enjoyment and appreciation of one of the world's most pleasurable beverages. Here are some simple steps to help you develop your wine-tasting ability:

1. OBSERVE COLOR AND APPEARANCE

- You can tell a lot about a wine from its color. The easiest way to evaluate color in wine is against a white backdrop, ideally a tablecloth. Tilt the glass slightly away from you to get a better angle.
- In white wines, a clear, pale, or straw color should indicate a lighter style wine in the mouth; a more golden color suggests either an older or more full-bodied wine.
- With red wines, lighter shades, such as ruby and crimson, indicate lighter to medium body; scarlet, dark red, and purple usually indicate either a youthful or more full-bodied wine. As red wines age, they turn slightly brickish-orange around the rim of the glass.
- By swirling the liquid slightly in the glass and observing the "legs" (the rivulets of wine that run down the side of the glass), it's possible to assess the wine's body as well. An oily coating that runs slowly down the glass usually indicates a full-bodied wine that is often slightly higher in alcohol than less full-bodied wines.

2. SWIRL TO OPEN UP AROMATIC ELEMENTS

- Place the glass on the table with just an ounce or two of wine in it. Take the bottom of the stem of the glass between your thumb and first two fingers. Using a steady, consistent motion, move the glass in small circles. This allows the wine to swirl around the glass in a similar manner. (You might want to practice on something other than Grandma Minnette's white embroidered tablecloth!) The complex aromatic components of the wine are exposed to air, making the wine much easier to smell. In wine terms, it "opens up."

3. SMELL FOR SUBTLETY—"THE NOSE"

- Bring the wine to your nose immediately after swirling and take a long, slow inhalation.
- Let the wine make its aromatic impression on you. The bouquet of the wine is called "the nose," and it is an important part of the wine's subtlety, personality, and taste.
- As a point of differentiation, "aroma" usually refers to the smell of the varietal grape itself, whereas "bouquet" refers to the subtleties that emerge from the winemaking process, such as exposure of the wine to small oak barrels for aging.
- Use free association to describe the wine: Is it like a freshly cut green apple? A cigar box? Grandmother's sachet drawer? A bowl of cherries? A slice of pineapple? A basket of peaches? Childhood references often work; so do food associations.
- Write down your impressions; this helps to establish "taste memory" and develop better recall.
- Since the sense of smell, called the olfactory sense, is directly connected to the sense of taste, these first impressions you get from the nose will greatly magnify the "taste" of the wine.

4. TASTE THE WINE

- Immediately after smelling the wine, take a small taste. Gurgle the wine softly on your tongue. This allows the wine to interact with air and cover the entire mouth. Swallow and evaluate.
- Notice how the wine strikes you. Is it light or heavy? Dry or sweet? Tart or smooth? Does it have layers of flavors or just one dimension? Does it seem balanced or unbalanced? Try to describe the flavors you're experiencing just as you did with the wine's aroma and bouquet. Let the wine speak to you.
- All wine is a combination of five basic components of taste, each experienced in a different place on the tongue. The ideal wine is a perfect balance of these components:

Sweet: Tip of the tongue (shows residual sugar)
Sour: Side of the tongue (indicates acidity and tartness)
Salty: Center of the tongue (rarely experienced in wine)
Bitter: Back of the tongue (results from tannin, which is derived both from the skins of grapes as well as the exposure of wine to oak barrels)
Peppery or pungent: Front part of the tongue (often associated with earthy red wines)

5. EVALUATE THE FINISH

- Swallow the wine and keep your concentration on it. Do the flavors persist and stay on your tongue a long time, or do they dissipate quickly? Do you notice other elements in the wine that you didn't when you first tasted it? Are these pleasant or unpleasant? The "persistence," or length of the finish, is another good indicator of the wine's quality.
- What is your overall impression? After you've analyzed the finite points, let your own taste determine: Quite simply, did you like the wine or not? What foods does it suggest? How does it compare to other similar wines that you've tried? What do you think of its quality and price compared to other wines you have tasted?

TEN QUICK TIPS FOR PERFECT FOOD AND WINE PAIRING

There is only one reason for knowing the "right" wines to pair with the "right" food: Wine and food that complement each other enhance the flavor of both; wine and food that don't complement each other detract from both. That's it. That's the only reason.

The tips below work because they explain the experience of consuming particular foods and wines together. In other words, you can taste for yourself when a wine that you love, eaten with a certain dish, suddenly tastes sour, or when a wine, drunk alongside a familiar food, suddenly makes that food sing; these tips explain why this happens.

1. Foods that are high in natural acids (tomatoes, citrus fruits, goat cheese) are best suited to wines with higher acids: Sauvignon Blanc and certain styles of Chardonnay, Riesling, Gewürztraminer, Zinfandel, Pinot Noir.
2. Richer and fattier foods (duck, lamb, beef, cheese) go well with either slightly oaky white wines, such as Chardonnay, or with young red wines, such as Cabernet Sauvignon or Zinfandel.
3. Spicy, salty/smoky, and more heavily seasoned dishes are best paired with light, fruity wines, whether red or white, such as Gewürztraminer, Johannisberg Riesling, Gamay Beaujolais, Pinot Noir, and certain Zinfandels.
4. Foods with some sweetness (meat and poultry dishes with fruit sauces) are best paired with wines that offer some sweetness (Gewürztraminer, Johannisberg Riesling, White Zinfandel) or sufficient ripeness (Cabernet Sauvignon or Zinfandel). If the food is sweeter than the wine, it will often make the wine taste dry, oaky, or tannic.
5. Generally, wines (like courses) should follow a natural progression from dry to sweet. However, if a dish with some sweetness comes early in the meal, it's best to serve a slightly sweet wine with it.
6. The "texture" of a wine, its body and weight in the mouth, is as important as its flavor to matching it successfully with food. (A heavy, full-bodied wine is going to overpower a simple salad.)
7. Obvious opportunities for pairing food and wine occur when a particular wine is used in the cooking process, such as in a marinade or a sauce. The table wine should mirror the dish.
8. Great food and wine combinations come not only from matching flavors, textures, and taste components but also from contrasting them.
9. Successful food and wine pairing is highly subjective and individual — an experimental, dynamic art form more than a science. Don't be afraid to follow your own instincts.
10. Most important, the food should not overwhelm the wine any more than the wine should overpower the food. Ideally, the result is synergistic: Food and wine together are far more enjoyable than either food or wine by itself.

COOKING WITH HERBS AND WINE

At the heart of wine country cuisine is the use of fragrant, fresh herbs. Whether in sprightly salads with flavored vinaigrettes, in aromatic marinades for grilled vegetables, seafood, poultry, or meats, or in naturally reduced sauces, the creative use of herbs and wine plays a pivotal role in enhancing both the aroma and flavor of many wine country dishes.

Herbs often provide the magical connection to tying wine to a dish since many herbal qualities are found in fine varietal wines. These tips will help make that connection and show you that by cooking with herbs and wine even the simplest dishes can be enlivened as never before.

BASIL (SWEET BASIL; *OCIMUM BASILICUM*)

Large, fragrant, green leaves; rich spicy, mildly peppery flavor with a trace of mint and clove. White edible flowers. Aromatic garnish.

Pesto, salad dressing, tomato-based pasta sauces, butters, eggplant, zucchini, stews, ragouts, tomatoes, vinegars.

White Zinfandel, Gamay Beaujolais, Zinfandel, Cabernet Sauvignon, Sauvignon Blanc.

CINNAMON BASIL (O.B. 'CINNAMON')

Bright-green leaves; spicy flavor and pungent cinnamon-clove scent. Flavor intensifies with cooking. Edible white flowers. Store in oil or vinegar.

Use as you would sweet basil. Infuse in crème anglaise sauces for desserts, or add to biscotti.

White Zinfandel, Gamay Beaujolais, Zinfandel, Cabernet Sauvignon, Sauvignon Blanc.

OPAL BASIL (O.B. PURPURASCENS)

Shiny, dark-purple leaves with red veins. Similar smell but spicier than sweet basil, with edible lavender flowers. Flavor lost with prolonged heat. Colorful garnish.

Use as you would sweet basil. Turns brown in pesto but is excellent in vinegar.

White Zinfandel, Gamay Beaujolais, Zinfandel, Cabernet Sauvignon, Sauvignon Blanc.

BAY (SWEET LAUREL; *LAURUS NOBILIS*)

Glossy, tough, dark-green leaves; warm, slightly spicy, somewhat sweetish flavor.

Rub to release flavors. Cook slowly to free powerful, earthy aroma. Use fresh or dried, then remove.

Spanish, Creole, and French soups, sauces, stews, marinades, game, shellfish, tomato sauces, grains, beans, fruit punches.

Cabernet Sauvignon, Zinfandel, Sauvignon Blanc.

CHERVIL (*ANTHRISCUS CEREFOLIUM*)

Green, dainty, fernlike leaves; elegant, warm anise-parsley flavors are lost in long cooking. Pretty garnish—unusual white flowers.

Delicate French sauces, soups, green salads, fish and chicken dishes, carrots, egg dishes.

Sauvignon Blanc, Chardonnay, Johannisberg Riesling, Gewürztraminer, White Zinfandel.

CHIVES (*ALLIUM SCHOENOPRASUM*)

Long, thin, dark-green leaves; mildest of the onion family. Tangy, sometimes hot taste. Cannot stand heat, best used raw; add last in cooking or as a garnish. Round, pale-purple edible flowers.

Potato salads, green salads, butters for fish or chicken, vegetable casseroles, omelets, cheese bread.

Sauvignon Blanc, Zinfandel, White Zinfandel.

CORIANDER (CILANTRO; *CORIANDRUM SATIVUM*)

Green, multileafed stems; intense and very aromatic parsleylike aroma with bold sage flavor and tangy citrus taste. Use fresh leaves or dried seeds. Roots have added nutty flavor.

Mexican salsa, chutneys, chicken marinades, salad dressing, Asian stir-fry, spicy dishes.

Gewürztraminer, Sauvignon Blanc, Zinfandel.

DILL (*ANETHUM GRAVEOLENS*)

Pale, blue green feathery leaves; long, hollow stalks. Intense herbal aroma, spicy with mild aniseed flavor. Use fresh or stronger dried form. Snip with scissors.

Fish, especially salmon, light sauces, butters, carrot soup, breads, deviled eggs, pickles, cucumbers.

Sauvignon Blanc, Chardonnay, Johannisberg Riesling.

FENNEL (SWEET FENNEL; *FOENICULUM VULGARE*)

Deep-green feathery leaves; a softer, nuttier version of anise with sweet aroma. Use fresh tender stems as you would celery; grind seeds. Mince stalks and bulbs for salads and soups. Fragrant garnish, with yellow edible flowers.

Salads, soups, vegetable casseroles with Parmesan cheese, seafood, breads.

Chardonnay, Zinfandel, Sauvignon Blanc.

HYSSOP (*HYSSOPUS OFFICINALIS*)

Rich-green, spiky leaves. A member of the mint family, slightly bitter with strong camphorlike aroma. Best fresh. Edible blue violet flowers. Especially fragrant garnish.

Roast chicken, lamb stew, vegetable soups, fruit salads, teas.

Chardonnay, Gewürztraminer, Johannisberg Riesling, Cabernet Sauvignon.

LAVENDER (*LAVANDULA OFFICINALIS*)

Small, perfumy, edible lavender flowers with fresh, astringent flavor and aroma. Use sparingly, even as a garnish. Excellent combined with pepper.

Dry marinades (rubs) for poultry and game birds, jams, stews, soufflés, ice cream, sorbets. Infuse sugars, vinegars, gelatins, honeys.

Zinfandel, Pinot Noir, Petite Sirah, Cabernet Sauvignon, Chardonnay.

MINT (GARDEN MINT; *MENTHA SPICATA*)

Long, green, narrow, spear-shaped leaves; sharp, cleansing taste and distinctive aroma. Fresh leaves or sprigs for garnish.

Lamb, sautéed vegetables, fruit-based soups, Middle Eastern salads and rice dishes, desserts, fruit beverages, chocolate, teas, coffees.

White Zinfandel, Cabernet Sauvignon, Zinfandel, Gewürztraminer.

OREGANO (*ORIGANUM VULGARE*)

Small, round, green leaves; hot, peppery flavor, warm savory taste, and pungent aroma. Good dried. Garnish with whole stems.

Vegetable soups, zucchini and eggplant dishes, marinade for beef and lamb, pizza and pastas with tomato-garlic sauce, cheese and egg dishes, breads.

Sauvignon Blanc, Zinfandel, Cabernet Sauvignon.

PARSLEY (*PETROSELINUM CRISPUM*)

Green, flat or curly leaves; fresh aroma, mild, herbal flavor. Flat-leaved preferred. Add last to avoid bruising, use entire stem in stocks and soups, then remove. Garnish with whole or minced form.

Grilled or sautéed meats, tomato-based pasta, butters for seafood, omelets, sauces for fish, relishes.

Johannisberg Riesling, Sauvignon Blanc, Gamay Beaujolais, Cabernet Sauvignon.

ROSEMARY (*ROSMARINUS OFFICINALIS*)

Dark, green gray, needlelike leaves; pungent, piny, mintlike, with a slight ginger finale. Crush or mince leaves or use whole, then remove. Freeze whole. Use pale-blue flowers or sprigs as a garnish.

Marinade for beef, pork, lamb, hearty soups, tomato-garlic sauces, roast chicken, breads.

Cabernet Sauvignon, Zinfandel, Petite Sirah.

SAGE (GARDEN SAGE; *SALVIA OFFICINALIS*)

Silver green velvet leaves; lemony, pleasantly bitter, and aromatic, with balsamic flavor. Dried has a stronger, musty taste.

Poultry stuffings and game dishes, liver, sausages, cheese soufflés, vegetables, breads, teas.

Chardonnay, Sauvignon Blanc, Cabernet Sauvignon, Zinfandel.

SORREL (FRENCH SORREL OR DOCK; *RUMEX SCUTATUS*)

Narrow, long, bright-green leaves with slightly lemony taste and sharp, acidic bite. Powerful flavor is best mixed with other herbs. Use whole leaves as garnish.

Soups, salads, cream sauces, egg dishes, salmon, as a puréed side dish, with spinach.

Sauvignon Blanc, Zinfandel.

TARRAGON (FRENCH TARRAGON; *ARTEMISIA DRACUNCULUS*)

Small, greenish white leaves; savory anise flavor with hidden tang; overpowers other flavors; bitter if cooked long. Best fresh, frozen, or stored in white vinegar.

Cream soups, bearnaise and hollandaise sauces, mayonnaise, salad dressings, roasts, ragouts, butters, shellfish, olives.

Chardonnay, Cabernet Sauvignon, Sauvignon Blanc.

THYME (*THYMUS VULGARIS*)

Tiny, gray green leaves with pale underside; distinctive sweet aroma, pungent flavor with faint clove aftertaste. Use white lilac flowers and sprigs as a garnish.

Soups, stocks, marinades for meats, vegetable dishes, shellfish, beans, lentils.

Sauvignon Blanc, Zinfandel, Cabernet Sauvignon, Chardonnay.

LEMON THYME (*T. CITRIODORUS*)

Dark-green, glossy leaves, broader than thyme; pronounced lemon aroma. Use sprigs with pink flowers as a garnish.

Use as you would thyme. Seafood and poultry dishes, eggplants, bell peppers, lamb stew, sweet foods, teas.

Sauvignon Blanc, Zinfandel, Cabernet Sauvignon, Chardonnay.

SILVER THYME (*T. VULGARIS ARGENTEUS*)

Like thyme, but plant is completely silver tinged. Classic sweet thyme fragrance with soft, lingering clove flavor. Use whole stems as a garnish.

Use as you would thyme. French, Creole, and Cajun dishes, seafood chowders.

Sauvignon Blanc, Zinfandel, Cabernet Sauvignon, Chardonnay.

WINTER SAVORY (*SATUREJA MONTANA*)

Deep-green, glossy, lance-shaped leaves; strong, peppery, piny aroma with spicy, slightly bitter flavor. Use with other strong flavors.

Mediterranean stews, grilled or roasted poultry and game, eggplants, peas, beans, sauces, vinegars.

Zinfandel, Cabernet Sauvignon, Sauvignon Blanc.

CHOICE OF A WINEGLASS

Most people know that it is traditional to serve different wines in different glasses — at least to the extent of having different styles of glasses for red wine, white wine, and sparkling wine. But did you know that there are particular styles of glasses for Chardonnay or Cabernet?

Here are my suggestions. It's not really so terribly important which glass you use unless you're a serious traditionalist. The single exception is the glass you choose for sparkling wine or Champagne. For these you want a tall, straight-sided, flute-shaped glass, which encourages and shows off the bubbles. Never, never use the flat, round, saucer-shaped glass (even if it is supposedly a re-creation of Marie Antoinette's breast). For still wines, choose a glass that allows you to perform the three S's easily: that is, Swirl, Sniff, and Sip. You want a good-sized bowl on the glass so that when you swirl you won't spill wine all over you, and swirling helps develop the aroma. Finally, the bowl needs to be big enough for even the largest nose to fit in, to enjoy the liberated aromas while you sip.

Remember also to choose glasses that are perfectly clear, so you can enjoy the color of the wine.

FOOD AND WINE PAIRING CHART

	STYLE	AROMAS / FLAVORS	CLASSIC FOODS
Chardonnay	Light yellow, light body, emphasis on fresh fruit, crisp	Green apple, lemon, orange, grapefruit	Appetizers, soups, shrimp salad, glazed roast chicken
	Medium yellow, medium-full body, oak influence	Apple-spice, pineapple-tropical fruit, citrus, buttery, toasty	Roast turkey, roast chicken with Dijon mustard, seafood with sauces
	Medium-dark yellow, full-bodied, rich with oak emphasis	Pineapple-tropical fruit, vanilla, nutty, toasty, buttery, spicy	Crab cakes, lobster, fettuccine Alfredo, seafood with cream sauce, soft cheeses
Gewürztraminer	Dry-sweet, light-medium yellow, medium body, often a hint of sweetness	Apricot, peach, Asian spice, tropical fruit, honey	Spicy appetizers, baked ham, roast turkey, prosciutto and melon, Asian foods, picnic foods
Johannisberg Riesling	Dry-sweet, light-medium yellow, medium body, often a hint of sweetness	Apricot, peach, pear, honey, floral, metallic	Appetizers, baked ham, lighter poultry, smoked salmon, fresh fruits, picnic foods
Sauvignon Blanc or Fumé Blanc	Medium yellow, medium body, oak influence	Fig, melon, orange, lemon, vanilla, herbal, grassy, dill	Lighter seafood, chicken with olives, steamed clams, pasta with pesto, vegetarian dishes
Cabernet Sauvignon	Crimson-medium red, medium body, smooth, fruity, soft	Cherry, berry, spice	Roast or grilled meats, beef or lamb stew, veal roast, game with fruit sauces
	Medium-dark red, medium-full body, oak influence, more complex	Cherry, currant, chocolate, cedar, mint, vanilla	Grilled meats, roast rack of lamb, roast pork or veal, hearty game
	Dark red-purple, full-bodied, strong oak influence	Currant, chocolate, cedar, tobacco, mint, vanilla, pepper	Grilled meats with peppercorn crust, hearty game, aged cheeses
Gamay Beaujolais	Ruby red, light-medium body, lively, very fruity	Raspberry, strawberry, flora	Appetizers, baked ham, roast turkey, pizza
Merlot	Medium-dark red, medium body, soft, round mouth-feel	Berry, cherry, orange zest, tea, vanilla, cedar	Roast poultry, meat-based pastas, hearty cheeses
Petite Sirah	Dark red purple, full body, tannic	Blueberry, raspberry, jammy, spice, pepper	Pepper steak, stews, grilled meats, venison chili, hearty cheeses
Pinot Noir	Ruby-medium red, light-medium body, soft, fruity	Cherry, spice, cedar, coffee, earthy, mushrooms	Roast chicken, grilled salmon or tuna, mushroom tart, vegetarian pastas, soft cheeses
Zinfandel	Medium-dark red, medium-full body, lively	Blackberry, raspberry, jammy, spice, pepper	Pasta with garlic-tomato sauce, grilled meats and ribs, hearty cheeses
White Zinfandel	Pink coral, light body, hint of sweetness, lively	Strawberry, orange zest	Appetizers, barbecued chicken, pasta salad, Asian dishes

NEW WINE VARIETALS

California's history of varietal wine grapes has focused on the more popular varietals—Chardonnay, Sauvignon Blanc, Fumé Blanc, Gewürztraminer, Johannisberg Riesling, and Chenin Blanc in the whites; Cabernet Sauvignon, Zinfandel, Pinot Noir, Petite Sirah, and Merlot in the reds. Both retail wine stores and restaurant wine lists have featured these varietals for the past few decades to the increasing curiosity of consumers.

Recently, new varietals with origins in Europe have burst onto the California wine scene and offer opportunities for wine lovers to experience a wider range of flavors. These new varietals are well suited to the assertive style of many wine country dishes. Many of these wines offer forward fruit and lower tannin, oak, and alcohol than some of the traditional wines of California.

GRENACHE

Grenache is native to Spain but is best known in southern France, where it flourishes in the Rhône region, particularly in Bandol and Châteauneuf-du-Pape. In California, Grenache is often used in innocuous rosés that exemplify little character, but it is now being combined with Syrah and Mourvèdre to create distinctive New World blends. Grenache is most known for its ability to provide a lush, fruity quality to these blends.

MARSANNE

Marsanne is a dry southern French white wine varietal that is often blended with another varietal, Roussane, to make stunning wines with a slight earthy-mineral character. Only a few producers from California are currently experimenting with Marsanne.

NEBBIOLO

Nebbiolo is the noble red grape of the Piedmont region of northwest Italy, known for making intense, full-bodied, long-aged red wines. Used predominantly in the Barolo and Barbaresco areas, Nebbiolo has been slow to catch on in California. When grown in the right locale, it offers a distinctive earthy, mushroom-like aroma that is very well suited to hearty braised dishes.

PINOT BLANC

Best known in the Chablis region of France, where it is often planted with Chardonnay, and in the Alsace region, where it is widely acknowledged for producing wines of delicacy and finesse, Pinot Blanc is a fine dry white wine with a long heritage in California. Despite its pleasing qualities, Pinot Blanc has not generated much enthusiasm in California and is unfortunately viewed as a stepchild of Chardonnay.

SANGIOVESE

A great varietal from the Tuscany region in Italy, which produces Chianti, Sangiovese is a world-class grape with a great future in California as well. In Italy, Sangiovese has been blended for many years by law with other red and even white wine grapes. More recently, top producers in both Italy and California are experimenting with nontraditional blends of Sangiovese and Cabernet Sauvignon and with Sangiovese on its own, and they are achieving considerable success. Sangiovese complements a wide range of rustic Italian dishes as well as other full-flavored foods.

SYRAH

Syrah is one of the noble red grapes of the Rhône region in southern France. While often confused with Petite Sirah, it is not related. Syrah has been grown successfully in California for a number of decades and has many fans due to its peppery, spicy quality and intense, full-flavored fruit. Syrah is often blended with Grenache and Mourvèdre, another Rhône variety, to make New World red blends that resemble Châteauneuf-du-Pape. It is often made without blending as well.

Syrah is well suited to red meat dishes, particularly grilled and braised preparations with full, robust flavors.

VIOGNIER

Viognier is a gloriously decadent white wine grape that is grown primarily in the Condrieu region of southern France. It is quite rare and thus commands steep prices, which has prevented it from becoming better known in California. Over thirty producers are now making Viognier in California, and there is considerable optimism for high-quality wines at lower prices than their French counterparts.

Viognier offers a gorgeous, seductive aroma, often reminiscent of apricots, peaches, and honey-suckle. It has a lush mouth-feel and captivating flavors, making it an enjoyable diversion from Chardonnay. It is sometimes aged in oak, which adds a buttery quality to the already creamy texture of the varietal.

Enjoy Viognier with full-flavored seafood and poultry dishes and on its own as a sipping wine. The search for this rare varietal will be well worth it, as it offers pure hedonistic pleasure. This is definitely a varietal for the future.

SULFITES IN WINE

In the mid-1980s, in response to concern about how sulfites can affect asthmatics, the U.S. government began requiring a sulfite warning statement on wine labels. It is unclear how long sulfur has been used in winemaking, but it has certainly been around for several hundred years. A small amount of sulfites occurs in all young wines, since they are a natural by-product of fermentation. Something in the neighborhood of ten parts per million are usually present.

Winemakers historically added sulfur or sulfites to wine to help stabilize it and improve its longevity. Sulfites have both fungicidal and antioxidant properties. Back in the days before clean, modern equipment and fermentation practices, more sulfur was added than is typically used today. U.S. law allows up to 350 ppm, but most wines today are being produced at levels of less than 100 ppm.

Wine isn't the only food from which we get sulfites. Most dried fruits contain much more sulfur than wine. Wine writer Dan Berger has noted that "you can get as much sulfite from one dried apple as from four full bottles of wine." Sulfite solutions are also often used at restaurant salad bars to keep greens bright and fresh looking.

In my view, unless you are one of the estimated 1 percent of the population sensitive to sulfites, the more important issue is other agricultural chemicals used to grow grapes, such as herbicides, pesticides, and fungicides. Labeling laws at present don't require any warning labels about residues of these substances.

Finally, there is the issue of red wine, headaches, and sulfites. Scientists say that there doesn't appear to be any connection between sulfites and headaches. Why headaches are more associated with red wine rather than white is still being explored.

APPENDICES

EDIBLE FLOWERS

Edible flowers have had a continuing role in wine country cuisine for many years. Although it may seem like a new trend, edible flowers have had a long history in many countries:

- Roses and orange flowers in Middle Eastern and Persian foods
- Lilies in China
- Cherry blossoms and chrysanthemums in Japan
- Lavender in France and England
- Saffron in Spain and the rest of the Mediterranean

Flower petals can add wonderful color and sparkle to a plate, and many—such as daylilies and nasturtiums—have bold, interesting flowers.

Not all flowers, however, are edible. Cathy Barash in her book *Edible Flowers from Garden to Palate* offers these guidelines:

TEN COMMANDMENTS OF EDIBLE FLOWERS

1. Not all flowers are edible—some are poisonous.
2. Eat only those flowers that you can positively identify as safe and edible.
3. Eat only edible flowers that have been grown organically.
4. When eating out, do not eat flowers on your plate unless you are sure they are edible and safe to eat. (See Commandments 2 and 3.)
5. Do not eat flowers from florists, nurseries, or garden centers. (See Commandment 3.)
6. Remove pistils and stamens from most flowers before eating. Eat only the petals of most flowers.
7. If you have hay fever, asthma, or allergies, do not eat flowers.
8. Do not eat flowers picked from the side of the road. (See Commandment 3.)
9. You don't have to like all edible flowers. Flowers may vary in taste when grown in different locations. Different varieties of the same flower may vary in taste.
10. Introduce flowers into your diet the way you would new foods to a baby—one at a time and in small quantities.

FLOWERS FOR THE EATING

Here is a list of edible flowers I have used over the years, with my tasting notes:

NAME	TASTING NOTES
Anise hyssop	Licorice
Apple blossom	Slight floral
Arugula	Spicy, peppery
Bachelor's button	Mild
Basils (various kinds)	Strong, spicy, herbal
Beans, snap or pole	Beany, floral
Bee balm (*Monarda didyma*), **purple and red**	Strong, hot, minty
Begonia (tuberous)	Crisp, lemony
Borage	Mild, light cucumber
Calendula (pot marigold)	Mild, vegetal
Carnation	Clovelike, floral
Chamomile, German	Slightly bitter, for teas
Cherry	Sweet, floral
Chervil	Warm anise-parsley flavors
Chicory	Slightly bitter
Chives	Tangy, oniony
Chrysanthemum	Mild to strong, bitter
Cilantro, coriander	Bold sage flavor and tangy citrus taste
Citrus (lemon, orange, lime)	Tangy, rindlike
Clover, red	Herbaceous, slightly bitter
Collard greens flower	Sweet, mild
Cress	Peppery

NAME	TASTING NOTES
Dandelion	Mild to strong
Daylily (true lilies only, not calla, Aztec, or other so-called lilies, which are poisonous)	Mild, sweet, crunchy
Dianthus, pinks	Mild vegetal to sweet spice
Dill	Herbal aroma, spicy, with mild aniseed flavor
English daisy (*Bellis perennis*)	Mild, vegetal
Fennel	Mild, anise
Forget-me-not, cynoglossom*	Mild
Fuchsia	Acidic
Garlic, chives	Pungent, garlic flavor
Geraniums (scented, including apple, lime, lemon, rose, etc.)	Floral
Hibiscus	Tart, citrus, cranberry, tropical
Hollyhock	Vegetal, okralike, bland
Honeysuckle	Sweet nectar, mildly bitter floral
Hyssop	Slightly bitter, strong camphor like aroma
Impatiens*	Citrusy
Jamaica flower	Cranberry
Jasmine	Slightly sweet
Johnny-jump-up	Mild, cinnamon or root beer
Judas tree (redbud)	Mild, slightly bitter

*Not all edible flower references agree.

NAME	TASTING NOTES	NAME	TASTING NOTES
Lavender	Herbal, strongly perfumed	Scarlet runner	Mild bean, slightly crunchy, sweet
Lilac	Floral, strong tarragon	Shasta daisy	Mild, vegetal
Mints (chocolate, apple, spearmint, peppermint)	Slightly sweet, herbal, refreshing	Snapdragon*	Mild, vegetal
Mullein	Mild, vegetal	Sorrel	Citrus, herbal
Mustard	Pleasantly hot	Squashes	Mild, vegetal
Nasturtium	Peppery, hot spicy flavor	Stock, mathiola*	Floral, sweet, perfumed
Oregano	Herbal, warm savory taste	Strawberry	Mild
Pansy	Mild, sweet flavor, wintergreenish	Sunflower	Mild, vegetal
Passionflower	Mild, sweet	Tarragon	Herbal, savory anise flavor
Pea (not sweet pea)	Sweet, faintly floral	Thyme, various	Herbal, taste varies with variety
Petunia*	Mild vegetal, sometimes bitter aftertaste	Tulbaghia (tricolor)	Garlic
Pineapple guava	Sweet spongy-marshmallow flavor, floral	Tulip (do not eat bulb)	Mild, floral, crisp
Plum blossom	Sweet floral, faint cherry flavor, slightly bitter	Vegetable blossoms (All EXCEPT tomato, potato, eggplant, peppers, and asparagus)	Mild, vegetal
Poppy—Shirley poppy only (use only petals: avoid opium poppies)	Mildly bitter, floral	Viola	Mild perfume
Portulaca	Mild, vegetal	Violet	Sweet, very floral
Primrose	Mild, floral	Woodruff, sweet	Distinctive herbal-floral flavor
Prune	Mild, fruity	Yucca	Sweet, herbal
Rocket	Sharp, strong, peppery		
Rose	Mild, floral; perfume varies		
Rosemary	Herbal		
Safflower	Slightly bitter, earthy		
Sage (winter & summer)	Herbal, spicy, slightly bitter		

*Not all edible flower references agree.

FARMSTEAD CHEESE PRODUCERS OF AMERICA

The word "American," when applied to cheese, generally has negative connotations. It brings to mind the typically artificially colored, tasteless, processed, and uninteresting version we see in the supermarkets and fast-food industry. In reality, American farmstead cheeses are quite the opposite of those orange horrors. Their superb quality matches that of European rivals. Produced on farms throughout the country, our American cheeses are made with fresh high-protein milk from cows, goats, and sheep. They are handled with great care and reflect the regions in which they are produced.

As with the fine wines of America, American farmstead cheeses have finally come of age.

CALIFORNIA

Achadinha Goat Cheese — goat's milk: achadinha.com
Andante — goat's and cow's milk: andantedairy.com
Bellwether Farms — Jersey cow and sheep's milk:
  bellwetherfarms.com
Bodega Goat Cheese — goat cheese:
  bodegagoatcheese.com
Bravo Farms — cow's milk: bravofarm.com
Capricious Cheese — goat's milk: capriciouscheese.com
Cowgirl Creamery — cow's milk: cowgirlcreamery.com
Cypress Grove Chevre — goat's milk:
  cypressgrovechevre.com
Fagundes Old World Cheese — cow's milk:
  oldworldcheese.com
Fiscalini Farmstead Cheese — cow's milk:
  fiscalinicheese.com
Gioia Cheese Co. — cow's milk: gioiacheese.com
Harley Farms Goat Cheese — goat's milk: harleyfarms.com
Laurel Chenel's Chevre — goat's milk: 707-996-4477
Marin French Cheese Co. — cow's milk:
  marinfrenchcheese.com
Matos Cheese — cow's milk:
  joematoscheese@sbcglobal.net
Mozzarella Fresca — cow's milk: mozzarellafresca.com
Point Reyes Farmstead Original Blue — cow's milk:
  pointreyescheese.com
Redwood Hill Farms — goat's milk: redwoodhill.com
Spring Hill Jersey Cheese — Jersey cow's milk:
  springhillcheese.com
Three Sisters Farmstead Cheese — Jersey cow's milk:
  threesisterscheese.com
Vella Cheese Co. — cow's milk: vellacheese.com
Winchester Cheese Co. — cow's milk:
  winchestercheese.com

HAWAII

Surfing Goat Dairy — goat's milk: surfinggoatdairy.com

OREGON

Alsea Acre Goat Cheese — goat's milk: 1-888-316-4628
Fraga Farm — goat's milk: fragafarm.com
Oregon Gourmet Cheeses — Jersey cow's milk:
  oregongourmetcheeses.com
Rogue Creamery — cow's milk: roguecreamery.com
Silver Falls Creamery — goat's milk: 508-881-9911
Tumalo Farms — goat's milk: tumalofarms.com
Willamette Valley Cheese Co. — Jersey cow's milk:
  wvcheeseco.com

WASHINGTON

Appel Farms Artisan Cheese — cow's milk: appel-farms.com
Beecher's Handmade Cheese — cow's milk:
  beecherscheese.com
Black Sheep Creamery — sheep's milk:
  blacksheepcreamery.com
Estrella Family Creamery — goat's and cow's milk:
  efcchesse@aol.com
Golden Glen Creamery — cow's milk:
  goldenglencreamery.com
Gothberg Farms — goat's milk: gothbergfarms.com
Monteillet Fromagerie — goat's and sheep's milk:
  montecheese.com
Quillisascut Cheese — goat's and cow's milk:
  quillisascutcheese.com
Sally Jackson Cheeses — goat's, cow's, and sheep's milk:
  sallyjacksoncheeses.com

IDAHO

Ballard Family Dairy and Cheese — Jersey cow's milk: ballardcheese.com
Hoo Doo Valley Creamery — cow's milk: 208-255-4388
Rollingstone Chevre — goat's milk: chevre@mac.com

COLORADO

Bingham Hill Cheese Co. — cow's and sheep's milk: binghamhill.com
Haystack Dairy — goat's milk: haystackgoatcheese.com
James Ranch Artisan Cheese — cow's milk: jamesranch.net/cheese
MouCo. Cheese Co. — cow's milk: mouco.com
Shepherd's Way Farm — sheep's milk: 507-663-9040

MIDWEST

Antigo Cheese Co. (Wisconsin) — cow's milk: antigocheese.com
Bleu Mont Dairy Co. (Wisconsin) — cow's milk: cheeseforager.com/bleumont
Buckeye Grove Farm Cheese (Ohio) — Jersey cow's milk: buckeyegrovefarmcheese.com
Capri Creamery Cheese (Wisconsin) — goat's milk: capricheese.com
Capriole Goat Cheese (Indiana) — goat's milk: capriolegoatcheese.com
Crave Brothers Farmstead (Wisconsin) — cow's milk: cravecheese.com
Fantome Farm (Wisconsin) — goat's milk: fantomefarm.com
Maytag Dairy Farms (Iowa) — cow's milk: maytagblue.com
Michigan Farm Cheese Dairy (Michigan) — cow's milk: andrulischeese.com
Uplands Cheese Co. (Wisconsin) — cow's milk: uplandscheese.com

EAST

Berkshire Cheese Makers (Massachusetts)—Jersey cow's milk: 413-445-5935
Blythedale Farm (Vermont) — Jersey cow's milk: 802-439-6575
Boggy Meadow Farm Cheese (New Hampshire)— cow's milk: boggymeadowfarm.com
Cabot Creamery (Vermont) — cow's milk: cabotcheese.com
Calabro Cheese (Connecticut) — cow's milk: calabrocheese.com
Catapano Dairy (New York) — goat's milk: catapanodairyfarm.com
Cato Corner Farm (Connecticut) — Jersey cow's milk: catocornerfarm.com
Champlain Valley Creamery (Vermont) — cow's milk: cvcream.com
Coach Farm (New York) — goat's milk: coachfarm.com
Cobb Hill Cheese (Vermont) — cow's milk: cobbhill.org/cheese
Grafton Village Cheese Co. (Vermont) — Jersey cow's milk: graftonvillagecheese.com
Great Hill Dairy (Massachusetts)—cow's milk: greathillblue.com
Jasper Hill Farm (Vermont)) — cow's milk: jasperhillfarm.com
La Fromagerie du Royaume (Vermont)) — cow's milk: lafromagerie.biz
Lakes End Cheeses (Vermont)) — goat's and cow's milk: lakesendcheeses.com
Lively Run Goat Dairy (New York)) — goat's milk: livelyrun.com
Old Chatham Sheepherding Co. (New York)) — sheep's milk: blacksheepcheese.com
Rustling Wind Creamery (Connecticut) — cow's milk: rustlingwind.com
Shelburne Farms (Vermont) — cow's milk: shelburnefarms.org
Silvery Moon Creamery (Maine) — cow's milk: smilinghill.com
Smith's Country Cheese (Massachusetts)— smithscountrycheese.com
Sugarbush Farm (Vermont) — Jersey cow's milk: sugarbushfarm.com
Taylor Farm Cheese (Vermont) — cow's milk: taylorfarmvermont.com
Thistle Hill Farm (Vermont) — cow's milk: thistlehillfarm.com

Vermont Butter & Cheese Co. (Vermont)—goat's and
    cow's milk: vtbutterandcheese.com
Vermont Shepherd (Vermont)—cow's milk:
    vermontshepherd.com
Westfield Farm (Massachusetts)—goat's milk: chevre.com
Willow Hill Farm (Vermont)—cow's and sheep's milk:
    sheepcheese.com
Woodstock Water Buffalo (Vermont)—water buffalo:
    woodstockwaterbuffalo.com

SOUTH AND SOUTHWEST

Blue Ridge Dairy (Virginia)—cow's milk:
    blueridgedairy.com
Coon Ridge Organic Goat Cheese (New Mexico)—goat's
    milk: coonridge.com
Goat Lady Dairy (North Carolina)—goat's milk:
    goatladydairy.com
Mozzarella Cheese Co. (Texas)—cow's milk: mozzco.com
Sleeping Dog Ranch (North Carolina)—goat's milk:
    sleepingdogranch.com
Sweet Grass Dairy (Georgia)—goat's milk:
    sweetgrassdairy.com
Sweet Home Farm (Alabama)—cow's milk:
    southerncheese.com
True Ewe Dairy (Virginia)—sheep's milk: TrueEwe.com

ARTISANAL CHEESES RETAIL AND INFORMATION SOURCES

American Cheese Society: cheesesociety.org
Artisanal Premium Cheese: artisanalcheese.com
Bodega Blue Artisan Cheese (Florida):
    bodegabluecheese.com
California Artisan Cheese Guild: cacheeseguild.org
CHEESE.COM—All About Cheese!: cheese.com
Cheesecraft (New Mexico): cheesecraft.com
The Cheesemaker's Daughter: cheesemakersdaughter.com
Cow Girl Creamery: cowgirlcreamery.com (visit their Library
    of Cheeses online)
Great American Cheese Collection: greatamericancheese.com
Great New England Cheeses: newenglandcheese.com
Igourmet Specialty Cheeses and Fine Foods: igourmet.com
Murray's Cheese: murrayscheese.com
New England Cheesemaking Supply Co.:
    cheesemaking.com
New York State Farmstead and Artisan Cheese Makers
    Guild: nycheese.org
Pacific Northwest Cheese Project: pncheese.com
Real California Cheese: realcaliforniacheese.com
Resident Cheesemonger: residentcheesemonger.com
Vermont Cheese Council: vtcheese.com
Wisconsin Cheese Makers Association:
    wischeesemakersassn.org

ASIAN

Amazon: amazon.com/gourmetfood
Asian Foods: asiafoods.com
Lee Kum Kee (authentic Chinese products): usa.lkk.com
Pacific Rim Gourmet: pacificrim-gourmet.com

INDIAN

Ethnic Grocer World Market: ethnicgrocer.com
Namaste Indian Groceries: namaste.com
Spices Store: spices-store.com

LATIN

Gourmet Sleuth Gourmet Food: gourmetsleuth.com
Kitchen Market: kitchenmarket.com
Mex Grocer: mexgrocer.com

MEDITERRANEAN

Etruria Gourmet: etruriagourmet.com
Formaggio Kitchen (small-production foods and handmade
    products): formaggiokitchen.com
Joie de Vivre French Specialties: frenchselections.com
La Tienda Spanish Foods: tienda.com
The Spanish Table (all things from Spain):
    thespanishtable.com
Urbani Truffles USA Ltd.: urbani.com

MIDDLE EASTERN

Kalustyan's Fine Specialty Foods: kalustyans.com

GLOBAL

Chef Shop: chefshop.com
Ethnic Grocer World Market: ethnicgrocer.com
Food411: food411.com
Gourmet Sleuth Gourmet Food: gourmetsleuth.com
Surfas Gourmet Food and More!: surfasonline.com

DRIED HERBS AND SPICES

Penzeys Spices: penzeys.com
San Francisco Herb Co.: sfherb.com
Vann's Spices: vannsspices.com
Whole Herb Co.: wholeherbcompany.com

SPECIALTY OILS AND VINEGARS

ChefShop (global pantry of oils and vinegars): chefshop.com
Corti Brothers Grocers and Wine Merchants: 916-736-3800
DaVero Olive Oil Co.: davero.com
Katz & Co. (specialty olive oils and vinegars): katzandco.com
McEvoy Ranch Olive Oil: mcevoyranch.com
Spectrum Organics (oils and vinegars): spectrumorganic.com
The Olive Press (olive oils and vinegars): theolivepress.com
California Olive Oil Council (olive oil Information): cooc.com

FINISHING SALTS AND PEPPERS

The Salt Traders (global salts): salttraders.com
ChefShop: chefshop.com

RICE, GRAINS, LEGUMES

1-800-gourmet foods: 1800gourmet.com
Indian Harvest (rice, grains, and beans): chefnet.com
Phipps Country Store and Farm: phippscountry.com
Purcell Mountain Farms (beans, seeds, nuts):
    purcellmountainfarms.com
Surfas Gourmet Food and MORE!: surfasonline.com
Zursun (specialty legumes): 1-800-424-8881

MUSHROOMS

Fresh
Earthy Delights: earthy.com
Foods in Season: foodsinseason.com
Gourmet Mushrooms: gourmetmushrooms.com

Dried
Earthy Delights: earthy.com
Gourmet Store, featuring D'Allasandro gourmet
    ingredients: gourmetstore.com
Marky's Caviar: markyscaviar.com

DRIED CHILES

Rancho Gordo Specialty Foods: ranchogordo.com
The Chile Guy: thechileguy.com
Tierra Vegetables: tierravegetables.com

MEAT, GAME, AND POULTRY

Niman Ranch (ethically raised meats): nimanranch.com
Nueske's (ham and smoked meats): nueskes.com
Preferred Meats (specializes in organic beef, Kobe beef, naturally raised beef, Berkshire (Kurobuta) & Duroc pork, lamb, game birds, game meats, fresh sausages, and specialty cured and smoked meats): preferredmeats.com

CAVIER AND SMOKED FISH

Katy's Smokehouse (100% natural smoked fish): katyssmokehouse.com
Marky's Caviar: markyscaviar.com
Shuckman's Fish Co. and Smokery (smoked fish and caviar): kysmokedfish.com
Sterling Caviar (one of the very few American producers of premium farm-raised sturgeon caviar): sterlingcaviar.com

LINKS FOR INFORMATION ON SEAFOOD SUSTAINABILITY

The Monterey Bay Aquarium's Seafood Watch Consumer Guide can be downloaded at this site: mbayaq.org or montereybayaquarium.org or telephone (831) 648-4800. Any changes to seafood recommendations are posted on the Web immediately and the wallet-sized printed guides are updated regularly. There are now individual versions developed for major regions of the country. You can also get information on all the extraordinary programs and activities of the aquarium.

The Seafood Choices Alliance is a free subscriber service providing current information on environmental issues in the seafood industry. It includes the Seasense database, a handy tool in making sustainable seafood choices: seafoodchoices.com

The Environmental Protection Agency posts advisories on all kinds of fish and recommendations on both what to eat and what not to eat: epa.gov/ost/fish

Sea Web is a nonprofit public education organization whose aim is to raise awareness of the ocean and the life within it: seaweb.org

Aquaculture Network Information Agency includes a comprehensive list of links and organizations: aquanic.org

Environmental Defense Fund: Click on the Seafood Selector to get information on choosing fresh environmental-friendly fish: environmentaldefense.org

The National Audubon Society is active in supporting sustainable practices and publishes a beautiful and informative book called *The Seafood Lover's Almanac*: seafood.audubon.org

WEBSITES WORTH A VISIT AND GUIDES FOR FINDING SUSTAINABLE PRODUCTS IN YOUR AREA

Edible Communities — Provides information to those who want to connect, in a more direct way, with the food resources in their region, with an emphasis on sustainable agriculture, small family farmers, and artisanal food producers: ediblecommunities.com

Eat Well Guide — Provides a free guide to sustainably raised meat, poultry, dairy, and eggs from your local stores, restaurants, and farms: eatwellguide.org

The Meatrix — Critically acclaimed video that cleverly portrays the thought-provoking issues around factory-farmed meat: themeatrix.com

Local Harvest — A guide for sustainably grown produce and products in your area: localharvest.org

Learn more about sustainable food at Sustainable Table: sustainabletable.org

GARDEN SEED SOURCES

Artistic Gardens: artisticgardens.com

Bountiful Gardens: bountifulgardens.org

Cook's Garden: cooksgarden.com

Johnny's Selected Seeds: johnnyseeds.com

Native Seed Search: nativeseeds.org

Nichols Garden Nursery: nicholsgardennursery.com

Renee's Garden: reneesgarden.com

Ronnigers Seed Potatoes: ronnigers.com

Seed Savers Exchange: seedsavers.org

Seeds of Change: seedsofchange.com

Territorial Seed Co.: territorial-seed.com

The Gourmet Gardener: gourmetgardener.com

The Tasteful Garden: tastefulgarden.com

HERB AND SEEDLING SOURCES

Caprilands Herb Farm: caprilands.com

Companion Plants: companionplants.com

Emerisa Gardens: emerisa.com

Garden Place: gardenplace.com

Mountain Valley Growers: mountainvalleygrowers.com

Nichols Garden Nursery: nicholsgardennursery.com

Seeds of Change: seedsofchange.com

The Herb Cottage: theherbcottage.com

Thompson & Morgan: thompson-morgan.com

Vermont Bean Co: vermontbean.com

White Flower Farm: whiteflowerfarm.com

Information

The Herb Companion: herbcompanion.com

WINERY ASSOCIATIONS

CALIFORNIA

Alexander Valley Winegrowers: alexandervalley.org

Amador Vintners Association: amadorwine.com

Anderson Valley Winegrowers Association: avwines.com

Calaveras Winegrape Alliance: calaveraswines.org

Carneros Wine Alliance: carneros.com

Central California Winegrowers: ccwinegrowers.org

Central Coast Wine Growers Association: ccwga.org

Clarksburg Winegrowers Association:
clarksburgwinegrowers.org

El Dorado Winery Association: eldoradowines.org

Lake County Wine Grape Growers Association:
lakecountywinegrape.org

Livermore Valley Winegrowers Association:
livermorewine.com

Lodi Appellation Winery Association: lodiwine.com

Madera Vintners Association: maderavintners.com

Mendocino Winegrowers Alliance: mendowine.com

Monterey County Vintners & Growers Association:
montereywines.org

Napa Valley Vintners: napavintners.com

Nevada County Wineries Association: ncgold.com

Paso Robles Vintners & Growers Association:
pasowine.com

Placer County Wine & Grape Association: placerwineand-
grape.org

Russian River Valley Winegrowers: rrvw.org

Russian River Wine Road: wineroad.com

San Benito County Winegrowers' Association:
sbcwinegrowers.org

San Luis Obispo Vintners & Growers Association:
slowine.com

Santa Barbara County Vintners Association:
sbcountywines.com

Santa Cruz Mountains Winegrowers Association:
scmwa.com

Sierra Grape Growers Association: sierragrapegrowers.org

Silverado Trail Wineries Association: silveradotrail.com

Sonoma County Wineries Association: sonomawine.com

Sonoma Valley Vintners and Growers Alliance:
sonomavalleywines.com

Temecula Valley Winegrowers Association:
temeculawines.org

The Wine Institute (California wines): wineinstitute.org

Wine Artisans of Santa Lucia Highlands: montereywine.com

OREGON

Oregon Wine Center: oregonwine.org

Oregon Wineries and Wines: oregonwines.com

WASHINGTON

Columbia Cascade Winery Association:
columbiacascadewines.com

Columbia Valley Winery Association:
columbiavalleywine.com

Puget Sound Winegrowers Association: pswg.org

Spokane Winery Association: spokanewineries.net

Walla Walla Valley Wine Alliance: wallawallawine.com

Wine Country Washington: winecountrywashington.org

Woodinville Wine Country: woodinvillewinecountry.com

Yakima Valley Winery Association: wineyakimavalley.org

NEW YORK

Finger Lakes: fingerlakeswinecountry.com

Uncork New York: newyorkwines.org

For updates and current source information, visit
chefjohnash.com

BIBLIOGRAPHY

Ash, John, and Sid Goldstein. *American Game Cooking*. Reading, MA: Addison Wesley/Aris Books, 1991.

Ausubel, Kenny. *Seeds of Change: The Living Treasure*. San Francisco: Harper San Francisco, 1994.

Barash, Cathy Wilkinson. *Edible Flowers: From Garden to Palate*. Golden, CO: Fulcrum Publishing, 1993.

Bayless, Rick, and Deann Bayless. *Authentic Mexican*. New York: Morrow, 1987.

Bell, Mary. *Complete Dehydrator Cookbook*. New York: Morrow, 1994.

Bissell, Frances. *The Book of Food*. New York: Henry Holt, 1994.

Cader, Michael, and Debby Roth. *Eat These Words*. New York: HarperCollins, 1991.

Castle, Coralie, and Robert Kourik. *Cooking from the Gourmet's Garden*. Santa Rosa, CA: Cole Group, 1994.

Child, Julia. *Mastering the Art of French Cooking, vol. 1*. New York: Knopf, 1961.

Creasy, Rosalind. *Cooking from the Garden*. San Francisco: Sierra Club Books, 1988.

Corriher, Shirley. *Cookwise*. New York: Morrow, 1987.

Davidson, Alan. *The Oxford Companion to Food*. New York: Oxford University Press, 1999.

Devi, Yamuna. *The Art of Indian Vegetarian Cooking*. New York: Dutton, 1987.

Dille, Carolyn, and Susan Belsinger. *Herbs in the Kitchen*. Loveland, CO: Interweave Press, 1992.

Dumas, Alexandre. *Dictionary of Cuisine*, ed. and trans. by Louis Colman. New York: Simon & Schuster, 1958.

Ferrary, Jeanette, and Louise Fizer. *Season to Taste*. New York: Simon & Schuster, 1988.

Field, Carol. *The Italian Baker*. New York: Harper & Row, 1985.

Fisher, M. F. K. *An Alphabet for Gourmets*. San Francisco: Northpoint Press, 1989.

Fisher, M. F. K. *The Art of Eating*. New York: Macmillan, 1971.

Gerard, John. *The Herball: A Historie of Plants*, ed. by Marcus Woodward. London: Senate, 1994. First published in 1597.

Gibbons, Euell. *Stalking the Wild Asparagus*. New York: McKay, 1978.

Goldstein, Joyce. *Back to Square One*. New York: Morrow, 1992.

Hazan, Marcella. *Marcella's Italian Kitchen*. New York: Alfred A. Knopf, 1987.

Hensperger, Beth. *Baking Bread*. San Francisco: Chronicle Books, 1992.

The Herb Companion, published bimonthly by Interweave Press, Loveland, CO.

Hillman, Howard. *Kitchen Science*. Boston: Houghton Mifflin, 1981.

Kilham, Christopher S. *The Bread and Circus Whole Food Bible*. Reading, MA: Addison Wesley, 1991.

Madison, Deborah. *The Savory Way*. New York: Bantam Books, 1990.

McGee, Harold. *On Food and Cooking: The Science and Lore of the Kitchen*. New York: Scribner, 1984. Revised and updated edition, 2004.

Medrich, Alice. *Chocolate and the Art of Low-Fat Desserts*. New York: Warner Books, 1994.

National Audubon Society. *The Seafood Lover's Almanac*. Boston: Audubon's Living Oceans Program, 2000.

Pollan, Michael. *The Botany of Desire: A Plant's-Eye View of the World*. New York: Random House, 2001.

Rodale's Illustrated Encyclopedia of Herbs, ed. by Claire Kowalchek and William H. Hylton. Emmaus, PA: Rodale Press, 1987.

Rombauer, Irma S., Marion Rombauer Becker, and Ethan Becker. *The All New, All Purpose Joy of Cooking*. New York: Scribner, 1997.

Root, Waverly. *Food*. New York: Fireside Books, 1980.

Rosengarten, David, and Joshua Wesson. *Red Wine with Fish*. New York: Simon & Schuster, 1989.

Schneider, Elizabeth. *Uncommon Fruits and Vegetables: A Common Sense Guide*. New York: Harper & Row, 1986.

Shepard, Renee, and Fran Raboff. *Recipes from a Kitchen Garden*. Felton, CA: Shepard's Garden Publishing, 1991.

Simmons, Marie. *Rice, the Amazing Grain*. New York: Henry Holt, 1991.

Stockli, Albert. *Splendid Fare*. New York: Knopf, 1970.

Tatum, Billy Joe. *Billy Joe Tatum's Wild Foods Cookbook and Field Guide*. New York: Workman Publishing, 1976.

Toussaint-Samat, Maguelonne. *A History of Food*, trans. by Anthea Bell. Oxford: Blackwell Publishers, 1992.

Visser, Margaret. *Much Depends on Dinner*. New York: Collier Books, 1988.

Vongerichten, Jean-Georges. *Simple Cuisine*. New York: Prentice Hall, 1990.

INDEX

TABLE OF EQUIVALENTS

The exact equivalents in the following tables have been rounded for convenience.

LIQUID/DRY MEASURES

U.S.	Metric
¼ teaspoon	1.25 milliliters
½ teaspoon	2.5 milliliters
1 teaspoon	5 milliliters
1 tablespoon (3 teaspoons)	15 milliliters
1 fluid ounce (2 tablespoons)	30 milliliters
¼ cup	60 milliliters
⅓ cup	80 milliliters
½ cup	120 milliliters
1 cup	240 milliliters
1 pint (2 cups)	480 milliliters
1 quart (4 cups, 32 ounces)	960 milliliters
1 gallon (4 quarts)	3.84 liters
1 ounce (by weight)	28 grams
1 pound	454 grams
2.2 pounds	1 kilogram

OVEN TEMPERATURE

Fahrenheit	Celsius	Gas
250	120	½
275	140	1
300	150	2
325	160	3
350	180	4
375	190	5
400	200	6
425	220	7
450	230	8
475	240	9
500	260	10

LENGTH

U.S.	Metric
⅛ inch	3 millimeters
¼ inch	6 millimeters
½ inch	12 millimeters
1 inch	2.5 centimeters